WILD JUSTICE

Wild Justice

THE EVOLUTION OF REVENGE

Susan Jacoby

HARPER COLOPHON BOOKS
Harper & Row, Publishers
New York, Cambridge, Philadelphia, San Francisco
London, Mexico City, São Paulo, Singapore, Sydney

A hardcover edition of this book is published by Harper & Row, Publishers, Inc.

Grateful acknowledgment is made for permission to reprint:

Excerpt from THE WORLD ACCORDING TO GARP by John Irving. Copyright © 1976, 1977, 1978 by John Irving. Reprinted by permission of the publisher, E.P. Dutton, Inc.

Lines from "To Lycomedes on Scyros" from JOSEPH BRODSKY: SELECTED POEMS translated by George L. Kline. English translation and Introduction copyright © 1973 by George L. Kline. Reprinted by permission of Harper & Row, Publishers, Inc. and Penguin Books, Ltd.

Lines from *Agamemnon* by Aeschylus from AESCHYLUS: THE ORESTEIAN TRILOGY, translated by Philip Vellacott (Penguin Classics, Revised edition, 1959). Copyright © Philip Vellacott, 1956. Reprinted by permission of Penguin Books, Ltd.

Lines from HOMER: THE ILIAD translated by E.V. Rieu (Penguin Classics, 1950), pp. 177–178. Copyright © The Estate of E.V. Rieu, 1950. Reprinted by permission of Penguin Books, Ltd.

Lines from "Requiem 1935–1940" by Anna Akhmatova from SELECTED POEMS by Richard McKane (Penguin Modern European Poets, 1969), pp. 90, 104–105. Translation copyright © Richard McKane, 1969. Reprinted by permission of Penguin Books, Ltd.

First HARPER COLOPHON edition published 1984.

Designer: Sidney Feinberg

Library of Congress Cataloging in Publication Data

Jacoby, Susan.
  Wild justice.

  Bibliography: p.
  Includes index.
  1. Revenge. I. Title
BJ1490.J32 1983   179'.8   83– 47537
ISBN 0-06-091181-6 (pbk.)

84 85 86 87 88 10 9 8 7 6 5 4 3 2 1

To Robert and Irma Broderick Jacoby

Contents

Acknowledgments : ix

I. Taboo : 1

II. Written in Blood : 14

III. In the Beginning Was the Word : 66

IV. Letters of the Laws : 114

V. Revenge as Metaphor: New Image Makers : 150

VI. Sexual Revenge : 183

VII. Life for Life : 233

VIII. On Crimes and Punishments : 290

IX. The Quality of Mercy : 331

Notes : 363

Index : 375

Acknowledgments

I was greatly assisted in the completion of this book by financial support through research fellowships sponsored by the Ford Foundation and the Rockefeller Foundation. I particularly wish to thank Richard Sharpe and Joel Colton, who were in charge, at Ford and Rockefeller respectively, of the fellowship programs during the periods in which I received my grants. Both men were unusual in their recognition of the need to extend foundation resources to independent scholars and writers who are not affiliated with academic or government institutions.

I am also indebted to the New York Public Library for the special services it offers to writers who use the Frederick Lewis Allen Room and for maintaining its tradition of free public access at a time when most great cultural institutions are charging ever-increasing fees.

Henry Schwarzschild of the American Civil Liberties Union, the best-informed man in the United States on the subject of capital punishment, was unfailingly helpful in offering the benefit of his extensive research on issues of crime and punishment. Dorothy Rabinowitz provided me with her transcript of the U.S. Immigration and Naturalization Service hearings concerning the deportation of Hermine Braunsteiner Ryan —a public document, but one that is exceedingly difficult to obtain. Dr. Harvey Lomas, chief of psychiatry at the Veterans Administration Hospital in Cincinnati, Ohio, gave me the benefit of his extensive clinical experience as well as access to unpublished papers on the relationship between psychiatry, the criminal-justice system, and revenge. Rabbi Marc Tannenbaum of the American Jewish Committee also offered me access to his unpublished papers on the historical role of the passion play in Jewish-Christian relations.

I also wish to thank Anthony Astrachan for his helpful suggestions regarding several chapters.

I am especially indebted to my editor, Aaron Asher, for his unfailing encouragement, perceptive criticism, and meticulous attention to detail at every stage of the editorial process.

For their personal support, I wish to thank Susan Brownmiller, Johanna Kaplan, and Linda Wolfe.

WILD JUSTICE

1 | Taboo

Revenge is a kind of wild justice, which the more man's nature runs to, the more ought law to weed it out.

FRANCIS BACON, *Essays,* "Of Revenge"

Accidents don't happen to people who take accidents as a personal insult.

MARIO PUZO, *The Godfather*

Forgive and forget. This admonition surely ranks as one of the most foolish clichés in any language. Remembrance is unquestionably a form of revenge, but, in one of the great paradoxes of civilized life, it is equally indispensable to the attainment of true forgiveness. The concept of "just deserts," which was not a philosophical abstraction but a fact of life throughout most of human history, evokes a deep unease in modern men and women. Who wants to be confronted by an Old Testament prophet, whether across the dinner table or on the evening news? We are more comfortable with the notion of forgiving and forgetting, however unrealistic it may be, than with the private and public reality of revenge, with its unsettling echoes of the primitive and its inescapable reminder of the fragility of human order.

Justice is a legitimate concept in the modern code of civilized behavior. Vengeance is not. We prefer to avert our eyes from those who persist in reminding us of the wrongs they have suffered—the mother whose child disappeared three years ago on a New York street and who, instead of mourning in silence, continues to appear on television and appeal for information about her missing son; the young Sicilian woman who, instead of marrying her rapist as ancient local custom dictates, scandalizes the town by bringing criminal charges; the concentration-camp survivors who, instead of putting the past behind them, persist in pointing their fingers at ex-Nazis living comfortable lives on quiet streets. Such people are disturbers of the peace; we wish they would take their memories away to a church, a cemetery, a psychotherapist's office and allow us to return justice and vengeance to the separate compartments they supposedly occupy in twentieth-century life.

In 1972, a primly dressed middle-aged woman named Hermine Ryan was brought before a court of the United States Immigration and Naturalization Service to answer charges that she had lied about her past when she entered the country after World War II. At the time of the hearing, she was an ordinary housewife—one of many German women who married American servicemen after the war—living in a modest residential neighborhood of New York City. In an earlier, less ordinary life, she was known as Aufseherin Hermine Braunsteiner, a dreaded officer of the Maidanek death camp. Most of the witnesses at the deportation hearings were Maidanek survivors. All of them were asked by Ryan's attorney whether they were "out for revenge"; all replied in controlled, dispassionate tones that they only wanted justice. They were obviously aware, as one writer later observed, of the cultural convention that makes it unacceptable to acknowledge any form of vengeance as a motivation.[1]

The force of this convention—as prevalent in everyday life as it is in courtrooms—was revealed in an exchange between a newspaper reporter and the only witness who displayed open anger on the stand. "Why are you here?" the reporter asked in the soothing, patronizing tone characteristic of social workers, psychotherapists, and teachers of small children. "Why am I here?" the witness responded in an incredulous tone, suggesting that the questioner was the one in need of psychiatric help. "I am here for our dead." Later in the day, the same journalist told a colleague, "You can see the woman's become unbalanced by the quest for revenge." Some years earlier, when reports of his wife's former occupation surfaced in the press, Ryan's husband expressed a similar opinion of those who wished to exact retribution for old crimes. "These people are just swinging their axes at random," he said. "Didn't they ever hear the expression 'Let the dead rest'?"[2]

I was one of many reporters assigned by newspapers and magazines to follow the case, but I found myself more fascinated by what the proceedings revealed about contemporary attitudes toward justice and revenge than by the specific fate of Hermine Braunsteiner Ryan. An assumption that revenge and justice are mutually exclusive was implicit in the interrogation of the witnesses, in the journalist's doubt about the mental health of one who had displayed anger, in Mr. Ryan's comments about the motives of those who had tracked down his wife. The strength of this assumption is underlined by the fact that the form of "vengeance" at issue in the Ryan case was not the uncontrolled fury of vigilantes but the truthful testimony, in a formal proceeding, of witnesses to crimes committed by a woman who helped run a Nazi death factory.

A decade after Ryan's deportation to face trial in Germany, American correspondents felt obliged to make a similar distinction between objective justice and personally motivated vengeance in their reports on French reaction to the capture of Klaus Barbie, who was known as the "Butcher of Lyons" for his extreme brutality as Gestapo chief in that city during the Nazi occupation of France. One account quoted the president of the Jewish Federation in the Lyons region: "Every Jewish family in Lyons has a loved one, a father or a grandfather, who was a victim of Barbie. No one among them has forgotten." The report then commented that "for former Resistance leaders and for Mr. Barbie's other victims, his trial, if it takes place, will be less a matter of settling old scores than of establishing the truth." The juxtaposition of these two observations is somewhat puzzling; it seems to imply a contrast, even an opposition, between families who have not forgotten their murdered relatives and those who are interested solely in "establishing the truth." Barbie's lawyer, like Ryan's American attorney, will undoubtedly attempt to cast just such a shadow of doubt regarding the credibility of victims and their families. Ugo Iannucci, a lawyer representing a group of French citizens deported by Barbie to concentration camps, spoke out forcefully against those who have suggested that such legal actions constitute useless vindictiveness. "There are people now saying, 'Why do you bother this poor old guy?' Well this poor old guy didn't respect women or children. . . . He tortured people. He must be brought to justice."[3]

The very word "revenge" has pejorative connotations. Advocates of draconian punishment for crime invariably prefer "retribution"—a word that affords the comfort of euphemism although it is virtually synonymous with "revenge." In this century, which has produced a new dictionary of terms like "resettlement," "special treatment," "protective reaction strike," and "re-education centers," euphemistic language has come to be regarded primarily as a tool of governments and officials attempting to conceal or at least to blur the outlines of their evil deeds. But euphemism is as likely to be the product of confusion as of design—especially when it concerns ethical dilemmas that fall within the realm of private as well as public behavior. The relationship between "retribution" and "revenge" is analogous to the only recently obsolete substitution of "protection" for "birth control": it has less to do with good and evil than with ambivalence about violations of social piety and propriety grown so widespread that they have become the rule rather than the exception.

The proper relationship between justice and revenge has been a major preoccupation of literature, religion, and law throughout the recorded history of the West. Establishment of a balance between the restraint that enables people to live with one another and the ineradicable impulse to retaliate when harm is inflicted has always been one of the essential tasks of civilization. The attainment of such a balance depends in large measure on the confidence of the victimized that someone else will act on their behalf against the victimizers. Laws are designed not to weed out the impulse toward revenge but to contain it in a manner consistent with the maintenance of an orderly and humane society. Even the classic Christian statement on the subject—"Dearly beloved, avenge not yourselves, but rather give place unto wrath: for it is written, Vengeance is mine; I will repay, saith the Lord"⁴—usually cited as an injunction against revenge, is as much a pledge of divine action as a prohibition of human retribution. In the absence of a divinity who dispenses floods, fires, and plagues to punish offenders, civil authorities have been regarded as legitimate stand-ins. How that legitimacy may be established is a separate question, whether it is framed in secular or religious terms.

One measure of a civilization's complexity is the distance between aggrieved individuals and the administration of revenge. But distance alone is not sufficient to establish a society's control over the vengeful impulses of its members, and it is certainly no measure of a civilization's humaneness. In determining the role of retribution in society, the ultimate aim of punishment is no less important than the procedure by which it is imposed. The fact that a judge rather than a mob designates drawing-and-quartering as a proper mode of execution is, in strict legal terms, an advance in the social control of revenge, but it also means that the values of those who control the social order are scarcely more advanced than those of the mob.

The United States Supreme Court evaded this issue when, in a 1976 decision upholding capital punishment, it described executions of murderers as an expression of a deep emotional need for retribution that is "neither a forbidden objective nor one inconsistent with our respect for the dignity of men."[5] One might easily construct an argument in which society's deep emotional need for retribution can only be satisfied by subjecting murderers to precisely the same torments they inflict on their victims. Until the eighteenth century, judicial bodies in England and continental Europe did exactly that. The question the Court ought to have addressed is not whether retribution *per se* is a "forbidden" objective of criminal justice but which forms of revenge are consistent with the aims of a just society.

Many opponents of the death penalty miss the same point, albeit from another direction, when they attack executions on the ground that they constitute "legalized revenge"—as if the very word "revenge" offered sufficient evidence of the barbarism of taking a human life. The word "retribution" would not serve the polemical purpose here, just as "revenge" does not suit those who try to construct elaborate theoretical justifications for capital punishment. The death penalty is certainly a form of legalized vengeance—revenge writ large—but so is any lesser punishment if a crime is unlikely to be repeated. Jean Harris, the distraught, jealous schoolmistress who shot her former lover, "Scarsdale diet doctor" Herman Tarnower, is not in prison because the jury feared she would kill again but because her action was viewed as a crime grave enough to demand some form of punishment—the defendant's remorse and bleak future, in or out of prison, notwithstanding. There are people who believe the offender's sense of guilt is "punishment enough" for this type of crime, but I suspect they are in a small minority. Remorse may wipe the slate clean with the gods, but men and women generally demand a more tangible penance. Nevertheless, the proper role of retribution—inside and outside courtrooms—has become a source of individual and institutional confusion. In countless instances, we see the tragicomic spectacle of victims (it makes little difference whether they are survivors of death camps or of muggings) who must deny any animus if their testimony is to be considered credible and who, like the witness at the Braunsteiner hearing, leave themselves open to bargain-basement analysis if they allow their disinterested masks to slip in public.

Jack Henry Abbott, a literary protégé of Norman Mailer, was tried for murder in 1982 in circuslike proceedings that highlighted the issue of revenge. A long-time convict who had been paroled partly as a result of Mailer's enthusiasm for his prison letters, Abbott had killed a young waiter in a senseless dispute the very week his collection of writings, *In the Belly of the Beast,* was published to enthusiastic reviews. (At the trial, Abbott—who had already killed a man in prison—claimed that his brutal experiences as a convict led him to think that the waiter intended to attack him.) The victim's father-in-law, Henry Howard, was understandably embittered by Mailer's role in obtaining parole for Abbott. Responding to the criticism at a boisterous press conference, Mailer expressed the hope that Abbott would not receive the maximum sentence and declared that he had "never been sympathetic to the idea that people have the right to demand blood atonement."[6] But the anguished father-in-law had never demanded "blood atonement"; he only insisted that Abbott should be returned to jail for life. He *was* asking for revenge, but he was not suggesting that Abbott pay with his own blood for the life he had taken. However, he made the mistake of displaying his anger in public: his style was too raw, too direct, too reminiscent of a prophet crying in the wilderness.[7]

Vindictive emotions are a highly marketable commodity in spite of, or because of, the disreputable aura surrounding them. The popularity of revenge as a theme in modern mass entertainment would have gladdened the hearts of both major and minor Elizabethan and Jacobean dramatists, who delighted in elaborate dissection of every conceivable form of human retribution before calling down divine judgment on avengers as well as on those whose actions aroused others to the crime of private vengeance. In their semi-pornographic fascination with acts they theoretically deplore, many of the minor seventeenth-century revenge tragedies strike a familiar chord in a contemporary reader; their authors would be at home today in the world of B-movies and television police dramas.

In the mid-1970s, to sit through a showing of the movie *Death Wish* in a darkened New York theatre was to be shaken by a display of the vengeful emotions that are not permitted in brightly lit courtrooms. A box-office hit in Europe as well as the United States, the movie features an avenging hero played by a mustachioed Charles Bronson. After his wife is murdered and his daughter raped by a trio of teenaged hoodlums, he embarks on a quest for revenge. The police, unwilling to arrest someone who has become a kind of Robin Hood to the crime-weary public, finally dispatch the Bronson character to Chicago (after some banter about the need to get out of town by sundown). In the final scene, Bronson turns his flinty gaze on a young tough who is annoying a woman at the airport and cocks his trigger finger in meaningful fashion. The audience cheered each time he pulled out his gun and dispatched yet another teenager who gave him a shifty glance or walked with an aggressive swagger. As the satisfied patrons left the theatre, one portly man in a Chesterfield coat turned to his wife and said, "I tell you, we're going to learn how to use a gun whether we can get a permit or not."

Although an aspiring censor would certainly suggest otherwise, the point is not that such movies drive legions of solid citizens to arm themselves. The powerful appeal of the revenge theme in mass entertainment is simply one more manifestation of the gap between private feelings about revenge and the public pretense that justice and vengeance have nothing, perish the uncivilized thought, to do with each other.

One need not turn to the realm of escapist entertainment to perceive both the moral and pragmatic conflicts arising from the notion that there is, or ought to be, an absolute dichotomy between justice and revenge. The pages of any newspaper will suffice. In Florida, a respected black businessman is somehow shot and killed by a white policeman who has stopped him for a routine traffic violation. The police officer is acquitted of any wrongdoing, and rioting ensues in the poorest black neighborhoods of Miami. After the street killing of a rabbi in New York, hundreds of Hasidic Jews occupy the local police station—overturning desks, shouting at officers, and bringing police business to a halt—because they do not believe the authorities are moving vigorously enough to bring the murderer to justice. In England and the United States, a number of battered wives who have repeatedly sought help from the police and been refused deal with their heavy-fisted husbands by picking up knives, guns, and torches.

On one level, all of these manifestations of vindictiveness may be viewed as extreme responses to everyday failures in the administration of criminal justice. But failures of social justice are also involved; the difficulty of bringing those in positions of traditional authority to account—whether they are police officers who have violated laws they are sworn to uphold or men who have abused their power within the family—is a historic source of private vengeance. It is difficult to separate specific legal penalties from larger questions of equity.

On a practical level, the human desire for retribution requires no elaborate philosophical rationalization. A victim wants to see an assailant punished not only for reasons of pragmatic deterrence but also as a means of repairing a damaged sense of civic order and personal identity. Deterrence and retribution are hardly identical, but the former invariably involves an element of the latter. In the United States, and to a lesser but increasing extent in Western Europe, there is a widespread perception that the judicial system is becoming less effective as a deterrent to crime. In Europe, where ordinary street crime is much less pervasive than it is in America, skepticism about the effectiveness of the police and judiciary tends to focus on the difficulty of dealing with political terrorism. The importance of this issue has been recognized by the Italian government in its determined, long-term effort to penetrate the Red Brigades, and the first concrete evidence of success—the freeing of the kidnaped American General James Dozier, followed by the swift trial of his abductors—was responsible for a significant surge of confidence in institutions that had long appeared helpless in the face of politically motivated assaults on both public officials and private citizens. The perception that governmental authority is unable to protect victims of violence —whether of a political or ordinary criminal nature—poses a serious threat to a social contract in which individuals agree to restrain their impulses toward revenge for the greater good.

Stripped of moralizing, law exists not only to restrain retribution but to mete it out—and to mete it out on behalf of individuals whose rights have been violated as well as in the interests of society as a whole. These functions exist in a state of tension rather than opposition; within that tension, great legal battles are fought and civilization is defined anew. A society that is unable to convince individuals of its ability to exact atonement for injury is a society that runs a constant risk of having its members revert to the wilder forms of justice. No one has a right to exact blood atonement, but everyone has a right to expect that the guilty receive punishment commensurate with the seriousness of their crimes.

It is simple-minded to suggest that anyone who believes in proportional punishment must therefore adhere to a strict "eye for eye" code of justice, leading inevitably to support for capital punishment. But it is equally absurd to maintain, as neo-conservative spokesmen frequently do, that opposition to the death penalty—which represents the outermost limit of *legalized* revenge—is invariably motivated by the soft-hearted, witless conviction that there is no such thing as a bad boy. In his famous essay "Reflections on the Guillotine," Albert Camus emphasized that his opposition to the death penalty was not founded on any illusions about the natural goodness of human beings.

I do not believe . . . that there is no responsibility in this world and that we must give way to that modern tendency to absolve everyone, victim and murderer, in the same confusion. Sentimental confusion is made up of cowardice rather than generosity and eventually justifies whatever is worst in this world. If you keep on excusing, you eventually give your blessing to the slave camp, to cowardly force, to organized executions, to the cynicism of the great political monsters: you finally hand over your brothers. This can be seen around us. But it so happens, in the present state of the world, that the man of today wants laws and institutions suitable to a convalescent, which will curb him without breaking him and lead him without crushing him.[8]

There is, or ought to be, a vast middle ground between belief in the death penalty and acceptance of a system that allows too many killers to "pay" with only a few years of their own lives —or to escape retribution altogether through legal and psychiatric loopholes—for a life they have taken from another. One of the great dangers of failing to acknowledge the legitimacy, and the psychological and social necessity, of measured retribution is the disappearance of a tenable middle ground.

The resurgence of support for capital punishment during the past decade, after a lengthy period of declining popular approval in the United States and Europe, is a striking example of the frustrations that may be released when people lose confidence in the ability of their society to exact appropriate limited retribution. Although proponents of capital punishment are fond of elaborate statistical arguments attempting to set an objective deterrent value on executions, support for the death penalty is based on emotion rather than logic. In a culture that regards "legalized revenge" as a term of opprobrium, there is a deep need to ascribe vengeance to other, more socially acceptable motives; rationalizing the death penalty as a form of deterrence fulfills this emotional need.

In a discussion of vindictiveness as neurosis, Karen Horney takes a utilitarian view of the role of social institutions designed to regulate the expression of revenge: "While they implicitly acknowledge the general existence of needs to retaliate, they also take these needs psychologically out of the hands of the individual by rendering them a civic duty."[9] Horney's observation embodies much of the contemporary psychiatric approach to the question of revenge. In this view, the urge to retaliate may be universal but it is unhealthy, and retributive institutions are important primarily because they remove the psychic burden of vengeance from individuals whose vindictiveness might otherwise endanger themselves as well as others. Although no one would deny that excessive vindictiveness can become a destructive obsession and a form of mental illness, the therapeutic sensibility (to borrow Christopher Lasch's phrase) has done much to confuse the social issues inherent in the relationship between justice and revenge. Retributive institutions were established not to promote mental health but to enhance public safety. They remove the practical, not the psychological, burden of revenge from individuals. If they fail—or are seen to fail—in the fulfillment of their practical function, they are likely to increase rather than decrease the psychic burden of vengeance. The fact that civilized men and women adhere to a social contract requiring them to settle disputes in courtrooms instead of at the corral before sundown does not mean that the impulse toward revenge has been eradicated—any more than the institution of marriage implies the disappearance of sexual impulses directed toward anyone other than one's lawful spouse.

The taboo attached to revenge in our culture today is not unlike the illegitimate aura associated with sex in the Victorian world. The personal and social price we pay for the pretense that revenge and justice have nothing to do with each other is as high as the one paid by the Victorians for their conviction that lust was totally alien to the marital love sanctioned by church and state. The struggle to contain revenge has been conducted at the highest level of moral and civic awareness attained at each stage in the development of civilization. The self-conscious nature of the effort is expectable in view of the persistent state of tension between uncontrolled vengeance as destroyer and controlled vengeance as an unavoidable component of justice. The replacement of this rigorously attained awareness by taboo is a curious development in a century that has experienced its own full measure of revenge, expanded beyond old limits by modern science and technology. Like all prohibitions honored mainly in the breach, the revenge taboo contains a disturbing potential for social regression. It is an enemy of the restraint it is mistakenly thought to encourage.

II Written in Blood

What though the field be lost?
All is not lost—the unconquerable will,
And study of revenge, immortal hate,
And courage never to submit or yield:
And what is else not to be overcome.
JOHN MILTON, *Paradise Lost*

Something of vengeance I had tasted for the first time. An
aromatic wine it seemed, on swallowing, warm and racy, its
first after-flavour, metallic and corroding, gave me a sensation as if I had been poisoned.
CHARLOTTE BRONTË, *Jane Eyre*

I believe in consequences.
CHARLES MCCARRY, *The Tears of Autumn,* 1974

Revenge, like love and the acquisition of worldly goods, is one
of the grand themes of western literature, a fountainhead of epic
and drama. It appears in every guise known to man and woman:
as comedy and tragedy; as a sickness of the soul and as emotional liberation; as disgrace and as honor; as an enemy of social
order and a restorer of cosmic order; as mortal sin and saving
grace; as destructive self-indulgence and as justice. Unlike jealousy—which, in literature as in life, invariably manifests itself
as a corrosive and futile emotion—revenge is a mixed substance. It has both a private and a public aspect; its effects on
the individual and on society are sometimes at odds.

Like the acts of retribution they carry out, actors in dramas of revenge, especially those created by writers of genius, tend to be mixed characters. Fictional heroes are always undone by jealousy but they are occasionally restored to sanity—or manage to restore themselves—through vengeance. Even when vindictiveness is seen as a ruinous force, destructive to individuals as well as social institutions, the literature of revenge is shaped by a persistent tension between moral condemnation and psychological fascination.

Writing at a time when the suppression of private revenge was one of the most critical tasks faced by secular and religious authority, Milton managed to create a devil whose seductiveness stemmed not only from pride but from the unremitting pursuit of vengeance directed against divinity itself. It is not surprising that the famous couplet "Revenge, at first though sweet,/Bitter ere long back on itself recoils" is one of the most misquoted (for unconscious as well as conscious reasons) passages in English literature. It is frequently transformed into a contrary aphorism: *Revenge is sweet.* Defenders of the faith have not been mistaken in their contention that Milton made the devil altogether too appealing to inspire sufficient fear of hell. Judged by human standards, Satan is the most recognizable actor in Milton's drama of pride and vengeance; his quest for recognition is, unmistakably, a human endeavor and his spirit remains unbroken in "dubious battle."

> Or if our substance be indeed divine,
> And cannot cease to be, we are at worst
> On this side nothing; and by proof we feel
> Our power sufficient to disturb his Heaven,
> And with perpetual inroads to alarm,
> Though inaccessible, his fatal throne:
> Which, if not victory, is yet revenge.[1]

From the earliest Semitic and Greek epics through the late Victorian era, the moral tension engendered by the subject of revenge has preoccupied artists catering to every level of public taste and intellect. This preoccupation has not abated in the twentieth century but it has lost some of the moral and literary stature formerly attached to questions of vengeance and honor. Nineteenth-century readers might address the problem of revenge on the level dictated by their literary tastes—in *Wuthering Heights, Jane Eyre,* and *Moby Dick* or in the cliffhanging serials of the penny dreadfuls. Seventeenth-century theatrical audiences could choose to grapple with the psychological complexities of a *Hamlet* or content themselves with the straightforward body count of *The Revenger's Tragedy* (enhanced by ingenious methods of dispatch, such as the concealment of a skull with an alluring poisoned mask in order to beguile the enemy into a fatal kiss). In classical Athens, one may safely assume, the audiences of Aeschylus, Sophocles, and Euripides were also drawn to less lofty productions by artists whose works did not survive the political and cultural upheavals of the ancient world.

In our own century, revenge, with its complicated and shifting relationship to honor and justice, occupies a much narrower band within the spectrum of artistic endeavor. For the most part, vengeance is relegated to the territory of detective and spy novels, which—however seriously they may be taken by their readers and authors—are not taken seriously by most arbiters of culture. Detective fiction is generally regarded as escape reading; the dilemmas of its heroes and villains are thought (or wished) to have only the most tenuous connection with "the real world." Detective and spy stories are accorded literary respect only insofar as they depart from the mechanics of crime and punishment to concentrate on the interior landscape of the spymaster, detective, or criminal.

The constriction of literary interest in a theme that has fascinated great writers for millennia clearly indicates a significant shift in cultural values. One possible explanation for this change is the fact that the impulse toward revenge, like so many other disturbing human drives, has come to be regarded more as a form of mental illness than as a conscious combination of motivation and action with sufficient moral weight to demand a reckoning. When the question of revenge is raised today, it is usually discussed within the context of psychological and social deviance. The equation of vengeance with aberrant behavior offers one explanation for the theme's frequent appearance in murder mysteries and its comparative rarity in literary works concerned with more ordinary crimes of the heart.

Contemporary writers are, of course, as interested as their predecessors in deviant behavior, but true artists are generally drawn to forms of deviance that are clearly related, whether closely or distantly, to behavior that is considered normal. Without a standard of health, pathology has no meaning. Deviant sexual behavior, we now believe, exists on a continuum with "normal" sexuality; for writers (indeed, for anyone) much of the subject's endless fascination lies in the struggle to define boundaries. To make sex interesting, one need not write a novel about incest or rape; relations between consenting adults offer enough possibilities for the active literary imagination. The boundary between the licit and the illicit is always shifting but it never vanishes—not, at any rate, for an extended period of time—from our moral and emotional landscape.

Unlike sex, the many forms of revenge do not arrange themselves on a moral continuum in the contemporary imagination. Regarded as the sick vestige of a more primitive stage of human development, vengeance naturally falls within the province of detectives and other specialists in abnormal psychology. Revenge, like cannibalism or infanticide, is seen as perversion—suitable fodder for movies made to be shown on commercial television but not an appropriate subject for those who wish to be considered genuine artists.

The diminution of literary interest in revenge may be a relatively new phenomenon, but the projection of vengeful impulses onto more primitive peoples and cultures has always been a literary commonplace. In analyzing classics of revenge, successive generations of writers have abandoned common sense and suggested that the Greeks (or the Romans, or the Elizabethans) were preoccupied with the theme of vengeance because—bloodthirsty savages that they were!—they saw nothing wrong with hacking someone to pieces in defense of honor. Thus, critics in the third century A.D., or in the sixteenth century, or in the pre-Holocaust period of the twentieth century, have been inclined to pat themselves on their backs and thank the gods (or God) that they were fortunate enough to have been born into a truly civilized world.

A 1929 edition of *Hamlet,* edited by Joseph Quincy Adams, offers a perfect example of the "we-must-realize-how-uncivilized-they-were-back-then" school of criticism. One of the best-known Shakespearean scholars of his generation (although his rigid brand of Victorian criticism has condemned him to obscurity today), Adams takes unnamed predecessors to task for suggesting that Hamlet's indecisiveness arises, at least in part, from Shakespeare's desire to condemn private revenge. "The notion that it was morally wrong for a son to avenge his father's murder . . . was not entertained in Hamlet's time," he argues. "On the contrary, revenge was believed to be necessary to the eternal rest of the murdered one. . . . We must be careful not to import into the play modern conceptions of ethical propriety. To the people of his own time, and even to the audience of the Elizabethan age, Hamlet was called upon to perform a 'dread' (=sacred) duty."[2] One imagines a scholarly critic of the twenty-third century, writing of Philip Roth's *Portnoy's Complaint:* "The notion that a son ought to pay attention to his mother's rules for sexual conduct was not entertained in Portnoy's time. On the contrary, casual sex was believed to be necessary for the mental health of men (and, in the latter half of the twentieth century, of women as well). We must be careful not to import into the novel modern conceptions of ethical propriety. To the readers of the twentieth century, Portnoy was called upon to perform an essential duty."

There is no surer guide to any epoch's ethical and political preoccupations than the recurrence of an issue in literature. (Perhaps it is more accurate to state that there was no surer guide before the advent of electronic communications media.) Aeschylus, Sophocles, Euripides, Kyd, Shakespeare, Webster, Milton, and Racine were not drawn to the theme of revenge because it was a socially acceptable, albeit bloody, commonplace of their times but because it was a source of intense, deeply felt moral and social controversy. The projection of revenge onto geographically or historically distant races is not a bias confined to critics of narrow vision; until the rise of drama with bourgeois heroes and settings, this tendency was an unbreakable convention of revenge tragedy. As the distinguished Italian scholar Mario Praz told an audience of his English colleagues, "In the same way as the Italian Senecans placed their gruesome plots among barbarian peoples, the English dramatists chose for their favorite scene of their horrors, 'the darkened Italian palace, with its wrought-iron bars preventing escape; its embroidered carpets muffling the footsteps; its hidden, suddenly yawning trap-doors; its arras-hangings concealing masked ruffians; its garlands of poisoned flowers.' "[3] While the authors of Elizabethan and Jacobean revenge tragedy were depicting florid Italian and Spanish scenes, Italian and Spanish dramatists of the same period chose equally exotic (to them) Turkish settings. This relegation of revenge to distant and mythic worlds was motivated by political as well as aesthetic considerations, in much the same manner as officially published Soviet writers are apt to couch their criticisms of commissars in attacks on Tsarist nobles and bureaucrats.

In the world of the Renaissance, the removal of vengeance to an alien and bygone setting was not politically motivated in the narrowest sense, although it is certainly true that an Elizabethan playwright might reasonably have anticipated a firsthand taste of royal retribution were he to write about vendettas in Elizabeth's court instead of misunderstandings be-

tween noble families in fourteenth-century Verona or machina-
tions of eleventh-century Danish royalty. Rather, the projection of revenge was politic in the primary dictionary definition
(i.e., prudent), not merely because it kept the author's head
safely attached to his neck but because it afforded a measure of
psychic distance between the audience and a profoundly disturbing subject.

Modern critics who believe that blood revenge was a
"given" for audiences four hundred years ago are simply mistaken, in the usual fashion of those who wish to assert the
superior moral vision of their own moment in history. Both
theologians and literary critics (it is not always possible to
distinguish between them) of the sixteenth century, in their
eagerness to proclaim the superiority of Christian "forgiveness"
to both paganism and Judaism, labored under analogous misconceptions about the views of revenge embodied in Greek
tragedy and in the Biblical and rabbinical writings of the Jews.

The revenge tragedy of classical Greece is of course fundamental to subsequent western interpretations of the relationship
between justice and vengeance. Even today, proponents of capital punishment hark back to the concept of homicide as pollution to support their contention that bloodstains in the fabric
of society can only be expunged by state-ordered shedding of
more blood. Moving beyond relatively narrow issues of criminal justice, the acts of vengeance woven through the plots of
Attic tragedy have been transformed, in the post-Freudian
world, into metaphors for the psychic underpinning of all
human behavior.

In the modern imagination, Greek tragedy is invariably
associated with a highly deterministic view of vengeance as a
constant in the moral universe. It is generally asserted—and not
only in the survey courses in western civilization forced upon
college freshmen—that the action of Greek drama must be
viewed within a context allowing little or no latitude for human

beings to affect their own destinies. In this interpretation, vengeance—like most other human acts—is presented not as a choice but as a moral imperative, a divine command to restore order when order has been violated. Blood cries out for blood, as capital-punishment advocates might (and do) say.

This view is not entirely accurate even when applied to the deterministic works of Aeschylus and Sophocles, but it is a totally inaccurate description of Euripides, the last (although he was outlived by the nonagenarian Sophocles) of the trio of Athenian playwrights usually lumped together as "the Greeks." As the great scholar Moses Hadas observed, the Greeks all look alike to a near-sighted reader leafing through the collected plays. On second glance, though, it is clear that Euripides, while as obsessed with the revenge theme as Aeschylus and Sophocles, was concerned not with the place of vengeance in divine order but with its consequences in the world inhabited by real men and women. His characters "do not invite tragedy in order to illustrate the operation of some grand ethical abstraction and to achieve heroism; theirs is the humbler aim of surviving as tolerably as may be amid conventional constraints which make tolerable existence difficult."[4]

The gods exist, but they are not always benign—and they do not provide sufficient justification for the vengeful passions that animate an Orestes or a Medea. Oh, there are *explanations* for the murderous violence. Euripides' Orestes is something of a thug, and Medea is a wife and mother driven to savage acts by a society that offers no legal recourse for women or foreigners. But these explanations are not justifications, any more than a scientist's observation of a fatal bacillus under the microscope is a justification for the organism's existence in the universe. Although the revenge tragedies of Euripides are based on classic myths, his empirical voice conveys a startlingly modern sensibility. One can more easily imagine him in conversation with Sand, Ibsen, or Shaw than with most of the Elizabethan and Jacobean dramatists. (It would of course be ridiculous to suggest that Euripides "saw" women, or conflicts between men and women, in the same way as Shaw or Ibsen. However, it seems to me that the weight of evidence—both literary and historical—supports those critics who maintain that Euripides' relationship to his own society was more analogous to Ibsen's than to, say, Shakespeare's.)

Euripides was born in 484 and died in 406 B.C. Thucydides was to describe the period as an era in which "men tried to surpass all the record of previous times in the ingenuity of their enterprises and the enormity of their revenges." Sophocles, who was born in 496, survived his younger rival by some months— long enough to dress his chorus in mourning garments when the news of Euripides' death reached Athens from Macedonia.

The apocryphal story of Euripides' death is itself a revenge tragedy—one the playwright might have considered a comedy. According to legend, Euripides died near a Macedonian village where he interceded with the king on behalf of some poor, hungry Thracians who had killed and eaten one of the royal Molossian hounds. The king decreed a penalty of a talent apiece for each villager, but Euripides persuaded him to cancel the fine because the Thracians could not afford to pay it. Soon afterward, some other Molossian hounds were set loose for a hunt; when they found the meddling Euripides sitting peacefully in a wood outside the village, they tore him to pieces. They were the children of the original hound, whose death had gone unavenged as a result of Euripides' well-intentioned interference.

As one might expect, there is no historical evidence supporting this tale of canine blood vengeance. Euripides did, however, die in Macedonia. It is believed that he left Athens in sheer aggravation at the drama critics of his day, who, by their dismissal of much of the poet's work, left incontrovertible evidence that the Golden Age of Greece produced its share of short-sighted cultural commentators—members of a species that did not acquire a definitive description until the nineteenth century, when Charles Dickens came up with "the lice of literature."

Euripides and Sophocles both spent their young manhood and middle age in the period of prosperity and cultural glory that followed the Athenian defeat of the invading Persian armies, and they both lived to see the economic, military, and moral decline of Athens in the exhausting Peloponnesian War, which began in 431 and ended with the victory of Sparta in 404 B.C. Although no writer as great as Sophocles could have been impervious to the upheavals of his civilization, he cast his lot with the moral universe of the past. His vision of the limited ability of mortals to influence a fate ordained by the gods, outlined most starkly in the drama of Oedipus, is close to that of Aeschylus (525–456 B.C.), who did not live to see the wrenching effect of the war on the civilization that had formed his art.

Although Euripides never explicitly rejected the old gods, he did not see them as the determining force in human behavior. He was interested in justifying neither the ways of the gods to men nor the ways of men to the gods, but of men and women to themselves. This is the sensibility that strikes us as modern; it also explains why Euripides, who received relatively little acclaim in his lifetime, was performed in the ancient world long after the works of Aeschylus and Sophocles had come to seem as remote to subsequent generations of Greeks and Romans as minor Jacobean drama does to us today. (The persistent popularity of Euripides for several centuries after his death may also explain why eighteen of his plays survive, while we have only seven texts apiece from Aeschylus and Sophocles. In the winter of 1981, seven separate productions of plays by Euripides were staged in New York theatres, including a presentation of *The Bacchae* in Japanese.)

Blood revenge is a central theme of all Greek tragedy, but Euripides' attitudes differ markedly from those of Aeschylus and Sophocles. In conformity with the conventions of the Attic stage, he retained the names and stories of classical myth—but that is as far as his conformity went.

As Hadas observes, Euripides imagined and developed his characters as contemporaries subject to contemporary pressures. The bloody acts of revenge committed in his plays are not the results of a preordained plan, either in the classic Greek religious or the modern psychoanalytic sense. The characters do what they do out of a combination of social pressures and individual strengths and weaknesses. The gods exist, but they are not to be blamed for the follies of men and women. Acts of revenge—whether initiated by individuals or by states exchanging the usual pretexts in defense of their honor—are neither glorious nor inevitable. They are the products of lust, greed, braggadocio, and the absence of social mechanisms to regulate expressions of vengeance.

Medea is the first work in western literature to examine a woman and her dreadful act of revenge within the context of women's lack of access to legal means of redressing grievances. The message is not that revenge is sweet but that vengeance is what we can expect in the absence of a system of justice that incorporates an element of measured retribution. In retrospect, the most remarkable aspect of *Medea* is the fact that Euripides, in raising questions about the social forces that might drive a woman to the horrifying decision to murder her own children, was not a generation or two but twenty-three centuries ahead of his time. His unjustified reputation as a misogynist is based entirely on revulsion at the acts committed by some of his female characters. But these acts—unlike, say, the tragedy of Oedipus—are neither inevitable nor are they the product of "treacherous" feminine nature. They are appalling, even crazed, but they are the product of a specific social order that places women at a grave disadvantage. Euripides does not approve of or admire Medea's actions, but he understands them.

Medea saves Jason's life and enables him to capture the Golden Fleece; she deceives those who trust her, betraying family and homeland for Jason, on whose behalf she is "more than fond and less than wise." After their return to Corinth, where she bears him two sons, he leaves her for a younger woman of his own tribe—and a king's daughter. The future children of his new marriage, unlike those of his union with a foreigner, will be eligible to inherit the throne of Corinth. Medea, knowing that Jason has every right to abandon her under the laws of his own land, seeks revenge not by slaying him but by destroying his future, in the persons of their own sons as well as of his new bride. The only innocents in this revenge tragedy are the children. Jason, who has pompously informed Medea that she has no grievance because being an abandoned wife in civilized Hellas is preferable to being the honored princess of a savage race, deserves what he gets (or at least ought to expect what he gets). Misogyny is in the eye of the beholder, not the vision of the author.

Medea is essentially a social drama; the act of vengeance at the center of the play is at once a violation of the codes that govern familial relations and a logical outgrowth of those codes. Individual character does play a role in the action: Medea has the strength and heartlessness to act as other women do not, or cannot, and Jason is something of a dullard in his failure to perceive the vengeful force of his wife's nature. Nevertheless, the characters—and the act that transforms their lives—are products of a social system in which a married woman is her husband's property, to be retained or cast aside as he wishes. The gods have little to do with this tragedy. (The theatrical tour de force of Medea's departure in a chariot drawn by winged dragons is nothing more than a splendid opportunity for special-effects men to display their talents; it is "intentionally incredible."[5])

In his later work, Euripides united character and conventional myth in the treatment of revenge. The qualities which distinguish him from Aeschylus and Sophocles—and which give his view of vengeance a crucial importance—are most apparent in *Electra*, the second drama in the Oresteian trilogy. It is the only segment of the trilogy that has been preserved in interpretations by all three Greek dramatists. The philosophic distance between Euripides and the parallel versions offered by Aeschylus in *Choëphoroe* and Sophocles in his *Electra* is much greater than, let us say, the gap between Arthur Conan Doyle and Dorothy L. Sayers. Those who share Edmund Wilson's low opinion of detective fiction will regard this comparison as an example of *lèse-majesté*. Nevertheless, all revenge tragedy has a strong detective element; *Oedipus the King* is the first detective story in literary history. For the Greeks, the detection was purely psychological, since the one thing everyone in the audience knew was who committed the crime. The gap that separates Euripides from Aeschylus and Sophocles looms especially large in light of the familiarity of the Oresteian legends upon which every dramatic interpretation is based. Untroubled by the need to construct a whodunit, the Greeks were free to explore the question of why terrible deeds occur (or are permitted to occur). Aeschylus and Sophocles ask: Under what circumstances is revenge ordained by the gods as human fate? Euripides asks: *Is* revenge ordained? By whom? Why?

The myth that forms the backdrop of the *Oresteia* is never made explicit in the plays, since it was familiar to all Greek audiences. Atreus, king of Argos, banished his brother Thyestes, whom he suspected of plotting against his throne. Thyestes eventually returned to Argos under religious protection (a kind of moveable sanctuary), which prohibited his brother from harming him directly. But Atreus devised a plan more cunning than any open attack: he killed Thyestes' children and arranged for them to be served to their father at a banquet. When Thyestes realized what his brother had done, he cursed the entire house of Atreus. The Oresteian trilogy follows the curse as it unfolds over several generations. For Aeschylus and Sophocles, acceptance of religious convention imposed inevitability upon every ensuing act of vengeance.

It is easy, even when one is familiar with the Greek myths,

to forget who does what to whom in the *Oresteia*. (Who, apart from Biblical scholars and the truly pious, remembers the birth order of King David's sons or the name of the first disciple to see Jesus after the resurrection?) Agamemnon, slain at the beginning of the trilogy, is Atreus' son. He is murdered by his wife, Clytemnestra, in revenge for his sacrifice of their daughter Iphigenia. Iphigenia had to die because a seer informed Agamemnon that the Greek fleet would be destroyed before reaching Troy without the sacrifice of the king's own daughter. In Aeschylus' and Sophocles' universe, the sacrifice of Iphigenia is a reasonable act, performed by a monarch who chooses public obligation over private feeling. For Euripides, such an act can never be justified; it belongs to a sequence of vengeful folly that ensues when human beings assume roles inconsistent with human capabilities and limitations.

When the body of Agamemnon is discovered in Aeschylus' version, the chorus tries to fix the blame for the disaster on Helen of Troy and the Trojan war. No, says Clytemnestra. The curse is responsible, and the curse not only explains but justifies the murder of Agamemnon. Clytemnestra's lover, Aegisthus (recognized by the Greek audience as one of Thyestes' offspring who escaped being cooked in the fateful banquet), appears and exults over the deed:

> O happy day, when Justice comes into her own!
> Now I believe that gods, who dwell above the earth,
> See what men suffer, and award a recompense:
> Here, tangled in a net the avenging Furies wove,
> He lies, a sight to warm my heart; and pays his blood
> In full atonement for his father's treacherous crime.[6]

The gods not only sanction vengeance; they demand it. Revenge is not only related to justice; it *is* justice. In the second part of the trilogy, Aeschylus and Sophocles never question the righteousness of burdening the next generation with the curse of blood revenge; Euripides does. The outline of the plot is, of course, virtually identical in all three versions: Agamemnon's and Clytemnestra's son Orestes returns to avenge his father's death by killing his mother. (The young Orestes was stolen away from the palace by his tutor to escape certain death at the hands of Aegisthus, who had taken Agamemnon's throne along with his wife.) Orestes' sister Electra, who is treated as a virtual slave by her mother and wicked stepfather, lives in the hope of her brother's return. When he does return, he carries out the mandate of the gods by murdering Clytemnestra and Aegisthus.

In both Aeschylus and Sophocles, the heroes have the noble stature decreed by myth. They are dignified, carrying out the will of their ancestors and their gods. Other characters, who advocate compromise or pragmatism, are seen as pitiable at best and contemptible at worst. An exchange in Sophocles between Electra and Chrysothemis (who, unlike Orestes, was still hanging around her evil stepfather's palace and, unlike Electra, had chosen to hold her tongue) illustrates this attitude. Electra is, as usual, calling for revenge against her mother. Chrysothemis admonishes her:

> What have you come to say out of doors,
> Sister? Will you never learn, in all this time,
> Not to give way to your empty anger?
> Yet this much I know, and know my heart, too,
> That I am sick at what I see, so that
> If I had strength, I would let them know how I feel.
> But under pain of punishment, I think,
> I must make my voyage with lowered sails,
> That I may not seem to do something and then prove
> Ineffectual. But justice, justice,
> Is not on my side but on yours. If I am
> To live and not as a prisoner, I must
> In all things listen to my lords.

Electra answers:

It is strange indeed that you who were born
Of our father should forget him
And heed your mother. All these warnings
Of me you have learned from her. Nothing is your own.
Now you must make a choice, one way or the other,
Either to be a fool
Or sensible—and to forget your friends.
Here you are saying: "If I had the strength,
I would show my hatred of them!" You who, when I
Did everything to take vengeance for my father,
Never did a thing to help—yes, discouraged the doer.
Is not this cowardice on top of baseness? . . .
I do not want to win your honor.
Nor would you if you were sound of mind.[7]

When he returns, Orestes fulfills his sister's vision of the noble avenger. Aeschylus draws a particularly awe-inspiring portrait of Orestes in *Choëphoroe,* showing him temporarily losing his mind after the murder of his mother. Obedient to the injunctions of patriarchy and divinity, he carries out the task, but his human nature rebels at what he has done. He is only restored to himself by divine absolution in *Eumenides,* the conclusion of the trilogy.

In Euripides' *Electra,* the characters are far from noble—in the spirit or the flesh. Orestes finds his sister in the hut of a peasant, to whom she was given by Aegisthus in order to prevent a match with a man of noble stature whose children might grow up to lay claim to the throne. This Electra is more concerned with regaining the clothes, accommodations, and status of a princess than with the honor of her family. Before Orestes reveals his identity to her, she admonishes his traveling companion to tell her brother "of the insults heaped on me and on him. Tell him of my clothes, like a farm-hand's. Tell him of the filth with which I am laden. Tell him the sort of house I live in—I that come from royal halls. I work at my own clothes with my shuttle, or I should have none to cover my own naked body. I carry water from the spring with my own hands. I have no part in the holy festivals. I am deprived of a share in the dances. . . . But my mother sits on a throne amidst the spoils of Phrygia, and about her seat are stationed captive Asiatic women whom my father won; they wear Idaean robes clasped with brooches of gold."[8]

Euripides also cuts Orestes down to life size from his earlier heroic proportions. He is not an evil figure, but rather a braggart with an unruly young man's taste for violence. Unlike Aeschylus' Orestes, who carries out the vengeful murders in a religious fervor but whose nature would not ordinarily be disposed to such acts, Euripides' Orestes takes a personal satisfaction in his task—especially in the murder of his mother's consort—that can hardly be seen as virtuous. When he tells his enraptured sister that he has disposed of Aegisthus, he announces: "I come from a battle of deeds not words. I have killed Aegisthus. To set this forth clearly for all to know I bring you the dead man himself. If you like, expose him to the wild beasts to devour, or impale him on a high stake to be plunder for the birds, the children of the sky. He is now yours."[9]

But Orestes does not display the same relish when he murders his mother. He knows it is his duty to kill Clytemnestra, but he hesitates as Electra goads him on. This Electra envies her brother his right to take up the sword as she envies her mother her jewels, clothes, and slaves. Even after he has done what he believes to be his duty, Orestes has regrets. "Did you see how the poor thing threw her dress aside," he asks in an exchange with Electra and the chorus, "how she bared her breasts as she was being murdered—ah me—how those limbs, our mother's limbs, lay on the ground? And her hair I. . . . This was her cry, when she put her hand upon my chin: 'My child, I implore you.' Her hands clung to my cheeks, so that my weapon nigh fell from my hands." How did Orestes manage to endure the sight of his mother's suffering and finish the deed? "I threw the mantle over my eyes," he says.[10]

For Euripides, this is the essence of violent revenge, whether carried out in the private drama of family quarrels or the public drama of war: bloody corpses and living men and women mouthing pieties in the midst of the ruins they have created. In *Electra,* the *deus ex machina* poses even more of a challenge to common sense than Medea's chariot. Castor and Pollux appear in the sky and promise a troubled Orestes that everything will be fine when he is tried for and acquitted of murder by a divine tribunal. *If you believe this,* Euripides seems to be saying, *I have a wonderful bargain for you, this bridge across the Aegean, only a hundred talents down.*

In view of the striking differences between Euripides' *Electra* and the versions of Aeschylus and Sophocles, it would be fascinating to know how he presented the trial of Orestes in his conclusion of the trilogy (given the conventions of Greek drama, it is reasonable to assume that he wrote such a conclusion but that its text did not survive). We do know how Aeschylus absolved Orestes and restored him to sanity. Moreover, Aeschylus' *Eumenides* is more than a dissertation on which forms of vengeance are sanctioned by the Olympian religion and which are not; it is also an explicit statement of civilized misogyny, equating female vengeance with slyness and male vengeance with justice.

In Aeschylus' trial, the Furies, a chorus of female deities, speak for Clytemnestra. They remind the Olympian gods that Clytemnestra killed her husband only after he had sacrificed their daughter for victory in the Trojan war. This observation carries no weight with Athena, who makes a point of the fact that she sprang full-blown from the head of Zeus and owes no loyalty to mothers. The murder of a woman who is guilty of killing her husband, she asserts, is a matter of no importance.

She casts the deciding vote to acquit Orestes before the divine tribunal; he leaves with his honor and sanity intact. This scene tells us as much about the force of patriarchy in the ancient world as it does about the complicated Greek view of blood vengeance.

It is no accident that Aeschylus and Sophocles, rather than Euripides, are the chief sources for so many of our psychological metaphors. In the Freudian world, neurosis is the price of civilization; in the world of Aeschylus and Sophocles, the temporary disruption of human lives is the price of a divinely ordained moral order. These two artists were fully aware of the human cost of elevating duty over emotion (without such awareness, the tragedies could scarcely have retained their psychological resonance for so long), but human cost was not their fundamental concern. Sophocles' Antigone is a heroine because she stands for an unchanging moral order in opposition to the pragmatism (or opportunism) of Creon; her love for her dead brother is incidental. Sophocles' Clytemnestra is a villainess because she does not recognize the public obligation Agamemnon accepted in sacrificing their daughter; her maternal love is as incidental as Antigone's sisterly devotion. It cannot justify her revenge against Agamemnon; it cannot command the understanding of her other children or stay the vengeful hand of Orestes. The characters play out their assigned roles; they cannot do otherwise. Individual acts of vengeance are abstractions, ritualized, albeit essential, punctuation marks in a larger moral scheme. They take their ordained places in our cultural unconscious.

In Euripides, acts of vengeance and their bloody consequences are not abstractions. Blind adherence to customs that have lost their original meaning—not gods or ancient curses—are responsible for the unfolding tragedies. To a modern audience, the posture of Euripides' Orestes is analogous to that of the unfortunate Japanese soldiers who were left behind on isolated Pacific islands at the end of World War II and who emerged ten, fifteen, even twenty-five years later, still believing it was their obligation to fight and die for the Emperor. In *Trojan Women,* which remarkably was first performed at the height of Athenian enthusiasm for the Peloponnesian War, the shattered survivors can hardly remember the quarrels and curses and vows of retribution that brought them to ruin.

Revenge is not taken for granted in Euripides, and that, too, is remarkable within the context of his age. "Free will," as understood in both Jewish and Christian tradition, is as absent from Euripides' drama as it is from Aeschylus' and Sophocles'. But Euripides, unlike his predecessors, invites us to consider the alternatives. What if Jason hadn't been a bully and something of a fool? What if women had some socially sanctioned way of defending their honor? What if Orestes had listened to the more gentle voice of his heart, rejected Electra's call to vengeance, and decided to drop the vendetta, leaving to the gods the fulfill-ment of the curse on the house of Atreus—if that was their will? Of the three great Greek poets, Euripides alone asks: *Must it come to this?*

Euripides does not deny the authority of the gods (although he was frequently accused of sacrilege by his rivals), but he does question human interpretation of divine orders. Moreover, he suggests nothing resembling the hierarchical distinction be-tween public and private revenge that lies at the heart of Eli-zabethan drama—in which private revenge is always wrong because man is usurping the authority of God but public re-venge is frequently right because it is carried out by God's authorized agents. In Euripides, the morality of revenge is de-termined by its human consequences—and those consequences are seldom a delight to behold. There is no assumption of an intrinsic moral distinction between public and private revenge, between justice sanctioned—no, ordered—by the gods and ven-geance prohibited by divine law. Revenge is never treated as a purely symbolic ritual; it is always, finally, a matter of mangled flesh. The audience can never throw the mantle over its eyes.

In the Elizabethan era, with its inescapable Christian theology, the distinction between godly public revenge and sinful private vengeance was basic to literature, religious thought, and historical analysis. To understand the revenge tragedies of the sixteenth and seventeenth centuries, it is necessary to comprehend the grave error implicit in widespread modern assumptions about the moral indifference of Elizabethan and Jacobean audiences as they contemplated bloody dramatic spectacles of vengeance. Although the bonds linking revenge, justice, and honor have been persistent themes of all western literature, no other era has produced such an extraordinary outpouring of revenge tragedy, beginning with the crude, Senecan-descended melodramas of the early Elizabethan stage. Such preoccupation could never have emerged from a climate of moral indifference. The misconceptions of so many critics on this subject (perfectly embodied in Adams' 1929 introduction to *Hamlet*) can only be attributed to an understandable desire to deny vengeful impulses by relegating them to a more barbarous and distant past. For there is surely no lack of historical evidence demonstrating the deep concern over the morality of personal and political revenge that pervaded the sixteenth and seventeenth centuries.

For England, France, and much of western Europe, the period between the mid-sixteenth and late-seventeenth centuries saw an unparalleled unity of civil and religious preoccupation with the control of private revenge. Vendettas conducted by powerful nobles were a threat to the hard-won authority of monarchs in England and France and to the more fragile rule of satraps throughout the European continent. The Reformation, of course, provided a strong motive for bloody revenge against religious foes on the part of those who claimed to believe in Christian mercy, but condemnation of private revenge was nevertheless a basic tenet of both Protestantism and Catholicism. As Lily B. Campbell noted in one of her brilliant essays on the social context of Elizabethan drama, the great tragic theme of sixteenth- and seventeenth-century religious teaching is God's revenge for sin—"and all Elizabethan tragedy must appear as fundamentally a tragedy of revenge if the extent of the idea of revenge but be grasped."[11]

The moral hierarchy was clear: God's just revenge (sometimes too slow to suit human beings but always certain); public revenge permitted to God's authorized representatives on earth (whether embodied in capital punishment, torture, or a "just war"); private revenge forbidden to kings and commoners alike. In the Christian doctrine of the age, private vengeance was a mortal sin not because of its human consequences but because it usurped the divine prerogative. The divine right of kings was a public doctrine, encompassing the official role of monarchs believed to derive their authority from God himself. Kings, too, could be guilty of the mortal sin of private vengeance if they acted from personal rather than divinely authorized public motives. (Queen Elizabeth's authorization of the execution of Mary Queen of Scots was naturally regarded by Roman Catholics as an unlawful act of private revenge rather than as the lawful public duty of a monarch.)

The unparalleled scope and depth of sixteenth- and seventeenth-century revenge tragedy is attributable to the juxtaposition of clear-cut religious injunctions against private revenge, rooted in the more orderly world of medieval Christendom, against a background of religious and political upheaval that characterized the world of the Renaissance and Reformation. How was one to distinguish between prohibited vengeance and "retributive justice" when more than one king (and more than one church) laid claim to the title of God's legitimate representative on earth? Was it permissible for subjects to rise up and avenge themselves upon a monarch who had abused his (and God's) authority? What were individuals to do if, through official corruption or ineptitude, they were denied the satisfaction of lawful public revenge? If God's retribution was certain, were men and women required to accept indefinite delay if they were the victims of evil?

In a psychological sense, these questions seem somewhat less modern than the dilemmas of Greek tragedy. In a civic sense—if one substitutes human for divine law—they are completely modern. The revenge tragedies of the Renaissance derive much of their force from the tension between these civic considerations and the passionate depths of the human impulse toward vengeance. The lure of revenge, in spite of its damning consequences for the immortal soul and civic order, is woven throughout the literature of the era—and this dramatic seductiveness makes it easy for a modern critic to overlook the equally strong note of moral condemnation. The revenge tragedians dwell on revenge in near-pornographic fashion, lingering voluptuously over the object of their censure. Tourneur's *The Revenger's Tragedy* (one of the few minor dramas from this period to turn up on the modern stage with some regularity) offers a scene which highlights the lurid appeal of vengeance— a *danse macabre* between a lustful duke and a painted, masked corpse whom he believes to be a woman proffered for his pleasure. The avenger on the stage watches with glee as the duke kisses the poisoned mask, realizes he has been deceived, and doubles over in agony. The pleasure of the moment outweighs the undeniable moral message of the play—that all private vengeance turns its authors into a species as loathsome as those who committed the original crime.

What distinguishes the major from the minor literature of revenge—in drama, prose, and poetry—is not merely the glory of the language but the lofty balance between the emotional pull of revenge and its grave moral and civic consequences. In both Shakespeare and Milton, for instance, the subject of revenge engenders a high moral tension that is somewhat diminished— if not altogether absent—in the works of their lesser contemporaries. The difference lies not in the moral judgment regarding vengeance—all Christian writers were unswervingly negative in their conclusions—but in the weight accorded opposing arguments. No writer has ever painted a more terrible portrait of the consequences of revenge motivated by pride than Milton does in *Paradise Lost,* yet it is the devil whom we remember and the devil whom we understand. Satan's words move us; he would not be a true demon if his explanation left us indifferent.

> From what highth fallen: so much the stronger proved
> He with his thunder: and till then who knew
> The force of those dire arms? Yet not for those,
> Nor what the potent Victor in his rage
> Can else inflict, do I repent, or change,
> Though changed in outward lustre, that fixed mind,
> And high disdain from sense of injured merit,
> That with the Mightiest raised me to contend,
> And to the fierce contention brought along
> Innumerable force of Spirits armed,
> That durst dislike his reign, and, me preferring,
> His utmost power with adverse power opposed
> In dubious battle on the plains of Heaven,
> And shook his throne.[12]

Later, the devil justifies his temptation of men and women in terms of his quarrel with God.

> Thank him who puts me, loath, to this revenge
> On you, who wrong me not, for him who wronged.
> And, should I at your harmless innocence
> Melt, as I do, yet public reason just—
> Honour and empire with revenge enlarged
> By conquering this new World—compels me now
> To do what else, though damned, I should abhor.[13]

Writing more than a century after the publication of *Paradise Lost,* Blake observed that "the reason Milton wrote in fetters when he wrote of Angels and God, and at liberty when of Devils and Hell, is because he was a true poet and of the Devil's party without knowing it."[14] In a secular age, it is necessary to remind ourselves that much of the fascination inherent in the contest between Satan and God arises from a theology in which the devil is a fallen angel—and man only a little lower than the angels. In an age of faith, the drive toward revenge was regarded not as an alien intruder but as an integral part of the human soul. Control of this powerful drive—alluring precisely because of its appeal to divine aspirations in men and women —was essential for salvation.

In every era, the greatest revenge tragedies raise questions —implicitly or explicitly—about the relationship between justice and revenge and the validity of the distinction between just and unjust forms of revenge. These questions assert themselves as insistently in Shakespeare, who accepted the basic moral assumptions of his age, as they do in Euripides, whose views ran counter to those of his more popular contemporaries in classical Athens. Shakespeare would never have questioned the divine prerogative of revenge (the demand that God justify his ways to man was Milton's—and contained enough blasphemy to justify Blake's comment), but his tragedies are filled with characters who, because they are God's appointed agents, firmly believe in the legitimacy of each of their vengeful acts. These beliefs may sometimes be justifiable according to the moral standards of their day (Hamlet, for example, *is* the lawful heir of the murdered king), but the heroes frequently founder on the shoals of unregulated passions that drive them to acts of revenge far beyond anything an Elizabethan God might be expected to sanction—even in his designated representatives. These heroes also founder out of doubt and judgment, a reluctance to go too far dictated at times by mercy and at other times by prudence. One of the most important distinctions between Shakespeare and his lesser contemporaries is the fact that his tragic heroes are brought down by the best as well as the worst in their natures, and nowhere is this more evident than in the acts of revenge—usually committed in the name of justice—that complete their downfall. Before murdering Desdemona, Othello laments:

> Ah, balmy breath, that dost almost persuade
> Justice to break her sword! One more, one more.
> Be thus when thou art dead, and I will kill thee,
> And love thee after. One more, and this the last:
> So sweet was ne'er so fatal. I must weep,
> But they are cruel tears: this sorrow's heavenly;
> It strikes where it doth love.[15]

Othello offers a perfect example of Lily Campbell's contention that all sixteenth- and seventeenth-century tragedy must be viewed as revenge drama. Any college freshman would surely say that *Othello* is a play "about" jealousy—and, of course, it is. But the fatal unfolding of the action depends on vengeance, motivated in the first instance by Iago's envy of Othello and in the second by Othello's jealousy of Desdemona. The classic crime of passion requires a rush to judgment on the basis of unsupported evidence and "unwritten law." Like many of Shakespeare's romantic tragedies, *Othello* is not simply a study of powerful emotions but of circumstances—among them, the absence of a formal proceeding to establish guilt or innocence—that unleash their destructive force. There is a telling contrast between the violent ending in Desdemona's bedchamber and an early scene in the Venetian council chamber, when Desdemona's father accuses Othello of seducing his daughter by force and witchcraft. In council, with witnesses speaking freely in the light of day, the ridiculousness of the father's vengeful accusation immediately becomes apparent.

> She gave me for my pains a world of sighs:
> She swore, in faith, 'twas strange, 'twas passing strange,

'Twas pitiful, 'twas wondrous pitiful:
She wished she had not heard it, yet she wished
That heaven had made her such a man: she thanked me
And bade me, if I had a friend that loved her,
I should but teach him how to tell my story,
And that would woo her. Upon this hint I spake:
She loved me for the dangers I had passed.
And I loved her that she did pity them.
This only is the witchcraft I have used:
Here comes the lady; let her witness it.[16]

Had the "evidence" of Desdemona's infidelity been examined in the same public light as the evidence of Othello's seduction, there would have been no acts of murder and revenge —and, of course, no tragic downfall in the last act of the drama. Unlike *Medea, Othello* is not identified with a single, horrifying act of revenge, yet the consequences of vengeful emotions, unrestrained by formal procedures to attain justice, are as evident here as in other Shakespearean tragedies, including the histories, that deal with more obvious public concerns. The importance of revenge in human conduct was taken for granted in the Elizabethan era, but many modern thinkers have confused that acknowledgment with approval. In fact, the Elizabethan awareness of the emotional importance of revenge was responsible for the high civic importance attached to its control. Private revenge was a threat to everyday order as well as to the expanding authority of the nation-state—not to mention the immortal soul—but the Elizabethans would have been astonished at the idea that it might be possible to restrain private vengeance in the absence of public retribution. As Campbell notes, the Pauline injunction against vengeance implies both a command and a promise. The restraint of individual impulses toward revenge depended in large measure on the public conviction that God, or God's representatives, would handle the grievance. That conviction is as essential to public order today as it was in the more "primitive" universe of our ancestors.

Philip Massinger's *The Fatal Dowry,* first performed in 1632, casts a particularly interesting light on the complexity of Elizabethan and Jacobean attitudes toward vengeance (although, in purely literary terms, it does not deserve to be classed with the works of Marlowe and Webster, much less Shakespeare). Unlike most dramas of the period, it features characters who might easily have been members of the audience —not kings and queens from distant legends or distant lands but lawyers, creditors, debtors, and members of parliament. This is a bourgeois revenge tragedy; the only distance is afforded by the setting of the action—not the familiar English countryside but the more exotic (to London audiences) locale of Dijon. But France, unlike the courts of Venice or Byzantium, was a real place, albeit enemy territory, to the English. The characters were as familiar to a seventeenth-century audience as the distraught parents in *Kramer vs. Kramer* or the cheerful, quarrelsome family in *Cousin, Cousine* are to twentieth-century American and French audiences. Bourgeois greed, not the struggle for a throne, sets the action in motion.

A marshal who once rendered great services to the state dies in debtors' prison; his son, Charalois, offers to imprison himself so that the creditors will release his father's body for Christian burial. One of the creditors urges his fellow body-snatchers to accept the offer and notes that the handsome Charalois might easily avenge his father's death by seducing their wives and daughters.

> Accept it by all means. Let's shut him up:
> He is well shaped, and has a villainous tongue
> And, should he study this by way of revenge,
> As I dare almost swear he loves a wench,

We have no wives, nor never shall get daughters
That will hold out against him.[17]

After many twists and turns of the plot, Charalois marries a beautiful young woman named Beaumelle, who commits adultery with Novall, son of a creditor involved in his father's death. Charalois kills Novall in a duel; he also stabs Beaumelle to death. The friends of both young men become involved in the quarrel; eventually, everyone is brought to court to answer for his actions. The one act of vengeance that does not fall within the jurisdiction of the court is Beaumelle's slaying. The death of a woman at the hands of her husband or father might be a human tragedy, as it is in *Othello,* but it only became a matter of civic importance when it led to demands for satisfaction and acts of revenge committed by the men of the family. Both the moral and civic importance of the act, in literature and in life, depended on the woman's virtue; Othello's tragedy is not that he killed Desdemona but that he was mistaken about her guilt. The death of the adulterous Beaumelle is a matter of minor import. *The Fatal Dowry* is concerned with the great civic question of legitimacy: Who has the right to exact retribution on behalf of victims? In the course of the debate before the court, Charalois receives a fatal wound from a friend of the dead Novall, and the avenger is himself stabbed to death by a friend and champion of the unfortunate Charalois. The final avenger is addressed sternly by a judge in the closing lines of the play:

We are taught
By this sad precedent, how just soever
Our reasons are to remedy our wrongs
We are yet to leave them to their will and power
That, to that purpose, have authority.
For you, Romont, although in your excuse,
You may plead what you did was in revenge
Of the dishonour done unto the court,

Yet, since you had no warrant for it,
We shall banish you from the state: of these, they shall
Be set free, or suffer punishment.[18]

The issue is not the morality of revenge but assignment of the responsibility for revenge to duly constituted authority. This question of legitimacy, in both the civic and moral realms, is central to all of the great revenge tragedies. When the burden of revenge is assigned to lawful authority, victims still have the psychic satisfaction of seeing their assailants' punishment, but society is protected from the violent passions of unchecked avengers and avengers themselves are protected from a weight that frequently proves too great for the more gentle side of human nature. Hamlet's indecision, like Othello's jealousy and Iago's evil cunning, is usually stressed as the key to his dilemma. But the real greatness of *Hamlet* lies in its depiction of a man undone by the responsibility of carrying out a vengeful assignment unsuited to his nature. An incomparable description of Hamlet's plight is offered by Goethe in the novel *Wilhelm Meister,* when the young hero becomes engaged in a passionate literary debate with his friends.

"Imagine this, you," he cried, "this son of a prince, represent to yourselves right vividly his condition and then observe him, when he learns that the spirit of his father is visible; stand by him in that terrible night when the venerable spirit itself appears before him; an unspeakable horror takes hold of him; he addresses the miraculous form, sees it beckon, follows it and listens. The fearful accusation against his uncle rings in his ears, the challenge to revenge, and the pressing, oft-repeated prayers: 'Remember me!' and when the ghost has vanished, whom do we see standing before us? A young hero, panting for revenge? A prince by birth, who feels himself fortunate in being called out against the usurper of his crown? No! Astonishment and trouble overwhelm the young man in his solitude, he is bitter against smiling villains, swears that he will not forget the departed spirit and closes with a significant sigh: 'The time is out of joint: O cursed spite,/ That ever I was born to set it right!'

"In these words, it seems to me, lies the key to the whole behavior of Hamlet, and it is clear to me that Shakespeare wished to describe the effects of a great action laid upon a soul which was unequal to it. . . . Here is an oak tree planted in a costly vase which should only have borne pleasing flowers, but the roots expand and the base is shattered."[19]

The impossible is demanded of Hamlet—not, Goethe emphasizes, what is impossible in itself but what is impossible for *him*. The gods who absolve Orestes cannot meet to restore Hamlet. In this respect alone, Shakespeare has more in common with Euripides—though not with Aeschylus and Sophocles—than is generally recognized. Both poets were concerned primarily with human morality and human social arrangements, even though the Christian God of Shakespeare is omnipotent in a way the Olympian deities are not. Another quality shared by Shakespeare and Euripides is the mixed, shaded nature of their heroes—a sharp contrast to the abstraction of character that permeates so many of the minor Elizabethan and Jacobean revenge tragedies. *The Revenger's Tragedy,* for instance, is scarcely more sophisticated or less schematic than the morality plays of the Middle Ages. How is one to take seriously the moral quandaries of characters named Vindice, Ambitioso, Supervacuo, and Lussorioso?

In fact, many of the revenge tragedies I classify as "minor" —without denying their importance in literary history—would have been far more effective as revengers' comedies than as revengers' tragedies. Few of the characters and plots of Kyd, Tourneur, and Massinger are sturdy enough to bear the weight of tragic revenge that seems appropriate in so much of Shakespeare, Webster, and Racine. *The Fatal Dowry,* for instance, begins with an irresistibly comic situation one can easily imagine in the hands of Molière: a living man is jailed in order to free a corpse. What a fine twist this might have been on the conventional use of ghosts in Elizabethan revenge tragedy! Instead of the spirits of the dead exhorting the living to avenge them, a live man becomes the object of vengeance intended for the prisoner who had escaped his mortal coil.

In comic revenge, blood need not be spilled. Trickery, infidelity, simple humiliation will serve well enough as punishments to fit the crimes; proportionality, in both its private and public meanings, comes to the fore. Falstaff does not have to die for his ludicrous attempts to seduce Mistresses Page and Ford in *The Merry Wives of Windsor.* The women pretend to arrange an assignation, tell Falstaff he can only escape the wrath of their husbands by being smuggled out of the house in a basket of dirty laundry, and unceremoniously dump the basket into the Thames. The husbands, instead of pursuing Falstaff with their swords, decide the whole affair is a good joke and arrange another tryst in which Falstaff is persuaded to disguise himself with a buck's head in order to meet the women in the park. The revelatory dialogue when Falstaff pulls off the head is a classic of comic revenge:

> MISTRESS FORD: Sir John, we have had ill luck; we could never meet. I will never take you for my love again; but I will always count you my deer.
>
> FALSTAFF: I do begin to perceive that I am made an ass.
>
> FORD: Ay, and an ox too: both the proofs are extant.[20]

Elizabethan comedy provides an important counterpoint to the prohibition of private revenge that underlies so much of Elizabethan tragedy. The Elizabethan disapproval of revenge was directed less toward the impulse itself than toward the social consequences of its violent expression; in comedy, getting even and getting hurt (in any permanent way) are far from synonymous. The comic notion of revenge is truly sweet, because punishment—while it may be exquisitely appropriate—

is never allowed to magnify the importance of a trivial offense. A man who behaves like an ass is treated like an ass, and that is the end of the matter.

But comic resolution is inappropriate when it dismisses the question of responsibility for serious crimes. *Measure for Measure* is a perennially disturbing and unsatisfying play precisely because no real retribution is exacted for acts that are—by the standards of our own day as well as Shakespeare's—truly evil. The classic comic ending, in which everyone is forgiven and married off, is scarcely appropriate to the complex moral drama of hypocrisy, lust, and betrayal of public responsibility that Shakespeare has set in motion. A ruler's sworn deputy, having revived an ancient law specifying the death penalty for premarital seduction, offers to spare the young man in question if his sister will abandon her virtue and satisfy his lustful desires. The duke, who eventually pardons his deputy and everyone else, is deeply implicated, because he has disregarded his responsibilities as a ruler in order to view the results of an experiment in justice conducted under the auspices of his frail surrogate. Indeed, the duke deserves to be punished for having cast himself in the role of observer and *deus ex machina* instead of fulfilling the responsibilities of his office. Because of this disparity between the tragic dilemma and the comic resolution, the flaw in *Measure for Measure* is keenly felt.

In the minor revenge tragedies, with their abstract characters and predictable plots, there is no flaw to perceive because the plays work well enough on their own terms. What they lack is the unresolved dialogue concerning degrees of responsibility for crime and punishment—a dialogue that is equally lacking in the cops-and-robbers shows of television. The greatest revenge tragedies have a tantalizingly inconsistent quality; their authors always seem to be asking, "What if?" even as they assert, "It could not be otherwise."

Racine's *Phèdre,* an avowed imitation of Euripides' *Hippolytus,* written at the end of an era of great revenge tragedy, embodies this characteristic in the same way as the portrait of the devil in *Paradise Lost*. By introducing the character of Aricia as the object of Hippolytus' romantic interest, Racine actually improved upon Euripides: his Hippolytus is pure but also engenders more empathy than the inhumanly chaste youth of Greek myth. Euripides' Hippolytus, in his single-minded devotion to the goddess of the hunt, is the sort of boy more likely to have been teased to death by his schoolmates than destroyed by the lust of a guilty stepmother. Like Hippolytus, Racine's Phaedra is a more shaded character than the Phaedra of Greek tragedy. She oscillates between the tormented, "What if?" and an equally anguished acceptance of her fate, and her sense of personal guilt and responsibility coexists with a sense of predetermined destiny. (*Phèdre* was written while Racine was in the early stages of returning to his Jansenist religious faith, which is of course founded on the paradox of belief in predestination vis-à-vis the obligation to act as if one's fate might be changed by personal rectitude.) When Phaedra begs Hippolytus to avenge his father by killing her, she is asking him to free her from a desire so destructive and overwhelming that it appears to be a form of divine vengeance.

> I burn with love. Yet, even as I speak,
> Do not imagine I feel innocent,
> Nor think that my complacency has fed
> The poison of the love that clouds my mind.
> The hapless victim of heaven's vengeances,
> I loathe myself more than you ever will.
> The gods are witness, they who in my breast
> Have lit the fire fatal to all my line.
> Those gods whose cruel glory it has been
> To lead astray a feeble mortal's heart.
> Yourself recall to mind the past, and how
> I shunned you, cruel one, nay, drove you forth.
> I strove to seem to you inhuman, vile;

The better to resist, I sought your hate.
But what availed my needless sufferings?
You hated me the more, I loved not less.
Even your misfortunes lent you added charms.
I pined, I drooped, in torments and in tears.
Your eyes alone could see that it is so,
If for a moment you could look at me.
Nay, this confession to you, ah! the shame,
Think you I made it of my own free will?
I meant to beg you, trembling, not to hate
My helpless children, whom I dared not fail.
My foolish heart, alas, too full of you,
Could talk to you of nothing but yourself.
Take vengeance. Punish me for loving you.
Come, prove yourself your father's worthy son,
And of a vicious monster rid the world.[21]

Another great theme of revenge tragedy is the connection between the thirst for vengeance and the thirst for justice. Revenge and justice were not seen as antipodes but as regions of the same moral territory: one might all too easily move from the permitted to the prohibited zone. This proximity is responsible both for the force of the religious injunction against vengeance and increasing awareness of the need for social institutions to dispense just retribution. In the sixteenth century, these institutions were thought of in relatively narrow terms—mainly as instruments of social order and criminal justice. Social justice, as we understand the term today, did not emerge as an explicit theme in literary investigations of revenge until the Enlightenment—and no writer would equal Euripides' grasp of the relationship between vengeance and the absence of social justice until the nineteenth century.

In nineteenth-century novels and plays, there is a character who once believed implicitly, or was brought up to believe, in the righteousness of social institutions—in their ability to punish the guilty and protect the innocent. The character is often a woman who, by virtue of special circumstances (which turn out to be not-so-special when she realizes the dependency of her sex), becomes the victim of a society that was supposed to shield her from harm. At this point, she embarks on a course of rebellion, and one measure of her character is the fine distinction between a passion for justice and a passion for destruction.

Facing the fact of her subservient position in a male-dominated society, Ibsen's Nora is as angry as Hedda Gabler, but while Nora burns with a just desire to control her own life, Hedda burns with a vindictive drive to dominate the lives of others. Retributive motives are present in both women, but Nora's actions appear, from a modern vantage point, as constructive attempts at self-definition while Hedda remains a study in pathology. (The one reproach still leveled at Nora is "How could she leave her children with a man like Torvald?" —not the simpler nineteenth-century criticism, "How could she leave her children?") Nora's answer, of course, is that she cannot be a fit mother to her children while she is still a child herself. But there is no destructive violence, no trace of Medea, in her quest for justice. Hedda, on the other hand, *is* a Medea.

Charlotte Brontë raises the question of justice, and its connection with vengeance, in the opening scenes of *Jane Eyre.* An orphan living on the charity of her aunt, Jane is locked in her room after she responds with fury when a bullying cousin tells her she has no right to use the family library. "Wicked and cruel boy!" she cries. "You are like a murderer—you are like a slave-driver—you are like the Roman emperors!" Later, with her head still aching from a blow delivered by her cousin, she burns for vindication. " 'Unjust!—unjust!' said my reason, forced by the agonizing stimulus into precocious though transitory power; and Resolve, equally wrought up, indicated some strange expedient to achieve escape from insupportable oppression—as running away, or, if that could not be effected, never eating or drinking more, and letting myself die." But Jane does not turn her anger inward; instead, when informed she is to be sent away to a school that specializes in disciplining recalcitrant, impecunious orphans, she turns upon her aunt and accuses her of being a deceitful hypocrite. When Jane sees that her aunt has been wounded by the truthful accusation, she enjoys her first taste of vengeance—followed by the sensation that she has been poisoned. But she resists the impulse to ask for forgiveness, because she realizes, "partly from experience and partly from instinct," that she would be aroused to further anger and vengeance by the self-righteous response the aunt would surely deliver.[22]

Questions of justice and revenge loomed large in the minds of those nineteenth-century writers who stripped their heroines of the meekness that was regarded as an innate and essential feminine trait. When one has been a victim, the quest for justice is frequently difficult to distinguish from the quest for revenge; the delineation of that distinction is an important, and frequently overlooked, element in the Victorian novels and dramas that offer a multilayered picture of the pressing social and economic questions of their day.

The dangerous proximity of justice and revenge is the single, unadorned theme of Heinrich von Kleist's remarkable *Michael Kohlhaas,* written in the first decade of the nineteenth century, before Victorian moralism and economic development demanded a more socially complex treatment of the subject. So stark are the contours of this short novel that it resembles a medieval allegory in form, but its sensibility is more akin to ours—specifically, to those periods of our century in which men and women, under pressure of morally unintelligible events, have been loosed from traditional ethical moorings.

In the German-speaking world, this tale of justice, honor, and revenge has survived in one form or another for more than four hundred years. The real Kohlhaas, actually named Hans not Michael, was born in 1532. An early chronicle recounting the events upon which Kleist based his version was circulated in 1595; another adaptation was published in 1731. Kleist's novel appeared in 1806. Read today, the story appears as a chilling precursor of the sense of unredressed grievance that played such a fatal role in twentieth-century German and European history.

"About the middle of the 16th century," Kleist's account begins, "there dwelt on the banks of the River Havel a horse-dealer named Michael Kohlhaas. The son of a schoolmaster, he was at once the most upright and most terrible of human beings."

> Until his 30th year, this extraordinary man might well have served as the model of a good citizen. In a village that still bears his name he possessed a dairy-farm that provided him with a modest living through his own hard work. The offspring which his spouse had presented him he brought up to be god-fearing, diligent and loyal. There was not one of his neighbors whose troubles had not been lightened by his benevolence or honesty. In short, posterity would have had cause to bless his memory, had not one of his virtues led him into excesses. For it was his strong sense of justice that made of him a robber and a murderer.[23]

The story opens with Kohlhaas's refusal to pay a bribe to a squire who has refused to allow him customary and legal free passage across his land. Kohlhaas vows to take up the matter with the proper authorities, and the squire detains two of his horses to assure his return. When Kohlhaas does return (without having obtained satisfaction from the appropriate officials), he is further enraged to find that his horses have been abused, underfed, and worked in the fields by the squire. In his quest to gain restitution for the mistreatment of his animals, Kohlhaas eventually destroys his business and his marriage (his wife is killed by the enemies he has made); burns down the squire's house; murders innocent inhabitants of the castle; and incites a revolt that lays waste to much of the surrounding countryside. In the end, Kohlhaas is executed for his actions, which are defined as bloody, unlawful vengeance even though the authorities have, by this time, acknowledged the justice of Kohlhaas's original claim regarding the animals.

Kohlhaas is not mistaken about the nature of the original injustice done him; he simply lacks any sense of proportion about the gravity of the injury. One is reminded, inevitably, of minor territorial disputes that mushroom into major wars—disputes of honor that consume the honor of everyone involved. The honor of the ruling nobles of Saxony does not emerge more intact than the honor of the enraged Kohlhaas; their less-than-scrupulous attention to just retribution acts as a spur to Kohlhaas's vindictiveness. In its warning about the private and public consequences of unchecked vengeance, the novel harks back to sixteenth-century revenge tragedy. Martin Luther appears as a minor character when he admonishes Kohlhaas, "How can you claim that your rights have been denied you, you whose wrathful heart, tempted by the desire for shameless vengeance, gave up all attempts to obtain justice after your first thoughtless efforts failed?"[24] But the heart of the story is the character of Kohlhaas, a man unhinged by the malfeasance, or nonfeasance, of institutions that had always inspired his profound faith. He becomes an outlaw when his society fails to live up to its own standards of justice. In this respect, he is a familiar figure to the twentieth-century reader. (The character Coalhouse Walker in E. L. Doctorow's novel *Ragtime,* is spiritually as well as etymologically related to Michael Kohlhaas.)

In our own time—especially in the second half of the century —a loss of confidence in the ability of public institutions to dispense measured retribution is central to any discussion of revenge. Revenge tragedy in the sixteenth and seventeenth centuries paralleled the rise of civic procedures designed to convince the populace that "retributive justice" was best left to duly constituted authority. These institutions gave new strength to traditional religious injunctions, which, in the absence of appropriate secular restraint, had been honored mainly in the breach.

The view of revenge reflected in twentieth-century literature has been influenced by a number of long-range social changes: a diminution of religious faith—especially the kind of faith that regards God as the ultimate judge who will surely repay evil; declining confidence in the efficacy of the criminal-justice system; the rise of what Thomas Szasz calls "psychiatric justice," with its blurring of individual responsibility for crime; and the recent emergence of a new feminist political analysis regarding issues of sexual revenge that have always been, in some senses, beyond the law.

It is also impossible to overestimate the importance of that singular event, the Holocaust, in reshaping the modern view of the relationship between justice and vengeance. One need not enter the degrading debate over whether the systematic extermination of six million Jews was really the worst abuse of human beings in history to recognize that it is the classic example in our own time of an evil for which there can be no adequate retribution. As a result of modern communications technology, the Holocaust became the first mass assault on human life to be revealed in detail and in fairly short order (in comparison to other major historical disasters) to the remaining inhabitants of the planet. Such widespread revelation was bound to exert a profound influence on public views of justice and retribution. How is a survivor to respond to the question, posed at the Braunsteiner hearings, of whether he or she is "out for revenge"? How is any adequate retribution possible? How not? These questions recur with great frequency in the modern literature of revenge, and not only in the large number of detective and spy novels concerned with the aftermath of the Nazi era.

Avengers are beyond the law in modern fiction, but in quite

a different way from their counterparts in revenge tragedy. From the Middle Ages until the mid-nineteenth century, all revenge drama—regardless of its literary merit—is essentially tragic in spirit: those who act on impulses of private vengeance do so in spite of the fact that their purposes would be better served by God's justice in the spiritual realm and by civic authority, resting on divine sanction, in the temporal realm. Most modern avengers are not tragic figures. In the cruder examples of the genre, they may be beasts—but no tragedy is possible because they began as beasts. In the more sophisticated and serious fictional conceptions of revenge, the protagonists gain dignity by taking the law into their own hands because it is assumed that leaving the law in someone else's hands will make it impossible to obtain either justice or vengeance. The modern avenger is not a wildman like Kohlhaas, nor is he necessarily in the wrong. In Mario Puzo's *The Godfather,* an international bestseller, Michael Corleone explains to his innocent fiancée his father's psychology in terms of justice rather than vengeance; she admonishes him that we would be "back in the times of the cavemen" if everyone tried to redress his own grievances.

> The trouble is all that damn trash in the movies and newspapers. . . . You've got a wrong idea of my father and the Corleone Family. . . . My father is a businessman trying to provide for his wife and children and those friends he might need someday in a time of trouble. He doesn't accept the rules of the society we live in because those rules would have condemned him to a life not suitable to a man like himself, a man of extraordinary force and character. What you have to understand is that he considers himself the equal of all those great men like Presidents and Prime Ministers and Supreme Court Justices and Governors of the States. He refuses to accept their will over his own. He refuses to live by rules set up by others,

rules which condemn him to a defeated life . . . society doesn't really protect its members who don't have their own individual power. In the meantime he operates on a code of ethics he considers far superior to the legal structures of society.[25]

It is obvious that many of the portrayals of revenge in modern fiction run counter to the prevailing cultural myth of a dichotomy between justice and vengeance. These portraits are commonly and mistakenly viewed as simple escape reading, but they actually employ a time-honored device to put some distance between presumably civilized readers and the primitive theme of vengeance. The world of the spy and detective, like that of the Mafia, is a reliably exotic locale, offering a whiff of brimstone without the flames; it helps bridge the gap between private emotions and the public posture of "justice, not revenge." Mystery and spy novels provide an emotionally acceptable framework for discussions of revenge because their heroes, by virtue of their profession, receive dispensations from everyday rules of conduct. They live dual lives, if only for limited periods of time. As Clark Kent, they conform to the norms that prohibit revenge. As Superman, they can do anything.

Charlie Heller, the hero of Robert Littell's *The Amateur,* is a mild-mannered code expert with the Central Intelligence Agency. On the side, he uses CIA computers to search Shakespeare's plays for ciphers to support the persistent speculation that Shakespeare was only a pseudonym and someone else was really the Bard of Avon. In the middle of an ordinary day, he learns that his fiancée has been seized as a hostage by terrorists in the waiting room of the American consulate in Munich, where she was handling a simple passport problem. She is the first hostage shot by the terrorists. After the murder, he is told the CIA knows the identity of the killers—international hit men financed by the Soviet secret police—but will do nothing to retaliate because of potential diplomatic repercussions. He cannot accept the fact that the terrorists will go unpunished, and his unfocused anger crystallizes into a plan of revenge when his fiancée's father, a Nazi-concentration-camp survivor, tells him how he managed to reconstruct his life after the war.

It is an unusual variant on the Holocaust theme in novels of revenge—instruction in the theology of vengeance from the survivor of one disaster to the survivor of another. "To survive the death of people close to you," the old man lectures Heller, "you need ritual. In the camps there was no possibility of ritual —no corpses, no funerals, no sending or receiving condolences. So I created a ritual appropriate to the situation in which I found myself. . . . I spent three years tracking the doctor who sent them to the gas." Heller asks what he did when he found the doctor. "I created one last ritual," he replies. "With these hands I strangled him." Only then, he informs the young man, was he able to begin a new family and a new life. "It didn't bring them back from the dead," Heller says. The man answers, "It brought *me* back from the dead."[26]

Heller uses the computer to find top-secret messages about CIA involvement in foreign assassinations and blackmails his boss into providing training that will turn him into a field agent who can track down and kill the terrorists himself. What he does not know—and finds out in a final confrontation in Prague with the terrorist who actually shot his fiancée—is that the man himself is a CIA employee, trained to infiltrate guerrilla movements around the world. The operation in which Heller's fiancée died was designed to prove the agent's reliability to his terrorist colleagues; that, of course, is the reason the CIA does not want him killed. Heller shoots the man and avoids the punishment planned for him by his former bosses with the assistance of a Czech intelligence officer who had been engaged in his own Oresteian quest for vengeance. The dead terrorist's father, it seems, had betrayed the Czech to the Gestapo during the war. Since the young man's career of violence suggested that he was a case of "like father, like son," the Czech felt justified in pursuing revenge against him.

> Heller pushed his eyeglasses back up along his nose with a forefinger.
> "You were after revenge too?"
> "Just so."
> "Was it worth it?" Heller asked.
> The Professor's eyes seemed to cloud over. "It was . . . very satisfying. And you?"
> . . . "I wouldn't do it again," he confessed, "but it was just as advertised. It brought me back from the dead."[27]

There is something of Michael Kohlhaas in these modern avengers. At first, they assume the institutions of their society will punish the guilty; their personal resolve to vengeance hardens only as they realize there is no justice to be had from the authorities in whom they have always believed. Yet there is also a quality reminiscent of Aeschylus and Sophocles—minus the depth and poetic grandeur, of course—in the mechanistic unfolding of these stories. Questions of legitimacy never arise, because the characters are removed from the realm of ordinary human experience. They are not so removed, though, that it is impossible to identify with them. There is no longer any implausibility in the idea that a loved one might be the victim of impersonal political violence; the only implausibility lies in the notion that one might be in a position to strike back at those responsible.

In some instances, the heroes are not themselves avengers but become actors in the drama by virtue of an Oedipus-like dedication to solving a riddle. Charles McCarry's novel *The Tears of Autumn* offers one of the best examples of the genre. A spy winds up totally outside the law as he pursues clues to the assassination of President Kennedy. The instigators turn out to be the Ngo family, intent on vengeance for the death of its three sons in the CIA-aided coup that resulted in the 1963 overthrow of Ngo Dinh Diem's government in Saigon. And, of course, the Vietnamese interpretation of *lex talionis* requires the death of not one Kennedy brother but three. . . .

Like spies, the members of the Corleone family in *The Godfather* exist outside ordinary codes of American behavior. The actions of the Corleones are motivated by tribal concepts of identity and honor that seem primitive indeed, but they are usually set in motion when the wider, ostensibly more civilized society is stripped of its pretensions. In the opening chapter, an old friend who has kept his distance from Don Corleone out of a desire to be a "good American" comes to beg the Don for justice. His daughter has been brutally beaten in an attempt to defend herself from rape by two young men, one of them her boyfriend. Her father takes the case to court and the judge, after sternly reprimanding the youths, gives them a suspended sentence. "America has been good to me," the anguished father cries out. "I wanted my child to be American."

> The Don clapped his hands together with decisive approval. "Well spoken. Very fine. Then you have nothing to complain about. The judge has ruled. America has ruled. Bring your daughter flowers and a box of candy when you go visit her in the hospital. That will comfort her. Be content. After all, this is not a serious affair, the boys were young, high-spirited, and one of them is the son of a powerful politician. No, my dear Amerigo, you have always been honest. I must admit, though you spurned my friendship, that I would trust the given word of Amerigo Bonasera more than I would any other man's. So give me your word that you will put aside this madness. It is not American. Forgive. Forget. Life is full of misfortunes."[28]

The inevitability of Michael Corleone's involvement in his father's world is also reminiscent of Greek tragedy. In the hills of Sicily, where he flees after killing a rival Mafioso who tried to murder his father, Michael comes to understand the forces that shaped his father's, and in the end his own, destiny. He sees a society in which authority has always been so alien and oppressive that no one would think of turning to any public institution for justice. The landowners existed to exact tribute from the peasants in this life, the church to offer salvation in the next. Neither existed to redress grievances in the world of ordinary men and women. "A woman whose husband had been murdered would not tell the police the name of her husband's murderer, not even of her child's murderer, her daughter's raper. Justice had never been forthcoming from the authorities so the people had always gone to the Robin Hood Mafia."[29] *The Godfather* glosses over the process by which the "Robin Hood Mafia" was transformed into a strangling authority of its own. It is essentially a romantic portrait of tribal solidarity, of a world in which the rules of crime and punishment—harsh though they might be—are bearable because everyone knows what to expect. The atavistic emotional appeal of *The Godfather* is powerful and undeniable.

In one sense, twentieth-century men and women accept the preaching of both traditional religion and modern psychiatry—that one must abandon the drive toward vengeance in order to attain emotional peace. But we also believe in the importance of retribution to civic and moral order, and this sense of righteousness is violated by the taboo attached to revenge. Both our negative and positive perceptions of retribution are satisfied by literature that is preoccupied with the subject of revenge but relegates it to the semi-legitimate world of spies, police, and Mafiosi.

There is one fictional universe in which acts that would not be out of place in Greek tragedy are committed by the boy and girl next door. Domesticity gone mad is the theme of this fiction; most of its authors are women, and they are concerned with rape, wife beating, child abuse—crimes that so often fall beyond the power of the law because they are committed by acquaintances or intimates. In *Good Riddance,* by Barbara

Abercrombie, a newly divorced woman is raped by a man who has walked her home from a dinner party at her next-door neighbor's. He is drunk; she gives him a cup of coffee to help him sober up; when she says, "It's time you were leaving," he rapes her. The next day, she imagines walking into a police station and charging the man with rape. "The policemen would ask questions. . . ."

> Did she see his face?
> (Of course. She had dinner with him earlier that evening next door.)
> How had he gotten into her house?
> (She had let him in. He had walked her home.)
> Walked her home? Didn't she live just next door?
> (True. But he said that a gentleman always walks a lady home.)
> Did he force his way in, then?
> (Not exactly. He said he wanted a cup of coffee.)
> And did you give him a cup of coffee?
> (Yes.)
> And then he attacked you?
> (No. First he had brandy.)
> And did you have brandy also?
> (Yes.)
> How late did he stay?
> (Very late.)
> Why didn't you tell him to leave?
> (It was easier to let him stay.)
> And the charm would melt away and they would think: Whore. Vindictive bitch.[30]

Believing that no policeman, judge, or jury will ever be convinced by her story, she decides to kill the man. It's easy to set up the victim, because—after an initial hesitation due to the fact that *he* knows he raped her—he assumes she has changed her mind and wants a repeat performance. So she shoots the man and devises a plan that almost—but not quite—enables her to avoid being caught. The murder, which had begun to free her psychologically, will imprison her physically: there is no winged chariot to carry her away from the forces of the law. Her act is not so outrageous as Medea's—she has not, after all, killed an innocent—but it is prompted by the same dilemma. Like Euripides, Barbara Abercrombie never suggests that the woman has committed an admirable act. She is merely saying, "This is what you get when you push people too far." The connection between justice and vengeance, in both its positive and negative senses, commands more attention here than it does in the exotic novels of revenge. Abercrombie's heroine is the sort of murderer of whom stunned neighbors always say on the television news: "She was such a nice lady, always took the kids when it was her turn in the car pool/He was just a regular guy, always clowning around. . . ."

A "regular guy" is the pathological avenger in Joy Fielding's *Kiss Mommy Goodbye.* After failing to obtain custody of his children in a divorce suit, he warns his wife, "Even if you win, you'll lose." He plays the model father for some months, always behaving in the friendliest possible fashion when he picks up the children for their weekend visits. Then he disappears with his son and daughter, surfacing only to make periodic phone calls to his former wife to tell her he has convinced the children their mother doesn't want them. The police won't help; they tell her this is a "legal kidnapping." Although the father has violated a court order, they cannot treat him as a criminal because he is the children's natural parent. When the desperate mother finally manages to locate him, she discovers that her six-year-old son has indeed learned to hate her. There is a "happy ending" when she returns home with the children, but one is left with the sense that the father might easily turn up on her doorstep once again—with murder instead of kidnapping on his mind.

Although domestic settings offer a more recognizable, plausible frame of reference than the underworld of spies and detectives, most modern novels of vengeance—regardless of their setting—lack the moral tension that defined the great revenge tragedies of earlier epochs. One exception is *Innocent Blood,* an appropriately titled novel by the well-known English detective writer P. D. James. This is not a conventional detective story (although the intricate plot bears the stamp of an accomplished mystery writer's craft) but a psychological exploration of the contending forces in human hearts that have experienced unrightable wrongs.

Philippa Rose Palfrey, the adopted daughter of a sociology professor, sets out at age eighteen to track down her natural mother. She finds—the nightmare of those who oppose open adoption records—that her mother was a murderer, about to be released from prison for collaborating with her dead father in the killing of a small girl. Because the father was a child molester, the reader is led to believe that the mother was drawn into his crime by accident. Philippa, who also believes this version of the story, agrees to live with her mother for several months, primarily because she wishes to fill in the details of her own identity. Meanwhile, a government clerk named Norman Scase, the father of the child who was killed, is stalking Philippa's mother with murder in mind. He does not believe ten years in prison is sufficient punishment for the killing of a child. But retribution is not his only motive. He is also in search of identity—an identity he lost when his daughter was brutally murdered. His wife, now dead of cancer, had withdrawn from the world; as she lay dying, he promised her that he would carry on their pact to avenge the death of their child.

Now, sitting in the sun with his few belongings on the ground between his feet, he accepted again the burden laid upon him. He would seek out his child's murderess and kill her. He would try to do it without danger to himself, since the prospect of prison terrified him, but he would still do it, whatever the cost. The strength of this conviction puzzled him. The will for the deed was absolute, yet the justification eluded his questing mind. . . . Was it, perhaps, that after nearly fifty-seven years of living he needed to prove himself, nonentity that he was, capable of courage and action, of an act so terrible and irrevocable that, whatever happened to him afterward, he could never again doubt his identity as a man? He supposed that it might be so, although none of it seemed relevant to him. But surely it was ridiculous, this sense that the act was inescapable, pre-ordained. And yet he knew that it was so.[31]

At this point, the contrived coincidences of a detective plot end and James returns to the more terrible coincidences of ordinary life. Philippa naturally assumes that her mother gave her up for adoption because she had no choice after being convicted of murder, but she learns from her adoptive father that the papers were signed several weeks before the child's death. Her mother, it seemed, had brutally beaten Philippa and nearly killed her; she had given up her daughter out of a fully justified fear of her own violent impulses. So the death of the other child might have been no more of an accident than the beating of Philippa. "This is where you belong," her adoptive father tells her. "I've got an adoption order to prove it. And if that legalistic conveyance of possession lacks the emotional charge of the blood tie, hasn't your family had enough of blood?"[32]

Not yet, Philippa answers. She comes to hate her mother as fiercely as does the pathetic Norman Scase; then, in a psychological reversal, she decides to make the effort to forgive her for the crime of abandonment. She has no interest at all in that other, more final crime—the murder of a small girl. Philippa, intent on some form of emotional reconciliation or retribution —we are never entirely sure which—and Scase, intent on murder, converge on the woman's apartment. They are both cheated, because she has already committed suicide. Philippa realizes that Scase intended to murder her mother but stabbed her after she was already dead. They are both freed from the burden of revenge by the suicide, more logical than a *deus ex machina* but equally effective. When Philippa and Scase meet one last time, she is graduating from college and he is about to remarry. The closing lines of the book have an elegiac quality that recalls the fatalistic, albeit less optimistic, tone of Greek tragedy: "If it is only through learning to love that we find identity, then he had found his. She hoped one day to find hers. She wished him well. And perhaps to be able to wish him well with all that she could recognize of her unpracticed heart, to say a short untutored prayer for him and his Violet, was in itself a small accession of grace."

This novel occupies an unusual position in the modern literature of revenge because, although it is a meditation on emotional reconciliation and restoration, it does not treat vengeance as a purely pathological phenomenon. Philippa's involvement with her mother is a form of revenge directed against her adoptive parents; Scase's attempted murder is vengeance not for his daughter but for his own lost years. The scales must be balanced before either character can move beyond revenge to create a new life.

James neither takes the easy route of removing vengeance from ordinary social settings nor does she adopt the conventional formula of "justice, not revenge." Her approach places the Biblical formulation "Vengeance is mine; I will repay, saith the Lord" in a different light. This declaration has always been seen as both a prohibition and a pledge of divine justice. For the characters in *Innocent Blood,* the traditional religious injunction would be a psychological release, a blessing, an "accession of grace."

But most modern chronicles of revenge are concerned with men and women who have no expectation that anyone, human or divine, will assume their psychic burden. They must discharge the burden themselves or be crushed themselves—and discharge it in a world that seems to lack any legitimate outlet for rage, any way of transforming revenge into justice. P. D. James offers her characters a way out, but the protagonists of most modern dramas of revenge cannot forgive in a world where others have forgotten.

III In the Beginning Was the Word

Ye have heard that it hath been said, An eye for an eye, and
a tooth for a tooth: But I say unto you, That ye resist not evil:
but whosoever shall smite thee on thy right cheek, turn to
him the other also.

MATTHEW 5: 38–39

But Gods providence and justice . . . is as different as miraculous; for sometimes he protracts and defers it of purpose,
either to mollify or to harden our hearts, as seems best to his
inscrutable will and divine pleasure; or as may chiefly serve
and tend to his glory, yea, sometimes he makes the murderer
himself as well an instrument to discover, as he hath been an
actor to commit murder, yea, and many times he punisheth
one sin by and in another, and when the murderer is most
secure, and thinks least of it, then he heaps coals of fire on
his head, and suddenly cuts him off with the revenging sword
of fierce wrath and indignation.

JOHN REYNOLDS, *The Triumphs of Gods Revenge against
the crying and execrable sin of wilful and premeditated
murder,* 1704

Religion has played a crucial and, at times, a contradictory role
in the evolution of revenge from the collective, hereditary vendetta that prevailed in the earliest stages of civilization to a
system of law in which crime becomes an insult to the community as well as to the family or tribe and punishment becomes
a public rather than a private duty. On the one hand, we have
the gods and prophets of mercy and love, on the other, the

vengeance so often imposed in the name of deities whom we have created in our own image.

Murder, treason, and sacrilege (not necessarily in that order) are the most grave crimes in every society; the latter two have always been regarded as public transgressions demanding public retribution. Murder, however, was regarded as a family matter for countless generations in the early epochs of human history. In the long transition from tribal vendetta to measured legal retribution, it is impossible to overestimate the importance of the religious concept of murder as a stain upon a land and its entire people and an offense against its gods. The "pollution doctrine" of homicide, which supplanted earlier tribal beliefs at roughly the same point in Greek and Semitic cultures (during the seventh century B.C.),[1] was both a religious concept and a response to the political needs of peoples in the process of establishing a communal identity that transcended more parochial loyalties. Because bloodshed posed such a grave threat to social order, neither the state nor its religious arbiters could continue to treat murder as a family affair.

The concept of murder as an insult to the highest religious authority suggests that something more than, or distinct from, blood vengeance is required to expiate the crime; indeed, unrestrained revenge offers yet another insult to the higher order. In this respect, the post-Homeric Greeks and the Jews of Biblical times, rabbinical judges from later eras of Jewish history, and theologians from the early centuries of the Christian era through the Renaissance—though separated from one another by chasms of culture and time—all belong more to our own age than to the early period of tribal vendetta, when "a single deed of blood provokes an endless series of retaliations: a hideous orgy of revenge . . . an orgy which no one may escape; for old men and women and children perish, whether one by one, or in a general massacre."[2]

Yet there is no denying the paradox underlying religious attitudes toward revenge. All western religions, in varying degrees, have rendered a service to social order by rejecting human revenge on the ground that it usurps the prerogative of God, but they have simultaneously conferred approval on vengeance thought to serve God's purposes and conducted by his agents. A religious distinction is therefore established between sinful human revenge and righteous divine vengeance, just as law distinguishes between unsanctioned vigilante justice and court-ordered punishment. Like law, religion effects a compromise between the urgent personal impulse to punish the guilty and the need to contain the impulse in a civic order that also protects the innocent.

The difficulty is that divine vengeance, in the absence of natural disaster, can only be interpreted and exacted by human beings—and it is much more difficult to restrain those who assert their rights as God's chosen avengers than to restrict those who have been appointed or elected by fallible mortal peers. Moreover, the invocation of divinity on behalf of one side or another in a human dispute is as likely to incite vengeance as to contain it. This was true even in times when the distinction between religious and secular law was much less clear than it is today. Control of unlawful revenge is a basic tenet of both Judaism and Christianity, but revenge on behalf of religion itself has been a bloody *leitmotif* of western history.

The consequences of this contradiction have manifested themselves in so many times and places, in such varied and terrible forms, that the God of Vengeance frequently seems more real than the God of Mercy. One of the most devastating and emblematic of these manifestations has been the role of the Christian churches in persecutions of Jews for the last millennium—a sequence of events that might reasonably be considered the longest-running revenge tragedy of western civilization. The assignment of eternal blame to the Jews for the crucifixion of Jesus—a view that has been explicitly repudiated by the major Christian churches only in the second half of the twentieth century—represents a reversion to the hereditary vengeance that both Christianity and rabbinical Judaism have done so much to overcome in other contexts. The historical tendency of religion (though replete with anomalies like the Calvinist theory of predestination) has been to fix both the blame and the punishment for sin on the individual and to repudiate the tribal concept that the sins of the fathers are inevitably visited upon the children. The notion of Jewish culpability in the death of Jesus, which extends from the early Christian era through the twentieth-century re-examination forced by the Holocaust, is an anomaly of such intensity and duration that it can scarcely be considered an aberration. Rather, it demands a re-evaluation of the relationship between all religious teaching and revenge.

In a philosophical sense, the vengeful posture of proselytizing religions vis-à-vis those who refuse to accept the faith stands in direct opposition to the religious effort to control vengeance within the fold. In a practical sense, sanctified revenge against outsiders is one way of turning vengeful impulses outward— and away from the society the religion wishes to preserve. This practical motivation is not a function of Christian (or any other) theology but of unions between religion and politics, with their tendency to turn plowshares into swords. The contradictions inherent in the combination of compassionate religious preaching with vengeful action—in theocratic states from the ancient world through the present era—have played a major role in the formation of ambivalent attitudes toward revenge.

In the long retreat from uncontrolled vendetta, which characterized human life in its most savage stages, measured tribal retribution, blessed by tribal gods, was a major advance in the domestication of revenge. Among the Greeks, punishment by written law was still unknown when the Olympian religion was outlined in Homer's epics (now thought to have been written around 700 B.C.). Vengeance, as the story of the Trojan war clearly tells us, was a tribal function, but tribal revenge was subject to strong social controls. These restraints are illuminated in a scene that takes place on the plain outside the walls of Troy, where Achilles had brought his fellow warriors to near-disaster by refusing to fight. With rage and vengeful pride aroused by the loss of a concubine to King Agamemnon, Achilles remains unmoved when the king's emissaries offer to restore the woman to him and to concede many other rich prizes as well. One of the emissaries chides Achilles for his relentless enmity and reminds him that much greater insults are ordinarily regarded with greater restraint by the wounded party:

> I cannot help reflecting, on the combination of rancor and arrogance that Achilles has displayed. Ruthlessness too. Not a thought for the affections of his comrades, who made him the idol of our camp! The inhumanity of it! After all, even in cases of murder it is quite common for a man to accept blood-money for a brother or maybe a son. The killer does not even have to leave the country if he pays up to the next of kin, whose pride and injured feelings are eased by the indemnity. But you, Achilles—God knows why—have worked yourself up into this implacable fury over a girl, a single girl.[3]

Both the *Iliad* and the *Odyssey* were, of course, created out of legends that already belonged to the mythic past in Homer's time, but the passages referring to tribal payment as a substitute for blood vengeance—like many descriptions in both epics—undoubtedly refer to social customs that existed in the author's own lifetime. (Anachronisms of this sort occur in nearly all of the dramas of Aeschylus, Sophocles, and Euripides, who—unlike Homer—lived and wrote in a society that left a historical record of its own legal practices.) Restitution, or tribal *Wergeld,* was a commonplace of many cultures—a stage between vendetta and the elevation of murder, through the new religious doctrine of pollution, to the status of an offense against society as a whole. Even after the appearance of the pollution doctrine, *Wergeld* remained as a form of retribution for lesser crimes as well as a condition for religious purification.

Although the *Iliad* is, on one level, a saga of revenge on a grand scale, there were many limitations on vengeance of the sort implied in the emissary's reproach to Achilles. When Achilles' friend Patroclus is slain in battle, he is completely justified, according to the codes of both tribes, in his retaliatory slaying of Hector. But Achilles goes too far by desecrating Hector's corpse and by burning the corpses of twelve Trojan warriors along with the body of Patroclus. The gods themselves intervene to bring Hector's father, King Priam, safely into the enemy camp—but Achilles has already decided to return the body. He orders Hector's corpse to be anointed in another part of the house because he fears that Priam, seeing it, might lose his self-control in the presence of his son's killer and that he, Achilles, might himself fly into a rage and kill the old man, thereby sinning against Zeus.

The killing of an aging, unarmed king who has braved the enemy camp to claim his son's body would have been an offense against the codes of conduct accepted by most civilized tribes in the Mediterranean world. The concept of a specific murder as an insult to tribal custom was far removed from the subsequent religious doctrine of all murder as pollution. Nevertheless, it was a vital link between the old tribal order and the new religious and political definition of bloodshed as pollution, which took hold in Greece shortly after the age of the author (or authors) known as Homer.

The doctrine of murder as pollution—with all it implies about the social, as distinct from the personal, status of crime and punishment—appears in parallel legends among the Greeks and Hebrews. The Biblical account of Abel's murder by his brother Cain sets forth the pollution doctrine after Cain speaks the famous line, "Am I my brother's keeper?"

And he [the Lord] said, What hast thou done? the voice of thy brother's blood crieth unto me from the ground. And now art thou cursed from the earth, which hath opened her mouth to receive thy brother's blood from thy hand; When thou tillest the ground, it shall not henceforth yield unto thee her strength; a fugitive and a vagabond shalt thou be in the earth. And Cain said unto the Lord, My punishment is greater than I can bear.[4]

Thucydides tells the story of Alcmaeon, who murdered his mother and was condemned by Apollo to wander the earth until he came to a land not yet in existence—"not seen by the sun"—at the time of the slaying. The rest of the earth was accursed to him, as it was to Cain. Finally, Alcmaeon came to a deposit of silt near the mouth of the river Achelous—a deposit caused, Thucydides explains with characteristic precision, by the position of a small group of islands between the mainland and the river's mouth. When Alcmaeon saw the silt, he concluded that he might settle there because it must have accumulated after his mother's death, during the long period in which he had obeyed Apollo's command to wander the earth. There is, of course, a strong resemblance between Alcmaeon's resting place in a land far from his ancestors and the end of Cain's exile in "the land of Nod, on the east of Eden." (Many scholars have speculated that contact between Semitic and Greek traders might account for the symmetry of the two tales. In any event, the penalty of exile for a murderer who pollutes the land was characteristic of many early cultures and religions.)

The parallel between Greek and Judaic concepts of murder as pollution is most striking in its earliest stages; in both cultures, the pollution doctrine should be viewed primarily as a bridge between tribalism and written law. In the Biblical era, Jewish definitions of good and evil, of justice and revenge, emerge from a covenant between the one God and his chosen people. God's power is absolute; he never changes; the prerogative of dispensing vengeance or mercy is eternally, unalterably his. Sin, or crime, is seen as a violation of divine edict. In the Hellenic world, with anthropomorphic deities whose relationship to human beings is never entirely stable, concepts of good and evil arise from a general sense of moral order, or fitness, rather than from a specific set of divine edicts. Although the pollution doctrine clearly arose from analogous religious and political impulses in both cultures, it had assumed quite different shapes by the closing decades of the sixth century B.C., which marked the beginning of the "Golden Age" in Athens and the return of the Jews to Israel from the Babylonian exile. In the Hebrew writings of this period, it is impossible to imagine anything like the trial of Orestes which concludes Aeschylus' *Oresteia,* in which contending gods argue over the question of whether it is worse to kill one's husband or one's mother.

The Greek pollution doctrine, unlike that of the Israelites, did not constitute an absolute prohibition of all murder or even of all premeditated murders. This is clearly indicated by the justification for matricide in Aeschylus' version of the Oresteian trilogy. The disparity between Euripides' interpretation and that of his predecessors suggests that the concept of greater and lesser degrees of religious pollution must have posed a substantial philosophic (and legal) problem for Greeks of the classical period. Individual moral responsibility, as understood in both Jewish and Christian tradition, scarcely enters into the definitions of pollution dramatized by Aeschylus and Sophocles.

The story of Oedipus offers the most obvious and famous illustration of this point, for he is not "guilty" in any sense that would have been accepted by early talmudists, much less by modern Christian and Jewish theologians. It is a basic tenet of both rabbinical Judaism and non-Calvinist Christianity that there can be no guilt, and therefore no just retribution, without awareness of and consent to sin on the part of the offender. (In both religions, willful rejection of awareness complicates the question of guilt.) For Oedipus, though, there can be no escape:

he is polluted even though he has no advance knowledge of his sin. It is the inevitability of tragic fate that links Sophocles more closely with Freud than with religious thinkers who proclaim the doctrine of free will.

Oedipus' pollution is no less complete because he fails to understand the blind prophet Tiresias when he declares, "I say thou art the murderer whom thou seekest." As the prophet warns him, his failure to recognize the truth only makes the retribution that awaits him more certain:

> And when thy father's and thy mother's curse
> With fearful tread shall drive thee from the land,
> On both sides lashing thee,—thine eye so clear
> Beholding darkness in that day,—oh, then,
> What region will not shudder at thy cry?[5]

The importance of the pollution doctrine in establishing the primacy of the state and its gods and laws over older tribal practices is most clearly defined in the Oresteian trilogy. Orestes is, to some extent, defiled by the murder of his mother, even though Apollo himself ordered the deed. In every version of the legend, he is filled with the horror of his act and must wander the earth, pursued by the vengeful Furies (who represent the more ancient female deities of tribal culture), until the younger, more powerful—and, not incidentally, male—god Apollo conducts him safely to an Olympian tribunal. In Euripides' *Electra*, Clytemnestra's brother Castor tells Orestes: "For her part, she has received justice, but what you have done is not just. And Phoebus, Phoebus—but he is my king and so I am dumb. Clever he is, but what he required of you was not clever. But we must accept these things. Henceforth, you must do what Zeus and fate have decreed for you."[6] (This passage— "clever he is, but what he required of you was not clever"— underlines Euripides' skepticism about certain aspects of the Olympian religion.)

In Aeschylus' *Eumenides,* the trial of Orestes establishes the pre-eminence of public over private concerns and the ascendancy of the newer patriarchal gods. One of the Furies addresses Apollo:

> You plead for his acquittal: have you asked yourself
> How one who poured out on the ground his mother's blood
> Will live henceforth in Argos, in his father's house?
> Shall he at public altars share in sacrifice?
> Shall holy water lave his hands at tribal feasts?

And Apollo answers:

> This too I answer; mark the truth of what I say.
> The mother is not the true parent of the child
> Which is called hers. She is the nurse who tends
>   the growth
> Of young seed planted by its true parent, the male.
> So, if Fate spares the child, she keeps it, as one might
> Keep for some friend a growing plant. And of this truth,
> That father without mother may beget, we have
> Present, as proof, the daughter of Olympian Zeus:
> One never nursed in the dark cradle of the womb;
> Yet such a being no god will beget again.

The Furies appeal to Athena in vain: she casts the deciding vote to acquit Orestes, in one of the most stunningly misogynous statements ever issued by a female (human or divine) in western literature.

> My duty is to give the final vote. When yours
> Are counted, mine goes to uphold Orestes' plea.
> No mother gave me birth. Therefore the father's claim
> And male supremacy in all things, save to give
> Myself in marriage, wins my heart's loyalty.
> Therefore a woman's death, who killed her husband, is,

> I judge, outweighed in grievousness by his. And so
> Orestes, if the votes are equal, wins the case.
> Let those appointed bring the urns and count the votes.[7]

These passages underline several aspects of the pollution doctrine as it was understood in classical Athens. There are degrees of pollution—that of a son who kills his mother is not as great as that of a woman who kills her husband. The idea, so deeply rooted in tribal culture, that nothing is so terrible as the spilling of kindred blood has given way to a broader view of civil order. The gods who represent the state—Apollo and Athena—take precedence over the Furies, who represent the older values of family and tribe. Religious and social order are firmly linked with male power. Orestes' murder is sanctioned by the gods, while Clytemnestra's slaying of Agamemnon is declared the treachery of a vengeful woman.

The hierarchy of guilt represented in the *Oresteia* must have posed a considerable philosophic problem—not only because it repudiated ancient blood loyalties but because it was somewhat at variance with the requirements of the pollution doctrine itself. Euripides' skeptical view of the motives of Orestes, which diverges from the interpretation of Aeschylus and Sophocles, represents what might easily have been contemporary objections to the dramatic acquittal of a son who had committed matricide. To a modern mind, the hierarchy of pollution reflected in the *Oresteia* is not obviously superior, in a moral or a legal sense, to earlier customs of tribal settlement. Nevertheless, the religious elevation of the crime of murder to a plane above personal or tribal interests was unquestionably a precondition for the development of law as we know it today.

Although the importance of the pollution doctrine is unquestionable, its significance has frequently been misunderstood and exaggerated by those who wish to claim the superiority of theology to jurisprudence or the supremacy of one religion over others. In western culture, both polytheistic and monotheistic creeds recognize a distinction (although the precise location of the dividing line has always been and remains a matter of intense controversy) between private sins and public crimes. Perhaps the best statement of this distinction was made in the twelfth century by Maimonides, in his exhaustive commentaries on rabbinical law. He warned against the payment of ransom to absolve a murderer of his crime, "even if he offers all the money in the world"—and even if the victim's closest relatives, entitled to blood vengeance in the earliest stages of Mosaic law, agree to financial restitution. "For the life of the murdered person," Maimonides asserted, "is not the property of the avenger of blood but the *property of God* [italics mine]. . . . There is no offense about which the Law is so strict as it is about bloodshed, as it is said, So ye shall not pollute the land wherein ye are; for blood, it polluteth the land (Numbers 35:33)."[8]

A sin, in this view, is not always a secular crime, but a crime is always a sin. Just as a fine can never repay society for the taking of a human life, a formal religious purification ceremony can never serve as a substitute for genuine spiritual atonement. For the Hebrews of Biblical times and for Greeks of the classical period, religious purgation was not a substitute for legal punishment but a symbolic rite accorded those who had already, as we would say today, paid their debt to society. As Hubert Treston notes, religious purgation for homicide was never permitted by the Greeks until the slayer "had re-established his normal equilibrium, had suffered the penalty prescribed by law, namely exile, temporary or perpetual, and was ready to resume religious communion with his fellow-men."[9] Both Jewish and Christian tradition are as insistent as the Greek pollution doctrine on punishment of the offender as a precondition for spiritual purification and reconciliation. Confusion between atonement and purification is a modern phenomenon, supported by none of the western religious traditions that have played such an important role in the restraint of personal vengeance.

Retribution as a requirement for reconciliation is a pillar of the fundamental covenants governing both Judaism and Christianity—a fact of religious history that has frequently been ignored by Christian theologians intent on proving the superiority of Christian mercy to Judaic vengeance. The great Jewish drama is the covenant between God and the children of Israel, God's wrath when his children violate the terms of the covenant, and the mercy that can only be obtained through the repentance and suffering of the Chosen People. It is a covenant that cannot be broken, even when the punishment has seemed too great to bear.

The great Christian drama is also one of sin, suffering, and redemption, albeit of a somewhat different nature. In Christian belief, there can be no resurrection without a crucifixion; through his agony on the cross, Jesus is believed to have atoned for the sins of all men and women. This conviction is embodied in the Roman Catholic sacrament of penance, in which the sinner must not only repent but take concrete steps to atone for the offense in order to be forgiven and—literally—return to the communion of the faithful. The words of the old Catholic act of contrition, recited in the confessional by penitents before the liturgical reforms promulgated in the 1960s by the Second Vatican Council, explicitly promise atonement as a condition of forgiveness: "I firmly resolve with the help of Thy grace to confess my sins, to do penance, and to amend my life. Amen." (In keeping with the contemporary retreat from emphasis on retribution, the words of the old act have been softened and made less explicit. Since the mid-1960s, many cards in confessionals have been imprinted with the slogan, "Today is the first day of the rest of your life." For a Catholic schooled in traditional theology, the card should have included the qualification, ". . . if you have paid for what you did yesterday.")

In the evolution of religious theory regarding revenge, the similarities between rabbinical Judaism and Christianity are more striking than the differences. The practical application of these theories is another matter altogether—and must be discussed within a political rather than a theological context.

The phrase "Old Testament vengeance" has frequently been used as a pejorative by Christian proselytizers to emphasize what they regard as the fundamental distinction between Judaism and Christianity; i.e., Christ's emphasis on forgiveness as opposed to strict Mosaic retribution. This mistaken view of Judaic revenge is partly attributable to the conviction that Christianity is the fulfillment of Hebrew prophecy and is, as such, the divinely ordained successor to Judaism. Before the development of modern anthropological methods of historical investigation, the stereotype of Judaic vengeance was also based on a general lack of knowledge about early tribal customs. The numerous accounts of savage revenge in the Bible, especially in (but not limited to) Genesis and Exodus, reflect the practices of most primitive tribal cultures rather than specific characteristics of the Hebrews. This point was forcefully made by a Catholic scholar, who observed in 1941 that "original Germanic customs of blood revenge were modified [both] through Christianity and by ancient Semitic traditions as embodied in the Mosaic law. The 'Avenger of Blood' figures largely in Jewish tradition in consequence of the extreme solidarity of tribal groups. . . . The same close family bonds mark all the early Christian civilizations of Europe."[10]

Even in the relatively primitive period of Mosaic law, the historical bent of Jewish tradition had been in the direction of limitations on human vengeance, and it is in this spirit that the famous "eye for eye" passage from Exodus—so often cited today in support of the death penalty—must be understood. It is significant that this famous verse is almost never cited in its Biblical context. The preceding verse concerns the hypothetical case of a pregnant woman who is injured by a man and suffers a miscarriage. If loss of the unborn child is the only consequence, the assailant is liable for a limited penalty determined by the woman's husband and the judges. If "mischief"—presumably a severe injury to or death of the woman—follows the miscarriage, only then do more stringent penalties come into play.

> If men strive, and hurt a woman with child, so that her fruit depart from her, and yet no mischief follow: he shall be surely punished, according as the woman's husband will lay upon him; and he shall pay as the judges determine. And if any mischief follow, thou shalt give life for life, Eye for eye, tooth for tooth, hand for hand, foot for foot, Burning for burning, wound for wound, stripe for stripe.[11]

The intent of this passage is clearly to forbid penalties, including death, that are greater than the original crime. (Opponents of legalized abortion are unlikely to derive comfort from this Mosaic admonition, since it makes a clear distinction between the unborn child and the living mother.)

Even the early books of the Bible, which prescribed much stricter retribution than did the rabbinical teachings at the time of Jesus, are filled with cautions against unlimited personal revenge. One of the most striking examples, exemplifying the Hebrew interpretation of the pollution doctrine, concerns "cities of refuge" to prevent blood revenge against those who have killed unintentionally. The cities of refuge were not a device to prevent all blood vengeance but a way of buying time to guard against the unjust exaction of revenge.

> Thou shalt separate three cities for thee in the midst of thy land, which the Lord thy God giveth thee to possess it. Thou shalt prepare thee a way, and divide the coasts of thy land, which the Lord thy God giveth thee to inherit, into three parts, that every slayer may flee thither. And this is the case of the slayer, which shall flee thither, that he may live: Whoso killeth

his neighbour ignorantly, whom he hated not in time past; As when a man goeth into the wood with his neighbour to hew wood, and his hand fetcheth a stroke with the axe to cut down the tree, and the head slippeth from the helve, and lighteth upon his neighbour, that he die; he shall flee unto one of those cities, and live: Lest the avenger of the blood pursue the slayer, while his heart is hot, and overtake him, because the way is long, and slay him; whereas he was not worthy of death, inasmuch as he hated him not in time past. . . . That innocent blood be not shed in thy land, which the Lord thy God giveth thee for an inheritance, and so blood be upon thee.[12]

That innocent blood be not shed. The Hebrews of this period did not, of course, take the same attitude toward the shedding of guilty blood. Failure to avenge the victim of unlawful murder polluted the land as surely as misguided vengeance against one who was innocent of intentional murder.

But if any man hate his neighbour, and lie in wait for him, and rise up against him, and smite him mortally that he die, and fleeth into one of these cities: Then the elders of his city shall send and fetch him thence, and deliver him into the hand of the avenger of blood, that he may die. Thine eye shall not pity him, but thou shalt put away the guilt of innocent blood from Israel, that it may go well with thee.[13]

The evidentiary requirements that made it extremely difficult for any rabbinical court to impose a death sentence were products of the talmudic thought of later eras. (The most notable of these restraints is the provision that no one may be put to death without the testimony of two eyewitnesses related neither to the victim nor to the accused assailant.) Many would consider it a violation of the soul of Judaism—which uses "the Law" interchangeably with the very word of God—to suggest the existence of a distinction between religious and civic prohibitions. Nevertheless, there is such a practical distinction in

Jewish tradition (if not in the eschatological structure of the Jewish universe) and it exists not only in talmudic debate but in the fundamental covenant between God and the children of Israel. It concerns the difference between the rules governing relations between God and his people, as opposed to those governing the relations of human beings with one another. This distinction between divine and human prerogatives appears in another form in Christianity; in both religions, the division is a major source of the philosophic tension that continues to shape western attitudes toward revenge.

Whatever restraints the Scriptures place on vengeance committed by God's creatures, they accord the unlimited and unquestionable right of vengeance to the creator of the universe. Dan Jacobson, in a provocative re-examination of the Biblical covenant, notes that the God of the Jews reserves his most boundless revenge for infidelity. He observes that "Yahweh is assumed to know *from within,* like his people, what it is like to suffer the fear of being passed over. He knows the privileges and the agonies of his own solitude, of the 'separation' he has imposed on himself, as well as on his people. He experiences all the dread of a lover who can never be certain that his love is wholly and exclusively reciprocated, and that whatever he gets from her will be all that she has to give."[14]

For the authors of the Bible, Jacobson notes, the loverlike qualities of Yahweh were underlined by the fact that he tolerated the worship of other gods by *other* peoples. "*Autres pays, autres dieux* seems to be his attitude. . . . But Israel was different. She was the solitary possession of this solitary God. On her he had to take a boundless revenge for any infidelity or wrongdoing. Where was she without him? And he without her?"[15]

The possessiveness and near-erotic element of Yahweh's relationship with his people leads to what Jacobson describes as a cycle of "remorseless reciprocity"—boundless revenge when Israel has been unfaithful to her God, boundless mercy when she reaffirms her exclusive devotion. This cyclical concept of divine vengeance and forgiveness was to become an equally potent force in Christianity. The Christian theme of God's revenge for individual sin is a logical extension of the Old Testament theme of God's revenge for the infidelity of his people. Jeremiah's prophecy that "the Lord God of recompenses shall surely requite" is almost identical to the Pauline promise that vengeance is the Lord's and he will repay.

The unchallengeable aspect of God's vengeance placed the children of Israel in a constant state of vulnerability (as the Calvinist theory of predestination would later affect Christians who accepted it). The concept that the sins of the fathers are visited upon the children is irreconcilable with the compassionate values of the Sermon on the Mount and the Golden Rule, and this contradiction permeates all religious views of revenge. For the drama of divine vengeance can only be acted out in human lives—and how is it possible to determine whether God's creatures are acting justly in his stead or are inflicting unjust, ill-conceived human revenge on the innocent? For the Jews of Biblical times, their position as the chosen people was accompanied by frequent, arbitrary displays of Yahweh's anger —a vindictiveness that was both collective and hereditary, punishing the innocent and the guilty alike. Yahweh was rarely as selective as he was in preserving Noah and Lot; most of the time, the just and the unjust perished together.

How, Jacobson asks, could the danger of Yahweh's vengeance not be omnipresent in the minds of his subjects. And who was the agent of this revenge? Those who had been driven from their land in favor of the Chosen People? How could one distinguish between the stranger who deserved compassion and the stranger who was so often used as an agent of God's revenge? "In the Hebrew Scriptures," Jacobson argues, "we can see all those impulses expressed: the compassionate or protective ('You know the heart of the stranger, for you were strangers in the land of Egypt'); and the guilty vindictive. In much the same way, *being* the victim or loser will produce a hunger

for justice that is virtually indistinguishable from a dream of
revenge and recompense; these, too, are to be found in the
Scriptures."[16] (This observation has, I believe, a startling pertinence to the endless cycle of vindictiveness and bloodshed that
has characterized relations between the modern state of Israel
and the Arabs—from both the Arab and Israeli points of view.)

There is, however, a strain in Jewish tradition that runs
counter to the unquestioning acceptance of God's unending
right of revenge. It surfaced after the destruction of Solomon's
temple in 587 B.C., when many of the Israelites were taken into
exile by their Babylonian captors. This is the period described
in the famous psalm that resonates with the yearnings of all
exiles:

> By the rivers of Babylon, there we sat down,
> yea, we wept, when we remembered Zion.
>   We hanged our harps upon the willows
> in the midst thereof.
>   For there they that carried us away cap-
> tive required of us a song; and they that
> wasted us required of us mirth, saying, Sing us
> one of the songs of Zion.
>   How shall we sing the Lord's song in
> a strange land?
>   If I forget thee, O Jerusalem, let my
> right hand forget her cunning.
>   If I do not remember thee, let my tongue
> cleave to the roof of my mouth; if I prefer not
> Jerusalem above my chief joy.[17]

Fear that they would lose their traditions in a strange land
gave the Jews an urgent reason for re-examining and codifying
ancient laws, many of which were already inscribed on scrolls
containing some of the material that now appears in the first five
books of the Bible. The Babylonian exile marks the beginning
of the period of rabbinical, or talmudic, Judaism, leading to the

completion of the Mishnah around A.D. 220 and the Gemara around A.D. 500. These vast commentaries constitute a sequel to the Biblical Hebrew scriptures.

The beginning of talmudic Judaism coincides with the appearance of the great prophets of the Babylonian exile, whose lives are recorded in the scriptures. One of these prophets, Ezekiel, departed radically from received opinion by rejecting the belief that the sins of the fathers are visited upon the children. It is ironic that he is remembered chiefly as a prophet of fire and brimstone, because his views on hereditary punishment were so radical in light of previous interpretations of the Jewish covenant that the Book of Ezekiel was almost omitted from the sacred scriptures. Almost . . . but not quite. For the ideas attributed to Ezekiel represent the side of Jewish tradition which is concerned not only with collective destiny but with individual accountability. Ezekiel envisioned a God who promised explicitly to judge "every one according to his own ways" and who declared, "I have no pleasure in the death of him that dieth."

> What mean ye, that ye use this proverb concerning the land of Israel, saying, The fathers have eaten sour grapes, and the children's teeth are set on edge?
>
> As I live, saith the Lord God, ye shall not have occasion any more to use this proverb in Israel.
>
> Behold, all souls are mine; as the soul of the father, so also the soul of the son is mine: the soul that sinneth, it shall die . . .
>
> Now, lo, if he beget a son, that seeth all his father's sins which he hath done, and considereth, and doeth not such like,
>
> That hath not eaten upon the mountains, neither hath lifted up his eyes to the idols of the house of Israel, hath not defiled his neighbour's wife,
>
> Neither hath oppressed any, hath not withholden the pledge, neither hath spoiled by violence, but hath given his

bread to the hungry, and hath covered the naked with a garment,

That hath taken off his hand from the poor, that hath not received usury nor increase, hath executed my judgments, hath walked in my statutes; he shall not die for the iniquity of his father, he shall surely live.

As for his father, because he cruelly oppressed, spoiled his brother by violence, and did that which is not good among his people, lo, even he shall die in his iniquity.

Yet say ye, Why? doth not the son bear the iniquity of the father? When the son hath done that which is lawful and right, and hath kept all my statutes, and hath done them, he shall surely live.

The soul that sinneth, it shall die. The son shall not bear the iniquity of the father, neither shall the father bear the iniquity of the son: the righteousness of the righteous shall be upon him, and the wickedness of the wicked shall be upon him.[18]

This vision of a deity whose punishments are specifically tailored to the sins of the individual is far removed from the sweeping reciprocity in which both the innocent and the guilty are caught up in Yahweh's inscrutable vengeance. But remorseless divine reciprocity *is* the dominant theme of the first five books of the Bible, so it is understandable that Ezekiel posed a dilemma for the rabbis. His vision implies a view of divine retribution and of history itself different from the one manifested in the opening chapters of what Jacobson calls "the story of stories." For if God's retribution is inflicted on each "according to his own ways," how is one to explain the sufferings of the innocent? This is the classic question of the skeptic, and it is particularly urgent in the history of a people whose worldly fate has always been linked with its spiritual covenant.

One pious answer was offered by those devout Jews, convinced that their fate under the Nazis was integral to the divine plan of atonement, who praised Yahweh as they went to their deaths in the gas chambers. The rabbi of the Polish city of Grodzisk, addressing his people before they were led to the ovens from the railroad station at Treblinka, declared that "these are the last real birth pangs of the Messiah. You are blessed to have merited the honor of being sacrifices and your ashes will serve to purify all Israel." This explanation for vengeance wreaked upon innocents has, of course, occurred to martyrs of all faiths, but martyrdom by choice is quite a different matter from martyrdom by involuntary extermination— which is not martyrdom at all but simply death.

An endless cycle of divine vengeance and forgiveness—to which one may or may not piously submit—is one possible outcome of the concept of reciprocity that permeates the early books of the Bible. Another possibility is the ethic of the Golden Rule taught by Jesus and his contemporary Rabbi Hillel, who said: *Do not unto others that which is hateful unto thee.* (A common spirit animates both the positive and negative formulations, but the latter seems somewhat more attuned to realistic human limitations.) There is, in any case, an awesome gap between the sensible, humanistic ethic of Jesus and Hillel and the cycles of unknowable divine vengeance that surface repeatedly in Judaeo-Christian thought from the early Biblical era through the Renaissance. Both Jews and Christians have attempted to bridge this chasm with the concept of free will, which bears directly on the legitimacy—or illegitimacy—of revenge.

On the night of conception, according to one talmudic legend, God decides over a drop of semen (the rabbis, in spite of their distaste for Hellenism, shared Aristotle's views on the irrelevance of female substance in the creation of a human being) whether the child will be poor or rich, stupid or intelligent, handsome or ugly, male or female. The only quality not determined by God is the child's moral character. The angel escorts the nascent soul through paradise, where the rewards of the righteous are displayed, and through Gehenna, where the wicked are lashed with scourges of fire. The child is then born and begins the life that will lead to eternal reward or eternal punishment, since "everything is in the power of Heaven except the fear of Heaven."[19] This legend (without the image of an angel giving the drop of semen a tour of the afterworld) would also accurately reflect the Christian view of free will: God knows all, but he does not force his desires on men and women.

Faith in free will, as opposed to predestination and more modern forms of psychological and sociological determinism, plays an important role in the formation of cultural attitudes concerning the relationship between justice and revenge. If divine power to reward and punish is limitless and independent of individual human acts, the relationship between crime and punishment is meaningless. As soon as one envisions, as Ezekiel did, a deity whose actions are directly related to the behavior of individuals, the distinction between just and unjust retribution comes into play. God himself is not exempt from the requirement of justice.

The Christian gospels, like many talmudic writings of the same period, are filled with contradictory attitudes toward retribution and forgiveness. Jesus certainly preached what was, for the most part, an ethic of compassion. Perhaps the most pertinent example is the story of the woman taken in adultery, who was brought before Jesus by Pharisees attempting to trick him into uttering heresy against Mosaic law.

> And the scribes and Pharisees brought unto him a woman taken in adultery; and when they had set her in the midst, They say unto him, Master, this woman was taken in adultery, in the very act. Now Moses in the law commanded us, that such should be stoned: but what sayest thou? This they said, tempting him, that they might have to accuse him. But Jesus stooped down, and with his finger wrote on the ground, as though he

heard them not. So when they continued asking him, he lifted up himself, and said unto them, He that is without sin among you, let him first cast a stone at her. And again he stooped down, and wrote on the ground. And they which heard it, being convicted by their own conscience, went out one by one, beginning at the eldest, even unto the last: and Jesus was left alone, and the woman standing in the midst. When Jesus had lifted up himself, and saw none but the woman, he said unto her, Woman, where are those thine accusers? hath no man condemned thee? She said, No man, Lord. And Jesus said unto her, Neither do I condemn thee: go, and sin no more.[20]

This story is often cited as an example of New Testament forgiveness, in opposition to Old Testament revenge. But Jesus (who was himself a Pharisee) was giving voice to the strong, pragmatic compassion that already existed in rabbinical Judaism—and was indeed at variance with the stringent prescriptions and proscriptions of early Mosaic law. Jesus did not confront his priestly challengers as antagonists; he merely asked them to search their own consciences. Thus, he was defending a point of view with which the other Pharisees were already familiar. This behavior, like nearly all of Jesus' acts in the gospels, is in line with his admonition "Think not that I am come to destroy the law, or the prophets: I am not come to destroy, but to fulfil."[21]

The Biblical Jesus was more interested in preaching positive charity than negative fear of retribution. The most explicit statement of this philosophy is, of course, the Sermon on the Mount.

Ye have heard that it hath been said, Thou shalt love thy neighbour, and hate thine enemy. But I say unto you, Love your enemies, bless them that curse you, do good to them that hate you, and pray for them which despitefully use you, and persecute you; That ye may be the children of your Father which is in heaven: for he maketh his sun to rise on the evil and on the good, and sendeth rain on the just and on the unjust. For if ye love them which love you, what reward have ye? do not even the publicans the same? And if ye salute your brethren only, what do ye more than others? do not even the publicans so? Be ye therefore perfect, even as your Father which is in heaven is perfect.[22]

It is always a shock to read these words, with their uncompromising idealism, in black-and-white instead of to hear them mumbled in a soporific, easily ignored liturgical format. One might have anticipated that such a prophet would be put to death, even if he had not run afoul of a colonial governor and native administrators trying to keep the lid on a discontented populace. For it has always been a difficult enough task, requiring persistent threats of civic retribution, to persuade men to refrain from doing violence to their adversaries. To persuade men to love their enemies is truly a task belonging to a kingdom and a king not of this world.

Although the Sermon on the Mount strongly resembles the rabbinical teachings associated with the school of Hillel, there is one point on which the Jesus of the gospels did depart substantially from Jewish prophets who preceded him: he defined "neighbor" more broadly. "Neighbor," as the term is understood not only in Mosaic law but in most early legal codes, means a member of the tribe. The legal gravity of a crime, and the penalty attached to it, were strongly influenced by the status of the victim. Retribution for a crime against a neighbor was far more stringent than for a crime against an outsider. The Jesus of the gospels argued for a more universal definition; he replied with the story of the good Samaritan when a lawyer asked, "Who is my neighbor?"

A certain man went down from Jerusalem to Jericho, and fell among thieves, which stripped him of his raiment, and wounded him, and departed, leaving him half dead. And by chance there came down a certain priest that way: and when he saw him, he passed by on the other side. And likewise a Levite, when he was at the place, came and looked on him, and passed by on the other side. But a certain Samaritan, as he journeyed, came where he was: and when he saw him, he had compassion on him, And went to him, and bound up his wounds, pouring in oil and wine, and set him on his own beast, and brought him to an inn, and took care of him. And on the morrow when he departed, he took out two pence, and gave them to the host, and said unto him, Take care of him; and whatsoever thou spendest more, when I come again, I will repay thee. Which now of these three, thinkest thou, was neighbour unto him that fell among the thieves?[23]

Jesus gave essentially the same answer that the God of Genesis gave Cain when he asked, "Am I my brother's keeper?" —but he expanded the definition of brother.

Although Jesus was primarily a prophet of compassion and forgiveness, he was also—like earlier Jewish prophets—a believer in proportional retribution. Like Ezekiel, he took an individual rather than a collective view of accountability for sin.

And the Lord said, Who then is that faithful and wise steward, whom his lord shall make ruler over his household, to give them their portion of meat in due season? Blessed is that servant, whom his lord when he cometh shall find so doing. Of a truth I say unto you, that he will make him ruler over all he hath. But and if that servant say in his heart, My lord delayeth his coming: and shall begin to beat the menservants and maidens, and to eat and drink, and to be drunken: The lord of that servant will come in a day when he looketh not for him, and at an hour when he is not aware, and will cut him in sunder, and will appoint him his portion with the unbelievers. And that servant, which knew his lord's will, and prepared not himself, neither did according to his will, shall be beaten with many stripes. But he that knew not, and did commit things worthy of stripes, shall be beaten with few stripes. *For unto whomsoever much is given, of him shall be much required: and to whom men have committed much, of him they will ask the more.* [Italics mine.][24]

Like the "eye for eye" passage in Exodus, Luke's story of the punishment for a faithless servant may be read in two ways. On the one hand, there is strict proportionality of crime and punishment. On the other, the gravity of the crime is determined, at least to some extent, by the situation of the servant (how much trust and authority was he accorded by his master?). These two aspects of Christian teaching, which extend from the gospels to the present day, are not necessarily opposed to each other—although sharp conflicts can and do arise when they are applied to civic issues, such as the question of whether a murderer from an impoverished background deserves the same punishment as one from a home of material comfort and privilege.

In Christian theology, the dual nature of Christ's teachings regarding punishment and mercy frequently appears as a conflict between the immutable "natural law" expounded by Thomas Aquinas and "situation ethics," in which the morality of an act is defined by the circumstances in which men and women find themselves. These two concepts are not as totally opposed as some modern thinkers have suggested. In the universe of Augustine and Aquinas, the intrinsic moral nature of an act never changes under *force majeure*, but the degree of just retribution is definitely linked with the intention of the sinner.

In spite of the emphasis on mercy and compassion in the teachings of Jesus, most thinkers from the early Christian era until the Enlightenment emphasized the vision of a God whose reciprocity and inevitable revenge are virtually indistinguishable from those of the vindictive Yahweh of the Old Testament. *The Triumphs of Gods Revenge against the crying and execrable sin of wilful and premeditated murder,* a bestseller published in numerous editions during the first decade of the eighteenth century, describes—with great relish—retributive torments precisely calibrated to the nature of the sin.

One emblematic tale, with the mysterious title "A Swedish History" (mysterious because the story is set in Switzerland), concerns the murder of a pious, wealthy widow by her profligate son. The mother, Christina, sends her son, Maurice, to the University of Lausanne in fulfillment of her late husband's wish that the boy become a scholar. Maurice, alas, is no scholar; he prefers to spend his days drinking and carousing under the influence of a Svengali-like tutor. When the mother refuses to send him any more money, he returns home and plays the part of a dutiful son. But he is only waiting for the right moment, which comes when he is able to alarm his good mother with the news that a neighbor's child has fallen down their well. The gullible Christina rushes into the yard and her son, "better like a fury than a man, and rather resembling a devil more than a son, fasteneth his left hand on the wellspout, and as she looks into the profundity thereof, with his right hand tips and throws her in; and so without any more doing, caps down the cover thereof; when rejoicing in his heart, that he has sent her to death."[25]

Maurice, of course, spends all of the money he inherits upon his mother's death and winds up in debtors prison, where he slips on the stairs while taking a walk and breaks his arm in two places. "It putrefies and rots," the tale exultantly concludes, "as for the preserving of his life, he within fifteen days is enforced to have it cut off a little below the shoulder; and this was the very same hand and arm which threw his mother into the well. A singular act of God's revenging justice, and just revenge shown therein."[26] If your right hand offends you and you do not cut it off yourself, God will do it for you.

Just deserts, one might say, as far as the evil Maurice is concerned. But *The Triumphs of Gods Revenge* articulates another singularly unappetizing aspect of the prevailing view of divine vengeance. To punish the sinner, God often inflicts evil on innocent bystanders. Consider the tale of Hautefilia, a woman who hated her brother and his wife because they had a happier, more prosperous marriage than she enjoyed. The sister tells her brother that his wife has been unfaithful with another man (whom she also abhors, because he has kept a lap dog his page stole from her). When neither the brother nor his "rival" is killed in a duel—and the brother decides his wife was trustworthy after all—Hautefilia arranges to have the wife poisoned by an apothecary. Then, so she will be able to inherit a large estate, she arranges to have the same apothecary do away with her witless brother.

"And now," the author informs his readers, "his blood-thirsty sister Hautefilia (the author of the murders and the tragedies) thinking herself freed of all her enemies, and all that stood in the way of her advancement and preferment (neither thinking of her conscience or soul, of heaven, or hell) domineers far more than before; yea, builds castles in the air, and flatters herself with this false ambition, that she must now be a duchess, or at least a countess; *but she reckons without God.*" (Italics mine.)[27]

And how does God avenge the deaths of the unfortunate brother and his wife? Why, the apothecary who carried out the sister's murderous orders rapes the twelve-year-old daughter of a tavern owner. After enduring torture on the rack and being sentenced to death for rape, he also confesses to the murders instigated by the perfidious Hautefilia. The rape victim, one assumes, went about praising God for allowing her suffering to be the instrument for uncovering the even greater crime of murder. God's ways are not to be questioned. Hautefilia is finally apprehended and placed on the rack herself; then her breasts are torn off with red-hot pincers and she is hanged. This was the Christian justice, circa 1700, that had replaced supposedly inferior Mosaic vengeance.

Of course, if the relatives of the victims had taken it upon themselves to dispatch the murderess, their acts would have been regarded as mortal sins that also merited the death penalty. The hierarchy of vengeance is clear. God's revenge is unchallengeable. The revenge of God's appointed magistrates, the proprietors of the rack, is also morally justifiable (unless they use their God-given authority to pursue private grudges). Private revenge is forbidden to all, regardless of social position. Belief in the divine right of kings provides a religious and political foundation both for the prohibition of private revenge and the sanction of public revenge.

The fullest exposition of pre-Enlightenment thought on the relationship between public authority and private revenge appears in the essays of Peter de la Primaudaye, whose works were translated almost immediately and were as influential in Elizabethan England as in France. Primaudaye recognized the problem posed by incompetent or evil rulers who failed to carry out God's plan for avenging injustice. Nevertheless, he argued, the only righteous course for Christian men and women is to wait, secure in the faith that God's plan of retribution will inevitably be revealed.

All private Revenge proceeding of envy, or of hatred, or of anger, is vicious and forbidden by God, who commandeth us to render good for evil, and not evil for evil. For he hath ordained the means, whereby he will have vengeance executed among men. Therefore he hath appointed Magistrates to execute it according to his law, and following his ordinance, not with any evil affection, but with just indignation proceeding from love and from true zeal of justice . . . so he would have them supply his place among men, unto whom he hath committed the sword for the defense of the good and punishment of evil doers, to follow his example. But *whether they do so or no,* there is no sin that can avoid punishment, and that findeth

not a judge even in him that committed it, to take vengeance
therefore by means of the affections, which God hath placed
in men to that end. [Italics mine.][28]

The cyclical view of God's revenge for sin is clearly evident
in Shakespeare's histories. Rulers may sin and use their God-
given authority for private ends, but their downfall invariably
comes in God's own time. In this view, war (which, like random
crime, affects the innocent as well as the guilty) is part of God's
plan of vengeance against an unworthy ruler. The difficulty of
trying to reconcile this cyclical Renaissance philosophy with
the Christian doctrine of free will is obvious: if atrocities inflicted by humans are part of God's revenge for sin, how can
men be held responsible? The answer of the gospels—one that
has never satisfied skeptics—is "Woe unto the world because of
offences! for it must needs be that offences come; but woe to that
man by whom the offence cometh!"[29]

The Biblical vision of God's inevitable revenge for sin (articulated in both Old and New Testaments) provided the foundation for the cyclical concept of history adhered to by most
thinkers of the Renaissance. It explains, as Lily Campbell notes,
"the recurrent round of events with which Tudor history and
particularly Tudor accounts of the War of the Roses were
concerned. An usurper seizes the throne; God avenges his sin
upon the heir through the agency of another usurper, whose sin
is again avenged upon the third heir."[30]

Thus, uprisings, feuds, civil war—all agents of social disorder and human misery—are part of God's plan of vengeance.
But revolt by individuals against unjust rule is, for most writers
of the period, both sinful and unlawful (even though it may play
a role in God's larger plan). The *Mirror for Magistrates,* a
widely known work concerned primarily with the moral and
civic obligations of governors and the governed, states this
viewpoint succinctly:

For whatsoever man, woman or child, is by consent of the whole realm established in the royal seat, so it have not been injuriously procured by rigor of sword and open force, but quietly by title, either of inheritance, succession, lawful bequest, common consent, or election, is undoubtedly chosen by God to be his deputy: and whosoever resisteth any such, resisteth against God himself, and is a rank traitor and rebel.[31]

Primaudaye goes even further: Even if a king has acquired his office by morally dubious means, the people still have no right to take it upon themselves to avenge their injustices: "This word, Tyrant, was . . . [used] for him that made himself sovereign prince of his own authority, without election, or right of succession, or lot, or just war, or special calling of God, yet we must not infer this consequence, that therefore it is lawful to kill every prince that exerciseth tyranny."[32]

The hierarchy of public and private revenge in Christian thought clearly falls within the territory where religion and politics intersect. Just as the ascendancy of the pollution doctrine among the Hebrews was linked with the self-definition of the Israelites as a people and a nation, and among the Greeks with the rise of city-states, so was the preoccupation of Renaissance theologians with controls on private revenge linked with the emergence of nation-states from the feudal period. The link between theology and politics is most evident in the antagonism of late Renaissance leaders of both church and state (in Protestant and Catholic countries) toward the *Realpolitik* of Machiavelli.

Machiavelli was no more in favor of uncontrolled private vengeance than were the most conservative Christian theologians. But Machiavelli's analysis of vengeance—like his approach to all of the passions affecting political life—was based on pragmatic rather than moralistic considerations. He was concerned with men and women as they are, not as they might be in an ideal and (as far as he was concerned) unattainable world of Christian mercy.

This is as true of *The Discourses,* which are concerned more with questions of liberty than of authority, as of *The Prince,* in which the preoccupations are reversed. The wise ruler, Machiavelli argues in *The Prince,* is one who swiftly interposes his own retribution between potential rebels and the state. Such a ruler, he suggests, is not only acting in his own interest but will in the end prove more compassionate than a weak prince who allows isolated acts of rebellion to erupt into general civil disorder. Christian theorists of the Renaissance were disturbed not by the actions Machiavelli advocated but by the fact that his recommendations were grounded in human political needs rather than the divine right of kings. The theological argument —that unlawful private vengeance was transformed into lawful public vengeance by the divine authority conferred on God's human agents—was absolutely irrelevant to Machiavelli. His approach could not be tolerated by those who sought divine justification for vengeance on earth.

The attitude of Christian Europe toward revenge was complicated by the Reformation, which was seen by the Church of Rome not only as a rebellion against God's magistrates but against God himself (since the right of kings was subject to the still more divine authority of the church). The attitude of Protestant leaders toward revenge did not differ significantly from that of Catholic authorities: they disagreed only over the question of which church, and which men, were in fact God's true representatives.

The unity of Catholic and Protestant views on the subject of private revenge became clear when the rebel religion became the state religion, as it did in England. Elizabeth's views on the divine right of kings and the legitimacy of public revenge were presumably identical to those of her father, Henry VIII, before his break with the Church of Rome. Although bloody retribution was not her favorite mode of government, she never hesitated to use it when she felt either her own power or the security of her realm to be at stake. Victims, not rulers, took the high road of compassion and forgiveness. Mary Stuart, during her trial for treason against Elizabeth, declared, "I do not desire vengeance. I leave it to him who is the just avenger of the innocent and of those who suffer for His Name under whose power I will take shelter. I would rather pray with Esther than take the sword with Judith."[33]

The fact that Christian theology served the purposes of the state by legitimizing public revenge and forbidding private revenge does not negate the genuine importance of religious teaching in the social containment of vengeance.

The history of vengeance committed in the name of God is not a function of any one religion but of the union of religious and political power. It is one of the great paradoxes of religious history that sacred injunctions designed to contain the worst impulses of men and women have, when wedded to secular power, so often been vehicles to express those very passions. The long history of Christian vindictiveness toward the Jews of Europe is the paradigmatic western example of vengeance committed in the name of divine justice. This history, usually viewed within the specific context of anti-Semitism, is also a case study highlighting the general difficulty of containing the impulse toward revenge. The Christianity preached by Jesus makes abandonment of vengeance a condition of personal salvation; the Christianity expounded by ecclesiastical authority has, at many points in history, made vindictiveness a condition of institutional survival.

Religious anti-Semitism stands in direct opposition to the concept of individual responsibility for sin that plays such an important role in the Christian theological condemnation of indiscriminate vengeance. The Jews, *as a people,* were charged with deicide for their role in the crucifixion of Christ. The accusation was foreshadowed in writings of the early church fathers; articulated fully by many Roman Catholic rulers and theologians in the Middle Ages; carried on by religious theorists of both the Reformation and counter-Reformation, and explicitly rejected by many Christian leaders only after the Holocaust. The repeated massacres of Jews charged with the "crime" of deicide have been the subject of many complicated religious, political, and economic analyses. All of these explanations have some validity, but none fully encompasses the irrational. Revenge is its own rationale. The charge of deicide as a rationalization for the "just retribution" inflicted on Jews offered a legitimate outlet for the vengeance that was, in most other circumstances, prohibited to those of the Christian faith. Like the ruthlessness of the armies of ancient Israel in the conquest of Canaan and the violence Protestants and Catholics wreaked upon each other in turn during the Reformation, the Christian vengeance against Jews exemplifies the worst consequences of the unrestrained human propensity for vengeance. The deicide charge is not simply a convenient camouflage for more rational economic and political motives. It lies at the heart of the historical Christian animus toward Jews. In its insistence on hereditary guilt and vengeance, it embodies the most retrograde aspects of the passion for revenge.

In the Gospel of Matthew, after Pilate washes his hands, the Jewish mob yells, "His blood be on us, and on our children."[34] These fateful words were to exert a much stronger influence on Christian thought than the following verses, in which Roman soldiers ridicule Christ, strike him and spit on him, place the crown of thorns upon his head, give him vinegar to drink instead of water, cast lots for his garments, and affix a sign to the cross with the legend "King of the Jews." (Many scholars have argued convincingly that the Romans may in fact have regarded Jesus as a political subversive.)

It is important to remember that the Gospels of John and Matthew were the last portions of the New Testament to be written, between A.D. 80 and 100. John's account of the crucifixion is the most antagonistic of the gospels toward the Jews, as is Matthew's description of the Pharisees. During this period —after the Roman destruction of the temple in Jerusalem in A.D. 70—the Pharisees formed the most cohesive remnant of traditional Jewry. Moreover, the Pharisees were successful missionaries and were in direct competition for converts with the Christians, who were beginning to define themselves as a separate religion rather than as a sect of Jews known as Nazarenes. In these circumstances, it is not surprising that the authors of the gospels felt the need to distinguish themselves sharply from the Pharisees. (In the parochial schools where I was educated during the 1950s, "Pharisee" was a purely negative description. It would have astonished the schoolchildren—and many of their teachers—to learn that Jesus was himself a Pharisee. The following passage, published by a Catholic press in the 1970s, would have been incomprehensible to a Catholic grammar-school class before the Second Vatican Council: "Self-criticism was common among the Pharisees. Their integrity demanded it. They fought hard against hypocrisy of all sorts. . . . Indeed, Jesus is most a Pharisee when he is attacking hypocrisy."[35])

The Gospel of John places much more emphasis than the other gospel accounts on the role of the Jewish high priests in convincing Pilate that Jesus should be executed.

> Then they led Jesus from Caiaphas unto the hall of judgment: and it was early; and they themselves went not into the judgment hall, lest they should be defiled; but that they might eat the passover.
>
> Pilate then went out unto them, and said, What accusation bring ye against this man?
>
> They answered and said unto him, If he were not a malefactor, we would not have delivered him up unto thee.
>
> Then said Pilate unto them, Take ye him, and judge him according to your law. The Jews therefore said unto him, It is not lawful for us to put any man to death:

That the saying of Jesus might be fulfilled, which he spake, signifying what death he should die.

Then Pilate entered into the judgment hall again, and called Jesus, and said unto him, Art thou the King of the Jews?

Jesus answered him, Sayest thou this thing of thyself, or did others tell it thee of me?

Pilate answered, Am I a Jew? Thine own nation and the chief priests have delivered thee unto me: what hast thou done?

Jesus answered, My kingdom is not of this world: if my kingdom were of this world, then would my servants fight, that I should not be delivered to the Jews: but now is my kingdom not from hence.

Pilate therefore said unto him, Art thou a king then? Jesus answered, Thou sayest that I am a king. To this end was I born, and for this cause came I into the world, that I should bear witness unto the truth. Every one that is of the truth heareth my voice.

Pilate saith unto him, What is truth? And when he had said this, he went out again unto the Jews, and saith unto them, I find in him no fault at all.

But ye have a custom, that I should release unto you one at the passover: will ye therefore that I release unto you the King of the Jews?

Then cried they all again, saying, Not this man, but Barabbas. Now Barabbas was a robber.[36]

Only the Gospel of Luke, written at a much earlier date than John or Matthew, records the words of Jesus on the cross: "Father, forgive them; for they know not what they do."[37] Nevertheless, even the gospels that place the greatest onus on the Jews have Roman soldiers doing all the torturing. In the medieval passion plays a thousand years later, the torturers were transformed into Jews.

In the world of medieval Christendom, it was firmly believed that the Jewish Diaspora was God's revenge for the sin of deicide. Many Biblical passages have been cited as proof that Jesus predicted the fall of Jerusalem to the Romans. One of these exchanges appears in Luke, as Jesus addresses a group of weeping women who are following him to Calvary. "Daughters of Jerusalem," he admonishes them, "weep not for me, but weep for yourselves, and for your children. For, behold, the days are coming, in the which they shall say, Blessed are the barren, and the wombs that never bare, and the paps which never gave suck. Then shall they begin to say to the mountains, Fall on us; and to the hills, Cover us. For if they do these things in a green tree, what shall be done in the dry?"[38] This is one of many verses cited in support of the belief that the sins of Jews at the time of Christ's death justified unending Christian revenge upon their descendants.

Although this interpretation of the destruction of the temple does appear in Christian writings during the first millennium, it does not take shape as a consistent motif—a rationalization for vengeance against "Christ killers"—until the Middle Ages. It was only in the eleventh century, with the beginning of the First Crusade, that retaliation against Jews for the death of Jesus came to serve as a unifying force in Christendom.

At the beginning of the eleventh century, the first rumors concerning desecration of Christian shrines by Moslem rulers of the Holy Land reached western Europe. Christians in Jerusalem were in fact being persecuted, and the patriarch of Jerusalem was beheaded upon the orders of the ruling Emir. The fact that the Emir hated Jews as fiercely as he hated Christians made no impression in Europe. In both France and Italy, massacre of local Jews was the initial response to reports of Christian blood being spilled in the Holy Land.

When the First Crusade was proclaimed in 1096, the armies of good Christian men began their march toward the land already sacred to Islam, Judaism and Catholicism by torturing and murdering Jewish "infidels" and "heretics" in the cities of Europe. There was no reason for these soldiers of the Lord to think they might be committing the sin of vengeance or murder, because they firmly believed they were God's lawful avengers. For the Crusaders, the reports that their holy places had been desecrated in Jerusalem were only one more event in a continuum that began with the Biblical account of Jesus' denunciation to the Roman governor by the Jewish high priest.

Jews who escaped being slaughtered by the Crusaders in France wrote to warn their German relatives, who responded with the standard assertion that such miscarriages of justice would never be permitted by the governing authorities in *their* towns. In May of 1096, a group of Jews—no longer sanguine about the prospects for protection from the populace—took refuge in the palace of Bishop Adalbert. When they refused to convert to Christianity, the bishop had them put to death.

A half century later, when the call came for a new Crusade, the massacres of Jews began again. At this point, the accusation of ritual murder against the Jews appears for the first time in both Jewish and Christian accounts. In the first volume of his exhaustive history of anti-Semitism in the West, Léon Poliakov points out that the Jewish chronicles of pogroms are permeated by a combination of rage and powerlessness. "But this fury remains impotent," he notes. "It is not possible to take vengeance on the persecutors; the disproportion of strength is so obvious that the calamities that overwhelm the Jews represent to its spokesmen an upheaval of nature rather than a struggle between two camps."[39] One is reminded of Dan Jacobson's observation about the cycles of Yahweh's vengeance in the Old Testament, that "being the victim or loser will produce a hunger for justice that is virtually indistinguishable from a dream of revenge and recompense."

The central importance of the crucifixion in religious rationalization for unending revenge against Jews is most clearly apparent in the passion plays, which re-enacted the suffering and death of Jesus in productions lasting for hours or days and involving casts of hundreds. Today, the old passion plays survive mainly as curiosities (albeit extremely popular ones), the best-known being the Oberammergau pageant, presented in Germany every ten years. Non-Jews—particularly in England, where the passion plays of the Middle Ages failed to establish themselves as a permanent tradition, and in America, where they have never played a conspicuous role in public religious life—are frequently bewildered when Jews raise periodic objections to the presentation of the Oberammergau play. Few English speakers actually know what is contained in the texts of the plays, and the history of these powerfully moving, quasi-liturgical mass entertainments is not widely known. It requires a considerable leap of the imagination for a twentieth-century audience to understand the response the passion plays engendered during the Middle Ages, when excited crowds would frequently leave the pageant and express their vengeful emotions in pogroms against the local Jewish communities. A modern translation of one of the most famous medieval French passion plays offers considerable insight into the emotional impact on medieval men and women.

In one scene, Jewish characters are gleefully torturing Jesus before he prepares to shoulder his cross (a description that does not appear in any of the gospels). "Let us play at pulling out his beard," says one of the tormentors, "That is too long anyway." "He will be the bravest," agrees his companion, "who gets the biggest handful." They proceed to tear out the beard and one of the men says proudly, "I have torn at him so hard/That the flesh has come too."*[40] It is not difficult to imagine the anger these passages must have engendered in

---

*The original text reads:

> Juons-nous à plumer sa barbe
> Elle est par trop saillant.

> Celue sera le plus vaillant
> Qui en aura plus grand poignée.

> Je lui ay si roide empoignée
> Que la chair est venue après.

medieval Christians, who believed implicitly in the religious truth and historical accuracy of the spectacle they were witnessing. And the passion plays were presented with highly realistic props—so realistic that simulated tortures were reported, in more than one instance, to have caused the death of the actor playing the role of Jesus.

The quasi-liturgical role of these plays was of fundamental importance. They recapitulated, in popular form and in the vernacular, events that were enacted in church in the official Roman Catholic liturgy. With the full sanction of the church, the passion plays conveyed an unalterable sense of collective guilt and the righteousness of hereditary vengeance against the Jews. Such acts would not have been regarded as sinful private revenge but as the just retribution of the faithful upon the descendants of a people held responsible for deicide. The revenge theme of the medieval passion plays was—like the vindictive side of the Old Testament Yahweh—rooted in a primitive religious mentality. However, the theme proved suitable for the twentieth-century purposes of the Nazis, who classified the Oberammergau Passion Play as "a racially important cultural document." On the pageant's three hundredth anniversary, in 1934, the seventeenth-century text was Nazified to represent Jesus and his followers as a band of Aryan heroes. After the war, the Oberammergau pageant returned to a nineteenth-century text written by a priest named Joseph Alois Daisenberger. The Oberammergau play has remained a sore point with Jews and many Catholics, who feel it violates the spirit of Vatican guidelines, issued in 1975, designed to eliminate anti-Semitism from church teaching. At a 1978 symposium sponsored by a group of distinguished German Catholic scholars, Rabbi Marc Tannenbaum of the American Jewish Committee observed that the Daisenberger text "is free from 19th and 20th century-style racism; but it abounds with anti-Jewish religious prejudices and misstatements—as well as demonological and satanic images of

Jews as being in league with the Antichrist—long established in the popular tradition."[41]

The theme of hereditary responsibility and revenge also surfaced in a famous Renaissance controversy over the role of the Talmud in religious scholarship. In 1516, Johannes Pfefferkorn, a German Jew who had converted to Christianity, published a pamphlet demanding that the Talmud be suppressed on the ground that it aroused Jewish opposition to "the true faith." Pfefferkorn actually obtained an imperial commission to seize and destroy Hebrew scrolls wherever he found them. Johannes Reuchlin, the first Christian Hebraic scholar in Germany, defended rabbinical writings as invaluable historical records and attacked Pfefferkorn on the curious ground that he had proved himself a true Jew by his vindictive zeal to destroy the Talmud! Reuchlin characterized Pfefferkorn as a "baptized Jew . . . who gaily abandoned himself to a perfidious revenge, according to the traditional manner of his ancestors."[42]

Throughout Europe, scholars lined up on both sides of the issue. Erasmus and the humanists were, as might have been expected, in favor of preserving the ancient Hebrew manuscripts. In one of the strangest arguments in the history of religious (and scholarly) vindictiveness, he revived the deicide charge in defense of the Talmud. Pfefferkorn's Jewish ancestors, Erasmus observed, "attacked Christ only, whereas he [Pfefferkorn] attacked many worthy and eminent men. He could render no better service to his co-religionists than by betraying Christendom, hypocritically claiming to have become a Christian."[43]

The words "revenge" and "vengeance" crop up repeatedly in these debates. Martin Luther's notorious anti-Semitic diatribes, delivered after it became apparent that German Jews were no more receptive to his proselytizing than they had been to the Church of Rome, make frequent references to the respon-

sibility of the Jews for the death of Christ. His first essay on the
subject, "Against the Jews and Their Lies," appeared in 1543.
Luther, who was sensitive to the general religious problem
posed by the sufferings of the innocent, addressed himself to the
persecutions endured by the Jews and came up with a comforting answer: the Jews are in fact guilty and have brought their
punishments upon themselves. This argument could, of course,
be applied to any seemingly inexplicable manifestation of
human misery. "For such ruthless wrath of God is sufficient
evidence that they [the Jews] have assuredly gone astray," Luther argued. "Even a child can comprehend this. For one dare
not regard God as so cruel that he would punish his own people
so long, so terribly, so unmercifully and in addition keep silent,
comforting them neither with words nor with deeds, and fixing
no time limit and no end to it. Who would have faith, hope, or
love toward such a God?"[44] Who, indeed?

Luther blamed the victim—a projection mechanism used to
justify revenge in political as well as religious contexts. Vindictiveness, in his view, was a specifically Jewish trait.

They wish that the sword and war, distress and every misfor-
tune may overtake us accursed Goyim. They vent their curses
on us openly every Saturday in their synagogues and daily in
their homes. They teach, urge, and train their children from
infancy to remain the bitter, virulent and wrathful enemies of
Christians. . . . They have been bloodthirsty bloodhounds and
murderers of all Christendom for more than fourteen hundred
years in their intentions, and would undoubtedly prefer to be
such in their deeds. . . . So we are even at fault in not avenging
all this innocent blood of our Lord and of the Christians which
they shed for three hundred years after the destruction of
Jerusalem, and the blood of the children which they have shed
since then (which still shines forth from their eyes and skin).
We are at fault in not slaying them.[45]

These essays have naturally proved a great source of embarrassment to Lutherans in the post-Holocaust era. In 1949, the U.S. National Lutheran Council published a paper objecting to the use of Luther's essays in an anti-Semitic pamphlet by the right-wing polemicist Gerald L. K. Smith. The council stressed that Luther's statements on the Jews should be viewed within the context of their age and not as representative of modern Lutheran teaching. The author took pains to dissociate Luther's religious attack from the racial anti-Semitism of the Nazi era: "The cause of the controversy between Luther and the Jews is Christ. Everything else is more or less incidental."[46] Of course. But religious vindictiveness would not have proved to be such a great obstacle to the social control of revenge if it had remained within the realm of theology.

In the history of Christian-Jewish relations, the 1961 trial of Adolf Eichmann in Jerusalem provided one of the most dramatic illustrations of the relevance of religious disputes to the larger issue of cultural attitudes toward revenge and justice. In 1960, when Israeli agents apprehended Eichmann in Argentina, controversy immediately erupted in both the religious and the general press. The religious press focused on the question of collective guilt *vs.* individual responsibility and frequently transformed the issue into a question of revenge *vs.* justice. In the general press, there was considerable controversy over the issue of Israel's legal right to try Eichmann and, as the American Jewish Committee noted in an exhaustive review of the commentary, there was an even division of legal opinion.[47] In the Christian press, however, opinion on the legal issue was largely unfavorable to Israel. (This negative perception was much stronger in the Protestant than in the Catholic press, which leaned toward the view that while it would be more desirable to try Eichmann in an international court, Israel had a stronger legal and moral claim than any other nation.)

A number of Protestant publications actually compared the

trial of Eichmann to the trial of Jesus—an analogy that ought to have bordered on sacrilege for devout Christians as well as Jews. William Stringfellow, writing in an Episcopal periodical, described the comparison as "scandalous" and then went on to make it.

> The defendant in the earlier case was rather different from the present defendant, but, nevertheless, he was accused, as Eichmann was, of subverting the Jewish nation. The authorities, as in Eichmann's case, had apprehended him by trick, and there was a dispute about who had jurisdiction to try him. He had to be tried, it was asserted, as in the recent trial, for the sake of the law, for the sake of the moral nurture of the people. And it was said in his defense, as Eichmann testified in his own defense, that he was being condemned for the sins of others.
>
> The difference in the two trials is that Eichmann's condemnation does not save a single man from bondage and service to death, while the condemnation of the other defendant set men free from death and from the power of death in their own sin.[48]

A Baptist publication asserted that the trial of Jesus loomed "like a depressing shadow" behind the trial of Eichmann. "Alas," the publication mourned, "on that day a nation rejected its King. And since, the path of the Wandering Jew down through the centuries has been marked by blood. This reference is penned by one who loves the Jewish people, realizing that through them have come the greatest gifts from God—the sacred Scriptures and the Savior. The blood-spotted path is part of the Mystery of the Jew."[49] (This declaration recalls Pascal's assertion that the Jews were allowed to survive as a people, in spite of their guilt, to serve as an example of sin, suffering, and retribution for the rest of the world.) That such statements could appear in prominent religious periodicals only fifteen years after the death camps is a tribute to the enduring power of religious metaphor and religious vindictiveness.

Many publications—of liberal and conservative theological bents—also revived the stereotypical charge of "Old Testament vengeance." *The Unitarian Register* declared that "the ancient God of just retribution seems to have won the upper hand."[50] The *St. Louis Review,* a Roman Catholic periodical, printed an interview with J. Norman McDonough, dean of the law school at St. Louis University. The interview said that "Dean McDonough doubted that there is substance in Jewish religious beliefs to support an 'eye for eye' basis for the trial of Eichmann by the Jewish nation. It is true that the Jewish religion holds that one who takes an eye deserves to lose an eye. But it is up to God and not man to judge if the execution should be made."[51]

That has not, of course, been the view of any religion on the question of punishment. Only God can judge the human heart, but only man can exact penalties on earth.

The tone of Christian commentary at the time of the Eichmann trial might have been much less censorious had the proceedings taken place a scant five years later, after the Second Vatican Council of the Roman Catholic Church explicitly repudiated the charge of deicide against the Jews. The Catholic bishops were not the first Christian leaders to abandon the deicide accusation, but their statement carried special weight—not only because of the church's world-wide influence but because the notion of hereditary Jewish guilt for the crucifixion had its earliest roots in Catholic teaching. The Vatican II declaration, spurred by the strong support of American, German, Belgian, and Dutch bishops, recognized the link between the deicide charge and persecution of Jews in the Christian era.

True, authorities of the Jews and those who followed their lead pressed for the death of Christ (cf. John 19:6), still, what happened in His passion cannot be blamed upon all the Jews then living, without distinction, nor upon the Jews of today. Although the Church is the new people of God, the Jews should not be presented as repudiated or cursed by God, as if such views followed from the holy Scriptures. All should take pains, then, lest in catechetical instruction and in the preaching of God's Word they teach anything out of harmony with the truth of the gospel and the spirit of Christ.

The Church repudiates all persecutions against any man. Moreover, mindful of her common patrimony with the Jews, and motivated by the gospel's spiritual love and by no political considerations, she deplores the hatred, persecutions and displays of anti-Semitism directed against the Jews at any time and from any source.[52]

The entire deicide controversy has an archaic ring to those who do not regard religion as an animating force in their personal lives. This is equally true of the Vatican II declaration and of the careful arguments by Jewish scholars focusing on the political situation in Judaea at the time of the crucifixion. (The Jewish analyses frequently stress the fact that the high priest did not represent Jews as a people—an observation that would seem to have about as much pertinence to modern attitudes as the statement that Achilles was not acting on behalf of all of the Greek people when he tried to desecrate Hector's corpse. But, then, Trojans have not marched Greeks off to gas chambers.)

The violent history of Christian-Jewish relations, unfolding from a trial and execution that were transmuted into a rationale for hereditary revenge, is not simply a story of the animus of one religion toward another but a paradigm of the complex relationship between religion and the historical effort to contain vengeance. Although the persecution of Jews by Christians has been defined by its own set of political and economic, as well as religious, characteristics, it is anything but unique in its demonstration of the vindictive potential of religion—in particular, of religion wedded to political power. One need not delve into ancient history for examples. The massacre of Moslems by Christians (and vice versa) in Lebanon during the past fifteen years—the most widely publicized one in 1982 in a Palestinian refugee camp of Beirut, while the Israeli army (as judged by its own government's investigatory panel) stood by and did nothing to halt the carnage—affords the most conspicuous recent example of the melding of religious and political vendetta.

The irony is that religious feeling provided the original impetus for the control of revenge so essential to the maintenance of orderly and humane society. By itself, respect for the prerogatives of God has restrained human vengeance, but the addition of political power to religious belief has frequently had the reverse effect. It has persuaded men that they will be rewarded in the next world for acts of revenge committed in this world. Dostoyevsky's formulation that "without God, everything is permitted" is an inadequate response to the problem of maintaining earthly justice. To restrain inhuman acts of revenge, human law is required.

IV Letters of the Laws

> The feelings for which the law makes no provision, are feelings for which it ought not to provide.
>
> THE REVEREND LYMAN BEECHER, Sermon Against Dueling, 1809

> No authority more useful and necessary can be granted to those appointed to look after the liberties of a state than that of being able to indict before the people or some magistrates of court such citizens as have committed any offense prejudicial to the freedom of the state . . . an outlet is provided for that ill feeling which is apt to grow up in cities against some particular citizen, however it comes about; and when for such ill feeling there is no normal outlet, recourse is had to abnormal methods likely to bring disaster on the republic as a whole.
>
> MACHIAVELLI, *The Discourses*

Legalized revenge. The expression invariably resounds as an indictment, embodying either the general conviction that vengeance has no place in modern jurisprudence or a more limited argument against specific legal penalties. The specific argument, most frequently directed against the death penalty or other cruel (though not necessarily unusual) punishments, rests squarely within the mainstream of progressive legal tradition—while the general argument is founded on excessive optimism about the prospects for modifying human behavior. The specific approach, which focuses on the attainable, has made the most enduring contributions to legal control of both private and public vengeance. In the struggle against the vicious punishments human beings repeatedly inflict upon one another, the most effective reformers rarely waste their words in pious pronouncements about the immorality of legalized revenge. Instead, they concentrate on defining the forms of retribution permitted by law and on limiting the powers of those who apprehend criminals, pass judgment, and pronounce sentence.

In societies—still few in number—with a highly developed concept of individual worth, law extends itself to uphold a wide variety of personal rights and liberties. This aspect of the legal system, which falls within the broad classification of "human rights," is a sophisticated, relatively recent addition to the three irreducible functions of law—punishment of the guilty, exoneration of the innocent, and deterrence of those who might, in the absence of sufficiently reliable and unpleasant penalties, sustain themselves by preying on their fellow citizens.

Insofar as humanly possible (and the task has often seemed humanly impossible), law attempts to remove personal animus from the process of apportioning blame and exacting retribution. It is the removal of private animus, not the absence of vengeance, that distinguishes the rule of law from the rule of passion. Laws may, of course, be unjust even though they are not founded on personal enmity; the old Jim Crow laws of the American South and the current apartheid laws of South Africa are cases in point. Inequitable retribution is one of the chief features of such laws; punishment is determined not only on the basis of what a person does but of what he or she *is*—or is perceived to be under the ruling biases of the land. Equitable retribution requires a fusion of libertarian and punitive concerns—a rare blend in a world that tends to regard freedom and order as natural antagonists. Retribution per se is an integral component of just as well as unjust legal systems. Legalized revenge, however repellent it sounds, is not an accusation but a fact.

There are a great many legal theorists who argue that retribution ought not to be a fact if it serves no other clearly defined purpose—that a woman like Jean Harris, whose personal history strongly suggests that she is unlikely to commit another violent crime, ought not to be imprisoned at all. I believe they are mistaken. Legal penalties are based on judgments of what a man or woman has done in the past, not on predictions of what he or she might do in the future. If a defendant can be set free on the basis of benign behavioral forecasts, he or she might as easily be imprisoned on the basis of unfavorable predictions —a disastrous practice from a civil libertarian point of view.

The crucial role of retribution in law does not contradict the principle that justice ought to be tempered with mercy, if that principle is interpreted in a strict legal rather than a broad ethical sense. Legal mercy involves considerations of motive, mitigating circumstances, and degrees of responsibility—not religious absolution or the forgiveness men and women may accord one another in their private lives. Those who administer the law have the right to punish or to determine that no punishment is required; they have neither the right nor the duty to forgive. This point is either ignored or misunderstood by conservative polemicists, who tend to regard all civil libertarians, beginning with the great figures of the Enlightenment, as naive optimists who see no need for legal retribution.

Although some eighteenth-century reformers did hold a ludicrously optimistic view of human nature, this perspective did not characterize those whose main concern was change in the legal system. Cesare Beccaria, whose 1764 treatise *On Crimes and Punishments* was to exert such extraordinary influence on the foremost figures of the Enlightenment in both Europe and America, was scarcely a Pollyanna when he wrote that "experience shows us that the majority of men adopt no stable principles of conduct, and only evade the universal principle of dissolution, which is to be observed in both the moral and physical world, if there exist motive forces which make an immediate impress on the senses and present themselves continually to the mind in such a way as to counterbalance the strong effect of passions whose bias is opposed to the general good."[1]

Beccaria's view of human conduct rules out both private punishment and private clemency as a substitute for public retribution.

> Some men escape punishment for a minor crime because the offended party forgives them: such an action conforms with mercy and humanity, but it is contrary to the public good; as if a private citizen, by his forgiveness, could do away with the need of an example in the same way he can remit the damages due for an offense. The right to punish rests not with an individual but with all citizens of the state or with the sovereign. The individual can renounce only his share of that right; he cannot annul that of others.[2]

The modern civil libertarian position on retributive justice is directly descended from Beccaria's argument. Aryeh Neier, for many years executive director of the American Civil Liberties Union, observes that "public forgiveness and private vengeance suffer from the same vice: They depreciate the victim. Respect for those who suffer requires that no one usurp the victim's exclusive right to forgive his oppressor. Similarly it requires that the duty to punish be assumed by everyone other than the victim. That is what is meant by the rule of law."[3] There is, in short, no inherent contradiction between belief in the necessity of legal retribution and the libertarian concern that the accused not be subjected to uncontrolled revenge. Furthermore, the separation of private forgiveness and public justice is an essential condition for the legal restraint of vengeance. From an individual standpoint, it seems harsh to prohibit the inclusion of private forgiveness in the public process of criminal justice: why should society punish if the victim forgives? From a civic standpoint, though, the principle of public retribution is not a philosophical abstraction but a cornerstone of public order and safety. In Athens—although the pollution doctrine of homicide had largely replaced private settlement for murder—an exception was made if the dying victim, in the presence of witnesses, forgave the killer. One can imagine the tableau and its possible consequences: a mortally wounded man forgives his slayer in the presence of relatives from both families; his anguished son knows there will be no legal penalty for the murder and decides, "Father wasn't in his right mind . . . if he hadn't been dying, he would have been the first to avenge the crime. . . . I'll go out and do it for him."

Compassion has never been the only, or even the primary, force of the movement to control revenge through law. The desire for more reliable punishment was as influential as any impulse toward mercy in the formation of early social compacts that removed the right of vengeance from individuals and families. The emergence of the Greek pollution doctrine, with its enormous significance for the control of private vengeance, was preceded by a century of savage disorder in which it was just as likely that murder would go unpunished as that it would be avenged in speedy, unrestrained, and brutal fashion. In an era of unfettered private retribution, one is as likely to become a victim as a righteous avenger.

In considering the relationship between vengeance and law, it is natural to think of the long-range historical transition from cruel penalties and investigative procedures to more humane, measured tactics—limitations on the imposition of the death penalty, replacement of physical mutilation by imprisonment, abolition of torture as a mode of interrogation. However, the assumption of retributive functions by the state frequently meant more rather than less severe penalties, at least in the early stages of civic development. "Early," in this context, is a deliberately ambiguous adjective. The modes of punishment and interrogation used by many twentieth-century states are obviously no more humane than those used by our less sophisticated ancestors—and they stand in opposition to the values that have, through a tortuous process of political change, set limits on the vengeful powers of the state. This struggle has produced tangible results at entirely different times in different cultures. Unevenness is the chief feature of the historical process that has imposed restraints on vengeance, enabling us to walk the streets with reasonable confidence that we will not be blamed for the crimes of our parents, siblings, and cousins. In the evolution of legal controls over revenge, the list of anomalies and inconsistencies is endless.

Tribal payment as homicide settlement, for instance, was abolished by both the Jews of Biblical times and by the Romans, but it survived until the late Middle Ages in many areas of Christian Europe.[4] The laws of Draco, which Plutarch tells us were written in blood rather than ink, specified such harsh penalties that we still speak of one who calls for overly severe measures against criminals as an advocate of draconian punishments. Yet Draco (insofar as he is known through fragmentary engravings on stone and the orations of Demosthenes three centuries later) prescribed lighter penalties for murder than for relatively minor offenses. This inconsistency led Solon, who is remembered as the architect of a more democratic, humane, and enduring Athenian legal code, to abolish all the laws of Draco *except* those relating to homicide.

In rabbinical courts at the time of Christ, restraints on cruel corporal punishments for minor crimes against property were far more advanced than they were in any European nation until the mid-eighteenth century. Until the Enlightenment, the general restraints on vengeance in rabbinical law—which the Jews of the Diaspora administered within their own communities— were far more developed than in the surrounding nations where Jews lived, or died, according to the will of the Christian majority.

(The relationship between the sophistication of Jewish law and the marginal civic status of pre-Enlightenment Jewry poses an intriguing, unanswerable historical question. Would the controls on revenge have developed in the same measure if Jews, like Christians, had enjoyed political power? In the "golden age" of Spanish Jewry under the caliphs, when Jews enjoyed freedoms unknown during the rest of their experience in Europe, contemporary rabbinical observers from other nations were aghast at the harshness of the Jewish courts. "When I first arrived here," wrote the German Rabbi Yehiel ben Asher, "I asked in amazement by what legal right Jews could today legally convict anyone to death without a sanhedrin. . . . In none of the countries that I know of, except here in Spain, do the Jewish courts try cases of capital punishment."[5])

The uneven pace of legal progress rules out a chronological approach to the history of retributive justice. Many advances in the legal restraint of revenge can be traced to specific times and places—the desert in which the Hebrews somehow managed to accept a code that enabled them to avoid slaughtering one another on the way to the Promised Land; the glorious, brief period of Athenian democracy between the overthrow of the tyrants and the outbreak of the Peloponnesian War; the hall in Philadelphia where the Bill of Rights was added to the American constitution. But the pieces do not fall neatly into place; the legal structure controlling vengeance resembles nothing so much as an English manor house with a Tudor core, Restoration addition, Georgian garden, and Victorian water closet. Even a well-defined period like the Enlightenment, which produced the theory that generated the widespread practical legal reforms of the next century, is filled with anomalies. Only in retrospect is it possible to identify the great conceptual changes in the legal approach to revenge—and many of those changes continue to generate intense social controversy today.

The conceptual shift upon which all legal restraint of revenge is based is the movement from diffuse to specific responsibility, from hereditary guilt and punishment to individual accountability. The concept of the "born" criminal—and particularly of the born political criminal—has proved to be one of the most tenacious in human history. During the age of Pericles, collective and hereditary vengeance had long been abolished for murder but a form of it still prevailed for the more serious (to the Greeks) crime of treason. No descendant of a convicted traitor could ever be permitted to live in or hold property in Athens. In thirteenth-century Florence, an aristocrat named Giano della Bella declared himself a commoner and led the political fight to widen the base of the electorate. He then promulgated a new code of laws making every citizen liable for the crimes of his or her relatives. Special boxes were set up to receive secret denunciations; dozens of prominent families were deprived of their civic rights; old aristocrats took plebeian names to disguise their identity, in much the same manner as the Jewish *conversos* did during the Spanish and Portuguese inquisitions.

The practice of imprisoning or executing relatives of alleged traitors is, of course, equally familiar in our own century. The Nazi procedure of *Sippenhaft* (which literally translates as "kin-arrest or apprehension"); Stalin's arrest of wives and children of real or presumed opponents as "class enemies"; the Red Guard attacks during the Chinese cultural revolution on relatives of scholars and former landowners or government officials —these instances proclaim the durability of the practice of government-imposed or institutionalized familial punishment.

Punishment of the relatives of political traitors might easily be viewed as a special case with no connection to the ordinary process of criminal justice. However, general standards of justice are profoundly affected by crimes thought to pose the gravest threat to social order—whether they are crimes of treason or crimes of violence. The Inquisition, originally applied to crimes of heresy and sacrilege, set a standard of criminal interrogation that prevailed throughout Europe until the mid-eighteenth century. (In John Reynolds' early-eighteenth-century bestseller, *The Triumphs of Gods Revenge,* the rack and thumbscrews are simply taken for granted as God-sanctioned means of uncovering crimes of murder, rape, and assault.) In Stalin's Russia, the practice of retaliating against "enemies of the people" by imprisoning their relatives was not even restricted to so-called political crimes; the distinction between ordinary crime and political crime lost much of its meaning in a society where petty pilferage from a factory could be construed as the treasonous act of "wrecking" the Soviet economy.[6] The Inquisition was responsible for a similar confusion between genuinely criminal acts and the political/religious offense of heresy. Sexual assault, in particular, was attributed to Jewish conspiracy, and there was no need to track down a specific criminal when revenge could be exacted from a collectively suspect group.

On the one hand, assignment of collective or familial responsibility is an excuse for unrestrained vengeance; on the other, it inhibits retribution directed against those who genuinely deserve to be punished. The belief that the sins of the fathers are visited upon the children invariably has both prescriptive and descriptive implications. Consider the Victorian expression "bad blood"; skull measurements by which the pioneering nineteenth-century criminologist Cesare Lombroso claimed to prove the existence of a "criminal type"; the inferences about racial predisposition to crime and violence drawn from some twentieth-century genetic research. The neo-racist pseudo-science of predicting individual behavior on the basis of genetic generalities bears about as much relationship to the real achievements of modern genetic research as the quackery of Stalin's favorite biologist, Trofim Lysenko (whose basic theory can be summarized by the statement that if you cut off a dog's tail, its puppies will be born without tails), did to real biology. However, the new pseudo-genetics does bear an amusing and depressing resemblance to the outward signs of hereditary guilt accepted by primitive tribal religions. Indeed, descriptions of black skin as the mark of Cain remained a staple of florid racist oratory into the early decades of this century.

Belief in hereditary responsibility has always impeded the

historical effort to place revenge within a legal rather than a mystical, quasi-religious framework in which "blood cries out for blood." Hereditary guilt is inextricably linked with hereditary punishment; the generalization can be applied to the most serious and the most trivial crimes. The decline of belief in hereditary responsibility for sin, or crime, was a pre-condition for what was probably the single most important advance in the legal control of revenge: the abolition of private settlement for murder.

The historical meaning of "private settlement" is an agreement between families, or tribal clans, on appropriate retribution and/or restitution for the death of a member of one of the groups. A group, not an individual, therefore becomes the injured party or the offender. Private settlement was itself an advance over unrestrained vendetta; without such settlement, human beings would undoubtedly have rendered themselves extinct. The obvious deficiency of private settlement is that it does not always work; instead of a murder's being settled by restitution and a peace agreement, it is settled by yet another murder and the always unsettling resumption of collective vendetta. One need not look to ancient history for examples; in cultures where *machismo* is an unwritten law unto itself, vendetta is alive and well in the 1980s. In 1981, the Brazilian military police were forced to assume control of a town named Exu after nine people were killed in the resumption of a thirty-two-year-old blood vendetta. A private settlement—a "moral pact of nonaggression" negotiated under the auspices of the Roman Catholic primate of Brazil—had broken down. The legal basis for the military takeover, the *New York Times* soberly reported, was the fact that the local city council could no longer produce a quorum.[7] Two members had been murdered in a four-month period and four resigned under death threats. One gave notice of his resignation by mail after he had fled to Rio de Janeiro, two thousand miles from Exu.

In the ancient world, as in the modern, the abolition of

private settlement was obviously intended to prevent members of the populace from killing one another. However, private settlement was not always ineffective, and the assumption of retributive powers by the state was frequently accompanied by more rather than less stringent penalties for crimes of bloodshed. Exile, not death, had been a standard penalty for murder in many tribal cultures. In Greece, the rise of the pollution doctrine and the prohibition of private settlement gave sanction to state executions for murder. In tribal cultures such as those depicted in the *Iliad* and the *Odyssey,* there was no provision for corporal punishment or restitution for manslaughter committed within the clan.* How could there be, when the only lawful recipients of restitution were kin to both victim and killer?

In Greece, the abolition of private settlement even injected the state into disputes between spouses—something that would have been unthinkable in tribal culture. When a husband or wife killed a spouse, either by accident or in a sudden rage, permanent exile from the family and temporary exile from the state were the legal penalties. According to Plato's *Laws,* composed in the fourth century B.C., a husband or wife who had slain a spouse could never return home to dwell with the family. (Greek law was more flexible on the issue of return to one's former abode if the victim and killer were not married.)

The abolition of private settlement made it difficult in all cultures, and impossible in some, to atone for the taking of a life by a payment of money or property. Both Hebrew and Roman law ruled out financial restitution as a substitute for corporal punishment of the slayer (although they did not rule out restitution in addition to legal retribution, just as modern law does not prohibit the bringing of a civil action for damages

---

*I use the term "manslaughter" in the modern sense, to denote a killing without premeditation. The concept of intent as a means of distinguishing among different types of murder was widely accepted in tribal societies.

following a criminal prosecution). The Covenant Code of the Israelites, the early legal structure established between the exodus from Egypt and the establishment of a monarchy in Jerusalem, explicitly forbade absolution (there was no difference at that point between the legal and religious meanings of the term) for murder through payment or through substituting another man's life for the life of the murderer. This represented an enormous advance over contemporary law codes in the Fertile Crescent, including those of the Assyrians and the Hittites, which allowed a powerful murderer to arrange the execution of someone else in his place. This prohibition was reinforced in later rabbinical law, which outlawed the settlement of any murder by financial restitution and which also emphasized the legal irrelevance of private forgiveness by the victim's relatives. "The court is warned against accepting ransom from a murderer," Maimonides emphasized, "even if he offers all the money in the world and *even if the avenger of blood agrees to let him go free*" (italics mine).[8]

The abolition of private settlement for murder was the first, crucial step in the long process by which the domain of the state was gradually extended to all crimes. For murder was not, of course, the only offense that could provoke revenge and civic violence—and the extension of state jurisdiction to lesser crimes has not been fully accomplished even now.

One of the most durable examples of the difficulty of imposing legal sanctions on private settlement was the custom of dueling, which survived well into the nineteenth century in both England and the United States (somewhat undermining Anglo-American boasts about their superiority to the hot-blooded Latins whose vengeance was immortalized in Elizabethan tragedy). In France, too, an extraordinary number of men found themselves unable to behave with the *savoir faire* of their countryman St.-Foix, who neatly avoided becoming involved in a duel as he sipped his *café* in a Parisian café. St.-Foix had provoked a man by asking him to move to another table. "Why so, sir?" the man inquired. "Because, sir, you smell," St.-Foix replied. "That, sir, is an insult. My seconds will wait on you, and you must fight with me" was the predictable response. St.-Foix answered, "I will fight if you insist, but I don't see how that will mend the matter. If you kill me I shall smell too. If I kill you, you will smell—if possible—worse than you do now." The duel never materialized, but the results of other duels—which could indeed be provoked by anything from an insult to a gentleman's appearance to a quarrel over a woman —were anything but a joke.

During the reign of the French Henry IV (1589–1610), some four thousand men were killed in spite of laws against dueling—and more than fourteen thousand royal pardons were issued on behalf of those who had broken the law.[9] At the beginning of the sixteenth century, the custom of dueling had been imported into England from France; in 1580, Queen Elizabeth's privy council sharply condemned the practice. In the eighteenth century, although the death penalty had been decreed for dueling, London newspapers carried frequent accounts of duels involving prominent personages. The social pressure to answer challenges of honor is evident from the fact that men like the Duke of Wellington, whose opposition to the practice was well known, nevertheless felt compelled to rise to the occasion when challenged to a duel.

In the United States, the forces opposed to dueling were strengthened by the famous 1804 duel in which Aaron Burr killed Alexander Hamilton. The Hamilton-Burr duel had taken place on a cliff overlooking the Hudson River, and anti-dueling associations were promptly formed in nearby localities. The Reverend Lyman Beecher, pastor of the Presbyterian Church of East Hampton, New York, one of the oldest congregations in the young nation, preached a widely discussed sermon in which he deplored the fact that New World democracy had persuaded ordinary men to take up dueling, which in the Old World had been largely restricted to the nobility.

> The feelings for which the law makes no provision, are feelings for which it ought not to provide—ungodly—sensations of haughty pride and relentless revenge; and which, instead of a dispensation for indulgence, deserve the chastisement of scorpions. . . . In Europe, where dueling originated, the great inequality of rank has usually prevented the practice from descending to the common walks of life. It is there the unenvied privilege of great men to kill one another. But in our own country, there is no such barrier. The genius of our government has inspired every man with a spirit of independence and self-importance—a spirit desirable, when duly regulated, but dreadful when perverted; and in young men, especially, very liable to be perverted.[10]

Thirty years later, as the frontier moved westward, similar sermons against dueling were still being preached and they still referred to the Hamilton-Burr duel as a prime example of unlawful private vengeance. One Indianapolis minister pointed out that a man who dies in a duel is just as responsible, from a moral and legal standpoint, as a man who kills, since the outcome might as easily have been reversed. Referring to Hamilton, he asserted that "the highminded friend of Washington,—the distinguished general, the able jurist, the tender husband,—was no less a murderer because he was deceived by the wickedness of the law of honor."[11]

In spite of a century of clerical and governmental opposition, the practice of dueling survived well into the twentieth century in the American South and Southwest. The real issue was not dueling, but the broad question of private settlement that appeared in the earliest legal codes of the western world. One focal point of anti-dueling legislation in the nineteenth century concerned the very issue that distinguished Hebrew and Roman homicide law from Greek law—the elimination of private forgiveness as a means of canceling out public penalties. Like the Jews and the Romans, nineteenth-century American legislators decreed that dueling should be punished, even if the loser survived and forgave his opponent. (Of course, this stern view was honored more in theory than in practice.)

The subject of dueling may seem anachronistic, but the issue of private settlement is very much alive today. The most notable survival of private settlement—a continuing source of legal and social controversy—involves "family matters" like wife beating and child abuse. Acts that would be crimes if they involved strangers are frequently removed from the process of legal retribution if they involve family members. Sexual crimes, especially rape, are also affected by the ancient toleration of private forgiveness.

A woman's forgiveness—if demonstrated by agreement to marry her assailant—was long regarded as an acceptable way of settling the crime of rape. As Susan Brownmiller points out in her pioneering study of rape, *Against Our Will,* the thirteenth-century English prohibition of the common-law custom of absolving a rapist through marriage represents one of the most important advances for women in legal history—even though the new law, like the prohibition of private settlement for homicide in the ancient world, was more a statement of principle than a practical reality.[12] Of course, the ambiguous status of the female victim in the eyes of male lawmakers made it far more difficult to establish rape—or any sexual offense— as a public infraction deserving public retribution than to establish murder as such a crime. The Statutes of Westminster, adopted during the reign of Edward I in the last three decades of the thirteenth century, restricted the abolition of private settlement to cases in which a lawsuit had been brought in the king's courts. However, the same statutes made it more difficult to relegate rape to the status of a private feud by providing that the right of prosecution automatically revert to the Crown if a raped woman or her relatives failed to institute suit within forty days. Before then, the failure of a woman or her family to instigate action automatically consigned the crime to private forgiveness or private revenge. As Brownmiller suggests, the main point of these laws was not the rights of the raped woman but the extension of royal authority—and the threat to public order posed by private exaction of vengeance.

Today, private settlement is no longer suggested as a way of dealing with rape, but it is frequently advanced as the best solution—to be facilitated by psychologists and social workers rather than police officers—to the crimes of child abuse and wife beating. Although such issues are generally examined within the context of modern sexual politics, they also belong to the long-standing debate over the proper relationship between public retribution and private forgiveness.

The movement toward abolition of private settlement is closely linked with another legal step in the containment of revenge— the concept of proportionality as a limitation on rather than a license for savage public penalties. Proportionality as limitation should not be confused with the popular misconception of proportionality as a mandate for punishments that replicate the original crime, exemplified by the "eye for eye" justification of capital punishment. Those who view law as a restraint upon the darkest human impulses have always understood that proportional punishment serves a dual function: it must be severe enough to reflect society's estimation of the seriousness of a crime, but not so harsh or excessive as to exceed the harm done by the offense. Among legal progressives, the latter concern has naturally outweighed the former, because most civilizations have been characterized by an excess rather than an insufficient amount of vindictive zeal. The view of proportional retribution as a limitation rather than an expansion of vengeance has surfaced repeatedly, in entirely different times and places. Although proportionality as limitation is generally associated more with secular than religious law, a number of exceptional religious leaders—men ahead of their time—have used their spiritual authority on behalf of civil leniency. Saint Augustine of Hippo, awaiting word in the fifth century A.D. on the fate of several men who had been convicted of murdering Christians in brutal fashion, admonished the Roman governor against excessive penalties.

> This news has plunged me into the deepest anxiety, lest perchance your Excellency should judge them worthy according to the laws, of punishment not less severe than suffering in their own persons the same injuries as they had inflicted on others. Wherefore I write this letter to implore you by your faith in Christ, and by the mercy of Christ the Lord Himself, by no means to do this or permit it to be done. . . . We do not wish to have the sufferings of the servants of God avenged by the infliction of precisely similar injuries in the way of retaliation. Not, of course, that we object to the removal from these wicked men of the liberty to perpetrate further crimes; but our desire is rather that justice be satisfied without the taking of their lives in any part. . . . This is indeed called a penal sentence; but who does not see that when a restraint is put upon the boldness of savage violence, and the remedies fitted to produce repentance are not withdrawn, this discipline should be called a benefit rather than a vindictive punishment?[13]

Augustine's view of the proper relationship between justice and vengeance is far removed from the gleeful vindictiveness of subsequent tracts by many other religious leaders on the support God's revenge ought to receive from legal authority—a vindictiveness that formed the foundation of legal systems throughout Europe at the beginning of the eighteenth century. In fact, Augustine's views on the importance of proportionality and restraint in punishment of criminals are closer to the legal thinking of the Enlightenment than to the received ideas of his own era, the medieval world, or the Renaissance.[14]

Eight hundred years after Augustine, Maimonides also explicitly rejected the idea that "an eye for an eye" meant an offender must be wounded in exactly the same fashion as he had wounded another. It is reasonable to assume, given the near-total separation of Christian and Jewish scholarship for most of western history, that Maimonides' exhaustive commentaries on Hebrew law were never considered by most of those who used "Old Testament vengeance" as a pejorative—or, on the other hand, by those who cited the Old Testament as justification for castrating rapists, cutting the hands off thieves, or burning arsonists alive. Maimonides could not have been clearer in his interpretation of the famous passages on retribution from Exodus.

> How do we know that when the Scripture says, concerning limbs, *An eye for an eye,* etc. (Exod. 21:24), it means compensation? It says in the context, *Stripe for stripe* (Exod. 21:25), and also says explicitly, *And if a man smite another with a stone or with his fist . . . he shall only pay for the loss of his time and shall cause him to be thoroughly healed* (Exod. 21: 18–19). We thus learn the word *for* . . . in the case of a *stripe* signifies compensation. The same conclusion applies to *for* in the case of the eye and other limbs.
>
> Although these rules appear plausible from the context of the Written Law, and were all made clear by Moses, our Teacher, from Mount Sinai, they have all come down to us as practical rules of law. For thus did our forbears see the law administered in the court of Joshua and in the courts of Samuel . . . and in every court set up from the time of Moses, our Teacher, until the present day.[15]

This passage is best interpreted not as an absolute prohibition of corporal punishment or incarceration but as a warning against using the Scriptures to rationalize punishments that replicate the original crime. Maimonides' argument is conceived in much the same spirit as Augustine's admonition to the

Roman governor: it is a statement of legal proportionality as a limitation on rather than a blueprint for penalties so brutal in their reciprocity that they would, if exacted by individuals instead of the state, be regarded as criminal acts rather than instruments of just retribution.

Until the Enlightenment, those who argued in favor of the idea of proportionality as limitation were very much ahead of their fellow citizens (and their rulers). In fact, strict proportional retribution would have been a considerable improvement over the legal doctrines accepted throughout the western world at the beginning of the eighteenth century. The great thinkers of the Enlightenment were born into a world that believed not only in legalized revenge but in revenge far in excess of all but the most monstrous crimes. Punishments for petty theft in the eighteenth century would be considered suitable for mass murder today. In 1785, Benjamin Franklin wrote to a friend from London, where he had been shocked by a newspaper article reporting the execution of a woman who was hanged for stealing some bandages worth approximately fourteen shillings and three pence: "If I am not myself so barbarous, so bloody-minded, and revengeful, as to kill a Fellow-Creature for stealing from me 14/3, how can I approve of a law that does it?"[16]

The situation Franklin described was as common in continental Europe as it was in England (where, thanks to the absence of an inquisitorial process of investigation, the accused actually enjoyed more rights than elsewhere). Disproportion between crime and punishment—especially when crimes against property were involved—was universal. In France, the death penalty could be imposed, at a judge's discretion, for *any* theft. In Italy, failure to pay a fine for a civil offense could also be punished by death. The legal archives of Florence, for instance, record a case involving two men who were executed because they failed to pay a thirty-lire fine within the twenty-four-hour period specified by law.[17]

The widespread use of the death penalty for crimes against

property affords a striking example of the uneven pace of development of legal restraints on revenge in different cultures. The earliest statutes of the Israelites—long before the period of rabbinical Judaism that began during the Babylonian exile—prohibited imposition of the death penalty for crimes involving the theft or destruction of property. (This prohibition, along with the provision preventing a murderer from escaping punishment by designating a slave as his substitute, was one of the major features distinguishing the laws of the Hebrews from the codes of their neighbors.)

The manner of punishment in pre-Enlightenment Europe was as cruel as the nature of punishment was excessive; the disproportion of legal revenge was a practical as well as a theoretical matter.

In Spain—where the Inquisition remained an active force in criminal law long after it had lapsed into disuse in the rest of Europe—the only defendants exempted from torture during the process of interrogation were children under fourteen, pregnant women, knights, nobles, and royal counselors (and children of the three latter groups). It was a common practice to imprison a pregnant woman and wait to question her until she had given birth and was again eligible for torture. In providing a hereditary exemption from torture for children of the nobility, the Spanish code offered an interesting corollary to the ancient concept of hereditary retribution.

In England, a legal procedure that originated in the twelfth century remained unchanged for five hundred years—the disemboweling, while still alive, of one who was being hanged for treason. In the eighteenth century, the punishment was modified so that the entrails could be pulled out after, rather than before, the heart had stopped beating. (Voltaire sarcastically described this procedural change as an enormous advance in the march of civilization.)

There is perhaps no stronger evidence of the disproportionate character of legal revenge in Europe than the legal penalties for those who attempted suicide and for the corpses of those who succeeded in killing themselves. Those who tried and failed at suicide were executed; for the corpses, violent desecration was prescribed by law. The widespread acceptance of this ghoulish retribution is not difficult to understand in view of the belief, so prominently enacted in Elizabethan revenge tragedy, in vengeance from beyond the grave, and in the propensity of the living to avenge the injuries of the dead. What is somewhat surprising, though, is the fact that punishment of would-be suicides by death survived well into the nineteenth century.

In 1869, Nicholas Ogarev, a Russian exile who was a close friend of Alexander Herzen, wrote a letter to his mistress, Mary Sutherland, about the execution of a would-be suicide in London. (His shocked tone may be partly explained by the frame of mind in which most Russian exiles of the period had left their native land: in the West, they hoped to find not only a more free but, above all, a more rational society in which to live and work.)

> A man was hanged who had cut his throat, but who had been brought back to life. They hanged him for suicide. The doctor had warned them that it was impossible to hang him as the throat would burst open and he would breathe through his aperture. They did not listen to his advice and hanged their man. The wound in the neck immediately opened and the man came back to life again although he was hanged. It took time to convoke the aldermen to decide the question of what was to be done. At length the aldermen assembled and bound up the neck below the wound *until he died.* Oh my Mary, what a crazy society and what a stupid civilization.[18]

In light of the savage and excessive criminal penalties that prevailed throughout Europe, it is hardly surprising that the legal thinkers of the Enlightenment attributed immense importance to the concept of proportionality as a limitation upon the vindictive powers of the state. For a man like Beccaria, whose chief concern was the law, optimism about the natural human capacity for self-control was not the primary point of contention with defenders of absolute clerical and monarchical authority. The real difference between the legal reformers of the Enlightenment and spokesmen for the status quo was the skepticism of the former concerning the state's capacity to restrain its own vindictive impulse. Beccaria, for instance, was not nearly as hopeful as Augustine on the matter of repentance by criminals. Repentance or, as modern criminologists would say, rehabilitation was irrelevant to Beccaria's rationalization of legal penalties. There was no trace of sentimentality about criminals, or about the likelihood of their being persuaded to change their evil ways, in Beccaria's opposition to the death penalty.

This unqualified position was not fully shared by his contemporaries, including Voltaire, whose skills as a propagandist had so much to do with spreading the less flamboyant Beccaria's ideas throughout Europe. In his treatise on crimes and punishments, Beccaria explained that his opposition to capital punishment was based mainly on "the barbarity of the example it gives to men. If the passions, or the necessity of war, have taught the spilling of human blood, the law, which is the moderator of the conduct of men, ought not to augment so cruel an example, made all the more grievous, the more legalized death is inflicted with deliberation and formality. To me it appears absurd that the laws . . . which detest and punish murder, should themselves commit a murder; and to deter citizens from killing, should ordain a killing in public."[19] Thus Beccaria sounded the beginning of a debate over capital punishment that has persisted to this day—an argument that comprises a chapter of its own in the history of cultural attitudes toward vengeance and justice.

Like the framers of rabbinical law, Beccaria adopted a double-edged approach to the question of proportionality: punishments should be neither excessive nor trivial in relation to the seriousness of a crime. He recommended corporal punishment or involuntary servitude for robbery by violence; in fact, he felt that all violent crimes should be answered by society with corporal punishment (not, however, with the torture and mutilation that were the standard penalties of his day). Beccaria placed crimes of violence in an entirely different category from nonviolent crimes involving property.

"Other writers before myself," he noted, "have pointed to the obvious confusion which arises if we fail to distinguish between punishment for robbery by violence and punishment for robbery by fraud, thus absurdly equating a large sum of money with a human life."[20] In another passage, strongly reminiscent of rabbinical law, Beccaria argued that the rich should not be able to escape legal penalties simply by paying off the poor: "To those who say that the same punishment inflicted on a nobleman and a commoner is not really the same because of the difference in their upbringing and because of the disgrace such punishment spreads through an illustrious family, I shall answer that punishment is measured, not by the sensibility of the guilty man but by the injury done to society, which is all the greater when he has been society's favorite."[21]

Beccaria's importance in the history of criminal law, as Marcello Maestro argues convincingly, lies not in the originality of any one idea (although several of his principles, especially his unqualified opposition to the death penalty, were revolutionary within the context of his era) but in the fact that he was the first thinker to articulate a systematic program for reform of the legal system. (He expressed many of the humanitarian ideals already embodied in Montesquieu's *Spirit of the Laws,* but Beccaria's slim treatise is a specific program for reform of every aspect of the legal system, while Montesquieu's famous work is a broad philosophical treatise covering many aspects of society.)

The connection between Beccaria and Voltaire (an intellectual rather than a personal link) proved to be of the utmost importance in the process of reform that established the concept of proportional punishment as a limitation on rather than a spur to the most extreme forms of legalized revenge. When the first French translation of Beccaria's treatise was published in 1765, seven editions sold out in a six-month period. Voltaire had, of course, long been concerned with the state of the legal system, but he tended to focus his attention on specific cases involving religious intolerance. After the publication of Beccaria's book in France, Voltaire broadened his approach to questions of criminal justice. He remained on the qui vive for cases involving religious fanaticism and ecclesiastical heavy-handedness, but his overriding concern focused on the disproportionate punishments that characterized the system as a whole.

There is no doubt about the influence of Beccaria on Voltaire's thinking. In 1766, he published a commentary *(Commentaire sur le livre des délits et des peines)* on Beccaria's work that concentrates on the issue of proportionality. There were some differences between the two men: Voltaire, unlike Beccaria, felt there were some legitimate uses for the death penalty and even for torture. In general, though, they were in agreement on the barbarity of a system in which a woman could be sentenced to lose a hand for snatching a hunk of meat from a butcher, or a man condemned to death for stealing a purse containing a gold coin. As the best-known writer of his day, Voltaire was responsible for greatly expanding Beccaria's audience. Throughout Europe, his *Commentaire* was frequently published with editions of Beccaria's original treatise.

Although eighteenth-century legal retribution—even after the reform movement took root in many countries—remained harsh by modern standards, the period encompassed what was, in many respects, the most significant legal advance in the containment of revenge since the emergence of the pollution doctrine in the ancient world. Frederick the Great of Prussia, a man truly ahead of his time, had abolished the death penalty for burglary in 1743. Gustavus III of Sweden decreed the abolition of torture within his realm in 1788. In the same year, Grand Duke Leopold of Tuscany developed a new legal code based—statute by statute—on Beccaria's concepts of proportionality; the code abolished both torture and mutilation.

Because they were enacted by the decree of enlightened and humane rulers—and might therefore be (and frequently were) reversed by unenlightened and inhumane successors—these reforms occupy a smaller niche in legal history than the changes enacted by representative bodies during the French and American revolutionary periods. When the Estates-General was convened in 1788, the *cahiers* (written instructions from electors to their representatives) emphasized the fundamental principle that legal retribution should be personal, not collective or hereditary. The basic law passed by the constituent assembly in October of 1789, like the French Declaration of the Rights of Man, stressed the concept of proportionality as limitation: law should inflict only those penalties that are strictly and clearly necessary. A month earlier, the first Congress of the United States had submitted for ratification to the states the amendments that later became known as the Bill of Rights—including, of course, the eighth amendment, prohibiting the imposition of excessive bail, fines, and cruel and unusual punishments.

The lasting significance of reforms enacted by elected representatives, as opposed to compassionate monarchs, is best demonstrated by the fact that the reaction to the political terror of the French Revolution modified but did not obliterate the positive legal changes of the period. The Napoleonic code, for instance, restored some of the discretionary power of judges that had been abolished during the revolution, but it did not restore their power to impose the most punitive measures imaginable. Rather, the principle of proportionality was maintained by allowing judges discretion within maximum and minimum sentences. Meanwhile, the process of limiting the vengeful powers of the state continued. The death penalty for political offenses was abolished in France in 1848, and new limitations were imposed on punishment by mutilation. During the 1830s, the British finally abolished the death penalty for theft of sheep, horses, and letters; damage done to houses and ships; and forgery and sacrilege.

In some circles today, it has become fashionable to denigrate the achievements of the Enlightenment by equating its libertarian side with mob violence, and its egalitarian impulse with the revolutionary terror. However, the legal thinking of the Enlightenment marks a critical stage in the domestication of revenge. The gradual abolition of private settlement—the transfer of retributive powers from the tribe to the state—flowed from the realization that antagonists, in the absence of external authority, were as likely to "settle" their differences by killing each other off as by tallying up damages and dipping into their purses and grain reserves.

The Enlightenment gave rise to the recognition that vindictive impulses could not be contained solely by prohibiting "private" revenge while sanctioning almost any form of "public" revenge. Men like Beccaria and Voltaire drew new boundaries for public retribution. In the post-Enlightenment world, the legitimacy of an act of retribution could no longer be established solely by the social authority of the avenger. The extreme nature of certain retributive measures stripped them of legitimacy—whether they were enacted by "the people," a representative assembly, a king, or God himself. The movement from collective toward personal accountability; the prohibition of private settlement; and the gradual acceptance of proportionality as a limitation on punishment were joined, finally, to the gradual secularization of law. The secularization process, by which a clear distinction has been established between civic and religious definitions of crime and punishment, was a source of intense controversy in the early stages of civilization and remains an unresolved issue today. It is intertwined with all of the important legal issues regarding the containment of revenge.

Guilt or innocence as determined by human law is quite separate from the issues of moral culpability and rectitude that lie within the domain of religion; the important role of religion in laying the ethical foundations of law has frequently obscured this vital distinction.

Adam and Eve committed the first sin in the Garden of Eden; Cain committed the first crime—the first homicide, to be precise—outside paradise. This distinction was summarized with moral and legal clarity by Maimonides, who argued that while there are more serious religious offenses than bloodshed, none causes such destruction to civilized society—"not even idolatry, nor immorality, nor desecration of the Sabbath. . . . For these are crimes between man and God, while bloodshed is a crime between man and man. If one has committed this crime, he is deemed wholly wicked, and all the meritorious acts he has performed during his lifetime cannot outweigh this crime or save him from judgment."[22]

In every stage of legal history, there is a division (no less genuine because it may be identifiable only in retrospect) between those who wish to exact retribution on the basis of an elusive inner morality and those who insist on external evidence. In the classical world, Plato was the foremost advocate of a philosophy of justice based on inner morality. In the *Laws* he argues that a single penalty must apply to all thefts. A thief must pay twice the value of a stolen article and, if he does not have sufficient property to make the payment, must be imprisoned until he somehow manages to raise the money (or until he is granted clemency). Plato's dialectical antagonist asks, "How on earth can we be serious, sir, in saying that it makes no difference whether his theft is large or small, or whether it comes from sacred or secular sources? Shouldn't a legislator vary the penalties he inflicts, so that he can cope with various *categories* of theft?"[23]

Plato replies that categories of crime are irrelevant. He sees lawmakers as tutors, whose function is to advise citizens on the nature of goodness and virtue and justice, not simply to determine penalties commensurate with specific crimes. In any event, the inner state of the criminal—not the external consequences of a crime—should determine the nature of the penalty. A man who steals a small sum may, for example, be consumed by a greed more intense than that of a man who steals a large amount of money. It is the sin of greed, not the crime of theft, that the law attempts to extirpate.

This is the classic religious, or theological, view of the fundamental aim of law and should not be confused with such matters as the practical distinction between intentional murder and involuntary manslaughter (which Plato, like his predecessors, contemporaries, and successors, recognized). However, the secular philosophy of law insists that intent, like crime itself, be assessed on the basis of evidence. Mosaic law—somewhat ironically, in view of its Biblical origins—takes the secular approach. In deciding whether a killing is murder or involuntary manslaughter, a judge must determine whether the slayer gave evidence of having hated his victim "in time past." (The evidentiary determination of intent, it should be noted, has nothing in common with modern psychological evaluations of the inner makeup of criminal defendants.)

The Platonic linkage of retribution with the innermost heart of the criminal is characterized by a curious combination of the punitive and the indulgent. Plato was, in the jargon of modern criminologists, a believer in rehabilitation.

> When anyone commits an act of injustice, serious or trivial, the law will combine instruction and constraint, so that in the future either the criminal will never again dare to commit such a crime voluntarily, or he will do it a very great deal less often; and in addition, he will pay compensation for the damage he has done. . . . We may take action, or simply talk to the criminal; we may grant him pleasures, or make him suffer; we may honor him, we may disgrace him; we can fine him, or give

him gifts. We may use absolutely *any* means to make him hate injustice and embrace true justice—or at any rate not to hate it. But suppose the lawmaker finds a man who's beyond cure —what legal penalty will he provide for this case? He will recognize that the best thing for all such people is to cease to live—best even for themselves. By passing on they will help others, too: first, they will constitute a warning against injustice, and secondly they will leave the state free of scoundrels. That is why the lawgiver should prescribe the death penalty in such cases, by way of punishment for their crimes—but in no other case whatever.[24]

Thus, Plato was not opposed to legal retribution but he believed that its main purpose was the instruction of the soul. Anything might be used to persuade miscreants to change their ways—a flogging, a prison sentence, a vacation, or a fine meal. And if the offender was truly beyond persuasion, death was better than continuing to live in a state of spiritual degradation. Better for everyone, in Plato's view—although the unrepentant criminal facing execution might not agree. (There are, of course, a number of examples of criminals who, like Gary Gilmore, agreed that they would indeed be better off dead.) However, one of the main differences between the secular and the religious concept of retribution is that secularizers do not believe legal retribution, or compassion, should be determined either by the inner moral makeup or by the preferences of the criminal.

For secularizers, the unknowable will of God is as irrelevant as the interior spiritual condition of the offender to the assessment of civic penalties. The law cannot determine the extent to which the souls of men and women are, in a Platonic sense, ruled by the desire to do evil; it can only ascertain whether evil acts have in fact been committed and whether they have inflicted severe damage on the community. Human laws, Beccaria insisted, are simply that—human. This view has always been anathema to those who claim a higher origin—in the name of God or "nature"—for the retributive measures devised by human beings. "The relationship between man and God," Beccaria observed, "is one of dependence on a perfect being and creator,

> who has reserved to himself alone the right to be lawgiver and judge at the same time, because he alone can be both without impropriety. If he has ordained eternal punishment to such as disobey his omnipotence, what insect will dare take the place of divine justice, will desire to avenge that Being who is sufficient unto himself, upon whom things can make no impression of pleasure or of pain and who, alone of all beings, acts without being acted upon? The gravity of sin depends upon the inscrutable wickedness of the heart. No finite being can know it without revelation. How then can it furnish a standard for the punishment of crimes?[25]

Or, one might add, for the dismissal of crimes.

The secular approach to crime and punishment did not originate with the Enlightenment, nor has the Platonic approach disappeared from the modern world. Sophocles, Aristotle, Aquinas, Rousseau, and a good many twentieth-century psychoanalysts clearly belong on the Platonic side of the argument, although most of them would have made impossible, rather than unlikely, bedfellows on just about any other issue. Euripides, Maimonides, Beccaria, Voltaire (most of the time), and Hobbes just as clearly belong on the secularist side. Maimonides presents the particularly interesting spectacle of a man who, for obvious reasons, framed his legal arguments within a strict religious context and nevertheless arrived at the fundamental secularist division between, as he put it, crimes pitting men against each other and those involving a man and his God.

The relevance of this ongoing argument to the question of revenge is frequently overlooked because it is lodged within the larger body of political theory. On this question, as on so many others, the most original and, even today, the most controversial contributor to the discourse is Machiavelli—not "the evil Machiavel" of the Elizabethan stage but Niccolò Machiavelli of Florence, the first political scientist. It is ironic that the very name became a kind of shorthand for manipulative vengeance in Elizabethan and Jacobean drama, for the man himself surely regarded private interest or passion as the worst possible reason for retribution on the part of a ruler. However, it is certainly true that Machiavelli rejected the moral hierarchy of divinely sanctioned public revenge and prohibited private revenge that formed the foundation of church and state authority in his own day as well as in the sixteenth and seventeenth centuries.

On the matter of retribution, as on all political questions, Machiavelli was the consummate secularizer. Princes, in his view, are subject to the same forces that govern other men; their retributive measures are to be judged on the basis of civic results, not on the presence or absence of divine support. *The Prince* was placed on the Vatican's Index not because it advocated stern retribution in some circumstances (such retribution was routinely practiced and glorified by Christian rulers) but because it assessed those measures solely on the basis of their impact on society. Depending on circumstances, the secularist view of law and government lends itself to mercy as easily as it does to vengeance. The dual aspect of this philosophy is clearly defined in two passages from Machiavelli's *Discourses*. One of these passages, a famous attack on the a priori equation of Christian morality with civic virtue, simply dismisses the theocratic world view held by nearly all of Machiavelli's contemporaries.

> And if our [Christian] religion demands in you there be strength, what it asks for is strength to suffer rather than strength to do bold things.
> This pattern of life, therefore, appears to have made the world weak, and to have handed it over as a prey to the wicked,

who run it successfully and securely since they are well aware that the generality of men, with paradise for their goal, consider how best to bear, rather than how best to avenge, their injuries. But, though it looks as if the world were become effeminate and as if heaven were powerless, this undoubtedly is due to the pusillanimity of those who have interpreted our religion in terms of *laissez faire,* not in terms of *virtù.* For had they borne in mind that religion permits us to exalt and defend the fatherland, they would have seen that it also wishes us to love and honor it, and to train ourselves so to be such that we may defend it.[26]

Machiavelli was not concerned with the issue that preoccupied most theorists of the Renaissance—the "rights" of the ruler and the ruled within God's overall plan. He does not speak, as Primaudaye does, about the unlawfulness of a people avenging itself upon a tyrant. For Machiavelli, one of the vital tasks of government, whether in a republic or monarchy, is to promote social conditions that minimize the vengeful passions of the governed as well as the need for retributive measures on the part of governors. Of course, Machiavelli did not hesitate to recommend fierce retribution whenever necessary, but he insisted that uprisings by the populace and counter-measures by rulers should be the exception in a well-governed state. Fairness and consistency—not sanction by divine authority—were Machiavelli's standards for public retribution. One of the most enlightening passages on this subject deals with the question of rewards and punishments.

Very great were the merits of Horatius by whose virtue the Curiatii had been overcome; yet so abominable was his crime of killing his sister and so distressed were the Romans by this murder, that they tried him for life, despite his deserts which were both great and recent. Superficially this would seem to be an instance of ingratitude of the populace. But if one examines the case more carefully, bearing in mind the kind of institutions that a republic should have, it will be seen that the populace was more to blame for letting him off than for wanting to condemn him. The reason is that no well-ordered republic allows the demerits of its citizens to be cancelled out by their merits; but, having prescribed the rewards for a good deed and punishments for a bad one, and having rewarded someone for doing well, if that same person afterwards does wrong, it punishes him, regardless of any of the good deeds he has done. And when such ordinances are duly observed, the city long enjoys freedom, but otherwise it will always be ruined. Because if a citizen who has rendered some signal service to the state, acquire thereby not merely the repute which the affair has brought him, but is emboldened to expect that he can do wrong with impunity, he will soon appear so insolent that civic life in such a state will disappear.[27]

This passage recalls Maimonides' comments on murder, in which he insisted that a murderer must be deemed wholly wicked, "and all the meritorious acts he has performed during his lifetime cannot outweigh this crime or save him from judgement."

Machiavelli is one of those remarkable figures in the history of ideas who not only managed to outrage his contemporaries but who also proposed theories that have continued to incite practical and philosophical controversy for more than five hundred years. The best explanation for the durability of this antagonism is offered by Isaiah Berlin in his brilliant essay "The Originality of Machiavelli." Berlin sees Machiavelli as a thinker who planted a deeply troubling "permanent question-mark in the path of posterity"; the question stems from the recognition that "ends equally ultimate, equally sacred, may contradict each other, that entire systems of value may come into collision without possibility of rational arbitration, and that not merely in exceptional circumstances, as a result of abnormality or accident or error—the clash of Antigone and Creon or in the story of Tristan—but (this was surely new) as part of the normal human situation."[28]

This quality of Machiavelli's thought explains why he was as repugnant to Voltaire as to the Christian theologians of the Renaissance. For Machiavelli, there are only appropriate methods for achieving particular sets of goals. Christian methods might be appropriate to the spiritual ends of Christianity, but they do not necessarily have anything to do with effective government; the same generalization might be applied to libertarianism, fascism, dialectical materialism. Machiavelli remains a disturber of the peace, Berlin argues, because his thought attacks "the sense of certainty that there is somewhere a hidden treasure—the final solution to our ills—and that some path must lead to it (for, in principle, it must be discoverable). . . . Surely in an age that looks for certainties, this is sufficient to account for the unending efforts, more numerous today [1953] than ever, to explain *The Prince* and the *Discourses,* or to explain them away."[29]

There is, however, another set of conclusions to be drawn from Machiavelli's arguments—conclusions that proved to be of the utmost importance in the revision of thinking about "legalized revenge" that was spurred by the Enlightenment. Tolerance and pluralism, Berlin argues, are equally logical outcomes of Machiavelli's thought—results he certainly did not foresee and undoubtedly would have deplored.

> If there is only one solution to the puzzle, then the only problems are firstly how to find it, then how to realize it, and finally how to convert others to the solution by persuasion or force. But if this is not so (Machiavelli contrasts two ways of life, but there could be, and save for fanatical monists, there obviously are, more than two), then the path is open to empiricism, pluralism, toleration, compromise. Toleration is historically the product of the realization of the irreconcilability of equally dogmatic faiths, and the practical improbability of complete

victory of one over the other. Those who wished to survive realized that they had to tolerate error. They gradually came to see the merits in diversity, and so became skeptical about definitive solutions in human affairs.[30]

Machiavelli, then, fired the opening salvo in a battle over the ends of law and government that continues to this day. The struggle frequently revolves around the distinction between civic definitions of crime and ethical, or religious, definitions of evil—and it extends far beyond ordinary issues of criminal justice. The eighteenth- and nineteenth-century disputes over abolition of criminal penalties for would-be suicides (and legally mandated desecration of the corpses of successful ones), like twentieth-century struggles over legalization of abortion, suggest the broad nature of the controversy between the secularists and the theocrats. The current legal and political battle over abortion, like the old controversy over suicide, pits those who wish to transform what they consider a sin into a criminal offense against those who insist that certain acts, however ethically dubious they may be from an individual standpoint, are essentially private matters that do not merit public retribution even though they elicit legitimate public concern. Abortion (again like suicide) is a religious issue, a medical issue, an emotional and psychological issue. It is also a feminist issue—not because it aligns men on one side of the battle lines and women on the other (many women, obviously, oppose legalized abortion and many men support it)—but because it cuts to the core of women's rights and responsibilities in society.

However broad the ethical implications of such issues may be, the more narrow question of retribution is critical to the attainment of political solutions. Society may, for instance, discourage abortions by failing to provide financial or bureaucratic support, but—as opponents of liberalized abortion laws in Italy and the United States have recognized—the critical question is whether the government is prepared to punish those who either undergo or perform the procedure. The secularist asks not whether an act is morally wrong but whether it inflicts the kind of social damage that demands legal retribution. This undoubtedly explains the appearance of the curious new epithet "secular humanist" as a synonym for "liberal."

The secular approach to law implicitly recognizes the fact that public retribution may be fueled by the same destructive emotions that animate private vengeance. In the West before the Enlightenment, legal codes were grounded, to a significant extent, on a vindictive interpretation of divine mandate; the secularization of law has, therefore, generally been associated with limitations upon the power of the state to exact legalized revenge. However, there is another aspect to legal secularization that seems, superficially, to run counter to its role in limiting the vindictive powers of the state but is in fact complementary rather than contradictory. Legal secularism insists on human retribution even in cases where no appropriate response is possible in a Platonic or religious sense. Secularists do not necessarily doubt the efficacy of spiritual codes as forces for the good, but they never rely on "nature" or divinity to restrain evil. Religion asks, "At Auschwitz, where was God?" Secularism asks, "Where was man?" Measured by what Beccaria called "the inscrutable wickedness of the heart," crime—whether it involves the murder of one or the murder of millions—can never be appropriately repaid.

The secularist measures crime by human standards and accepts, even embraces, the margin of error that would be unnecessary for a divine being to whom nothing is inscrutable. In a world of law, the absence of just revenge poses as great a threat to both liberty and order as revenge gone wild.

V Revenge as Metaphor: New Image Makers

> We are poking around the dark, secret niches of the human heart, and our medical chart resembles antique maps with the dread legends: "Terra incognita" and "Here be dragons."
> LAWRENCE SANDERS, *The Third Deadly Sin*

> Every vindictiveness damages the core of the whole being.
> KAREN HORNEY

> Thieves, pimps, prostitutes, muggers and drug dealers, BE-WARE!
> Advertisement for 1982 movie, *Fighting Back*

For twenty-five hundred years, religion, law, and literature provided the images that shaped, and were shaped by, the struggle to establish a balance between revenge and restraint. In the twentieth century, the traditional visions of vengeance and justice have been joined by two new sets of images. One is the creation of Sigmund Freud and his followers; the other is produced by marketers of aggression, for purposes of entertainment and political persuasion, with the aid of increasingly sophisticated tools of mass communication. The elaborate exegesis of the human personality that lies at the heart of classical psychoanalysis could not be more different, in its goals and methods, from the crude symbolic agitation of the Nuremberg rallies or "snuff" movies; the former attempts to bring the unconscious and irrational into the light, while the latter keeps the same impulses in the dark even as it tries to manipulate them. The common element in both visions is their view of human behavior as essentially nonrational. This emphasis on the irrational does not readily accommodate the tensions inherent in the long effort to incorporate vengeance within a framework of justice. It tends to blur the vital distinction between public and private retribution, between legitimate and illegitimate expressions of vindictiveness.

During the past fifteen years, psychiatric image makers have begun to focus more sharply on the public implications of revenge—largely, I believe, in response to growing concern over the incidence of vengeful impulses acted out against society as a whole (whether in the relatively benign form of graffiti or in the more pathological forms of violent personal crime and political terrorism). Classical psychoanalysis is so clearly suited to the exploration and explanation of revenge that the apparent lack of interest in the subject on the part of analysts during the first half of this century—measured by the relative infrequency of references to vengeance in the psychiatric literature—is something of a mystery. The reluctance of traditionally oriented psychiatrists to address social problems was nearly universal until the 1960s, but that does not explain the paucity of theoretical writings on the role of vindictiveness in individual behavior (especially in view of the importance of vengeance in the Greek myths whose characters pervade psychiatric nomenclature). Given the enormous influence of psychiatry in modifying our fundamental concepts of the human personality, the omission of attention to vindictiveness—in contrast to the attentive focus on eroticism—conveys a value judgment of considerable significance.

Classical Freudian psychoanalysis is, of course, only one strain in modern psychiatric theory and practice. (In this book, I use the term psychoanalysis in its specific sense, as it refers to the explanation of human behavior elucidated by Freud himself or closely derived from Freudian theory. "Psychiatry" is used in the popularly understood sense, encompassing a wide

variety of psychiatric practitioners—including psychoanalysts
—whose ideas may depart substantially from those of Freud.)
In examining the shift in cultural attitudes toward revenge,
special attention must be paid to the Freudian vision, which
remains central to most forms of modern psychiatry with the
exception of behaviorism. Like Judaism, Christianity, and
Marxism, Freudianism fundamentally reshaped our picture of
human motivation, rationality, and responsibility. And the
question of responsibility lies at the heart of the contemporary
confusion over the relationship between vengeance and justice.

Religion and law, although serving different social purposes
and themselves replete with the ethical contradictions that
shape our uses, and misuses, of revenge, have nevertheless manifested a high degree of pragmatism in their efforts to encompass the unavoidable tension between vindictive and compassionate impulses. "Ye know the heart of the stranger," the
Israelites repeatedly admonished themselves, "for ye were
strangers in the land of Egypt." And yet, they were the same
people who exulted over the vengeance their God had visited
upon the same Egyptians: "The depths have covered them: they
sank into the bottom as a stone. . . . And in the greatness of
thine excellency thou hast overthrown them that rose up
against thee: thou sentest forth thy wrath, which consumed
them as stubble."

After the abandonment of unrestrained vendetta, this unset-
tled, and unsettling, mixture of vindictiveness and mercy characterized nearly every human arrangement for the domestication of revenge. However bitter the disagreement over solutions, there was general agreement on the nature of the problem
posed by the vindictive drive. It was taken for granted that
human beings had a deep need—a need as sharp as hunger or
sexual desire—to avenge their injuries, to restore a sense of
equity when they felt their integrity had been violated. Different
cultures accorded differing degrees of legitimacy to this need,

but all societies took it upon themselves to regulate the vindictive impulse and, whenever possible, to bend it to some constructive purpose. The strong emotional appeal of vindictiveness was balanced by an awareness of the dangers unrestrained vengeance posed to orderly existence. In Judaeo-Christian tradition, this awareness was based on the assumption of free will —an assumption underlying the concrete restraints of the criminal justice system as well as the abstract moral framework separating legitimate from illegitimate expressions of the retributive impulse.

Free will has no place in—indeed, it is directly contrary to —the Freudian model of human behavior. Within the classical psychoanalytic framework, as Dr. Willard Gaylin has noted, "a man can no more be guilty of a crime than he can be guilty of an abscess."[1] The irrelevance of free will to the psychiatric vision of human motivation and behavior is central to the current controversy over the role of psychiatrists in the criminal-justice system—one area in which the profession seems to have abandoned its usual reluctance to become involved in the resolution of social issues. There is little point in discussing social arrangements for the domestication of revenge without the assumption of free will or, if that is impossible in an age shaped by so many deterministic philosophies, the adoption of an "as if" posture: without denying the constraints of heredity or environment, one may—indeed one frequently must—act as if one were free. The attempt to attain justice through law obviously requires the adoption of such a position. Successful psychotherapy also requires this assumption on the part of both patient and doctor, but it is psychiatric theory—not the dialectic that unfolds in the privacy of a therapist's office—that has exerted the strongest influence on popular culture.

The relationship between psychiatry and the law is, it must be noted, a much more serious issue in the United States than in the rest of the western world, where an *idée fixe*—unaccompanied by a history of pathological behavior—is rarely regarded as sufficient cause to absolve criminal defendants of legal responsibility.

I do not mean to imply that psychiatric defenses are never employed in complicated or notorious European cases or that they are always employed in analogous American trials. Rather, I am suggesting that American culture, for a number of reasons connected both with the prestige of "specialists" and with a historical attraction to the untried and untested, is particularly receptive to the use of psychiatric methodology in contexts—criminal trials among them—for which it was never originally intended. Had members of the Red Brigades kidnaped a general within the borders of the United States, defense lawyers might have argued that their clients were in need of psychiatric help and understanding rather than imprisonment (as they did during the celebrated trial of Patricia Hearst for her participation in crimes carried out by the California group calling itself the Symbionese Liberation Army). The American use of psychiatry in the courtroom, which has increased dramatically during the past twenty-five years even though it is not nearly as widespread as its critics have charged, might easily be considered a modern, secular substitute for the ancient practice of religious purification.

As I have already noted, the introduction of legal retribution as a precondition for purification represented a major advance in the social sophistication of the ancient world. Thus, the substitution of psychological interpretation for punitive action—the use of psychiatry to exculpate rather than to explain—might reasonably be viewed as a regressive rather than a progressive social development. This is particularly true in light of the relatively primitive state of medical knowledge about the workings of the human mind—a body of knowledge which, however much more advanced it is today than it was a century ago, is roughly equivalent to the scientific understanding of genetics during the long span between Mendel and the unraveling of the mystery of DNA.

The contrast between the fates of John Hinckley, whose shooting of President Reagan was motivated by his obsessive quest for the attention of a teenaged actress, and that of Mehmet Ali Agca, the man who nearly succeeded in killing Pope John Paul II, is instructive. Hinckley was subjected to nearly a year of psychiatric examination by both the prosecution and the defense. (A quirk of federal law, under which he was charged, requires that the burden of proving the defendant's sanity rests on the prosecution if an insanity plea is entered; in many states, on the other hand, the defense is required to prove insanity.) When Hinckley was finally tried, he was acquitted by reason of insanity and confined to a mental institution, from which he might someday be released should his psychiatrists decide, and a judge certify, that he has regained his mental balance. Agca, in contrast, was speedily tried, convicted, and sentenced to life imprisonment—a judgment delivered with the same dispatch as that against the kidnapers of General Dozier. (The political questions that have now been raised concerning Agca's involvement with the Bulgarian secret police were not raised at the time, when he appeared to be another of the lone fanatics involved in assassinations.)

In America, neither conspiracy nor terrorism precludes a psychiatric defense. The psychiatric concepts of brainwashing and "learned helplessness" (in which an individual, having been punished repeatedly, internalizes fear and can be manipulated through psychological rather than overt physical coercion) were advanced—unsuccessfully, as it turned out—to exonerate Patricia Hearst for crime committed after her kidnaping. If one accepts a broad concept of psychological factors that may diminish individual accountability, there is no intrinsic reason why a terrorist who believes in the righteousness of gunning down representatives of bourgeois order is any less (or more) disturbed, in a clinical sense, than a man or woman who guns down an unfaithful lover. The latter act, which would have been regarded as a straightforward example of sexual vengeance (though not necessarily a crime) in other eras, is sometimes described in psychiatric testimony today as a "transient psychotic episode."

Whether one regards psychiatric justice in a positive, negative, or ambivalent light, it is undeniable that the role of psychiatrists in the courtroom is to focus the attention of judge and jury on the defendant's state of mind rather than on his or her actions—an approach that tends to diminish individual accountability. The psychiatric vision has disturbing implications for the control of revenge, which has always depended on the assignment of specific responsibility. The insights of classical psychoanalytic theory render retribution useless or damaging in therapy, but—as a number of distinguished psychiatrists have themselves noted in recent critiques of the role their profession now plays in the American legal process—law and therapy pursue goals that are not only different from each other but are frequently in direct conflict. The metaphoric, symbolic, imaginative vision of psychiatry attempts to illuminate what an act of revenge may represent in the life of the spirit; the law is necessarily restricted to what an act *is* in the flesh.

The influence of psychiatric metaphor on popular attitudes toward revenge extends far beyond the law. The psychiatric profession generally categorizes vindictiveness as a neurosis (and, in its extreme forms, as a psychosis). This interpretation has the curious effect of making criminal acts of vengeance appear to be less (or less consciously) malign, while non-criminal acts of vindictiveness—such as the determination to track down ex-Nazis and bring them to trial—appear to be more malign (or, at least, less just and rational) than they do in the pre-Freudian universe. This attitude contrasts sharply with the Freudian placement of erotic impulses on a full spectrum encompassing health as well as sickness. The concept of revenge seen, at best, as a childish coping mechanism to keep darker forces at bay and, at worst, as a manifestation of serious psychic illness has entered the common culture and challenged traditional assumptions about the legitimate role of retribution in a larger scheme of justice.

Because psychiatry exists in a pluralist rather than a monist culture, its influence on attitudes toward rationality, responsibility, and retribution is not as overwhelming as the tale of Yahweh's vengeance was for the Israelites or the story of the gospels for medieval Christians. Nevertheless, the influence of the psychiatric creed—like that of earlier religions—extends far beyond those who adhere to its tenets or derive consolation from its promises of healing. The idea that vindictiveness is, inevitably, a manifestation of immaturity or illness is accepted by people who routinely accord sophisticated tolerance to a wide variety of sexual impulses. "I'll get even with you," we have all heard children promise one another, and we frequently adopt the attitude that all acts of revenge should be treated on the level of playground disputes.

When vengeance is not dismissed as a form of immaturity, it tends to be regarded as a manifestation of psychic disturbance. "You can see the woman's become unbalanced by the quest for revenge" was the newspaper reporter's comment on the camp survivor who displayed open anger in her testimony against Hermine Braunsteiner Ryan. Similar comments have often been made about vindictiveness in the works of Russian writers, such as Aleksandr Solzhenitsyn and the late Nadezhda Mandelstam, who suffered irremediable injury at the hands of the Soviet regime. At a reception for émigré Russian writers in London I heard a literary critic comment that "Madame Mandelstam displays an unpleasant tendency to keep score." "Someone must," replied a writer who had spent several years in Soviet camps and mental institutions.

Osip Mandelstam, the greatest Russian poet of the twentieth century, was arrested and died en route to one of Stalin's labor camps in 1938. His widow, Nadezhda, always one step ahead of the secret police, wandered around Russia for twenty years, committed her husband's poems to memory lest his manuscripts be destroyed, and survived to see them published in his native language (though not in his native land). Osip Mandelstam's arrest was itself a drama of revenge. He was imprisoned for the first time after reading a poem to several friends in his apartment—a poem that portrayed Stalin in graphically repulsive images (mustaches as cockroaches, a tongue savoring the taste of executions). Nadezhda Mandelstam notes that the informer must have been one of the friends who heard the poem read but says she made no effort to pinpoint the identity of the culprit. In any event, she says resignedly, a man with Mandelstam's talents and outlook on life would surely have wound up as a victim of Stalin—with or without the poem. In her mid-sixties, she began to write her own massive memoirs. There she named some names (though not nearly so many as she might have) and, as might have been expected, had a good deal to say on the subject of revenge.

> Several people who had been denounced [during the Stalin years] by the same woman, a professional informer, decided they would gatecrash a party she was giving on her birthday and expose her in front of her guests. When she opened the door and saw these grim-faced people in whose lives she had played such a part, she was quite aghast, clutched at her heart and slumped down on a chair in the hallway. Seeing her turn so pale, the people who had come to take their revenge got into a panic, dashed to the kitchen for water, and, when she had calmed down, went away without another word. . . . I am not an advocate of vengeance. In this country, for the last half century, not only individuals but whole categories and classes of people have continually been the object of vengeance, and we have all seen what a terrible thing it is. Yet, nevertheless, I believe there would be nothing wrong in the country "getting

to know its heroes" [a reference to a passage in Solzhenitsyn's novel *The First Circle* about the exposure of a camp informer], just so that it will be more difficult to recruit people for the job in the future. They need not be imprisoned or killed, but a finger should be pointed at them, and they should be named.[2]

In this passage, Nadezhda Mandelstam seems to be arguing that the exposure of informers constitutes not retribution but deterrence (a line of reasoning that suggests the extreme difficulty of separating the former from the latter, in a psychological as well as a social sense). Nevertheless, her statement seems to me a classic example of the distinction between constructive and destructive forms of retribution.

There is no question, Mandelstam's disclaimer notwithstanding, that pointing the finger, or naming names, is in fact a form of revenge. Her books, like those of Solzhenitsyn, were inspired to some extent by a desire for vindication and retribution. So, too, is the testimony of camp survivors who come forward as witnesses against those accused of Nazi crimes committed decades ago. The real question is not whether such acts manifest a drive for vindication but why they should, a priori, be considered morally and psychologically suspect. They are not the actions of a Michael Kohlhaas, whose boundless vindictiveness truly becomes a form of madness, but the carefully measured aggression of individuals whose desire for redress takes the form of truth telling. Pejorative psychiatric images of revenge—particularly as they are refracted in popular culture—have blurred this vital distinction. Of course, many of these images cannot be attributed to the influence of psychoanalysis; they are the products of half-digested Freud rather than of his genuine insights. Moreover, the mechanisms of repression and denial as elucidated by Freud undoubtedly have a good deal to do with the reflexive modern disgust triggered by any suggestion that there are strong ties linking revenge, truth, and justice.

There are, however, two fundamental aspects of classical

psychoanalytic theory (which, however many transformations and modifications it has undergone, remains the basis of modern psychiatry) that have a special bearing on the modern reluctance openly to confront the question of vengeance. One is the all-encompassing determinism that portrays human beings as less rational (and therefore less accountable for their actions) than they are in the eyes of the law and of traditional religion. The other is psychiatry's reliance on symbols and metaphors as keys to the mystery of human behavior.

Any attempt to encompass the complex structure of psychic determinism in a limited space must necessarily be oversimplified; however, psychoanalyst Willard Gaylin offers a concise, useful definition in his recent study of the legal and psychiatric issues involved in the trial of Richard Herrin for the brutal slaying of Bonnie Garland, his college sweetheart. "If each piece of behavior is causally related to the past," Gaylin summarizes, "if one does B because of an A ($A^1 + A^2 + A^3 + A^4$ ad infinitum) that preceded it, and if one is going to explain B on the basis of A, then one is forced to say that behavior is determined: You had to do what you did."[3]

The limitations on human choice inherent in the theory of psychic determinism—like the inexorable fates that unfold in the tragedies of Aeschylus and Sophocles—produce quite different attitudes toward retribution from those embodied either in western law or in the great monotheistic religions. External retribution is either pointless or superfluous if crime, or sin, is regarded as a form of self-punishment on the part of the offender, carrying equal weight with the punishment inflicted upon the victim. The idea that victims are inevitable accomplices to crimes committed against them is, of course, a corollary of the determinism that exculpates the overt offender. Traditional psychiatry is descriptive in its theoretical structure, however prescriptive it has always been in the therapeutic attempt to help men and women conform to accepted middleclass standards of conduct with diminished emotional pain.

Law and religion are unabashedly prescriptive in both theory and practice; they were designed to cast, or recast, human behavior within socially tolerable—and highly specific—molds. To that end, they dispense punishments and rewards. Psychiatry—with the exception of behaviorism—is supposed to do neither. (The attitude of behaviorists toward retribution is, it should be noted, far more amoral than that of traditional psychiatrists. Acts of retribution or, to put it more neutrally, stimuli that produce aversion reactions, are taken for granted in behavioral therapy; they are intended not to "punish," as the concept of punishment is understood in religion and law, but to produce a new, automatic set of responses.)

The psychiatric emphasis on the metaphoric and symbolic exerts a more subtle and complicated—though no less important—influence on popular attitudes toward revenge than does the general theoretical structure of psychic determinism. Symbols are, of course, the raw material of psychoanalysis. Actions are not only what they seem to be—and may be in an "objective" sense—but symbols of more profound desires, symptoms of disturbances flowing from the vast unconscious. Although Freud is reported to have said there are times when a cigar is just a cigar, psychiatry as a profession is more concerned with identifying situations in which a cigar stands for something else.

This tendency to view all human behavior in metaphoric and symbolic terms, so well-suited to analytic therapy, is ill-suited to confronting the consequences of antisocial acts in nontherapeutic contexts. For a therapist, it may be vital to understand that a man beats his wife and children as a symbolic act of vengeance against parents who once assaulted him. For those whose private or official duty demands that they put an end to the vindictive violence (the mother trying to save herself and her children, the police officer trying to remove the children from a situation that threatens their lives), an understanding of the symbolic psychological dimension of revenge is sadly irrelevant.

In a libertarian society, psychiatry cannot and should not be expected to serve as a mechanism of behavioral control; however, the metaphoric approach to revenge is as unsuitable a tool for understanding the full significance of vindictive aggression as for controlling it. The use of the Holocaust as an umbrella-like metaphor for evil and bestiality is perhaps the most prominent example of the inappropriate use of symbolism to encompass a horror that, however unimaginable it may have been before the fact, was embodied all too concretely in bricks, poison gas, fire, and human ash. Holocaust historian Lucy Dawidowicz notes that "people forget that Auschwitz was built to kill the Jews—it was not a metaphor for some unspecified evil." The use of metaphor in this way is related to the shifting of responsibility that occurs when repulsive manifestations of human behavior are dismissed as regressive aberrations rather than as powerful, ever-present drives that must always be respected lest they overwhelm us. Heinz Kohut, one of the few distinguished psychoanalysts whose work thoroughly explores the role of narcissistic rage in vindictiveness, suggests that it is pointless to fall back on metaphors of bestiality to describe behavior that is all too human.

> I do not believe that we can come closer to the understanding of the Nazi phenomenon by conceiving of it as a regression toward the biologically simple, toward animal behavior— whether such a regression be extolled, as it was by the Nazis themselves, or condemned and despised, as it was ultimately by the rest of the world.
>
> It would on the whole be pleasant if we could do so; if we could state—in a simplistic application of a Civilization-and-Its-Discontents principle—that Hitler exploited the readiness of a civilized nation to shed the thin layer of its uncomfortably carried restraints, leading to the unspeakable events of the decade between 1935 and 1945. But the truth is—it must be admitted with sadness—that such events are not bestial, in

the primary sense of the word, but that they are decidedly human. They are an intrinsic part of the human condition, a strand in the web of the complex pattern which makes up the human situation. So long as we turn away from these phenomena in terror and disgust and indignantly declare them to be a reversal to barbarism, a regression to the primitive and animallike, so long do we deprive ourselves of the chance of increasing our understanding of human aggressivity and of our mastery over it.[4]

Revenge, in both its constructive and destructive forms, is an expression of the aggressive drive. To paraphrase Kohut, it will not do to classify vengeance as merely childish, because it is decidedly adult.

Until the last fifteen years, which have seen a rise of psychiatric interest in narcissistic personality disorders (whether there has been a rise in the actual incidence of such disorders is uncertain), psychiatrists displayed little interest in analyzing the nature of vindictive aggression. Freud himself had relatively little to say on the specific problem of vindictive drives, although they certainly play a role in a number of the experiences he regarded as critical influences on human development. Freud's views on the traumatic significance of the primal scene are too well known to need any recounting here; it is, however, important to remember his assumption that a child witnessing the primal scene would be likely to interpret parental lovemaking as a violent assault by the man upon the woman. The child would be shaken by a sense of mingled helplessness, excitement, and desire—emotions that could not be expressed and would therefore be transformed into anxiety.

Thus, the primal scene becomes one of the original causes of sexual jealousy, anger, and vindictiveness. It contributes to the boy's oedipal desire to supplant his father and possess his mother, and to the girl's desire to replace her mother in her father's affections. (Modern revisions of Freud's interpretation of the primal scene, from inside and outside the psychiatric profession, are extensive. To me, one of the most persuasive of these critiques revolves around the simple fact that Freud was speaking from a Victorian bourgeois concept of the marital sex act. The idea that a child would view sex as an assault upon the woman presupposes the male always in the dominant position. It also assumes an inevitable absence of laughter or other indications of pleasure.)

In recent years, a number of psychiatrists have stressed the role of narcissistic injury, as distinct from traumatic anxiety, in the child's response to the primal scene. An obvious response —indeed, it may be the only one—to an injury inflicted upon one's deepest sense of identity is a need for redress that may be expressed in many forms of vindictiveness. The primal scene engenders feelings of exclusion and betrayal, Jacob Arlow argues, that are transformed into a sense of personal defeat. The child's immediate response is a wish to wreak vengeance upon the betraying parents; in adult life, this desire may be transformed into a tendency to humiliate parents, parental surrogates, or lovers. "Relatively underemphasized," Arlow suggests, "are those vengeful repetitions of the primal scene in which the individual causes others to be witness to his sexual activities. . . . In this repetition the role of the parent may be assigned to somebody else—spouse, child, lover, etc."[5]

The psychoanalytic focus on the primal scene as a generator of narcissistic anxiety and rage is refracted in popular culture in attempts to hold parents responsible for the actions of their children. In this simplistic view—one that is not, it should be emphasized, expounded by most reputable psychiatrists—the primal scene becomes a metaphor for a child's total relationship with his or her parents, and parents are blamed for whatever their children do. This motif was prominent in the trial of John Hinckley, whose troubled relationship with his father clearly did play an important role in the formation of his character. Hinckley Sr. broke down and wept on the stand when he described his refusal (on the advice of a psychiatrist) to let his son come home a few weeks before the Reagan assassination attempt. That he was, by his own account, a rigid father is clear. What else is one to think about a man who told his son he was no longer welcome at home, handed him several hundred dollars, and suggested he look for a room at the YMCA—although the young man was, by his father's account, incoherent and barely able to walk off an airplane. "In looking back on that," he testified, "I'm sure that it was the greatest mistake of my life. I am the cause of John's tragedy. We forced him out at a time when he just couldn't cope. I wish to God I could trade places with him right now."[6]

In spite of the distraught father's self-acknowledged failure as a parent, there was something discomfiting about the judgmental comments by prominent psychiatrists which appeared in countless newspaper and magazine articles after the testimony. "Most Psychiatrists Urge Not Abandoning a Child," headlined the *New York Times*. The president of the American Academy of Psychoanalysis flatly declared, "It doesn't matter what his [the child's] age is. What matters is how much need they have for love and some sort of emotional support." The director of an adolescent psychiatry program in Chicago theorized that young people like Hinckley, who remain overly dependent on their parents, are "hanging around the house, waiting for love to turn up" because they did not receive the love they needed when they were younger. The chairman of the American Psychiatric Association's Commission on Psychiatric Therapies warned that "the more disturbed the child is, the more cautious one should be about letting him go."[7]

In none of these interviews was there the slightest hint of compassion for a parent whose twenty-six-year-old "child" never managed to hold a job or finish school, whose main activities during the preceding ten years seem to have been inventing stories to obtain more money from his parents, taking drugs, watching violent movies, and nursing racial hatreds and fantasies about famous women. Then there was the inevitable psychological theorizing about how young Hinckley, in attempting to kill the President, was acting out his hatred of his father. This hypothesis is perfectly valid from a psychiatric perspective, but its symbolic reasoning does not, and cannot, address itself to the question of accountability. Who is responsible for this tragedy? Hinckley Jr.? Hinckley Sr.? Both? Neither? The psychological approach to revenge as a symbol of, and a metaphor for, deeper conflicts contributes little toward a useful approach to the consequences of adult vindictiveness.

Karen Horney, that supremely sensible (in both the French and English senses of the word) figure in the history of psychoanalysis, delivered a paper in 1948 in which she catalogued several major types of vindictiveness. In her attention to this question, as on many other issues, she was two decades ahead of most of her professional peers. Horney believed vindictiveness was the critical motivating force in personality trends psychiatrists generally classify under the label of sadism. The impulse toward revenge, she argued, can be expressed in an openly aggressive, self-effacing, or detached manner. Open aggression is the most recognizable form of vindictiveness—and the most likely to wind up in the criminal courts. "The person may aggressively strike out at others," Horney notes. "He is usually proud of this capacity, although, as mentioned, he does not experience the vindictive character of these actions. He may feel that he is simply more honest and straight than the others, that he is merely doling out justice, that his dignity refuses to be insulted with impunity."[8] From the extremity of an Ahab or a Michael Kohlhaas to the pettiness of a woman who tells her best friend she is looking a trifle pudgy, the figure of the avenger who perceives himself or herself as more righteous and honest than everyone else is a familiar one.

This quality was perfectly, albeit unintentionally, embodied in a published diatribe against the admittedly irritating modern speech habit of prefacing statements with phrases like "in all honesty," "frankly speaking," and "truthfully." The author had found a way of dealing with those who adopted this pernicious mode of speaking. Whenever an unsuspecting *raconteur* began a statement with "frankly" or "truthfully," she immediately intervened, "You mean that sometimes you are not 'truthful,' are not 'frank,' are not 'honest?' Is that why you have to tell me what you are?"[9] The author clearly saw nothing unusual about the vehemence with which she attacked others for their rhetorical sins; one suspects she will, one day, be the recipient of a frank punch in the nose.

Self-effacing vindictiveness, in Horney's lexicon, is more indirect and subversive. Suffering is used to make others feel guilty, as in the stereotype of the mother who says, "I'm too good." The person who specializes in self-effacing vindictiveness puts less stress on justice and "honesty" than the openly aggressive avenger and "experiences himself as a particularly good person who is constantly abused by others."[10]

Detachment is the third and least obvious form of vindictiveness described by Horney. Detached vindictiveness generally manifests itself in sins of omission rather than commission. Failing to listen to others when they are speaking or "forgetting" their expressed wishes are forms of this type of vindictiveness. Chronic lateness, particularly when the person being kept waiting is known to value punctuality, is a common weapon in the hands of the detached avenger.

These different types of vindictiveness, in societies as well as individuals, are closely related. Those who generally adopt a posture of open aggression are, I believe, equally willing to take on the protective coloration of self-effacement when it suits their purpose.

Openly aggressive seekers of revenge who regard their actions not as vindictive but as "honest" and "straight" are also likely to strike the "I'm-too-good" note of self-effacement when it seems appropriate to them. They see themselves not only as determined seekers after justice but as endurers of greater suf-

fering than their fellow men and women. And they may shift
with little warning from the "self-effacing" into the openly
aggressive category. The movement from self-effacement to
open aggression began to be apparent in Richard Herrin's letters to Bonnie Garland during the summer before the murder,
when she was traveling through Europe and did not even send
him a postcard. In the first letter, Richard takes a self-effacing
tone, and the desire to generate guilt in Bonnie by describing
his own loneliness could not be more obvious. "Good Morning
Sunshine!" the letter began.

> How's my sweet little hunk of beauty and inspiration doing
> today? I love you, Bonnie. . . . There's nobody around and
> nothing to do. I've been thinking about you all day, babe. I've
> been thinking about you all day every day, babe. I've never
> missed you so much.
>
> I've never yearned for you like I do now. That gives me a
> great idea for your Tour Break!! But no, don't do it, don't fly
> back to Ft. Worth, I'll survive. You know, sweetheart, as of
> today (Saturday) I still haven't heard from you. 10 days!!! I
> can't stand it. Why me?!!![11]

Then, two weeks later, he wrote several drafts of a letter he
never mailed. In these letters, the self-effacing tone began to
hint at rage.

> Hi,
> Remember me? June 8 and still no mail from you. If it takes
> more than 3 weeks for mail to reach here, it must take longer
> for it to reach any destination in Europe. . . . I at least hope
> you're safe. I'm not angry with the postal service, yet, and I
> hope they're the cause of the delay in me hearing from you. But
> 3 Weeks? I'm depressed and confused, and at times I feel like
> I'm getting fucked over. By the postal service or whatever. I'm
> sorry I can't be more cheerful. 3 damn weeks.[12]

At this point, according to the psychiatric testimony at the trial, Richard began to fantasize about mutilating Bonnie's genitals and cutting off her breasts. Gaylin notes that neither the prosecution nor the defense was interested in pursuing the psychological significance of Richard's vengeful fantasies—the prosecution because it wanted to depict the defendant as a bad, but sane, boy; the defense because it wanted to portray him as a model boy who cracked, with no warning and no explanation, after his girlfriend rejected him. Of course, model boys are not expected to entertain fantasies about the ripped genitals and severed breasts of their sweethearts—although such fantasies are, sadly, more "normal" in a statistical sense than is generally acknowledged. (More normal, at any rate, in this culture. *Hustler* magazine, which features explicit photographs of genital mutilation, has a circulation of more than six million.)

But the normality or abnormality of such fantasies is not the issue. The killing of Bonnie Garland was real. The determinism that is one of the pillars of Freudian psychiatry has contributed to the emergence of an ironic dichotomy in twentieth-century attitudes toward revenge: Although the psychiatric view of the vindictive drive is overwhelmingly negative, psychiatrists are reluctant to hold people accountable for acting on those drives. "We psychiatrists have followed an ostrich policy when it comes to a frank discussion of revenge," argues Harvey Lomas, a psychoanalyst whose work has brought him into frequent contact with Vietnam veterans who have difficulty controlling their vindictive anger. "Like sex before Freud, revenge is condemned as immature and undesirable and thus unworthy of serious scientific investigation. This hypocrisy neither does justice to our profession, nor does it contribute to a better understanding of destructive human aggression."[13]

In spite of her shrewd classification of the differing styles of vindictive expression, Horney fails to acknowledge the dual force of the explicit promise of divine revenge that accompanies

the Pauline injunction against human vengeance. After propos-
ing a psychoanalytic interpretation of the passage, in which the
avenger is "repaid" for vindictiveness by psychic suffering
("contrary to neurotic expectations we do not 'get by' with the
wrong solution of our inner conflicts"), she goes on to ask:

> But why the explicit warnings against revenge? Is it another
> way of asking us to offer the other cheek? No, we can hardly
> discard it that easily. We feel a deeper wisdom in it that is
> important for our lives.
>
> Another question arises: does it not mean asking the im-
> possible? Are not impulses to get back for injuries done univer-
> sal? Are they not even culturally sanctioned in many civiliza-
> tions? In Japan, for instance, elaborate rules exist for restoring
> injured pride by retaliatory measures. But there is another way
> of looking at such institutions. While they implicitly acknowl-
> edge the general existence of needs to retaliate, they also take
> these needs psychologically out of the hands of an individual
> by rendering them a civic duty. In this sense they rather
> confirm the principle expressed in the Bible.[14]

But the principle expressed in the Bible is not that all revenge
is wrong—or neurotic. It is that revenge is wrong when it is not
expressed through proper channels. In both Judaic and Christian tradition, those channels are presumed to have been authorized by none other than the creator of the universe. From
a psychological as well as a social standpoint, a truly critical
question is what happens to the reasoning and emotional balance of an individual whose need for retribution is not satisfied
through civilized channels.

But the therapeutic sensibility does not always acknowledge
the existence of a fundamental need to retaliate when an injury
has been inflicted. In the wake of the Hinckley verdict, there
were a great many public debates between therapeutic professionals over the question of whether human beings have a psychological "need" for retribution. There were a number of ref-

erences to non-western societies, including a tribe that resolves disputes by having antagonists compete with one another in giving away their possessions. The winner is the one who gives away the most. This sounds suspiciously like self-effacing vindictiveness; killing with kindness is, after all, a well-known and highly effective mode of vengeance in western as well as non-western cultures. In any event, the major cultures of both East and West rest upon equally elaborate, albeit highly various, social mechanisms for the control of revenge.

When there is a breakdown—whether real or perceived—in social mechanisms that permit carefully measured expression of the need for retribution, the Biblical injunction loses its psychological usefulness for individuals. A sense of helplessness in the face of unredressed injustice has, throughout history, produced a strong attraction to boundless vengeance. At every stage of this process, symbolic representations of the vindictive impulse play a significant emotional role. Religious prophecy and art are the traditional channels of symbolic vindictiveness; their effectiveness has, in the twentieth century, been greatly enhanced by the modern technology of mass communication. Lomas notes that the story of the handwriting on the wall in the Book of Daniel is a clear projection of the Jews' hatred for their Babylonian captors and of their desire that Yahweh avenge their wrongs as he had in the past. He believes the Biblical imagery served the same function as modern urban graffiti: a frustrated population, unable or unwilling to stand up and be identified, was saying, "Someone will get even with you."[15]

> Belshazzar the king made a great feast to a thousand of his lords, and drank wine before the thousand. Belshazzar, whiles he tasted the wine, commanded to bring the golden and silver vessels which his father Nebuchadnezzar had taken out of the temple which was in Jerusalem; that the king, and his princes, his wives, and his concubines, might drink therein. Then they

brought the golden vessels that were taken out of the temple of the house of God which was at Jerusalem; and the king, and his princes, his wives, and his concubines, drank in them. They drank wine, and praised the gods of gold, of silver, of brass, of iron, of wood, and of stone. In the same hour came forth the fingers of a man's hand, and wrote over against the candlestick upon the plaster of the wall of the king's palace: and the king saw the part of the hand that wrote. Then the king's countenance was changed, and his thoughts troubled him, so that the joints of his loins were loosed, and his knees smote one against another. The king cried aloud to bring in the astrologers, the Chaldeans, and the soothsayers. And the king spake, and said to the wise men of Babylon, Whosoever shall read this writing, and shew me the interpretation thereof, shall be clothed with scarlet, and have a chain of gold about his neck, and shall be the third ruler in the kingdom.[16]

Daniel told the king the writing meant, "Thou art weighed in the balances, and art found wanting," and predicted that the kingdom would be divided between the Medes and the Persians. And that is how, when Darius conquered the kingdom, Daniel became the chief counselor of the land.

A particularly dangerous form of symbolic revenge emerges when those who are firmly in control persistently represent themselves as victims in need of redress. This type of symbolism reflects a paranoid mind set that may originally have been based on real injuries (the conditions imposed on Germany by the Treaty of Versailles, for instance) and eventually becomes an instrument for generating and manipulating a generalized drive toward vengeance. The Nazis, of course, were masters of the tools of symbolic revenge. The use of fire and darkness, from the first book burnings through the elaborately choreographed Nuremberg rallies, is well known. The prime example of vengeful symbolism in which the conquerer is represented as a suffering victim whose honor must be redressed was the Oberammergau Passion Play of 1934, in which Hitler was implicitly equated with Jesus and the apostles were explicitly portrayed as Aryan guards. Dorothy Thompson, writing in *Harper's Bazaar*, recounted the response of a German onlooker who, when Jesus was hoisted on the cross, cried out, "There he is. That is our Führer, our Hitler!" When Judas was paid his thirty pieces of silver, she said, "That is Röhm, who betrayed the Leader."[17]

The political symbolism of revenge is frequently characterized by a confusion of identity between victim and aggressor and by the transformation of vengeance into a positive social value. In public spectacles, the confusion is subliminal, but it can easily be transformed by totalitarian states into an explicit rationale for acts of rage and vindictiveness. A paradigm of this sort of transformation appears in Heinrich Himmler's famous speech to a group of high-level SS officers, in which he commended them for their perseverance in the painful task of eliminating the Jews ("it's a dirty job, but someone has to do it").

I also want to refer before you here, in complete frankness, to a really grave matter. Among ourselves, this once, it shall be uttered quite frankly. . . .

I am referring to the evacuation of the Jews, the annihilation of the Jewish people. This is one of those things that are easily said. "The Jewish people is going to be annihilated," says every party member. "Sure, it's in our program, elimination of the Jews, annihilation—we'll take care of it." And then they all come trudging, eighty million worthy Germans, and each one has his one decent Jew. Sure, the others are swine, but this one is an A-1 Jew. Of all those who talk this way, not one has seen it happen, not one has been through it. Most of you must know what it means to see a hundred corpses side by side, or five hundred, or a thousand. To have stuck this out and— excepting cases of human weakness—to have kept our integrity, this is what has made us hard. In our history, this is an unwritten and never-to-be-written page of glory.[18]

A similar confusion between aggressor and victim, albeit in less pernicious form, is apparent in the use of revenge as a theme in late-twentieth-century mass entertainment. Although this symbolism is not political in intent—not, at any rate, in the same sense as government-orchestrated revanchist symbolism —it reflects a disturbing climate of political opinion.

Although there is nothing new about the frequency of vengeance as a motif in popular entertainment, a number of particularly unsettling elements are apparent in the glorified portraits of revenge that have appeared with increasing regularity on television and in movies made during the past decade. The avengers are stick figures who are about as complex as the comic-book superheroes of the 1940s—and a good deal less complex than the "primitive" blood avengers of Elizabethan and Jacobean drama. The avenging hero of *Death Wish* and the inevitable *Death Wish II* never sheds a tear when his wife is murdered and his daughter raped; he simply buys a gun and starts finishing off one young punk after another. All of this is justified by the fact that the police never caught the hoodlums who attacked his family. Moreover, there is a sharp contrast between the amoral framework of these movies and the warnings against revenge that permeate even the bloodiest Jacobean dramas—warnings that are unmistakable in spite of the gusto with which each act of vengeance is depicted.

The cheering audiences at *Death Wish* did not seem to perceive anything askew in the emotional makeup of a character who, in the quest to avenge his wife and daughter, starts riding the subways with bulging grocery bags designed to attract muggers. The hero, played by Charles Bronson, need hardly exert himself to attract beasts in the urban jungle; they are drawn to his scent in supermarkets and parks and airports. The only place where he fails to be assaulted is in the cemetery where his wife is buried—and grave robbing is just about the only crime he fails to encounter. When his daughter emerges from the catatonic state into which she had retreated after the rape, he moves her to Los Angeles, where she is promptly slaughtered by a gang of dope-crazed hoodlums. So much for starting over; Bronson takes to the streets once again with his trusty revolver. Such movies are enormously successful at the box office. *Death Wish II,* an even more lucrative venture than its predecessor, earned nearly a million dollars in the first three days of its 1982 New York run. A new wave of hard-line cops-and-robbers series earned more than $190 million for the three major American television networks in 1981–82, and the advertising revenues were expected to soar to more than $315 million in 1982–83—a bonanza in the midst of the most serious American economic slump since the Great Depression.[19]

One of the toughest new law-and-order series, *T. J. Hooker,* features a middle-aged policeman outraged by younger officers who try to "understand" criminals. (Hooker was played by the actor William Shatner, best-known to international audiences as the sensitive captain of the Starship *Enterprise* in the 1960s television series *Star Trek.* So much for Captain Kirk and his friendly crew of mixed races, religions, and planets.)

The glorification of vengeance in mass entertainment is frequently accompanied by hymns to the old sexual order in which men protect their women and women know their place. In one episode of *T. J. Hooker,* the dedicated policeman is using extraordinary means to trap a criminal who has become known as the "lunch-hour rapist." A female reporter accuses Hooker of violating the suspect's constitutional rights—and learns her lesson when she is added to his list of victims. Hooker arrives just a moment too late to save her (in spite of his almost supernatural talent for interrupting crimes-in-progress), and she tearfully admits she was wrong to suggest that extremism in the pursuit of criminals might be a vice. Scores are settled all around.

Like *Death Wish,* many of the new movies and television series endorse vigilante justice, but they are not quite prepared to endorse it for women. *Victims,* a made-for-television movie shown on the ABC network, featured an enraged heroine who decides to take matters into her own hands when a smirking rapist is released because of a technical error in police identification procedures (that nit-picking Constitution again). With the help of three other victims, the woman finds out where the rapist lives and begins to stalk him. A policeman advises her to forget about it and she replies, "I spent a year of my life trying to forget about it. For what? So you could let him go free? No. This time I'm not going to forget about it."

Then the plot takes on a different coloration. Under the pressure of her obsession with revenge, the heroine's relationship with her live-in lover begins to fall apart. He suggests she visit a psychiatrist and she says the only thing that will help her is to see the rapist behind bars. Then the rapist finds out that his former victim is shadowing him and begins to threaten her. After trying to take the offensive, she finds herself in danger of becoming a victim again. It seems that women cannot win in these modern dramas of revenge. The heroine of *Victims* is punished for trying to strike back at her rapist, while the female reporter in *T. J. Hooker* is punished for being soft on crime. Vengeance is the prerogative of men, whether they are lone vigilantes or officers of the law.

The barely concealed hostility toward women in these mass-entertainment fantasies is hardly surprising in view of the combination of atavistic needs they embody. Patriarchal order is essential to the creation of a world in which criminals receive their just deserts (deserts they always escape, the movies imply, in the real world). Obeisance to patriarchy, combined with the unfailing lure of the Mafia and sentimentalization of "ethnic roots," surely played a role in the enormous public success of Mario Puzo's novel and Francis Ford Coppola's movie adaptation of *The Godfather*.

The family takes care of its own and, especially, of its women; no Corleone wife or daughter will ever see her rapist go free because of bumbling police concern over the suspect's constitutional rights. Coppola, however, pulled a surprising switch in the movie sequel to *The Godfather:* There was, he suggested, a high price to be paid for the order and unending vendettas of *la famiglia.* Merciless retribution would be visited upon women who did not accept the terms of their own protection—on Don Michael's wife, who had an abortion when she could no longer close her eyes to her husband's activities, and on his sister, who couldn't quite accept the fact that her husband had to die for his offenses against the family. But *Godfather II,* with its shadings of doubt, is a conspicuous exception to the monochromatic portrait of revenge that dominates popular entertainment. Revenge, cautions a Sicilian proverb, is a dish that tastes sweetest when it is cold. Modern television and movie audiences have become accustomed to having their vengeance served hot from the fast-food grill.

The glorified image of revenge and vigilantism in popular entertainment is totally at odds with the psychiatric image of vindictiveness as neurosis. Indeed, the larger-than-life avenger of *Death Wish* may be an answer to the condescension that characterizes so many of the metaphors for vengeance in the psychotherapeutic lexicon, as well as a response to fear of crime. The avenger is omnipotent; his victims are anonymous and alien specks in a menacing urban landscape. In this undifferentiated orgy of getting even, the principle of individual accountability—tortuously established through the long, uneven evolution of legal and religious restraints of vengeance—is lost. Avengers are not expected to account for their actions, and their victims have no connection with the crimes being repaid. "The enemy is not just viewed as somebody who is at cross purposes," Lomas observes. "Rather he/she is perceived as a flaw (a dehumanized flaw) in a narcissistically perceived reality. Independent action is the provocation. Murder is the cure."[20]

At first glance, the images of revenge in psychiatry and in popular entertainment seem to have little in common. In psychoanalytic theory, men and women, in thrall to the narcissistic injuries they have suffered, act out their vindictive needs in ways that make them appear petty and childish at best and profoundly destructive at worst. In mass entertainment, avengers are unexamined heroes, keeping their integrity (as Himmler put it) in order to right wrongs the rest of us are too intimidated to address.

But both sets of images—the complicated picture developed by Freud and his successors and the cartoon universe of popular entertainment—lack sufficient respect for the revenge impulse. The mass entertainment machine has nothing to tell us about the perils of unrestrained vengeance; it ignores Nadezhda Mandelstam's warning about the horror of a world in which "not only individuals but whole categories and classes of people" are subject to conscienceless revenge. These screen images cannot be dismissed as trash catering to the idle daydreams of bourgeois audiences; their popular appeal is a clear indication that something is askew in the delicate social balance between retribution and compassion. Moreover, there is a profound conflict between the emotions expressed by cheering audiences at *Death Wish* and a public ethic that insists on a justice/revenge dichotomy.

If mass entertainment has little to say about the dangers of unrestrained vengeance, the therapeutic sensibility has little to say about the perils of a world in which measured revenge has lost its legitimacy. The "justice, not revenge" formulation is inherent in much of the psychiatric thinking of the past fifty years. "Undesirable behavior should, of course, be forbidden," wrote the influential Karl Menninger, "and if possible prevented. But how will 30 years of a prison regime do that? Will 30 years do it better than 30 months? Indeed—can it? The real question is, Can this man be deterred or not? Can he be changed? Can he be realigned and made again self-supporting

and community conforming?"[21] But that is not the real question
—not from a civic, as distinct from a therapeutic, perspective.
Leaving aside for a moment the criminological argument over
rehabilitation versus punishment, another "real question" remains: Ought rehabilitation, even if it is successful, be allowed
to cancel out the need for retribution? From an emotional as
well as a legal standpoint, are not certain forms of retribution
an integral part of any process of rehabilitation? The ancient
concept that an offender must pay a penalty before being restored to society embodies a profound psychological as well as
social need—and embodies it for the criminal as well as the
victim. It can be argued—indeed, many psychiatrists do argue
—that addressing social problems is not the proper business of
doctors; however, the entanglement of psychiatry with the
criminal-justice system during the past thirty years has made it
ethically, if not medically, insupportable for physicians of the
mind to adopt a *noli me tangere* posture with regard to questions of crime and punishment. Moreover, the conflict between
the idealized image of vengeance in modern entertainment and
the therapeutic view of vindictiveness as psychological regression has played a significant role in maintaining the private and
public taboos that impede serious consideration of the proper
relationship between justice and retribution. The nature of this
relationship is as much a psychiatric issue today as it has been
a religious and legal issue for the past three thousand years.

From an individual as well as a social perspective, establishing a distinction between legitimate and illegitimate expressions
of vindictiveness is of critical importance. Horney's assertions
that "every vindictiveness damages the core of the whole being"
and that "not 'liberating vindictive aggression' but overcoming
it is our therapeutic goal" are an inadequate and incomplete
statement of the problem.[22] In sharp contrast to the classical
psychoanalytic acceptance of a wide range of erotic impulses—
an acceptance that has greatly expanded our concept of health
as well as of pathology—the suggestion that every manifesta-

tion of vindictiveness is in some way destructive would seem to relegate all vengeance to the realm of the perverse. One can scarcely imagine a psychiatrist who would suggest that every form of eroticism, or even erotic aggression, is somehow damaging; the usual therapeutic goal is to overcome inappropriate, or hurtful, expressions of the erotic urge. Freud's interpretation of revenge as a means of resolving oedipal conflicts[23] is not helpful in establishing distinctions between constructive and destructive manifestations of vindictiveness—or between a specific, limited act of vengeance and the adoption of a generalized vengeful attitude that dominates every aspect of life.

Psychiatry's inability to solve "the riddle of symptom choice"—why one man responds to the mistreatment or absence of a father figure by becoming Winston Churchill and another by becoming Adolf Hitler—is both a therapeutic and a theoretical obstacle in addressing many kinds of human behavior. (This inability does not constitute an indictment of the profession; if psychiatrists knew why one individual who was a battered child grows up to repeat the cycle of abuse with other tiny victims, while another grows up to become a loving parent, they would be gods rather than practitioners of a particularly inexact branch of the inexact art—albeit an art with many scientific elements—of medicine.)

The combination of the oedipal metaphor of revenge with the opaque nature of the symptom-choice riddle poses a special problem with regard to revenge, because specific acts of vindictiveness cannot be understood in isolation from the injuries that triggered them. Proportionality, as the term is understood in both religion and law, is equally important in establishing a psychological distinction between constructive and destructive revenge. Many slights and injuries are not important enough to justify the vindictive energy required for redress, and most of us are familiar with the psychological conclusion that "it's just not worth it"—to punish a friend for revealing private information about us at a party, to establish the fact that the bank is responsible for the two-dollar error on our monthly statement, to lose a day's work by fighting a twenty-dollar parking ticket in court.

But there are situations, both ordinary and extreme, in which the gravity of an injury does justify the energy expended on a vindictive response. What if a friend has not only revealed private information about me but has seriously damaged my reputation in the process? What—to up the ante—if I am raped on a date by a man who refused to take no for an answer? What —to move into a realm of still greater injury—if my child is murdered and the killer is never caught? Or what if the murderer is caught and convicted, only to be released on parole within a few years?

Heinz Kohut argues that "just as it is true with man's sexual desires, so also with his narcissistic needs: neither a contemptuous attitude toward the powerful psychological forces which assert themselves in these two dimensions of human life nor the attempt at their total eradication will lead to genuine progress in man's self-control or adaptation."[24] Neither the aggrandized image of vengeance in popular entertainment—an image that ignores both the personal and public perils of promiscuous vindictiveness—nor the condescending therapeutic metaphor of revenge as an acting-out of childish rage can contribute to a new definition of the proper relationship between justice and retribution.

"Do good to them that hurt you" is an ethic for saints; to refrain from doing disproportionate harm would seem to be difficult enough counsel for most human beings to follow. In similar fashion, overcoming vindictive aggression would seem to be a utopian vision (and not everyone's idea of utopia, at that). To permit vindictive rage to dominate one's entire existence is assuredly destructive, but vengeful anger is at its most powerful and pervasive when there are no mechanisms for releasing it through legitimate channels. The ability to exact proportional, measured retribution is one way of denying promiscuity to the vindictive drive. Evil and retribution are far too powerful to be treated merely as metaphors.

VI   Sexual Revenge

Sweet is revenge—especially to women.
LORD BYRON, *Don Juan*

You, stupid man, who believe in laws that punish murder by murder, you who have no power of vengeance except in calumny and defamation! When you find a woman who knows how to live without you, your vain power turns to fury.

Your fury shall be punished by a smile, by an adieu, and by life-long unconcern!
GEORGE SAND, *The Intimate Journal*

When any writer disappears from the public prints for an extended period, he or she becomes accustomed to the question —posed by some acquaintances with genuine interest and by others with genuine malice—"What on earth have you been doing all this time?" For several years, my reply was "I'm writing a book about revenge." Interrogators of both sexes immediately perked up; their eyes began to gleam, and they probed shamelessly for a personal motive. "What a perfect subject for a woman," they would say, in conspiratorial tones conveying the assumption, celebrated in song and story for millennia, that the most cunning and conscienceless avengers are members of "the weaker sex." They unearthed a veritable treasure trove of stories, apocryphal and real, about the devious vengeance of women—a wife who slipped a raw egg instead of a hard-boiled one into her husband's lunch pail; a cook who sliced and diced her faithless lover and served him up in a savory stew; a divorcée who, having agreed to sell her husband's Mercedes-Benz and split the proceeds as part of their divorce settlement, signed over the car to the first bidder for $25 and sent a check for $12.50 to the enraged ex-spouse. (The last story was reported as fact in the Detroit newspapers—but, of course, you can't believe everything you read.)

Although the notion of revenge being especially sweet to women seems especially sweet to men, the convention of "hell hath no fury . . ." exerts a powerful hold on the thinking of both sexes. The depth and duration of this cultural assumption requires an explanation that is political in the broadest sense, encompassing the written and unwritten laws governing sexual relationships, which, because of their emotional nature, are generally treated as questions of passion rather than of power.

As men and women, we all understand the emotional vindictiveness of rejected lovers. As citizens, we share a heritage of "the unwritten law," which should be regarded not in its most obvious, limited sense—as a license for a man to murder an unfaithful wife caught *in flagrante*—but as a way of placing all hot-blooded crimes of sexual revenge in a different category from cold-blooded crimes. Anyone who sits on a jury in a murder case can understand and identify with the intense pain of sexual rejection, in contrast, say, to the bizarre fantasies of a Charles Manson, the cold professionalism of a hired hit man, or even the greed of an armed robber turned killer. Unfortunately, the hot-bloodedness or cold-bloodedness of the slayer makes no difference to the victim, whose blood is always spilled.

Murder, of course, represents sexual vengeance in its extremity. Rape, wife beating, and sexual child abuse are more common physical manifestations of sexual revenge (and, of course, of other violent drives). In the nonviolent, or, at any rate, noncriminal range of the spectrum, there are child-custody battles, alimony and "palimony" suits, adulterous liaisons: the list is endless. Finally, there are the everyday acts of domestic sabotage and humiliation that provide so much of the material for television situation comedies. This connection between the ordinary and the extraordinary, the familiar and the exotic, the legitimate and the illegitimate—a tantalizing range of possibilities that is one of the wellsprings of eroticism—generates uncertainty and ambivalence whenever the issue of sexual revenge is raised in private or in public.

It is curious that so much of the folklore of sexual revenge focuses on women, when men are so much more likely to be the instigators of sexual violence. The publicity devoted to a relatively small number of cases in which women have killed their husbands or lovers makes it necessary to emphasize what every police officer and criminologist knows: men are responsible for most violent crimes, regardless of whether the motive has anything to do with sex. (In the United States and Europe, local and national crime statistics indicate that women commit about 10 percent of all crimes of violence and 15 percent of murders —figures that have not changed since the advent of reliable record keeping in the nineteenth century. In America, there has been a significant rise in the number of women arrested for *all* crimes during the past twenty years, but nonviolent crimes, such as fraud and larceny, account for the greatest proportion of those arrests.)[1]

In only one sexual confrontation, the "domestic quarrel" ending in death, is a woman almost as likely to kill as to be killed. But the motives of men and women who kill in such circumstances are far from identical. When a woman kills her husband in a violent quarrel, the act is usually a desperate, final response to years of physical abuse. When a man kills his wife in a domestic setting, his act is a logical extension of the physical abuse he has been dispensing for years, an ultimate upping of the ante. On this issue, I do not share the position of some feminist leaders, who insist that a woman who kills under such provocation is legally blameless. (The views of some feminists are frequently, and mistakenly, described as *the* feminist position—a phrase that betrays an ignorance about the diversity of modern feminist politics analogous to some hilariously earnest American newspaper stories, in the spring of 1917, which attributed identical views to Lenin and Kerensky.) However, it seems indisputably true that the psychological motivation of a battered wife who turns on her husband is quite different from that of a brutal husband who finally batters his wife to death. Whether this psychological distinction should be translated into a legal one is an issue that has, in recent years, been raised repeatedly in the courts and has been resolved in widely divergent ways.

In view of the relatively low incidence of sexual violence on the part of women, what is one to make of the intense public fascination with murder cases involving brutalized wives or spurned mistresses, such as the celebrated slaying of Herman Tarnower, the "Scarsdale diet doctor," by his former lover Jean Harris? The comparative rarity of such cases is one obvious explanation; they fit the classic dog-bites-man definition of news. However, statistical infrequency cannot in itself sustain public interest in an event. Suicide, for instance, is statistically rare, surprisingly so, even among the terminally ill and those in other objectively "hopeless" situations. But an "ordinary" suicide—that is, a suicide committed by someone who is neither a rock star nor a millionaire—does not rate a line in the daily paper. The relatively high visibility of both the victim and the killer might account for the interest in the Tarnower-Harris case, but prominence is rarely a factor in cases of husbands killed by battered wives. Wife beating, child abuse, and sexual assaults by men are almost totally lacking in news value unless they are committed in a particularly bizarre fashion, but an assault by a mother upon her child rates bold headlines in the tabloids.

When a woman commits an act of violence—especially against those she is assumed to love and expected to nurture— she upsets our deepest notions of sexual and social order. As the chorus observes in *Medea,* "Streams of the sacred rivers flow uphill/Tradition, order, all things are reversed." The emotional force of *Medea* depends on its portrayal of a woman committing the most unwomanly act imaginable—slaying her own children. In the *Oresteia,* Clytemnestra is the only creature, human or divine, who calls her husband, Agamemnon, to account for the sacrifice of their daughter Iphigenia. The Olympian gods blame Clytemnestra for killing her husband in revenge for her daughter; they do not blame Agamemnon for the slaying of the innocent Iphigenia or Orestes for the retaliatory murder of his mother. The deeply ingrained double standard of morality, usually thought of in terms of its applicability to sexual behavior, is better understood as a code ceding broader powers of action—whether in pursuit of eroticism, authority, wealth, justice, or revenge—to men than to women. Under the double standard, it is scarcely surprising that any act of revenge by a woman looms larger, in myth and in reality, than a comparable act by a man.

A Jean Harris with a gun, like a Nat Turner with a blade, confirms the worst suspicions of the powerful about the vengeance that lies in the hearts of the weak. This suspicion is embodied in the traditional view that vindictiveness, *short of criminality,* is a feminine rather than a masculine trait. Cunning, lies, sorcery, cuckoldry, vindictive alimony demands—these are conventional feminine weapons that supposedly balance out superior masculine strength. This perception is not always a male distortion; deceit and trickery *are* the preferred weapons of the weak when they are the only ones available. When the double standard decrees that adultery is a grave insult to a husband but not to a wife, it is natural that adultery will be considered a woman's weapon. How can it be considered a man's weapon if it is regarded as a man's right, rather than as a forbidden form of assault? Throughout the millennia when worldly power belonged almost entirely to men, only the rarest sort of genius—detached, by some miracle of empathy, from conventional male assumptions—was able to encompass the complex despair, rather than simple malice, in the deceitful forms of vengeance traditionally ascribed to women. Before the tragic dénouement of *Othello,* Emilia tells Desdemona:

> But I do think it is their husbands' faults
> If wives do fall: say that they slack their duties
> And pour our treasures into foreign laps,
> Or else break out in peevish jealousies,
> Throwing restraint upon us; or say they strike us,
> Or scant our former having in despite;
> Why, we have galls, and though we have some grace,
> Yet have we some revenge. Let husbands know
> Their wives have sense like them: they see and smell
> And have their palates both for sweet and sour,
> As husbands have. What is it that they do
> When they change us for others? Is it sport?
> I think it is: and doth affection breed it?
> I think it doth: is't frailty that thus errs?
> It is so too: and have we not affections,
> Desires for sport, and frailty, as men have?
> Then let them use us well: else let them know,
> The ills we do, their ills instruct us so.[2]

Any man would be a fool not to sense the psychological relationship between the everyday sense of grievance that leads women to employ traditionally feminine modes of vengeance and the accumulated outrage that occasionally explodes in violence—just as any woman would be a fool not to sense the relationship between ordinary masculine possessiveness and the overwhelming anger that can impel a man to kill the object of his "love." The tendency to interpret violent acts of sexual revenge in a psychological or emotional rather than a criminal light is rooted in awareness, whether conscious or subliminal, of the role of vindictiveness in ordinary conflicts between the sexes. In historical periods like our own, when the rights and wrongs of women engender public as well as private passions, the double standard may, in some instances, work against justice for men as well as women. These cases, which tend to arise when the traditional balance of sexual power is being renegotiated, should not be allowed to obscure the patriarchal origins of the codes governing sexual revenge. The acquittal of Inez Garcia, who shot and killed a man twenty minutes after he helped to rape her, is a case in point.[3] Garcia had picked up a gun and pursued her assailants into the night; her lawyer argued that an "unwritten law" allows a woman "to take the law into her own hands to protect her integrity." A more conservative attorney would not have made the argument openly, since juries are sworn to uphold not unwritten but written laws. However, the unwritten law could scarcely have been invoked on behalf of a woman in a case like Garcia's had it not been invoked for centuries in defense of men who tracked down and killed the rapists of their wives, daughters, mothers, and sisters.

If jury verdicts and judicial sentences are reliable indicators of contemporary thinking—and I believe they are—there is no consensus today on how to deal with extreme acts of sexual revenge. The absence of such a consensus is expectable in view of the current climate of confusion and conflict about ordinary sexual mores. In one instance, an act of sexual vengeance may be regarded as temporary insanity, in another as premeditated murder, in still another as a form of self-defense. Jean Harris, the schoolmistress who shot Dr. Tarnower after she became convinced that she had no chance of winning him back from a younger woman, was convicted of premeditated murder and given the mandatory sentence (in the State of New York) of fifteen years to life. Three years earlier, in the same affluent community of Scarsdale, twenty-three-year-old Richard Herrin used a claw hammer to smash in the skull of his sleeping girlfriend, twenty-year-old Bonnie Garland, after she told him she wanted to end their relationship in order to be free to date other men. Herrin was convicted not of murder but of the lesser crime of manslaughter because the jury believed him to be acting under "extreme emotional disturbance." He will be eligible for parole when he is thirty-one.* Herrin and his supporters, citing the absence of a history of violence, considered this sentence far too severe in view of his deep love for Bonnie and his profound distress at her loss.[4] Herrin's expression of self-pity prompted a psychiatrist who interviewed him after the trial to recall the old joke about the man who has killed both his parents and begs the court to have mercy on him because he is an orphan.

Several explanations might be offered for the disparity between these verdicts, reached by juries in the same community in murder cases with a marked similarity: in both instances, the victim had spurned the killer's love. One explanation involves the simple fact that the two juries were composed of different people; the obvious element of human idiosyncrasy should never be overlooked in analyzing the outcome of criminal trials. Another explanation, forcefully advanced by a number of feminist writers, is that a woman like Jean Harris, who commits a crime with a traditionally "masculine" weapon, is likely to be treated more harshly than a man who commits a comparable act of violence. I do not believe this explanation stands up under close scrutiny, because a survey of recent jury verdicts in cases of battered wives who have killed their husbands reveals no consistent pattern of convictions or acquittals.

There is one discernible pattern, though, in murder cases involving sexual rage and jealousy: a psychiatric defense is the killer's best friend. Since the verdict in the Hinckley trial, public attention has focused on the classic insanity defense, which aims at absolute acquittal and holds out the possibility of release from a mental institution if the defendant is later declared

---

*In New York State, a jury may convict a defendant on a charge of manslaughter rather than premeditated murder if he or she is presumed to be acting under extreme emotional stress. This approach is not identical to the insanity defense, in which defendants are alleged to be mentally incapable of accountability for their acts, but it does present psychological factors as mitigating circumstances meriting a lighter sentence.

"cured" by psychiatrists. Many psychiatrists have defended their role in the criminal-justice system by pointing out that acquittals by reason of insanity are rare. Modern psychiatric defenses are not, however, limited to the straightforward insanity plea; they may be aimed, as Herrin's defense was, at conviction on a lesser charge justified by "transitory emotional disturbance." Harris's lawyer, for reasons that are unclear, employed no form of psychiatric defense, while Herrin's trial was saturated with psychiatric testimony. The concept of extreme but transitory emotional distress offers juries an easy way out in crimes where the killer is viewed not as a cold-blooded murderer but as a frustrated lover; the jury is able to consider a defendant with no previous pattern of unstable behavior and conclude that he or she was temporarily unhinged by romantic despair. And who among us is unacquainted with the particular, intense despair precipitated by sexual rejection? Romantic love has, after all, been described by generations of poets as a form of madness.

No lawyer or judge, as far as I know, has ever suggested that a Gestapo officer's pre-Nazi relations with Jews—real or imagined, positive or negative—ought to influence a sentence for crimes committed during the Hitler era. But a history of passion or "love" is repeatedly offered as a mitigating factor when a crime involves intimates or former intimates. On June 4, 1980, a young Chicago man named Wayne Birch shot and killed his former girlfriend, Venira Curtis, who was pregnant by and about to marry another man. Both victim and killer were black, and Curtis was a secretary. There was nothing glamorous about the case—no millionaire diet doctor to attract the attention of the national and international press. But the crime was both brutal and calculated. Birch had repeatedly threatened Curtis after she left him; he had broken her car windows and pulled a gun on her and her fiancé, promising to kill her if she brought charges against him. She and her father, who had urged her to testify, were on their way to court for the trial when Birch appeared at their house and shot his "true love" through the head.

The State of Illinois permits the death penalty in cases where the assailant has killed someone who planned to testify against him in a criminal trial. But the judge did not even hand down a life sentence; he sentenced Birch to twenty-five years, with eligibility for parole after eleven years, when he will still be a young man. Why? Not because the judge opposed life sentences but because the victim and the killer had once been romantically involved. The judge concluded that Birch killed his former girlfriend because he wanted her back and she was in love with another man—not to prevent her from testifying against him. In his view, the killing was a crime of the heart rather than an act of calculated vengeance—and his sentence reflected the social consensus that crimes of the heart and crimes of the head are to be judged by different standards.

The use of psychiatry to exculpate those who attack their intimates is a modern twist on the ancient unwritten law that grants a certain legitimacy to the impassioned cry "If I can't have you, no one will." In the past, that legitimacy was enjoyed only by men. Today, as a result of the changing balance of sexual power, some women have also been able to invoke the protection of a legal custom dictated by passion rather than reason.

The unwritten law: It does not belong within quotation marks, with their implications of skepticism, thoughtful consideration, distance. By definition, the unwritten law was engraved on no stone tablets; it originated in the deepest, most destructive human passions and was upheld by the strength and social authority of men. A simple tableau comes to mind—a cowboy returning early to his home on the range, surprising his wife with another man, pumping them both full of bullets. Although this surely is the classic example of socially sanctioned vengeance—one that survived well into the twentieth century in many cultures, including the Italian and American South—the unwritten law is best understood as a broad code covering many aspects of social, sexual, and familial relations between women and men.

These include the traditional patriarchal powers of husbands and fathers, which, as the continued prevalence of wife beating and sexual child abuse suggests, are extremely difficult to limit through written laws; seduction and its consequences, inside and outside of marriage; rape, inside and outside of marriage, and the vengeance exacted for rape by the male relatives of a violated woman. The historic difficulty, or absolute inability, of women to exact their own retribution for rape cannot be overestimated as a factor in the development of the tangled laws, written and unwritten, linking sex and revenge. It is hardly surprising that some women today are claiming an "equal right" to vengeance outside the law; the extra-legal rights long accorded to men—both as instigators and avengers of crimes of passion—laid the groundwork for the regressive and legally illegitimate invocation of the unwritten law as women's "right."

Rape is, in fact, the most powerful example of a violent act uniting passion, possessiveness, and vengeance—the possession of women by men, vengeance toward all women enacted upon the body of one. The understanding of rape as a product of vindictiveness rather than eroticism is one of the most important insights offered by feminist scholarship during the past decade. It is no longer possible to view rape as a crime of love or the rapist as a prisoner of love: the crime is one of hate, and the victim, not the attacker, is the prisoner.

As Susan Brownmiller points out, the only recourse for women against the assaults of some men was to seek protection from other men. "Once a male took title to a specific female body, and surely for him this was a great sexual convenience as well as a testament to his warring stature, he had to assume the burden of fighting off all other potential attackers, or scare them off by the retaliatory threat of raping *their* women."[5]

From early myth through today's news, countless stories of family feuds, murders, duels, vendettas, and full-scale wars begin with the rape of or insult to a woman. Sometimes the assault or insult is real and sometimes it is invented. Imaginary or invented insults, it must be emphasized, originate in the minds of men as well as women; they are not, as male tradition has it, the sole creations of vengeful females bent on ensnaring husbands or retaliating against men who have scorned them.

In any event, the question of whether a sexual insult is real or invented is largely irrelevant to the outcome of most sagas of sexual revenge. Retribution is the sole prerogative of men, and the fate of the injured woman becomes incidental. Two Biblical narratives, one in the Book of Genesis and the other in the history of King David's reign, illustrate these points.

Genesis describes the violation of Dinah, the daughter of Jacob and his unloved but fertile wife Leah, by a non-Jewish prince. Whether she was raped, as rape is defined today, is far from clear; in the early periods of Jewish tribal history, there was little distinction between rape and seduction—mutual or otherwise—if either was conducted in violation of the laws of Israel. By the rabbinical period, this distinction was well established and extremely important in assessing damages and penalties. (Whether Dinah was raped, as rape is defined today, is highly debatable. Brownmiller argues convincingly that *all* Biblical accounts reflect the Hebrew male version of reality. Who knows what the female version might have been? Had I been Jacob's daughter, accustomed to my brothers' hot tempers, I might well have said I was raped when I was discovered dallying with a man from outside the tribe.)

The subsequent behavior of Dinah's lover does not sound like the reaction of a rapist. The Bible, after telling us that when the prince saw Dinah, "he took her, and lay with her, and defiled her," goes on to acknowledge that "his soul clave unto Dinah the daughter of Jacob, and he loved the damsel, and

spake kindly unto the damsel." There is, of course, no report
of what Dinah said to or felt about him. Jacob's outraged sons,
unmoved by the prince's offer to make an honest woman of
Dinah, insisted that it was impossible to give their sister to an
uncircumcised man. The prince, who must have been wildly in
love, agreed to the painful procedure and persuaded the other
men of his tribe to follow his example so that they too might
be eligible to marry the daughters of Israel.

With the men weakened by their recent circumcisions,
Jacob's sons descended on the prince's house and recaptured
their sister. They killed all the men and took (the Bible classes
them together) their sheep, oxen, asses, wealth, children, and
wives (who were raped in retaliation for the deflowering of
Dinah).[6] Dinah disappears at this point from the story of the
house of Jacob. We shall never know whether she was in fact
raped, whether she wanted vengeance, or whether she wanted
vengeance to be wreaked upon the women as well as the men
of the house where she had been living. The unwritten law has
never been concerned with the feelings of women—only with
their status as male possessions.

These Biblical events took place long before the codification
of Mosaic law. The rape of Tamar, King David's only legitimate daughter, by her half brother Amnon, occurred long after
unwritten laws became The Law—and, unlike the taking of
Dinah, was unquestionably a rape, and a violation, as well, of
the more serious ban on incest. Amnon feigned serious illness
in order to coax David into sending his beloved Tamar to cook
for her brother. When Tamar perceived Amnon's real intention
(and his real sickness), she pleaded for time, as any frightened
girl would. Surely, she suggested to her brother, their father
would alter the law to enable them to have each other legitimately. But Amnon was not fooled by this tactic; he overpow-
ered her and raped her.

Then, the Bible records, "Amnon hated her exceedingly; so

that the hatred wherewith he hated her was greater than the love wherewith he had loved her." In disgust, he ordered her to leave the house. Tamar replied with great dignity: "There is no cause: this evil in sending me away is greater than the other that thou didst unto me."[7] These are heartrending passages; Amnon's revulsion deprived Tamar of any conciliatory alternatives that might have mitigated her disgrace. But Amnon left Tamar with no face-saving recourse; her only choice was to reveal her shame and turn to her full brother, Absalom, to avenge her honor.

And Absalom did avenge his sister, luring Amnon to his death after two years of pretending that all was forgiven, if not forgotten; he avenged his sister and did away with a rival for the throne in one stroke. There is a curious ambiguity in the Biblical account of King David's response to these events: he is said to be greatly angered but does not himself act against Amnon; he is thought to understand Absalom's reasons for avenging Tamar, yet Absalom feels it prudent to exile himself from court. Of course, the historical David, like most great monarchs, was a complex and cunning man, and letting his heirs fight among themselves, ostensibly over the body of his defiled daughter, was very much his style. One thing is certain: the rape of Tamar was as much an excuse as a catalyst for the events that followed. Like Dinah, the ravaged Tamar disappears from the story as soon as her violation is avenged.

In a historical novel reconstructing this story, Dan Jacobson imagines the subsequent fate of Tamar: "Her pride, her passion for revenge, and even more, her determination to impose her own unalterable order on the disorder that has overwhelmed her, all demand that she show herself, bedraggled and bloody in a torn dress, to the whole city. . . . But the price of it! Not just the hours she is about to go through in the streets of Jerusalem; but of the months and empty years to follow. . . . Does she see her nephews and nieces, and eventually their children too, looking sideways at her . . . at Aunt Tamar, an invaluable help around the houses of others, never her own. . . . Does she understand that she too is the part she is assigning herself?"[8]

Several aspects of the powerful Biblical narrative exemplify the bonds connecting sex, revenge, and the unwritten law which have exerted such a powerful influence on western culture. One of these is the anonymity of women and the absolute reliance on men to defend female honor. When Tamar rends her garments in front of Absalom, he tells her, "Hold now thy peace, my sister: he is thy brother; regard not this thing." The narrator, like his readers, knew that Absalom had no intention of allowing the outrage to go unpunished, but Tamar could not have known that with any certainty (although she might have suspected her brother of guile). Nevertheless, a reconciliation might have been achieved by the two brothers; an agreement to let bygones be bygones is not unknown when powerful men have their own interests to protect. In the event of such a reconciliation, Tamar would have been the only one punished as a result of the rape.

The most important social realities reflected in this story are the tangled relationships between written and unwritten law where matters of sex and family are concerned; the ways in which unwritten law is incorporated, by intent as well as unconscious assumption, into written law; and the ease with which unwritten law can undo the prescriptions and proscriptions of written law. Mosaic law is broken every which way in this narrative—not only by Amnon's rape of his sister but also by David's failure to pass judgment and by Absalom's taking the duty of revenge upon himself. More than twenty-seven hundred years before the introduction of psychiatry into the criminal-justice system, the tendency to view acts of sexual violence and sexual revenge from a psychological or emotional rather than a criminal perspective was already well established. The Israelites were far ahead of neighboring tribes in their devotion to written law, but they too were unable to deal with crimes of passion—especially when the *dramatis personae* were all in the family—as they dealt with other crimes.

The rationalism of written law is frequently disregarded in determining penalties for sex crimes because the acts are not *ipso facto* vile but become so by virtue of motive or of the relationship between the participants. A killing is always a disaster, even though it may not be a murder. But sexual intercourse is not ordinarily a disaster (not, at any rate, the sort of disaster with which law is concerned) unless it is the result of coercion. The physical process of rape is identical to that of seduction or mutually initiated sex; force alone distinguishes the former from the latter. If physical evidence of coercion is nonexistent, a jury must listen to the participants and decide which of them is telling the truth. It is sometimes difficult for an outsider to draw a line between the vengeful, criminal act of rape and "normal" sex; the vindictive element in everyday relations between the sexes creates considerable confusion for ordinary citizens who are expected to distinguish between what is unlawful and what is merely deplorable. Nevertheless, most of us are capable of separating the erotic twilight zone, with its mingling shadows of love and hate, from the dark world of sexual coercion and revenge. But we are capable of making these distinctions only when the same standards are applied to crimes of the heart as to crimes of the head. The unwritten law has no place in this process.

Because passion so frequently prevails over reason in matters of sex, written law is even more important to the control of sexual revenge than to other forms of vengeance. Even though laws were written entirely by men until the twentieth century—and therefore embodied a male standard of sexual morality and decorum—the codification of law has, over several millennia, worked in favor of women. In its earliest stages, law provided women with greater physical safety than they enjoyed in more primitive cultures. (If there was, as some feminist thinkers contend, a Golden Age of matriarchy before the

Fall, that lost idyll did not provide women with any tools to obtain justice after the Fall.) In its later stages, mainly in the last century, law has offered women the possibility to act rather than be acted upon. Written laws regarding sex—like the earliest laws concerning murder—impose public judgments on what once were considered private acts. What is written by man may someday be rewritten by woman; what is assumed to be dictated by "human nature" or divine edict is much more difficult to change. Nowhere is this distinction more evident than in the tortuous development of laws punishing rape.

Christine de Pizan, writing at the end of the fourteenth and the beginning of the fifteenth centuries, became the first literary woman to take up her pen in defense of rape victims. Drawing on the mixture of pagan myth and Christian allegory that was the *métier* of scholars in her era, she recounted the tribulations of the queen of the Galatians, who was taken hostage during the Roman conquest of her land and raped by a Roman officer.

> He entreated and coaxed her with fine presents, but after he saw that pleading would not work, he violently raped her. The lady suffered terrible sorrow over this outrage and could not stop thinking of a way to avenge herself, biding her time until she saw her chance. When the ransom was brought to deliver her husband and herself, the lady said that the money should be turned over in her presence to the officer who was holding them. She told him to weigh the gold to have a better count, so that he would not be deceived. When she saw that he intended to weigh the ransom and that none of his men would be there, the lady, who had a knife, stabbed him in the neck and killed him. She took his head and without difficulty brought it to her husband and told him the entire story and how she had taken vengeance.[9]

Christine relates this tale with great relish and approval, and she speaks with equal admiration of Roman and Christian women who took their own lives to demonstrate their detestation of rape. Christine, who may well have been the first woman in the western world to earn her living by writing (she was a widely-known lyric poet and official biographer to the French King Charles V), wrote her *Book of the City of Ladies* (*Le Livre de la Cité des Dames,* which appeared in 1405) in direct response to the male epic poems of the age of chivalry, which on the one hand idealized the purity and beauty of women and on the other portrayed them as the seductive, deceitful, and vindictive sex. For Christine, tales of women who killed their rapists or committed suicide to mitigate their disgrace were the logical answers to the male vision of the woman who "was asking for it." The scope of her learning did not extend to law. As a devout Christian writing at the close of the Middle Ages, she would hardly have been aware of the changes in Jewish law providing women with the tentative legal basis to demand retribution for rape. As an artist who was educated in Italy and spent her adult life in France, she would have been equally uninformed about English statutes that gave raped women legal standing before the king's courts—a weapon that would ultimately prove more useful to the victim than a knife turned upon her rapist in rage or herself in shame. Private vengeance is the preferred weapon of those who have no access to public retribution.

In the eleventh and twelfth centuries, talmudists took the first steps toward a Jewish view of rape as an injury to the woman herself rather than as a form of property damage inflicted on her husband or father. The changes in rabbinical interpretation appear, from a modern perspective, as picayune, grudging, even ludicrous modifications of a fundamentally unjust legal concept of women as property; nevertheless, they were genuine advances for Jewish women at the time. Ordinarily, the damages for rape were paid to a virgin's father. The problem that perplexed the rabbis of the Middle Ages was what to do about the rape of an "independent" virgin—one whose father was dead and who was unbetrothed. (The cyclical violence visited upon European Jews during the Crusades must have left a considerable number of fatherless virgins. Rabbinical law was, of course, enforced only when both the assailant and the victim were Jews; the talmudists could do nothing about rapes of Jews by Christians in the name of their God.) Maimonides argued that no virgin—with or without a father—had the right to collect damages for rape, since she did not "own" her body. However, he was overruled by other rabbis; it was one of the few battles lost by this then-dominant figure in Jewish thought.

From the twelfth century onward, the fine for rape was to be paid to the girl herself if she was independent. The standard penalty was fifty shekels, and it was clearly a punitive award, since—unlike other fines—the amount was fixed regardless of whether the girl came from a wealthy or a humble family. A "semi-independent" virgin was one whose father was still alive but who was betrothed (and had not yet celebrated her nuptials). As one Jewish scholar notes, there are opposing traditions concerning the question of whether a semi-independent. virgin is entitled to collect the fine herself. Some wildly progressive rabbis even argued that indemnity for the mental and physical anguish of rape should always be paid to the virgin herself, even if she was totally dependent on her father, but that view did not prevail.[10] The medieval rabbis chose a course between Maimonides' strongly anti-female views and those of talmudists who, far in advance of their time, maintained that a virgin's status in relation to her father or prospective husband should have nothing to do with her right to receive damages from her rapist. (Non-virgins could be raped with virtually no penalty. So could "statutory non-virgins"—a curious classification including all girls over age twelve-and-a-half and even those under twelve-and-a-half whose lives had exposed them to such license that they could not be considered virgins. A slave or a girl who had been kidnaped from her father's house fell into the latter category. A married woman could never demand a fine for rape; retribution might be exacted only by the husband.)

In England, the twelfth and thirteenth centuries greatly

expanded the *theoretical* power of women to demand retribution for rape. As Brownmiller observes, a woman had little chance of bringing a successful suit against her rapist unless she was a propertied virgin or a wife of impeccable reputation. Nevertheless, it is impossible to overestimate the importance of a comprehensive set of laws stating unequivocally that the woman, not her husband or father, was the aggrieved party in a rape. The Statutes of Westminster, enacted between 1275 and 1290, were devised to expand the power of the Crown rather than the rights of women; the latter proved to be an unintended effect of the former. In the overall relationship of law to the containment of revenge, the significance of the rape provisions in the Statutes of Westminster lies in their expansion of public, as opposed to private, settlement of grievances.

In the more limited matter of sexual revenge, two provisions are of particular importance. One is the abolition of the old common-law definition of a married woman's rape as a crime of less intrinsic seriousness than the rape of a virgin; the other is official injunction against absolving the rapist through marriage. In the twelfth century, women were permitted to bring only two kinds of appeals before the courts of the Crown— those concerning the rape of a virgin and the slaying of a husband within his wife's arms. Lesser offenses—like the rape of a married woman—were referred to lower manorial courts. The Statutes of Westminster extended the king's jurisdiction to cover the rape of married women as well as virgins. The prohibition of exoneration through marriage applied only to cases in which a suit had been instituted. A woman might choose to keep silent and marry her rapist without bringing suit and many men have seen this option as yet another form of feminine vengeance. In fact, it seems likely that such marriages were far more common in earlier times, when the punishment for rape was decided not by a court but by the violated woman's father and brothers. (Of course, as the story of Dinah shows, willingness—even eagerness—to marry was not always sufficient to stay the avenging hands of outraged male relatives.)

The absolution of a rapist by marriage is a classic example of the phenomenon denounced by Beccaria—the substitution of private forgiveness for public retribution. The prohibition of this custom by the Statutes of Westminster may have been— and undoubtedly was—widely ignored in the thirteenth century, but the ideal it embodied is of incalculable importance. It asserts that no crime is so private as to be beyond the reach of public justice—a principle that is not fully accepted even today when applied to violence within a family.

The nonacceptance, or nonexistence, of the principle of public retribution can either foster private vengeance or allow those who commit crimes of passion to go unpunished. In the latter event, the victim herself may become the object of another form of assault. In 1966, Franca Viola, the daughter of a tenant farmer, became the first woman in Sicilian history to bring legal charges against an assailant instead of marrying him as custom demanded. Filippo Melodia, a young member of the Mafia, had asked the girl's father for the right to court her, but she subsequently broke off their engagement. Then, in a time-honored technique for overcoming female resistance, the young man drove up to the Viola house with several friends and abducted his former fiancée at gunpoint. Regardless of whether the abductor actually rapes his victim in these circumstances, it is assumed that she will marry him because no other man will want her after she has been "dishonored."

When Viola was found and freed nine days after the kidnaping, she stunned her town by denouncing Melodia to the authorities and taking him to court instead of marrying him. A judge eventually sentenced Melodia to eleven years in prison and his companions in the abduction to four-year terms. However, the young woman and her entire family became the victims of a vendetta. Police were stationed outside the house twenty-four hours a day to accompany her and her relatives whenever they made excursions to town. The family's grape-vines and truck garden—the source of their income—were de-stroyed. In a panel discussion with a group of young people on Italian television, several men said they admired Viola for her courage but would not be willing to marry her.[11] Nevertheless, her gesture was far from ineffectual. Four other women imi-tated her and sent their abductors to prison, and the widely publicized prosecutions led to a substantial decrease in "bride capture" through abduction and rape. (By the mid-1970s, when I spent a month in a small town in the province of Apulia, a number of women told me such cases had occurred many times in the history of their families but that none had taken place since "*la revolta della Franca.*") This case highlights the rela-tionship between sexual vengeance and "the unwritten law." When laws against bride capture by abduction were passed in Italy, it was no doubt asserted that respectable southern Italian families would resist any state interference in their private affairs. Yet the law needed only one woman of courage to extend its influence throughout a region that had honored the primitive custom of bride capture for centuries.

It is a sad, ironic twist of history to hear the unwritten law —a concept that has done so much damage to women for millennia—invoked in defense of women who have, under ad-mittedly serious provocation, taken their own violent revenge. Inez Garcia, testifying in her own defense, admitted she had killed the man who abetted her rape and said she was glad. "I feel anyone who has been raped has the right to kill back," she said, adding that she was sorry she had only killed the man who stood by and watched and had not gotten the actual rapist as well.[12]

It is understandable that such assertions are unsettling to men—and not only to the rapists among them. From my femi-nist perspective, the claim of women's right to violent revenge is, for different reasons, equally disturbing. On the most practical level, the extension of social tolerance to a small number of women who carry out violent acts of sexual vengeance is of little use to the vast majority of women, who are neither physically nor emotionally equipped to select a weapon and pursue their rapists through the darkened streets. In a strictly legal sense, the tendency to place crimes of passion and intimacy outside the law can be turned against women—once again—as easily as it can be used to defend them. In the late 1970s, a few acquittals of battered wives who turned against their husbands and killed them generated enormous publicity; the exoneration of these women represented a reversal of the standards normally applied to wives and mothers. At the same time, other battered wives were being convicted of manslaughter or committed to mental institutions for taking action against their brutal husbands. These cases—being dog-bites-woman rather than woman-bites-dog stories—attracted no attention at all.

Meanwhile, there has been no diminution of the traditional leniency accorded men who commit crimes of passion. Wayne Birch escaped a life sentence because he and his victim had once been romantically involved. Richard Herrin, after hammering Bonnie Garland to death, was convicted of manslaughter rather than murder because the killing took place a day after Bonnie told him she wanted to be free to date other men. John Hinckley's obsession with the actress Jodie Foster certainly played a role in his successful insanity defense. All of the controversy surrounding the Hinckley verdict has focused on the role of psychiatrists in the courtroom; however, the romantic, sexual nature of Hinckley's primary obsession was from the beginning tailor-made for a psychiatric defense. Given the federal stipulation that the burden of proving sanity rests with the prosecution, it is probable that Hinckley would have been acquitted in any event. Nevertheless, it is interesting to speculate on the question of whether a jury would have been as convinced of Hinckley's insanity under the law if his main fantasy had been one of conquering the world instead of proving his love for a teenaged actress. "I don't know why love has to hurt so much," Hinckley declared in several bizarre telephone interviews with newspaper reporters. As a basis for rationalizing violence and revenge, references to "love" and "honor" have served men much more often than they have served women.

In utilitarian and legal terms, the claim of a female right to violent revenge is an ineffectual tool for righting the wrongs of women. In terms of female self-esteem, the assertion is a true disaster. Woman as uncontrolled avenger is the mirror image of woman as a prisoner of man. In both instances, her life is beyond her control.

Sexual revenge—in its most ordinary and most extreme manifestations, on the part of both men and women—is inseparable from established patterns of female dependency and male authority. This is as true when the traditional order is reversed as when it is upheld. When an unusual production of *Medea,* starring Irene Papas and adapted by the Greek director Minos Volanakis, opened in New York in the early 1970s, most male critics were offended by the production's concept of Medea as a seeker, albeit a murderous one, after justice. There were suggestions that Euripides' masterpiece had been distorted by the imposition of a militant perspective. The critics were more comfortable with earlier interpretations of Medea as a madwoman or a misogynist's dream; one dismissed Papas' Medea as "more nearly hausfrau than maddened magician." But Euripides' Medea *is* a rejected housewife; that is the whole point of the play. However unusual she may be, her position in relation to her husband is perfectly ordinary. The only power she has is the power to destroy. In a newspaper interview, Papas compared Medea to Othello; there is more to both characters, she noted, than jealousy and a quest for vengeance. "I don't think Othello is *only* jealous, any more than Medea is. He is married to a white woman. There is a racial and a class basis for this so-called jealousy."[13] Medea is married to a man—and that, she tells the chorus, is cause enough for despair.

Women of Corinth, do not criticize me. . . . The man who was everything to me, well he knows it, has turned out to be the basest of men. Of all creatures that feel and think, we women are the unhappiest species. In the first place, we must pay a great dowry to a husband who will be the first tyrant of our bodies (that's a further aggravation of the evil); and there is another fearful hazard: whether we shall get a good man or a bad. For separations bring disgrace on the woman and it is not possible to renounce one's husband. Then, landed among strange habits and regulations unheard of in her own home, a woman needs second sight to know best how to handle her bedmate. And if we manage this well and have a husband who does not find the yoke . . . too galling, ours is a life to be envied. Otherwise, one is better dead.[14]

Of course, Medeas are few and far between, in art and in life. But the occasional appearance of an openly vengeful woman— like any rebel from a group without access to conventional power—carries enormous symbolic importance. It stimulates fear on the part of those in authority that others will follow the example of the avenger. Men tend to regard a woman who carries out an act of violent revenge as a kind of miner's canary, a warning of the suppressed rage that may lie beneath the surface of the good mother, good daughter, and good wife who uses "second sight to know best how to handle her bedmate." When men who wish to uphold the traditional order come face to face with a woman's vengeance, they have two choices—to punish her severely or to deny the true meaning of her act. Medea is less disturbing as a madwoman than as a victim of injustice; in Euripides' portrait, she is both. A reluctance to confront the social implications of individual pathology in a member of a subjugated class may explain the persistence of the charges of misogyny leveled (almost exclusively by male critics) at Euripides. In literary criticism, the recognition that Euripides may simply have been "advanced" (by more than twenty-two hundred years) in his view of women did not surface until the late nineteenth century.

In the closing decades of the nineteenth century, there was an expanding awareness (on a theoretical if not a practical level) that the full range of human possibilities, for good or evil, might be embodied in either sex. Even in art, this awareness was more readily extended to ancient immortals than contemporary authors. Ibsen was accused of being a misogynist, as well as a libertine and an atheist, for his portraits not only of the madly vindictive Hedda Gabler but of the measured, moderate (in twentieth-century terminology) Nora. As far as upholders of patriarchal order were concerned, Nora might as well have poisoned her children as left them.

The inchoate awareness of the potential range of female aggressiveness, problematic as it was in art, was much more troubling when it surfaced in life. In the United States and England, several trials of female murderers embodied (and fueled) the fears generated by social agitation for change in the status of women. The most famous of these trials—a font of publicity equaled in the history of American crime only by the twentieth-century Leopold-Loeb and Lindbergh kidnap-murder cases—was the brutal slaying of Lizzie Borden's father and stepmother in 1892. Lizzie was acquitted of the hatchet murders, but the verdict has been repudiated in a rhyme chanted by generations of schoolchildren:

> Lizzie Borden took an ax
> And gave her mother forty whacks.
> When she saw what she had done
> She gave her father forty-one.

The Lizzie Borden trial was flamboyantly reported in both the penny dreadfuls and the respectable press of the day; it has since reappeared in countless pulp novels and even in a ballet, *Fall River Legend,* choreographed by Agnes De Mille. The best account of the case, drawing on every available source, appears in a book on female killers by Ann Jones.[15] In retrospect, the evidence pointing to Lizzie Borden's guilt appears overwhelming; both opportunity and motive (had the burghers of Fall River been able to recognize it) were present.

The viciousness of the attacks certainly suggested pathological rage; when people are killed in their customary environment with an instrument kept around the house for other purposes, police generally assume they were murdered not by a stranger but by someone who knew them well enough to be familiar with their domestic habits. (This reasonable, and ordinarily accurate, assumption can hamper criminal investigations into the relatively uncommon murder with all the characteristics of an "intimate" crime that turns out to be the random act of a stranger. For several months, the police misdirected their investigation into the Sharon Tate murders because, even in the twentieth century, the extreme rage that leads a killer to carve up bodies is not, as a rule, directed toward strangers. When a body is hacked to death with a kitchen knife, one looks for a jealous lover or a psychopathic relative rather than a Charles Manson.) So the theory that the Bordens were brutally murdered by a passing stranger flew in the face of a normal police assumption—or what would have been normal, had the notion that a "good daughter" might harbor such anger not been terrifying to the arbiters of Victorian morality. The reason why Lizzie was acquitted, Jones argues, was that the motive—overwhelming hatred of her father—was unthinkable to the judge, the defense lawyer, the jury, even the prosecutor.

Lizzie, who was thirty-two at the time, lived at home (as any Victorian spinster would) and was utterly dependent on her father for financial support. She and her older sister stood to inherit an estate of more than $250,000, but money was discounted as a possible motive because Lizzie had nearly $3,000 in bank accounts in her own name. (Although this was indeed a great deal of money for a woman to have accumulated in 1892, it was certainly not enough to support Lizzie, who neither was educated nor had shown any inclination toward the sort of work that might have been considered suitable for a lady at the turn of the century.) In any event, greed could not account for the particularly brutal nature of the murders. Morally and legally, there is no difference between murder by poison or letter bomb and a murder committed by personally hacking someone to death. Emotionally and psychologically, there is a difference; in the absence of overwhelming personal rage or true psychosis, most people simply cannot endure the spurt of blood and the crunch of bone. That is why the possibility of eradicating millions by pushing a button has such terrifying potential; it is less disturbing to the individual psyche to commit murder by remote control than to do the job in person.

The painful, and potentially infuriating, relationship of a dependent thirty-two-year-old woman to her father was beyond the imagination of the men who judged Lizzie Borden. Lizzie's attorney, John D. Robinson, a former Massachusetts governor, noted that Andrew Borden "was a man that wore nothing in the way of ornament, of jewelry but one ring, and that ring was Lizzie's. It had been put on many years ago when Lizzie was a little girl, and the old man wore it and it lies buried with him in the cemetery. He liked Lizzie, did he not?"[16] As Jones notes, "this evidence that Andrew was fond of Lizzie was construed by both sides to mean that Lizzie was fond of Andrew."[17]

The unthinkable nature of the crime of patricide was underlined by the defense attorney in his summation, which reminded the jurors, "You are out of families, you come from firesides, you are members of households, you have wives and daughters and sisters and you have had mothers." If Lizzie's daughterly devotion was a lie, what horrors might lie beneath the tender, respectful demeanor of anyone's daughter, anyone's wife? Even the prosecutor could not bring himself to suggest that a woman might be capable of premeditated patricide; he offered the hypothesis that Lizzie had only meant to kill her wicked stepmother and had murdered her father in a fit of desperation when he surprised her in the act.

It was indeed true that Lizzie had never gotten along well with her stepmother. Although her father, a widower, had remarried when Lizzie was seven years old, she continued to address her father's wife as "Mrs. Borden" for a quarter century. The premeditated murder of a stepmother was well within the imagination of the town fathers; after all, feminine jealousy of other women is a staple of the folklore of sexual revenge. (The murder of *Mrs.* Borden scarcely figured in the furious controversy surrounding the trial and in the popular accounts of the case for the next fifty years. This omission is consistent with the general tendency to treat crimes less seriously when both the victim and the assailant are members of a relatively powerless social group. There have been many studies showing that lighter sentences are meted out to black criminals whose victims are also black than to blacks who commit crimes against whites; I know of no significant legal research comparing crimes committed by women against other women to female crimes against men.)

We can never know—not, at any rate, with legal certainty —whether Lizzie committed the murders; what is certain is that Victorian assumptions about the nature of womanhood precluded any possibility of a full investigation and a fair trial. Lizzie Borden was a beneficiary of the unwritten law in its broadest sense—a law that, in defense of patriarchal values, occasionally finds it as expedient to deny the criminal rage of a woman as to excuse the criminal vengeance of a violent man. Given the weight of the evidence against her, Lizzie would probably have employed an insanity plea today.

Twentieth-century judges and jurors do not assume the existence of daughterly devotion, but they can be just as uneasy as their nineteenth-century counterparts in the face of openly expressed female violence and revenge. On March 9, 1977, Francine Hughes, a mother of four in a small town in central Michigan, poured gasoline around the bed of her husband and set fire to him as he slept in an alcoholic stupor. She drove away from the house with her children as the bed was engulfed in flames and immediately turned herself in to the police. No woman ever had more reason to kill a man than Francine Hughes did, and her case became a feminist cause célèbre.

The slain man was, in fact, Hughes's former husband, although newspaper accounts generally referred to him as her husband. She had divorced him in 1971 after seven years of marriage, mainly because she found his physical abuse unbearable. But it is understandable that the newspapers described James Hughes as her husband, because she continued to behave like a wife even after the bitter divorce. From her testimony at the trial, it was clear that she remained bound to him emotionally, on some occasions sexually, and always as a target for abuse.

He was living in the same house with his former wife at the time of his death because she had agreed, at his mother's urging, to nurse him back to health after a serious automobile accident. He had made a good enough recovery from his injuries to beat her up repeatedly. Hughes's continuing sense of obligation to a man who had systematically abused her is a striking example of the victimization that some women are bred to accept. It is impossible to imagine a man returning with concern to the bedside of a wife who had subjected him to physical torture. Unlike many battered wives, Francine Hughes had summoned up the courage to divorce her husband, but she was unable to sever the emotional tie.

On the day James Hughes was killed, he had already beaten Francine and forced her to have sexual relations with him; there was nothing unusual about that. He had also made a bonfire in the back yard of her school textbooks. Francine, who had dropped out of high school to marry, was taking business courses at a local community college; she wanted to be able to support her children, get off welfare, and move away from the small community where she had grown up. James had already threatened to kill her if she continued with her business classes.

And so Francine poured the gasoline around the bed and lit it. Her murder trial was held in Lansing, the nearby state capital, where a jury acquitted her on the basis of temporary insanity. After a short period of psychiatric testing, she was declared sane and released from custody. Many feminists were indignant because Hughes's lawyer had chosen the safer plea of temporary insanity in preference to a plea of self-defense. This view is expressed by Ann Jones, who argues that "the notion of the 'preventative strike,' so widely used in international conflicts, seems downright cowardly when applied to a battered woman who sneaks up on a man. Thus, Hughes's attorney, taking no chances, hedged on the self-defense principle so clear to feminists and argued instead, much like the attorneys of the seduced-and-abandoned maidens a century ago, that the woman was temporarily insane."[18]

Of course, this interpretation of self-defense is not at all clear to all feminists—any more than the idea of a preventive nuclear strike is acceptable to those who are not affiliated with the Dr. Strangelove School of International Relations. I believe Francine Hughes was fortunate to have a lawyer who was more interested in obtaining his client's acquittal than in making an ideological point. One can easily imagine a self-defense plea exonerating a woman who picked up a knife or gun to protect herself against a charging two-hundred-pound man—even if he was unarmed—since the male body, by virtue of its superior strength and physical training, is usually weapon enough to overcome an ordinary woman. But it would be extremely difficult for any jury, mindful of the traditional definition of self-defense as a response to imminent deadly force, to acquit a woman who set fire to a sleeping man—however brutal the man may have been in the preceding years or hours. Some lawyers and judges have argued that the traditional boundaries of self-defense should be broadened to recognize the special condition of a woman who has been terrorized by a man for years. But where does the broadening process stop? Inez Garcia, who was acquitted at her second trial after an initial conviction was overturned, killed an accomplice to her rape twenty minutes after her assailants had left the house. Would a self-defense plea have been recognized if she had "only" been beaten rather than raped? Would it have been accepted if she had killed the man the following day? The following week?

And if the law is to allow ex post facto killings in self-defense, why not broaden the definition of justifiable homicide? In 1980, Marianne Bachmeier walked into a courtroom in West Germany and fired seven bullets into the body of a man who was about to be tried for the rape-murder of her seven-year-old daughter. The killing was not motivated by sexual revenge in the narrow sense, but it does fall into the broad, special category of crimes in which intimate emotional bonds play a vital role. Bachmeier's act, like Francine Hughes's, is understandable. The prosecutor, undoubtedly aware that many people fully approved of what Bachmeier had done, reduced the original charge of murder to manslaughter. She was sentenced to six years in prison and is likely to be paroled long before she has served out her full time. Her lawyer, like Richard Herrin's, argued that she acted under extreme emotional stress. She might even have been acquitted had the judge who was to have presided over the trial of her daughter's killer not testified that he overheard her saying, "I wanted to shoot him in the face but I only got him in the back. I hope he's dead." To find such acts understandable, however, is not to find them acceptable in a civilized society. Both Hughes and Bachmeier were clearly animated by a thirst for "wild justice." Is it possible to exonerate those who take such action, without threatening the fragile barriers against uncontrolled revenge that were erected millennia ago in Greece and the Sinai Desert?

Insanity pleas and their variants (reduced charges on grounds of extreme emotional stress, for instance) raise a problem different from self-defense pleas. By obfuscating the motives and questioning the rationality of one who commits an act of revenge, they deny the avenger his or her dignity in exchange for freedom. Francine Hughes's killing of her ex-husband seems to me a demonstrably saner act than her long-term acceptance of his violent abuse—unless one accepts the assumption that all revenge is "sick." But who would wish to admit this in a world in which former concentration-camp survivors are unwilling to acknowledge any desire for retribution even in the controlled setting of a courtroom? At the Hughes trial, many observers (and some of the jurors) saw the killing not as an example of self-defense but of justifiable revenge, and they were happy to be let off the hook by the temporary-insanity defense.

The insanity defense enabled the jurors to avoid meting out more punishment to a woman they clearly felt had already been punished enough by life. This use of the insanity plea (temporary insanity in particular) is not, of course, restricted to cases with a revenge motif: it is expedient whenever the punishment demanded by the letter of the law seems to exceed retribution that is consistent with common sense and compassion. In recent years, juries have been grateful for the temporary-insanity loophole when they have been called upon to decide the fate of those who have performed "mercy killings" of terminally ill relatives. On the one hand, these loopholes attest to the flexibility of the jury system and of common-law tradition. On the other, they enable society to avoid facing up to disturbing moral and legal issues.

Perhaps new laws should be written to cover the cases of terminally ill patients who beg their relatives to let them—even to help them—die. But the debate over such laws would be profoundly unsettling; it is easier to declare a mercy killer temporarily insane. In similar fashion, it would be equally disturbing to pass a law stating that a woman has a right to kill a man who has raped her or that a battered wife has a right to kill a sleeping husband if she feels she can escape him in no other way.

After the verdict acquitting Francine Hughes, the victim's brother said, "I think this decision will give a lot of violent women an excuse to go out and commit violent acts . . . to take their revenge." That is unlikely; the social conditioning of women militates against violence, and the Hughes case attracted enormous attention precisely because it was so unusual. What the insanity defense does accomplish in such cases is the continuation of a long tradition of treating crimes of sexual passion and revenge differently from other crimes. In the past, this tradition worked more in favor of men than of women; today, it is used to blur the accountability of defendants of both sexes.

This point is illustrated by both the defense and prosecution summations in the trial of Richard Herrin for the murder of Bonnie Garland. The college love affair between Richard and Bonnie—and the way in which the twenty-year-old Bonnie had wavered in her feelings for Richard—were the keystone of the defense's contention that the young man was "not himself" when he killed his girlfriend with a claw hammer. After a summer abroad—a summer in which she never wrote him a postcard—Bonnie finally told Richard in a letter that she wanted to go out with other men. Uninvited, he traveled across the country to confront her directly in her own home; she reiterated what she had already said in the letter. Then—much was made of this by the defense—Bonnie held out her arms to him and they made love. This was supposed to explain Richard's disorientation the following night, when he crept up the stairs with the hammer and bludgeoned Bonnie to death as she lay sleeping. (He had been repeatedly asked to leave both by Bonnie and her mother.)

What a familiar ring this story has (until the murder) to anyone who has ever been through a breakup in which one person wanted to continue the relationship and the other wanted to end it! How many times do adults inadvisedly fall back into bed with a spouse or lover they are trying to leave!

The defense lawyer never painted Bonnie as the villain of the piece—that would have backfired, given the fact that she was the one who died—but the implication that she bore some of the responsibility for her own death was unmistakable. Jack Litman, a skilled defense lawyer, characterized the situation in this way:

> And Bonnie, clearly unintentionally—but nonetheless—is sort of dangling. She doesn't realize how precarious he [Richard] is at this time, because he doesn't express—he is just so overwhelmed with happiness, being in her presence. He cannot express his anger to her, because he is afraid of losing her.
>
> Yet, on July the 6th, as firm as ever, she tells him, "No. You know what I said yesterday, is the way it is going to be. You'll be one of the fellows." And he can't believe it, especially after what happened the night before. . . .
>
> Ladies and gentlemen, it is hard to say with specificity, obviously and exactly what is going on exactly in his overwrought mind at the time, of feelings of abandonment and the loss of self. Even as he consciously tried to agree with Bonnie's position, and had hopes for the next day. But, you know that his psyche did respond by pushing this thought, this inhumane thought into consciousness, a thought he could not and did not debate, a thought whose command he had to carry out. If he wasn't crazy, ladies and gentlemen, consciously, how can you not experience that terrible flood of emotions that are overwhelming you and directing you to kill, and to kill the person you love more than anyone in the whole world?[19]

The prosecutor, William Fredreck, saw matters in a different light, and he naturally kept reminding the jury that what the defense lawyer called "this inhumane thought" was a murder.

> Let me make myself perfectly clear. I'm not contending that this Defendant was rational when he killed Bonnie. Rational people don't kill. Or that he was normal. Our Penal Law

doesn't outlaw rational acts. It only outlaws the irrational acts. . . .

I told you at the outset, ladies and gentlemen, in my opening statement, that there would be a smoke screen put up before you. Was I ever right? Look, what is in issue here is the early morning hours of July 7th, 1977, and not the fact that Bonnie loved Richard Herrin at one point, that she sent him letters from Central America, that she called him from Panama.

"You can't deny the depth of their love," says Mr. Litman. Well, that is true. It is true as long as it was going the way the Defendant wanted it to go. But he showed his love in July of 1977, when a young girl 20 years of age, whom he loved, wanted to see other people. Then that love changed to possessiveness, revenge and vengeance.[20]

The jury ultimately found the defense's arguments more convincing than the prosecution's and convicted Herrin not of murder but of the lighter charge of manslaughter mitigated by extreme emotional disturbance. This verdict is partly attributable to the technical peculiarities of New York law (just as the Hinckley verdict rests on the federal ruling requiring the prosecution to prove sanity). However, the verdict in the Herrin case also flows from confusion between the less-than-admirable conduct (including vindictiveness) that many people display in their private love affairs and the criminal expressions of sexual vengeance that turn a private tragedy into a matter for public adjudication. It is this confusion—not the use of psychiatry in the courtroom—that is primarily responsible for the erratic response of public institutions in dealing with acts of sexual revenge. "Crimes of passion seem particularly tragic," Willard Gaylin notes in his insightful study of the Bonnie Garland murder, "because one always recognizes the ambivalence in them, the complexity of motive deriving from the unique relationship between the killer and the victim. A street thug and a paid killer are professionals—beasts of prey, if you will, who have disassociated themselves from the rest of humanity and can now see human beings in the same way that trout fishermen see trout."[21] This is an accurate description of the popularly accepted distinction between the cold-blooded killer and the man or woman who murders out of a combination of frustrated love and rage. However, it is unsettling to reflect upon the fact that, in the popular mind, one disassociates oneself from humanity by killing for money but not by killing for love. Or what passes for love.

Just as there has never been a shortage of psychological rationalizations for crimes of sexual vengeance, there has also been a plethora of physiological, or quasi-physiological, explanations. In 1906, Harry K. Thaw, a millionaire's son who lit his cigarettes with five-dollar bills, walked into a theatre and shot the famous architect Stanford White through the head in what would seem to be one of the clearest murders of sexual revenge on record. Thaw was married to Evelyn Nesbit, a beautiful chorus girl who he claimed had been seduced by White with drugged champagne. His lawyers argued that their client was a victim of "dementia Americana" and had shot White "in a brainstorm."

A new instance of a physiological rationalization for crimes of passion applies only to women, and involves "premenstrual syndrome" (PMS). The first two cases of PMS defense occurred in England. On November 10, 1981, a London barmaid named Sandie Smith was placed on probation after threatening a police officer with a knife. Smith, who had a long criminal record, was said by her attorney to have been transformed each month into a "raging animal." The following day, twenty-seven-year-old Christine English of Norwich, who had been charged with killing her lover by running him down with a car, was conditionally discharged by the court after she pleaded guilty to manslaughter. She, too, claimed to have suffered from an aggravated form of PMS. Premenstrual tension was considered a

mitigating circumstance justifying the reduction of the charge
to manslaughter, much as extreme emotional distress was considered a mitigating factor in the trial of Richard Herrin. Soon
afterward, the premenstrual defense crossed the Atlantic and
was employed by a lawyer defending a mother accused of beating her child in Brooklyn. (This line of defense was eventually
abandoned, partly because Brooklyn's outspoken District Attorney Elizabeth Holtzman made it clear that she regarded the
PMS defense as legally worthless. Holtzman is one of many
feminists who have lined up against PMS as a defense, but there
are many women on the other side of the issue.)

There is little question that PMS, once thought by male
doctors to be "all in the mind," is a physiological reality for
some women—just as there is no question that Richard Herrin
and John Hinckley are severely disturbed young men by any
standard. But the admission of mental and physical departures
from the norm does not answer the question of whether such
deviations render men and women unaccountable for criminal
acts.

Women have long suffered from accusations that their
monthly menstrual cycle makes them prone to overly emotional, rash judgments and therefore renders them unfit for
command, public office, or any other form of "man's work." In
1970, Dr. Edgar Berman, a member of the Democratic Party's
Committee on National Priorities, was widely ridiculed as a
quack for claiming that women are unfit for office because of
"raging hormonal imbalances." Having dismissed such claims
when they were used to justify discrimination against women
in education and employment, feminists can hardly be comfortable with a legal defense of a woman based on the argument that
her menstrual cycle turns her into a "raging animal" once a
month.

Moreover, one wonders why, if these female hormones are
so irresistible, the overwhelming majority of violent crimes are
committed by men. In fact, a physiological argument that

sounds remarkably like the PMS defense was used for many years to excuse the conduct of rapists. Male hormones and the male sex drive, the argument went, are so strong that society (and women) must make allowances for the effects on men of a constantly high level of sexual frustration. (Once again, there is a relationship between the use of this argument in a criminal context and its employment in ordinary male-female relations. Teenaged boy to a girl in the back seat of a car: "Do you know that a guy gets sick, *actually sick,* if you go this far and then say no? Do you know it actually *hurts?*") The physiological defense of rapists has fallen on hard times as modern criminological research, bolstered by the feminist analysis of rape, has suggested that rape is a crime motivated more by the need for power than by physical passion.

On the other hand, there probably are a few female—and male—criminals who are driven to their acts by physiological, or hormonal, syndromes over which they have no control. Should the hypothetical woman who does turn into a beast during her menstrual cycle be deprived of a legitimate defense simply because the argument might conceivably be extended to restrict women in other areas of life? And why should feminists be afraid that the argument will be extended to women as a group? After all, the romantic and sexual fantasies, coupled with violent aggression, of a Herrin or a Hinckley are not considered typical of men as a group. But the aggression of male criminals—rapists included—has never been linked with a routine, identifiable physical phenomenon that also manifests itself in normal men. A defense based on the menstrual cycle, which has been a source of negative attitudes toward women in so many cultures, cannot fail to have substantial implications for women as a class. The physiological symptoms of PMS—extreme muscle tension, depression, backaches, insomnia, severe headaches—are now well documented in medical literature, although researchers disagree on the cause. But a leap of faith —not science—is required to draw the conclusion that this

syndrome explains and excuses criminal behavior. In this respect, the PMS defense is anything but new; it is part of the
ongoing dispute over the nature of personal responsibility, retribution, and justice in our society. Moreover, it also belongs
squarely within the tradition of special pleading for defendants
who have been accused of crimes of passion. PMS has been
raised as a defense only when women have attacked their boy-
friends, husbands, or children. It is doubtful that any lawyer
would dare to make such an argument on behalf of a woman
accused of embezzling or bank robbery during the week before
her period. But, then, embezzling and bank robbery are regarded as cold-blooded crimes.

There is a curious, double-edged relationship between sexual vindictiveness and the law. When the issue is not a criminal
act but a human tragedy, the law frequently intensifies hunger
for revenge. The role of the adversary system in divorce and
child-custody cases exemplifies the process by which natural
and statutory vindictiveness feed upon each other. The fixing of
blame, which lies at the heart of the criminal-justice system, has
no place in conflicts that are violations of private rather than
public peace. Adultery, jealousy, emotional indifference—all
may be private sins, but none is a public crime, in the sense that
"crime" is generally understood today. And yet the law continues, however indirectly, to punish many of these sins as if they
were crimes.

At the same time, the law continues to treat genuine public
crimes as private disasters, simply because they take place
within a sexual and/or familial context. The sexual molestation
of children, for example, is generally regarded as a clear-cut
penal offense when the adult molester and the child are strangers, but a father who persuades or forces his ten-year-old
daughter into sexual intimacies is treated in quite a different
way. The "situation"—if it is brought to light—is frequently
thought to require the services of a therapist rather than a
law-enforcement officer. Pedophilia, whether directed at one's

own children or strangers, is certainly a sickness, but it is also, when acted upon, a legal offense. Even if it can be successfully treated in a family context—and medical treatment, unlike criminal law, does not involve the placement of blame—one wonders whether the elimination of accountability and punishment serves the victim as well as it serves the offender. The unwritten law regarding sexual passion and revenge is intertwined with issues of a complexity and variety undreamed-of in the days of frontier justice, but two issues recur in every era.

One is a purely legal question: ought people who are bound together, either by formal family ties or by the informal but emotionally binding ties of passion and intimacy, be allowed to take revenge upon each other in ways that would ordinarily be forbidden by law? The second question involves larger moral and social as well as legal implications: to what extent should the obsessed be held responsible for the consequences of their obsessions?

In 1859, Elizabeth Packard, the wife of a Presbyterian minister in a small Illinois town, was committed to a mental institution by her husband because she had dared to disagree with his strict adherence to the Calvinist theory of predestination. The Reverend Theophilus Packard became enraged when his wife not only challenged his opinions but aired her views while she was teaching a Sunday-school class—in *his* church. The good reverend found a swift remedy in Illinois state law, which allowed husbands to commit their wives (and infants) to insane asylums without the formal hearing required in all other cases of commitment. (This statute is, of course, a textbook example of the way in which unwritten assumptions about male authority were translated into written law.) Never before, the minister declared, "had Elizabeth persistently resisted his will or wishes —a few kind words and a little coaxing would always set her right; but now she seems strangely determined to have her own way, and it must be she is insane."[22]

The redoubtable Mrs. Packard survived four years in the

asylum and managed to obtain her release with the help of her son, who was able to take legal steps on her behalf when he reached the age of twenty-one. (One wonders what her fate would have been had she been unfortunate enough to have only a daughter on her side.) After extricating herself from her husband's psychiatric vengeance, Mrs. Packard wrote a remarkable book about her experiences as a mental patient (proving, like so many articulate dissenters before and after her, that writing well can be the best revenge).

Conditions for patients (or, as Mrs. Packard put it, prisoners) in the mental institutions run by the State of Illinois in the early 1860s do not seem to have been substantially worse—or better—than conditions in public institutions today. In place of the modern pharmacopoeia for tranquilizing the inmate population, there was laudanum. There was, of course, no Freudian psychoanalytic framework, but there was plenty of "talking therapy." In Mrs. Packard's case, the institution's chief medical officer seems to have been well aware that his patient was perfectly sane. He bent his efforts toward trying to put her in a forgiving frame of mind—in the hope, no doubt, of relieving himself of the responsibility for a recalcitrant patient in full possession of her wits and a vengeful husband not entirely in possession of his. When the Reverend Packard came to visit his wife after a year, she greeted him with a certain lack of enthusiasm. This distressed the doctor, who asked her, "Mrs. Packard, do you think it would be considered natural, for a true woman to meet one who had been a lover and a husband, after one year's separation, even if he had abused her, without one gush of affection?"[23] Mrs. Packard apparently felt that her response —to a husband who had committed his wife to an insane asylum as the result of a theological argument—was indeed natural.

Then the doctor asked her if she could not find it in her heart to forgive her husband, bearing in mind the extreme nature of his "delusions." No, she replied in an answer that would have met with Cesare Beccaria's approval, because "he is to blame for getting into this deluded state. He has resisted known light, and a persistence in his own folly has so blinded him that he cannot see correctly. . . . Like a drunkard, who unconsciously harms another, is guilty, for he ought not to have gotten into this unconscious state. *The good of society requires that [persons of] folly, as well as rascality, should be responsible for their own actions"* (italics mine).[24]

Mrs. Packard, a true Victorian in the firmness of her moral convictions, if not in her attitude toward feminine subservience ("It shall be said of me," she predicted, " 'She hath done what she could.' "), held a straightforward view of personal responsibility. Forgiveness, in her opinion, was for those who repented and amended their ways, not for those who persisted in imposing their destructive delusions on others. Her concept of the proper balance between retribution and forgiveness was rooted in the religious and legal traditions of the preceding 2,500 years. Her doctor, in contrast, was a premature advocate of the therapeutic sensibility.

After her release from the insane asylum, Elizabeth Packard launched a national campaign to repeal laws that allowed husbands to commit their wives at will. In 1865, the Illinois legislature passed a law requiring evidence of insanity in all commitments; two years later, an investigating committee (spurred by the tireless Mrs. Packard) found that 148 married women had been committed without evidence in spite of the new law. In 1867, the legislature passed a "personal liberty bill" which set criminal penalties for husbands who violated the law.

The relationship between ordinary sexual vindictiveness and revenge that would be a crime unless exacted in the name of love or family is exemplified by the Packard case. The Reverend Packard had a perfectly ordinary dispute with his wife. He was used to having her agree with him; when she disagreed— and on a theological point of considerable importance to him —he took the extraordinary step of packing her off to a mental institution. Although perfectly legal at that point in the nineteenth century, the commitment was a calculated act of sexual vindictiveness; it would have been illegal if the Packards had not been husband and wife.

Reason is a particularly fragile barrier against vengeance when the latter is motivated by familial or erotic passion. Vindictive impulses between husband and wife, parent and child, lover and lover are truly beyond the law, but many vindictive acts are not—or ought not to be. Legislation cannot produce morality, kindness, decency, love, or the slightest measure of empathy—but it can promote restraint. Law is most necessary where inner restraints are most likely to fail. Within the context of intimacy gone wrong—when sexual desire and protectiveness are transmuted into rage and possessiveness—internal controls are at their weakest.

No law, it is frequently argued, can ever deter an individual man or woman from committing a crime of passion and sexual revenge: the brutal husband will continue to beat his wife; the battered woman will wait for the moment when she can avenge herself upon a violent man; Othello will murder Desdemona; Medea will slaughter her children. But this argument ignores the extent to which individual actions are influenced by social expectations; the popular and legal distinction between acts of sexual violence and revenge committed within a family and the same acts committed within a more impersonal context cannot fail to affect the frequency of such incidents. One can neither prove nor disprove the hypothesis that fewer men would beat their wives if husbands were hauled off to prison with some regularity for the offense, because retribution is almost never imposed on men who assault "their" women. But the absence of such retribution conveys an unmistakable social judgment— a judgment that a man may, by virtue of his intimate relationship with a woman, inflict violence that would be punished if it were directed toward anyone else. And the corollary to the treatment of sexual violence by the powerful as a "special case" is the responsive vengeance that may be elicited in the weak.

Public safety demands abandonment of the special status that custom and law have long accorded acts of sexual vengeance and violence. As human beings, we may sympathize with the rejected lover who, in an agony of disappointment, kills the object of his or her frustrated passion; with the mother or father who, having been beaten as a child, abuses his or her own child in turn; with the rape victim who stalks her attacker in the night. As citizens, we cannot afford to exempt these acts from the normal process of crime and punishment. Bonnie Garland may well have been a fickle, indecisive young woman (adjectives that might be applied to most twenty-year-olds of either sex); Dr. Tarnower, a sixty-eight-year-old bachelor who tormented his middle-aged mistress with the knowledge that he also had a younger lover, may well have been an emotional sadist in his relations with women. But law must concern itself not with the failings of the victim but with the actions of the killer.

We can understand the emotions of a distraught lover as we cannot understand the emotions of a thug who kills a man for the five dollars in his wallet, but that identification should not be allowed to obscure the fact that the result is the same in both cases: an innocent victim is dead. In an emotional or psychoanalytic sense, true innocence is nonexistent, but victims are innocent under the law unless they are attacked while in the act of attacking another. Psychological or emotional rationalizations should carry no more weight in cases of sexual violence than in cases of bank robbery or drunken driving. Like Mrs. Packard, I am certain that men and women should be held accountable for acts of folly as well as rascality.

Even in the absence of blood or emotional ties, sex crimes have always been subject to a special standard. In the 1970s, the women's movement placed a high priority on changes in existing rape laws. For centuries, a paradox had characterized the legal treatment of rape: the theoretical penalties for rape were much more severe than for other forms of violent assault, but the practical rate of conviction was extraordinarily low. In the United States and Europe, the death penalty for rape survived well into the twentieth century. (In the early 1970s, several southern states still specified death for rape. Life sentences for certain kinds of rape are still on the books in many states, while nonsexual assaults of equal violence draw shorter sentences.) But the rules of evidence were so strict, and the victims' testimony so suspect, that few rape convictions were obtained at all. The two most common requirements were corroboration of the victim's account by another witness—a difficult standard to meet, since most rapists do not carry out their acts in view of independent third parties—and physical evidence of resistance, such as cuts, bruises, or tears in the vagina.

Susan Brownmiller, writing in 1975, outlined a feminist position that would remove the "special case" status from rape.

> When rape is placed where it truly belongs, within the context of modern criminal violence and not within the purview of ancient masculine codes, the crime retains its unique dimensions, falling midway between robbery and assault. It is, in one act, both a blow to the body and a blow to the mind, and a "taking" of sex through the use or threat of force. Yet the difference between rape and an assault or a robbery are as distinctive as the obvious similarities. In a prosecutable case of assault, bodily damages to the victim are clearly evident. In a case of rape, the threat of force does not secure a tangible commodity as we understand the term, although sex traditionally has been viewed by men as "the female treasure"; more precisely, in rape the threat of force obtains a highly valued sexual service through temporary access to the victim's intimate parts, and the intent is not merely to "take," but to humiliate and degrade.[25]

Rape, in this view, is neither the worst crime imaginable—the taking of "the jewel that is dearer than life"—nor a subject for trivialization of the "when rape is inevitable, relax and enjoy it" variety. This approach demands that society "must normalize the penalties for such an offense and bring them in line more realistically with the penalties for aggravated assault, the crime to which a sexual assault is most closely related."[26] In other words, men will not be hanged for rape—but neither will they go free.

During the past ten years, many rape laws have been brought into line with the laws governing other forms of assault. The two most common changes, in the United States and Europe, have been abandonment of the corroborating-witness requirement and of the demand that a woman supply physical evidence of her resistance. Feminists have argued, for the most part successfully, that women should no more be expected to jeopardize their physical safety by resisting rapists than bank tellers should be expected to produce blood or bullet holes as evidence that they resisted a bank robber. However, the special attitude toward sexual violence and revenge has a tenacious hold on the law as well as the popular imagination. In New York, the law was changed so that rape victims no longer had to produce physical evidence of resistance, but they still had to swear that they failed to resist because they were afraid for their lives. The issue was reopened in 1982 when a rape prosecution was dropped because the victim knew her rapist and was not prepared to swear that she was afraid he would kill her if she did not comply. Since many rape victims do know their attackers, this is a critical issue. Why should a woman have to justify nonresistance by saying she was afraid of death? Isn't it enough to be afraid of being hurt during the rape? Or to be afraid, period?

It ought not to be necessary to stress that public regulation of sexual revenge should extend equal protection to, and demand equal accountability from, both sexes. Centuries of rationalizing male vengeance have, however, bred entirely pre-dictable modern rationalizations for female vengeance. I believe it is outrageous to extend the definition of self-defense to exon-erate a woman who kills a rapist a half hour, or a day, or a week after he leaves her house—just as I believe it is, and always has been, outrageous to suggest that women "ask for it." Insistence on a gender-blind attitude toward sexual revenge should not be construed to imply acceptance of the nonsensical charge of "reverse discrimination," sometimes used to describe recent changes in laws concerning rape and wife beating. I feel obliged to point out, once again, that women are generally the victims rather than the instigators of sexual violence.

The special position of sexual revenge in law is merely an outgrowth of the mythicization of erotic violence that has al-ways played, and continues to play, such an important role in our culture. Sexual vengeance and violence (and I believe the latter is almost always motivated by the former) become sym-bols for atavistic notions of, on the one hand, civilized honor and, on the other, release from the normal constraints of civili-zation. Thus, the horrifying rape scene in the Stanley Kubrick movie *A Clockwork Orange* (based on the Anthony Burgess novel) was eulogized by one critic as an appeal "to something dark and primal in all of us. He [the hero] acts out our desire for instant sexual gratification, for the release of our angers and repressed instincts for revenge, our need for adventure and excitement."[27]

Not surprisingly, the myth machine is beginning to let women in on the fun of releasing *their* repressed instincts for revenge. Perhaps the most widely known recent contribution to the genre was created by a man, in the book-within-a-book rape scene of John Irving's *The World According to Garp.* A woman kills a rapist just as he reaches orgasm—in fact, his orgasm helps her achieve her goal. (Remember, this is a male fantasy.)

He was trying to push himself up off her, but his lower half was locked into the long-sought rhythm; his hips shuddered in little spasms he couldn't seem to control, while his chest rose up, off her chest, and his hands shoved hard against her shoulders. . . .

Then she scissored his pale ass. He could not stop pumping down there, though his brain must have known then there was suddenly another priority. "My knife?" he said. And she reached over his shoulder and (faster than she herself could see it happen) she slid the slim-edged blade of the knife across his throat. For a second, she saw no wound. She only knew that he was choking her. Then one of his hands left her throat and went to find his own. He hid from her the gash she'd expected to see. But at last she saw the dark blood springing between his tight fingers. . . .

She stabbed the long blade into him, just above his waist, thinking that perhaps a kidney was there, because the blade went in so easily, and out again. Oren Rath laid his cheek against her cheek like a child. He'd have screamed then, of course, but her first slash had cut neatly through his windpipe and his vocal cords.[28]

There is more. The lady is extricated from the bloody mess by a sympathetic police superintendent who is thrilled by the sight of blood and the rapist's severed internal organs because his own wife was raped and murdered in a laundromat. ("Her arms were in the dryer with her head, so she was helpless. Her feet couldn't even reach the floor. The spring door made her jounce up and down under all three of them.") This is a classic man's fantasy about woman's revenge, in the guise of sympathetic understanding of the true horror of rape. The only man in the novel who *truly* knows what rape means to a woman is the policeman, who was unaware that his own wife was being violated as he sat in a car and waited for her to emerge from the laundromat with the wash. The woman explains that she used the knife on her rapist because he was planning to use it on her. It doesn't matter, the police superintendent tells her: *"He meant that she should have killed him anyway—even if he hadn't been planning to kill her. To Arden Bensenhaver, there was no crime as serious as rape—not even murder, except perhaps the murder of a child."*

For both men and women, the unwritten law dies hard. And the revenge exacted in its name, however glorified in myth, is seldom sweet.

VII   Life for Life

We've turned the other cheek too long.
>   Pro-death-penalty political commercial, 1982

When all is said and done, a murder is
a murder. And we mortals have a duty
to take up arms against all monsters. Who
maintains that monsters are immortal? God
in secret—lest we pridefully assume
ourselves to be distinct from those we've vanquished—
subtracts all recompense at a remove
from the exultant mob. And bids us hold
our tongues. And so we fade away.
>   JOSEPH BRODSKY, "To Lycomedes on Scyros"

Let us dispense with the platitude that some punishments are
worse than death. For a human being with a reasonably sound
mind and body, there is no fate worse than death. Were this not
so, the fierce centuries-old debate over the social utility and
ethical propriety of the death penalty would have focused on
some other form of legalized revenge. In our bones and our
souls, we all know that death is the ultimate vengeance—
whether it is inflicted in violation of the laws of society or by
society itself in the name of law. That is why all of the moral,
legal, and emotional issues concerning the relationship between
justice and revenge are writ large in the controversy over capital
punishment—a practice that is, as its proponents constantly
remind us, as old as civilization. Why these ancient origins

should be advanced as a persuasive rationalization for continuing the practice today is something of a mystery.

To suggest, as some advocates of the death penalty have in recent years, that incarceration is a harsher punishment than execution is to obfuscate the issue with the murky sentimentality of upstanding citizens who have never caught sight of a gallows (or, to keep the image up-to-date, a hypodermic needle loaded with lethal chemicals—dubbed "the ultimate high" by prisoners on Death Row after the first American execution by injection in 1982). It is true that some convicted killers, like the late Gary Gilmore, have expressed a preference for death over imprisonment—but that preference is surely one more indicator of their alienation from customary human feeling. It has always seemed to me that the ability to commit murder requires, among other qualities, a lack of imagination. Most of us can imagine all too vividly what it might feel like to have our bodies invaded by a bullet or a blade, and this empathetic identification—as much as fear of discovery and punishment—prevents normal men and women from acting on the urge to kill a fellow creature. In any event, the preferences of those who do commit murder ought not to determine society's standards of retribution. The desires of a Gary Gilmore are as irrelevant to the punishment he should receive as is the more understandable desire of another killer for a five-year prison term instead of a life sentence.

I do not share the view of those jurists and philosophers who regard deterrence as the only legitimate end of legal penalties, nor do I agree with Lord Byron that punishment is necessarily immoral if its purpose is to take revenge upon rather than to correct the offender.* As I have already stated, I believe there

---

*See excerpts from Byron's journal in the autumn of 1821, reprinted in *Lord Byron: Selected Letters and Journals,* edited by Leslie A. Marchand (Cambridge, 1982), p. 278. In this passage, Byron advanced a skeptical view of the Christian doctrine of the resurrection of the body. His somewhat idiosyncratic explanation was that the only possible reason for corporal resurrection would be to inflict eternal tortures on the damned, and this would be nothing more than an act of revenge. That, of course, is

is a legitimate place for retribution—regardless of whether it deters the offender or anyone else from committing future crimes—in a scheme of social justice. The term "legalized revenge" does not, as far as I am concerned, have the same demonic ring as "infanticide," "human sacrifice," or "slavery."

But it does not follow that every form of revenge is wise—or even tolerable—because some forms are. The death penalty is not merely legalized vengeance but vengeance taken to its extremity. As a public issue, it raises the same question as extreme vindictiveness does in private life: at what point does revenge, legal or otherwise, deform and consume its agent along with its intended object? Capital punishment is an ancient practice that—unlike, say, human sacrifice—has thus far resisted attempts to relegate it to anthropology textbooks. Abolished in some civilized nations and retained in others, the death penalty is anything but a closed chapter in history; it is everywhere regarded as a legitimate subject of debate, an issue over which reasonable men and women may differ. Those who would abolish capital punishment do their cause a disservice by suggesting that the survival of the public executioner is simply one more manifestation of the persistent irrationality and bloodthirstiness of the human species. The death penalty is more than an emotional issue (although the struggle between vindictive and compassionate urges certainly plays a significant part in the controversy); it is also a political issue arising from the great tension between liberty and authority.

Those who support the death penalty—and they have generally comprised a majority of the body politic, although the size of the majority fluctuates according to the general climate of cultural opinion—assume that anyone who is opposed to

precisely what the theology of Byron's time intended to promise sinners in hell. Fear of hell might, in the parlance of modern criminologists, be a deterrent, but hell after the Last Judgment could only be pure revenge, given the absence of live sinners to be deterred. Interestingly, Byron envisioned the eternal life of the mind not as damnation but as a reward.

capital punishment must be opposed to all forms of punishment. Walter Berns sums up this point of view in an indictment of those he regards, in modern parlance, as "soft on crime"—a group in which he includes Beccaria and liberal politicians of our own era.

> In fact, the essential difference between the public and the abolitionists is almost never discussed in our time; it has to do with retribution: the public insists on it without using the word and the abolitionists condemn it whenever they mention it.
>
> The abolitionists condemn it because it springs from revenge, they say, and revenge is the ugliest passion in the human soul. They condemn it because it justifies punishment for the sake of punishment alone, and they are opposed to punishment that serves no purpose beyond inflicting pain on its victims. Strictly speaking, they are opposed to punishment. They may, like Beccaria, sometimes speak of life imprisonment as the alternative to executions, but they are not in fact advocates of life imprisonment and will not accept it. . . .
>
> The elimination of capital punishment must be followed by the elimination of all punishment for the sake of punishment alone; only when the law is purged of its punitive spirit can we solve the crime problem.[1]

Although this description does fit some opponents of the death penalty (Karl Menninger, for instance), it scarcely fits all of those who have been in the forefront of what Berns correctly defines as a perennially unpopular cause. One might as well argue that anyone who opposed the practice of disemboweling traitors while still alive—the customary penalty for treason in England until the soft-hearted men of the Enlightenment began to exert a serious influence on public policy—was therefore in favor of allowing spies and murderers to ply their trade without restraint. (This argument was, in fact, made during every public debate over the restriction of torture and mutilation as accompaniments to capital punishment.) There is not the slightest reason to suppose that Beccaria was insincere in advocating life imprisonment as a substitute for the execution of murderers and traitors, especially in view of his support for the imposition of *corporal* punishment (not merely imprisonment) on anyone who committed a crime of violence. To argue that anyone who opposes a particular form of punishment is therefore against all punishment is as ridiculous as it would be to suggest that Berns supports a return to disembowelment of the living because he favors restoration of the death penalty.

To dismiss such distinctions as "hair-splitting," as one capital-punishment advocate did during a recent public debate, is to display a profound insensitivity to the nature of law and legal history. I am against the death penalty, and I am against it not on compassionate grounds but because, in Beccaria's words, "to me it appears absurd that the laws, which are the expression of the public will which detest and punish murder, should themselves commit a murder." I also oppose the death penalty out of self-interest; I am disturbed by the confession of weakness implicit in a society's—my society's—insistence that it can only control its violent members by executing some of them. But I am not opposed to punishment per se; indeed, I believe the renewed popular support for the death penalty in the United States today is largely attributable to the increase in violent crime during the past twenty years and the public perception that the criminal-justice system has failed to impose lesser punishments with any degree of predictability or consistency.

It is certainly true, however, that there are few companions for those of us who believe in the legitimacy of retribution without believing in the ultimate form of legalized revenge. I share Willard Gaylin's view that a sentence with the possibility of parole after eight-and-a-third years is an inadequate penalty for the deliberate killing of a twenty-year-old girl—that such a sentence places too little value on the life of the victim. I am therefore sympathetic to Gaylin's argument that "the state must punish not just because it will do some good for some future other, but simply because the killer of our child deserves to be punished."[2]

But then Gaylin moves from his support of the general principle of retribution to a highly qualified statement of non-opposition to the death penalty—a statement so troubled that it cannot be called an endorsement.

> Practically, I find little in favor of capital punishment. Theoretically, I find little to oppose it. In the past I have been convinced that on a procedural basis it was unjust, although I have never shared most of my [psychiatric] colleagues' feeling that the principle of capital punishment is morally indefensible. In order to protect itself from real or imagined enemies from the outside, the state assigned thousands of innocent young men to certain death in war. I do not see any rationale that allows for this which would not allow the sacrifice of guilty men for reasons of internal security.
>
> If it were done trivially it would be offensive. It ought to be reserved for "capital crimes." If it were done casually, even for so serious a crime, as indeed it has been done in the past, it would be a moral outrage. But if it were deemed necessary for the internal operation of the state—and I am not saying the case has been made—I can find no moral position (short of a total commitment to pacifism) that would support an indictment of this procedure.[3]

This is essentially the same position adopted in the eighteenth century by Voltaire, in contrast to Beccaria's absolutist opposition to the death penalty. Voltaire campaigned against the then-widespread practice of imposing the death penalty for trivial crimes, and against the mutilation and torture that frequently preceded and accompanied state executions, but he was unwilling to say, *Never.* And here I cannot follow Gaylin or Voltaire, for the death penalty is not simply a logical extension of lesser punishments for lesser crimes: it differs from all other forms of retribution not in degree but in kind. Jacques Barzun, writing in defense of capital punishment, once advanced the novel argument that prison sentences are no more "revocable" than death sentences. It is true, of course, that what prison does to a man or woman cannot be undone, but the analogy remains a specious one. Prison may not be revocable, but neither is it inevitably final.

John Locke, in his *Second Treatise of Civil Government,* defined political power as "a right of making laws with penalties of death, and consequently of all less penalties." A state that claims the right to put its citizens to death must certainly assert the right to impose less severe punishments, but the reverse formulation does not necessarily apply; any government may defend its right to impose limited punishments without insisting on the right to exact the ultimate punishment. In view of the intrinsic difference between the death penalty and all other forms of state-imposed retribution, capital punishment would seem to qualify as one of the few political issues that demand an absolutist answer. Where death is concerned, ifs, ands, and buts lose their customary meaning and utility, and both supporters and opponents of capital punishment must be prepared to live with the finality inherent in their positions. Canadian Prime Minister Pierre Trudeau, in a parliamentary debate on a bill to abolish capital punishment in Canada, put the issue clearly:

> It is not open to anyone among us to take refuge in the comforting illusion that we are debating nothing more than an abstract theory of criminal justice, and that it will be the Cabinet's sole responsibility to decide the actual fate of individual murderers, if this bill is defeated. . . .
>
> At this moment, eleven men are being held in Canadian prisons under sentence of death for the murder of policemen or prison officials. Some have exhausted their rights of appeal. Others have not.
>
> Therefore, while it is impossible to pre-judge how the Cabi-

net will treat any individual case when the time comes to decide whether to invoke the royal prerogative of mercy and commute a death sentence to life imprisonment, it is inevitable that the defeat of this bill would eventually place the hangman's noose around some person's neck. To make that quite clear: If this bill is defeated, some people will certainly hang.[4]

And, of course, opponents of the death penalty must live with the fact that their stand would allow certain vicious criminals to go on living without experiencing—at any rate, at the hands of the state—some measure of the ultimate horror they inflicted on others.

I once discussed this issue with a Nazi-concentration-camp survivor who has been a leader in the struggle against capital punishment in the United States. "You'd even let Eichmann live?" I asked, choosing the worst-case possibility—the criminal whose guilt, and the enormity of whose crimes, is beyond question. "Even Eichmann," he answered. "In a way, especially Eichmann. There can be no proportional punishment for a crime of this nature. Since you can't kill anyone more than once, the question then becomes: what does a particular punishment say about the nature of the society that imposes it? But this is not to say that killing Eichmann isn't the worst thing you could do to him *personally*. To suggest otherwise is an evasion of the real issue."

What, precisely, is the issue? What accounts for the periodic revivals of popular support for the death penalty in western societies that have long shrouded the executioner from public view? How is one to explain the apparent fickleness of legislative bodies in abolishing, then restoring, then sometimes reabolishing the death penalty? The frequent swings of public opinion on the question of capital punishment suggest, at the very least, the absence of a moral consensus comparable to the one reached during the nineteenth century on the issue of slavery. In the United States and Europe, legislators who proposed a return to torture and mutilation would be treated as lunatics, but those who propose to restore the ultimate penalty of execution are considered perfectly sane, and their suggestions are sometimes enacted into law.

Clearly, the issue is not the right of society to punish. The American constitutional prohibition of cruel and unusual punishment—a principle embodied in the laws of every developed nation even though it is not always honored in practice—implicitly acknowledges the general right of society to punish. There would be no need to place limits on the types of punishment to be exacted if punishment itself were not considered a legitimate function of government. Many supporters of capital punishment—including American governors who have recently signed death-penalty bills providing for the "humane" practice of execution by lethal injection instead of electrocution —would be horrified by the suggestion that a sentence of death be carried out in such a manner as to cause maximum pain. (In the late nineteenth century, electrocution was regarded as a humanitarian advance over the gallows and the guillotine. Thomas Alva Edison, who was opposed to capital punishment, suggested that his competitor George Westinghouse's alternating current be used: it was more dangerous—therefore quicker and more humane—than Edison's direct current. The term "electrocution" had not yet been coined, and Edison also slyly suggested that the new method of execution be called "Westinghousing"—a word that, had it captured the popular imagination, would surely have presented an advertising problem for the Westinghouse Corporation. (The first man to be electrocuted, one William Kemmler, died on August 6, 1890.)

Sheer anger, rather than an assertion of society's right to punish its most violent members, would seem to be the most powerful psychological force underlying the perennial appeal of the death penalty as a particular form of punishment. For society as a whole, capital punishment is a symbolic issue involving a collective moral judgment that certain acts are so evil, and so dangerous to the public welfare, that the only adequate response to them is death. That is why Prime Minister Trudeau felt obliged to remind his parliamentary colleagues of the real lives at stake.

The outrage that translates into heightened support for capital punishment can be fueled by specific, notorious crimes as well as by general social unrest. After the kidnaped Lindbergh baby was found dead in 1932—an event accompanied by publicity unequaled at that point by any criminal case in American history—the death penalty was instituted for kidnaping in more than half of the forty-eight states. The penalty was generally attached to all cases of kidnaping for ransom and not only to kidnap-murders. (The Leopold-Loeb case, largely as a result of Clarence Darrow's brilliant defense, also received an enormous amount of publicity. However, the murder of the boy Bobby Greenlease did not generate the same widespread public outrage as the murder of the child of an American hero.)

The general, cyclical swings of public opinion in favor of capital punishment have more to do with a climate of fear, violence, and social unrest than with specific crimes, although crimes that seem tailor-made for the ultimate penalty have a way of occurring during such periods of history. There is no question that the resurgence of support for capital punishment in the United States during the past decade—after the issue was mistakenly thought to have been settled by the 1972 Supreme Court decision in the case of *Furman v. Georgia,* which invalidated all capital punishment statutes then in existence—is related to the enormous increase in violent crime since 1960.

In retrospect, the *Furman* decision now appears as the highwater mark of abolitionism in the courts, to be followed by pro-death-penalty decisions and the resumption of executions in the late 1970s. Moreover, it is clear from an examination of public-opinion polls that popular sentiment, which turned against capital punishment in the early 1960s, had begun to swing back toward the death penalty by the time the *Furman* decision was handed down. Indeed, the very successes of the abolitionist movement may have had something to do with this change of heart; people who had never given a moment's thought to the death penalty turned on the evening news to hear that capital punishment had (so it was said) been outlawed. Some of these people undoubtedly reacted in the classic manner of children admonished by parents not to stuff beans up their noses; they became extremely concerned about asserting a "right" they had never cherished in the past.

However, it is incontestable that the rising rate of criminal violence has strongly influenced American opinion on the question of capital punishment. The rate of "index crimes" listed by the Federal Bureau of Investigation (which include murder and non-negligent manslaughter, rape, robbery and burglary, larceny-theft, and motor-vehicle theft) rose by more than 230 percent between 1960 and 1980. Although a certain proportion of this increase can be attributed to changes in crime reporting (rape, for instance, began to be reported by more women in the 1970s as the feminist movement diminished the intense sense of shame felt by rape victims), the general rise in the rate of violent crime is indisputable. One may quarrel about statistics regarding specific crimes but not about the overall trend. Between 1960 and 1976, the number of reported murders in the United States more than doubled—from 9,060 to 18,780.[5] The reasons for the increase in the incidence of crime are complicated, but the emotional results of an increasingly violent environment are straightforward and predictable: fear and anger. This anger is translated into a general feeling that society must "get tough on criminals" and, I believe, into specific support for the death penalty.

The emotional climate that fosters support for capital punishment has been particularly influenced by the increase in the proportion of murders and assaults committed by criminals who are strangers to their victims. The majority of murders are still committed by people who have a previous connection to the victim—whether intimate, as in cases involving spouses and lovers, or situational, as in murders that follow barroom brawls or street fights. However, the percentage of "stranger murders" is rising inexorably—they account for more than a third of all killings in some large cities—and the police are much less likely to catch a man who kills a stranger than one who kills a spouse, lover, or drinking companion. The impact of "stranger murders" on public perceptions of crime is even greater than its real effect on public safety. A man does not feel especially unsafe if he reads about another man who was killed in a barroom argument—not, at any rate, unless he is himself a combative habitué of seedy bars—but he feels profoundly threatened when he reads about someone being shot by a mugger after turning over his wallet. A murder in a barroom brawl is the result of a specific way of life; murder by a mugger could be anyone's fate.

The paradigmatic crime of the late 1960s, and the most widely publicized crime since the Lindbergh case, was the group of "stranger murders" committed by Charles Manson and his followers. As the Lizzie Borden case touched on some of the most important pressure points of the late Victorian era, the Manson murders evoked some of the deepest fears of the late sixties—fears inspired by children in revolt, mind-bending drugs, impersonal sex, and random violence. In 1971, the prosecutor Vincent Bugliosi asked for and received the death sentence from a jury outraged by the accumulated grisly evidence of the Tate-LaBianca murders. He argued that the defendants deserved to die because they were not human—an argument he would not have had to make and indeed would not have dared to make in an earlier era, when pre-Freudian, Christian values insisted on a criminal's full humanity as a condition for just retribution. Declared Bugliosi:

> These defendants are not human beings, ladies and gentlemen. Human beings have a heart and soul. No one with a heart and soul could have done what these defendants did to seven vic-

tims. These defendants are human monsters, human muta-
tions. There is only one proper ending to the Tate-LaBianca
murder trial—verdicts of death for all four defendants.[6]

The death sentences handed down to Manson and his followers
were automatically commuted to life imprisonment when the
California Supreme Court abolished capital punishment in the
state in 1972. Manson is eligible for parole under California
law, although it is Bugliosi's opinion that he will remain in
prison for at least twenty-five years and quite possibly for the
rest of his life. Public awareness that even a man guilty of such
extreme crimes might someday be released from prison is
unquestionably involved in the shift of opinion that has taken
place since the mid-1960s.

In 1953, the Gallup Poll showed that 68 percent of Americans favored the death penalty for murder, with 25 percent
opposed and 7 percent undecided. This represented a slight
increase in support for capital punishment since 1936, when
Gallup found 62 percent in favor, 33 percent against, and 5
percent undecided. Between 1953 and 1966, however, popular
sentiment shifted strongly in the opposite direction. The 1966
Gallup Poll found 47 percent against capital punishment, 42
percent in favor, and 11 percent undecided. By 1972—the year
of the *Furman* decision—public opinion had once again reversed itself, with 57 percent for the death penalty, 32 percent
against, and 11 percent undecided. In 1976, the pro-capital-
punishment majority had grown to 65 percent, with only 28
percent against and 7 percent undecided—roughly the same
proportions as in the opinion polls of the early 1950s. A Harris
poll in 1977 produced similar results.

The rising crime rate of the past two decades may explain
the reversal of popular sentiment that took place in the late
1960s, but it does not explain why there was such strong support for the death penalty in the early 1950s—a period of
relative complacency and stability in American life. The expla-

nation is not particularly complicated: those who argue in favor of the death penalty are perfectly right in their contention that popular opinion has, for most of history, supported capital punishment for serious crimes. The exceptions are those periods—like the late 1950s and early 1960s—when abolitionist sentiments have gained ground. In America, the rise in criminal violence and general social unrest in the late 1960s brought at least a temporary halt to the progress of the abolitionist movement, as it did to other liberal trends in political life.

The disparity between popular sentiment in favor of capital punishment and the sentiments of those jurists, lawmakers, and philosophers who have led the long fight against the death penalty is as pronounced in countries with a relatively low rate of criminal violence as it is in the United States; the difference lies not so much in the distribution as in the intensity of public opinion. In Canada, where Parliament abolished the death penalty in 1976, the solicitor general, who had publicly said he would resign rather than sign a warrant for execution, acknowledged that 80 percent of those polled in a nation-wide study commissioned by his office were in favor of capital punishment.[7] In England, where the death penalty was ended in 1970, most polls showed a majority in favor of retaining capital punishment for certain cases of murder and treason. On the European continent, only the Scandinavian and Benelux countries have demonstrated a strong, well-established popular consensus against the death penalty, although most other European nations have also abolished it or made it virtually impossible to put into practice.

One reason for the surprising durability of these sentiments (surprising to an American who marvels at the relative freedom from ordinary crime that characterizes large European cities) may be the spread of violent political terrorism, which has affected a number of European, Middle Eastern, and Latin American nations far more than it has the United States. When capital punishment is invoked as an answer to terrorism, retributive outrage is always a motivating force even when it is cloaked in the language of deterrence. Every lesson of history teaches that martyrdom inspires rather than deters acts of violent fanaticism. Even if one accepts the dubious premise that fear of death deters "ordinary" murderers, it is hardly possible to imagine that the murderers of Aldo Moro or of the Israeli athletes at the Munich Olympics could have been deterred by any penalty—any more than the assassin of Tsar Alexander II or the members of the Stern gang were deterred by the executioners of the societies in which they lived.

Thus, Israel's theoretical revival of the death penalty in 1979 seems particularly ill-conceived in view of the fact that it was aimed only at political terrorists—and particularly ironic in view of Prime Minister Menachem Begin's background as a leader of the Irgun before the partition of Palestine. Begin can hardly have forgotten that those who wished to work for establishment of a Jewish state through guerrilla violence were inspired to new feats after the execution of two members of the Stern group by the British in 1947. (No Arab terrorist has actually been executed under the modified Israeli law. In the history of the State of Israel, only one defendant, Adolf Eichmann, has ever been tried and put to death, and Eichmann's sentence required a special act of the Knesset making an exception to the general ban on capital punishment. In France, there were demands for a "one-time" revival of the death penalty after the capture of Klaus Barbie in 1983.) Eichmann's fate, like the sentences at the Nuremberg trials, does present an unusual example of a "pure" retributive rationale for the death penalty. It was seldom suggested that Eichmann's death, or the earlier judgments at Nuremberg, would "deter" any future Nazis from devising plans for mass murder. Support for Eichmann's sentence, in Israel and internationally, was based on the principle of just retribution; anything less than the ultimate penalty would, in this view, have been an insufficient declaration of society's outrage at the horror of the crime.

Until recently, the retributive argument was generally limited to extraordinarily horrible crimes—acts that, in some way, defy the usual limits of human imagination. Belief in deterrence has generally dominated arguments in favor of capital punishment for "ordinary" murders—ordinary meaning something less pathologically bizarre than Manson's "Helter-Skelter" or less massive and calculated than the Final Solution. Such arguments are frequently preceded by the "common-sense-tells-us" formulation: common sense tells us that, whatever statistical studies say, human beings are less likely to kill one another if there is a possibility that society will defend itself by killing them in return. Although faith in the deterrent value of executions remains a powerful rationalization for the death penalty, the current wave of popular support for capital punishment has been accompanied by a marked shift from the usual deterrence rationalization to an unabashed exaltation of retribution as a moral and legal principle. There is nothing new about the glorification of retribution, but there is something archaic about its use, in this context, in the late twentieth century; a whiff of the everlasting hellfire and merciless earthly swords from *The Triumphs of Gods Revenge* drifts toward us from the past.

The Supreme Court, in the 1976 case of *Gregg v. Georgia* (only four years after the *Furman* decision was thought to have settled the issue of capital punishment), legitimized newer, more narrowly drawn death-penalty laws and opened the way for a resumption of executions in the United States. The court took the position that evidence of the deterrent value of executions was uncertain but that retribution was itself an acceptable legal objective. "The decision that capital punishment may be the appropriate sanction in extreme cases is an expression of the community's belief that certain crimes are themselves so grievous an affront to humanity that the only adequate response may be the penalty of death," the court majority asserted, while acknowledging that the results of statistical attempts to determine the deterrent value of capital punishment "simply have been inconclusive."[8] In a dissenting opinion, Justice Thurgood Marshall left open the possibility that he might authorize capital punishment if it could be proven that it did deter murderers (although he clearly regards such proof as unattainable). The most interesting aspect of Justice Marshall's opinion, however, is his recognition of the difficulty of separating deterrence from retribution.

> The concept of retribution is a multifaceted one, and any discussion of its role in the criminal law must be undertaken with caution. On one level, it can be said that the notion of retribution or reprobation is the basis of our insistence that only those who have broken the law be punished, and in this sense the notion is quite obviously central to a just system of criminal sanctions. But our recognition that retribution plays a crucial role in determining who may be punished by no means requires approval of retribution as a general justification for punishment. It is the question whether retribution can provide a moral justification for punishment—in particular, capital punishment—that we must consider. . . .
>
> As my Brother [Justice William] Brennan stated in *Furman,* "here is no evidence whatever that utilization of imprisonment rather than death encourages private blood feuds and other disorders." . . . It simply defies belief to suggest that the death penalty is necessary to prevent the American people from taking the law into their own hands.
>
> In a related vein, it may be suggested that the expression of moral outrage through the imposition of the death penalty serves to reinforce basic moral values—that it marks some crimes as particularly offensive and therefore to be avoided. The argument is akin to a deterrence argument, but differs in that it contemplates the individual's shrinking from anti-social conduct not because he fears punishment, but because he has been told in the strongest possible way that the conduct is wrong. This contention, like the previous one, provides no

support for the death penalty. It is inconceivable that any individual concerned about conforming his conduct to what society says is "right" would fail to realize that murder is "wrong" if the penalty were simply life imprisonment.[9]

The utilitarian concept of punishment as a deterrent to crime and the moralistic concept of punishment as a retributive statement of social values are closely related, for there would be no need to deter what is not considered evil. Opponents of capital punishment, beginning with the eighteenth-century reformers, have frequently weakened their case by insisting on a dichotomy between deterrence and retribution—distinct concepts in theory, but thoroughly intertwined in practice. But this entanglement does not mean the retributive principle cannot be embodied in one form of punishment as well as another, unless the punishment is ludicrously light in relation to the crime. In America, the lax enforcement of drunken-driving laws exemplifies the latter situation; the punishment of drunken drivers is so light that it neither deters nor expresses a sufficient degree of retributive outrage. A man who, while under the influence of alcohol, kills another by running over him in a car is much less likely to serve time in jail than a man who, while under the influence of alcohol, knifes another to death in a bar. From the standpoint of both deterrence and retribution, a suspended driver's license is an inadequate response to the crime of manslaughter; the success or failure of one legal objective is inseparable from the other.

The real issue is proportionality—not "legitimate" deterrence versus "illegitimate" revenge. Advocates of capital punishment frequently introduce proportionality as a corollary to their retributivist arguments: the death penalty, they insist, is the only proportional punishment for premeditated murder. But this argument loses its force in the cases of mass murderers, for there can be no proportional punishment for more than one killing. One is then forced back to the question of which forms of retribution adequately reflect the seriousness of a crime while conforming to contemporary standards of decency and justice. The complexity of this question has imbued the history of the death penalty with more anomalies and inconsistencies than any other aspect of retributive justice.

One authority on capital punishment has noted that the definition of crimes punishable by death has shifted according to the definition of power and authority within society.

> In a period of religious hegemony, death was prescribed first and foremost for religious crimes; in a time of expanding economic wealth, it was imposed primarily for offenses against property. Thus, whatever else its function, the death penalty appears to have been used to protect the interests and position of the dominant group in the social order—to punish those offenses defined as gravest by those in power.[10]

The use of exile rather than death as the penalty for murder in early tribal societies was founded not on the ethical considerations that dominate modern arguments for the abolition of capital punishment but on the preeminence of the group in relation to the individual.

The nature of tribal identity also ruled out restitution for damages caused by acts of violence within the clan, since the aggrieved parties were considered to be equally related to both victim and assailant. Authorization of public executions (as opposed to private vendetta), which accompanied the rise of the pollution doctrine in both Greek and Semitic cultures, was unquestionably related to a heightened regard for the life of the individual as well as to a new concern for the power of the state. Draco's code of laws, instituted between the Homeric and the classical period, offered a compromise between old tribal customs and the new pollution doctrine. The death penalty was decreed for theft, while the options of private restitution for involuntary manslaughter, and of exile for premeditated murder, were retained. From a modern perspective, Draco's code simply reflects a greater concern for property than for human life. To the civilization of his time, however, it must also have represented a gesture toward the collective identity of tribal society at a time when a new concept of the autonomous individual was emerging in the Hellenic world. When Solon abolished the death penalty for property crimes, he retained a full range of punishments—from execution to exile—for various forms of murder and treason.

The Hebrews had eliminated the death penalty for property crimes long before the Greeks, but they decreed it for a number of other offenses, including adultery and cursing one's parents with the special names for Yahweh. Like the Christian framers of Anglo-European law before the Enlightenment, modern advocates of capital punishment frequently cite Mosaic law in support of their views, and they criticize Jewish opponents of the death penalty for stressing the limitations of rabbinical tradition rather than the authorizations of Mosaic law.

In a dazzling leap across millennia, Walter Berns bolsters his argument in favor of capital punishment by citing the Mosaic death penalty for cursing one's parents; Maimonides' declaration that Jews are exempt from the usual requirement of sitting *shivah* for a dead relative if that relative had been condemned to death by a rabbinical court; and the Israeli execution of Eichmann—an execution authorized by religious as well as secular political parties in the Knesset as an exemption to the general prohibition of capital punishment in force at the time.[11] There is, of course, no satisfactory answer to those who cite scriptural authority for—or, for that matter, against—the modern practice of capital punishment. Citing the numerous capital offenses in Mosaic law to support continuation of the death penalty today is roughly on a par with suggesting that Christ's death on the cross sanctifies all executions. In fact, one commentator in a Christian periodical came perilously close to adopting this position when he observed that "it is significant that when Jesus voluntarily went the way of the cross he chose the capital punishment of his day as his instrument to save the world. And when he gave redemption to the repentant thief he did not save him from capital punishment but gave him Paradise instead, which was far better."[12]

Mosaic law, like traditional Christian doctrine, does permit capital punishment. In the eighteenth century, the first systematic assaults on theocratically based criminal law were the product of a secular mentality (as were Machiavelli's early-sixteenth-century treatises on government). It is entirely logical that both Machiavelli and Beccaria wound up on the Roman Catholic Index of prohibited books. In fairness, it must be noted that opponents of the death penalty sound as archaic as its supporters when they rely on religious arguments to support their cause. In both Jewish and Christian scriptures, there are ample quotations to bolster either position; one must look elsewhere for a moral posture consonant with a modern, secular sensibility.

Elucidation of the scriptures is central to rabbinical Judaism, and this process of religious interpretation and modification offers a number of interesting parallels to the secular process of legal reform that began in the eighteenth century. With regard to the death penalty, the chief concerns of the rabbis were virtually identical to those of latter-day reformers. These included strict evidentiary requirements; scrupulous impartiality; reservation of capital punishment for the most serious crimes; and elimination of the torture and degradation that accompanied executions in ancient times.

The evidentiary requirements of rabbinical law—rules that are fully delineated in the early books of the Bible—were so strict that, in the words of one authority on Judaism, "it is clear that with such a procedure conviction in capital cases was next to impossible, and that this was the intention of the framers of the rules is equally plain."[13] The most important requirement was that the testimony of two eyewitnesses, related neither to the victim nor the accused, was required to sentence a defendant to death. The inflexibility of this demand is underlined in a famous passage from Simeon ben Shatah, an influential rabbi in the early half of the first century B.C.

> I saw a man chasing another into a ruin; I ran after him and saw a sword in his hand dripping with the other's blood and the murdered man in his death agony. I said to him, You villain! Who killed this man? Either I or you. But what can I do? Your life is not delivered into my hand, for the law says, At the mouth of two witnesses shall he that is to die be put to death. But He who knows the thought, will requite the man who killed his fellow.[14]

Circumstantial evidence was not admitted at all, and witnesses were cautioned by the judges to testify only to what they had actually seen. All witnesses in capital cases were questioned separately, and if any material discrepancies were found in their testimony, the accused was automatically acquitted. The witnesses were also warned that they themselves would be liable to the death penalty should they commit perjury and the defendant be convicted on the basis of their false testimony; this provision was designed to prevent witnesses from conspiring in order to rid themselves of an enemy.

One authority on Judaism and the death penalty observes that "the sentiment against capital punishment is expressed in the Mishnah in an opinion which maintains that a court which executes one man in seven years is a destructive one. R. Eleazer ben Azariah maintained that a court is destructive if it executes one man in seventy years. R. Tarfon and R. Akiba said, 'If we had been in the Sanhedrin, no man would ever have been put to death.' "[15] This extremely negative attitude toward capital punishment was not, of course, held by every rabbi; the Jews in Spain, as we have seen, were criticized by visiting rabbis from other areas of Europe for their favorable attitude toward the death penalty. However, rabbinical tradition was much more antagonistic to capital punishment than were the other legal traditions of pre-Enlightenment Europe. The German rabbi Yehiel ben Asher's criticism of legal procedures in Spain ("in none of the countries that I know of, except here in Spain, do Jewish courts try cases of capital punishment")* implies that the Spanish Jews were exceptional in their readiness to impose death sentences.

Jewish supporters of the death penalty today frequently point out that the reluctance of rabbinical authorities to authorize executions does not mean they were absolutely opposed to capital punishment, and this is certainly true. From a modern, secular perspective, it seems to me that the primary significance of the traditional rabbinical reluctance to resort to the death penalty lies not in overstated assertions that the rabbis were unequivocally opposed to capital punishment but in the prophetic relationship of Jewish law to the general movement toward reform of the criminal justice system that began with the Enlightenment. (It is ironic that the great thinkers of the Enlightenment displayed virtually no awareness of the rabbinical tradition that was so in keeping with their own ideas and focused instead on the literal interpretation of Mosaic law that was the basis of the harsh criminal statutes of Christian Europe.)

In their insistence on eyewitness testimony, the rabbinical courts were far more restrictive than modern courts in admitting evidence that might condemn a defendant to death. In other respects, such as the presumption of innocence and the prohibition of double jeopardy, the Mishnah and the Gemara set forth requirements that were virtually identical to those specified in the American Bill of Rights and in eighteenth- and nineteenth-century statutory reforms in western Europe. Jewish law also offered every possibility for last-minute reprieves. After conviction and sentencing, a case might be reopened at any time—even as the condemned man was being led to the

*See page 120.

place of execution. A herald preceded the convict, calling out his name and the details of his crime and inviting anyone with new evidence to step forward. If new witnesses presented themselves, a stay of execution was automatically granted in order that their evidence might be heard. The seriousness with which the rabbis viewed any proceeding that might result in a death sentence was also reflected in a procedural distinction between civil and criminal cases. In civil cases, the senior judges of the rabbinical court delivered their opinions first. In criminal cases, the junior judges spoke first in order to prevent them from being influenced by the judgments of their senior colleagues.

In the twentieth century, procedural moves to restrict the use of the death penalty have frequently been opposed out of a suspicion that the "restrictionists" are really abolitionists at heart. This suspicion has sometimes been justified; procedural reforms have occasionally foreshadowed demands for outright abolition of the death penalty. Nevertheless, unequivocal opposition to capital punishment was relatively uncommon until recent years. Beccaria's absolutist position set him apart even from his contemporaries in the Enlightenment, and most of those who hold the position today are absolute civil libertarians —also a rare breed.

As for the general public, only a small proportion is prepared to face the implications of allowing an Eichmann or a Manson to live—although the proportion prepared to assume personal responsibility for administering a lethal injection or pulling the switch on the electric chair is equally small. One of the curious features engendered by proposals to abolish capital punishment is the fierce insistence on retaining a theoretical power that is, at this stage in history, rarely invoked. In his oral argument before the Supreme Court during the *Furman* case, Anthony Amsterdam noted that the number of executions in the United States had dwindled steadily long before the current campaign against capital punishment began in the early 1960s.

At that time, there were only about twenty executions per year in the entire country.[16]

As a result of the writings of men like Beccaria and Voltaire in Europe and Benjamin Rush in the United States, the early nineteenth century saw the beginning of a sharp reduction in the number of capital crimes. In the United States, England, and northern Europe, the secular reform movement began to limit the power of the state over life and death in much the same fashion as rabbinical tradition had modified Mosaic law. In England, pickpockets became the first group of petty criminals to be freed from fear of state-imposed death. Picking pockets had been a capital offense in England since 1565; in 1810, Parliament repealed the law "without opposition or comment." With somewhat more opposition and comment, the next three decades saw the abolition of the death penalty for theft of cattle, horses, and sheep (1832); housebreaking (1833); sacrilege (1835); theft of letters by postal employees (1835); counterfeiting and forgery (1836); and burglary in private dwellings (1837). At the turn of the century, there had been more than two hundred capital offenses in the British Isles. When Queen Victoria ascended the throne in 1837, the categories of crimes punishable by death had been reduced to fifteen.[17]

During this period, the reduction in the number of capital crimes was accompanied by increased use of the royal prerogative of clemency, resulting in the frequent commutation of death sentences. This use of clemency resulted in a situation similar to that described by Anthony Amsterdam 150 years later in the *Furman* argument—a society in which the number of criminals actually executed was much smaller than the number originally sentenced to death. As Hugo Adam Bedau points out, the widespread use of clemency was natural in view of the fact that English law specified mandatory death sentences for all felonies. When a judge suggested that a case was suitable for royal clemency, the plea was generally granted, and the convicts were frequently transported to the Crown colonies. In the last decade of the eighteenth century, more than two-thirds of death sentences in London and Middlesex were commuted to imprisonment or exile. Although there were several thousand death sentences a year before the movement to reduce the number of capital crimes took hold, there were only about seventy executions a year by the early 1800s.[18]

The practice of clemency was already a source of considerable ambivalence for legal reformers. For those condemned to death, clemency was the only recourse in an era of harsh penal codes, but it also had the effect of making the death penalty appear to be to less awesome a prerogative than it actually was (or would be in the hands of more punitive rulers). Beccaria considered it a serious mistake for society to place its faith in the "common sense" and compassion of rulers or judges.

> Nothing is more dangerous than the common axiom that we should consult the spirit of the law. This is to allow the dyke of law to be breached by the torrent of opinion—a truth which to me seems irrefutable, though it may appear a paradox to vulgar minds who are more impressed by an immediate modicum of disorder than by the remote disasters which follow when a false principle is allowed to take root in a nation. . . . Every man looks at things in his own way, every man thinks differently at different times. "The spirit of the law" will therefore depend upon the good or bad logic of the judge, upon his good or his bad digestion; it will depend on the degree of violence in his emotions, upon the feebleness of the sufferer in the case, upon the relations between the judge and the victim, or on all those minutiae of circumstances which alter the look of everything in the fluctuations of the human mind. Hence we might observe a citizen's fate changing many times in his progress from court to court, we might see the wretches' lives

victimized by false reasoning or the good or bad humor of a judge.[19]

In the American colonies, which had no uniform criminal code, the laws regarding capital punishment varied considerably and depended in large measure on the ethical bent of each colony's founders. Clemency and benefit of clergy, both used in England to mitigate the theoretical harshness of laws mandating the death penalty, were never as widely used in the New World. (The precise legal meaning once attached to the term "benefit of clergy" has all but disappeared today. The practice arose from the conflict between church and state in England, dramatically embodied in the twelfth-century struggle between King Henry II and Thomas à Becket, the archbishop of Canterbury, who was slain at the altar by Henry's soldiers for his insistence on the right of the church to try clerics for civil offenses. Benefit of clergy meant that priests and monks were to be tried by ecclesiastical rather than secular courts, even for felonious civil offenses. By the eighteenth century, the old principle of the church's right to try its priests had undergone a sea change; benefit of clergy meant that a first-time felony offender could be spared the death sentence if he was able to recite the opening lines of the fifty-first psalm—"Have mercy upon me, O God, according to thy lovingkindness: according unto the multitude of thy tender mercies blot out my transgressions." Known for obvious reasons as the "neck verse," the recitation was offered as proof of literacy and therefore of the condemned man's "clerical" status—a reminder of the days when only priests and monks could read. As Bedau notes, benefit of clergy became a "fictional device whereby first offenders were given a lesser punishment."[20] In the nineteenth century, American and English criminal laws began to use the phrase "without benefit of clergy" to indicate that there could be no commutation of a death sentence on the ground that the crime was a first offense.

This phrase was popularly misunderstood to mea   hat the condemned must face the executioner without the c   olation or absolution of a spiritual adviser. In the twentieth cent⌐ry, the meaning of the term has become even more confused; it is now used to describe an act—usually sexual—that takes place without formal sanction by a church.)

In America, the Puritan founders of the Massachusetts Bay Colony set forth a wide variety of capital offenses in statutes that equaled any of the theocratic codes of seventeenth-century Europe in their harshness. However, the Quaker founders of Jersey and Pennsylvania, with their pacifist beliefs, placed restrictions on the use of the death penalty that were not equaled in the rest of the world until the twentieth century. In 1646, the Crown charter for the colony of South Jersey did not specify the death penalty for *any* crime—and there were in fact no executions in the colony for nearly half a century. William Penn's basic code of laws for Pennsylvania, promulgated in 1682, permitted the death penalty only for treason and premeditated murder—an incomparably liberal view at the time. By the beginning of the eighteenth century, however, the Mother Country had required her colonies to adopt the death penalty for a variety of crimes comparable to capital offenses in England, and the reformist strain did not reappear in American law until the adoption of the Bill of Rights. The diversity of religious practice in the New World militated against the general use of benefit of clergy (*which* clergy?), and the death penalty—in spite of the early restrictions in some of the colonies —may have been more widely applied in mid-eighteenth-century America than in England.

After independence, Pennsylvania soon returned to the restrictions on capital punishment advocated by its Quaker founders. (Philadelphia was the home of Benjamin Rush, who was strongly influenced by Beccaria's treatise and was the first American to propose a systematic reform of criminal laws.) In

1794, Pennsylvania abolished the death penalty for all crimes except first-degree murder. As England began to limit the number of capital offenses in the 1820s and '30s, America saw the emergence of a full-fledged movement to abolish capital punishment.

In terms of popular sentiment against the death penalty, the 1830s and '40s were comparable to the 1950s and early '60s. Alexis de Tocqueville, writing in the 1830s, observed that "although the Americans have in a manner reduced selfishness to a social and philosophical theory, they are nevertheless extremely open to compassion. In no country is criminal justice administered with more mildness than in the United States. While the English seem disposed carefully to retain the bloody traces of the Middle Ages in their penal legislation, the Americans have almost expunged capital punishment from their codes."[21] By the late 1840s, most northern and eastern states had abolished the death penalty for all crimes except murder and treason. In 1846, the territory of Michigan eliminated capital punishment except for treason; Rhode Island and Wisconsin, in 1852 and 1853 respectively, abolished the death penalty altogether. Only in the South was capital punishment retained for a wide variety of crimes—especially sexual offenses. The selective racial application of the death penalty, particularly with regard to sex crimes, originated in the laws promulgated under slavery and remains an important influence on the capital-punishment debate in America today.

Tocqueville had, of course, spoken too soon. The movement against capital punishment soon came to a halt as its energies were channeled into the fight against slavery. After the Civil War, a cyclical pattern of public opinion emerged, roughly consonant with liberal and conservative shifts of sentiment on other domestic political issues. The Progressive Era saw the abolition of the death penalty in several states and reduction in the number of capital statutes in others, while the period from the end of World War I until the late 1930s saw the resumption of executions in a number of formerly abolitionist states and the addition of many new crimes to the list of offenses punishable by death (the kidnap laws in the wake of the Lindbergh case among them).

The inconsistency of American public policy with regard to capital punishment is attributable less to an inherent fickleness of public opinion than to the nature of the federal system, in which so many offenses fall within the scope of state rather than national law—at least until they reach the higher appellate courts. Most state legislators, like the members of the House of Representatives, must run for election every two years and four years is the maximum term of office; state lawmakers are thus vulnerable to short-term, emotional swings of popular opinion on a highly emotional issue. Between 1872 and 1961, eleven states abolished and then restored the death penalty. Of those states, five restored the death penalty within a three-year period. Only two of the "restoration" states waited more than a decade to act, and it is reasonable to conclude that the resumption of executions had little to do with any long-term social consequences of abolition and everything to do with short-range political vulnerability of lawmakers.[22]

Procedure and proportionality—from the rabbinical courts of the first century B.C. through the political debates of the past twenty years—have always been the main concerns of those who have labored to reduce or eliminate the use of capital punishment in peacetime. (Wartime executions have generally been treated as another matter altogether, although pacifists would, and do, argue that they ought not to be. Every nation with an army has different provisions for military and civilian justice, and countries that long ago abandoned the death penalty in time of peace—like the Scandinavian nations—have special provisions for the execution of traitors in war.) Proceduralists address themselves primarily to regulations that reduce the likelihood of condemning an innocent defendant to death, proportionalists to the fit between crime and punishment. Not all of these reformers are absolute abolitionists, but the philosophical and political tendency of their efforts is in the direction of abolition: although some wish to retain the theoretical possibility of capital punishment, most would end it in practice. In much the same fashion, those who opposed the extension of slavery into new territories in the 1850s were abolitionists at heart.

A third element of the movement for reform of capital punishment is much more ambiguous than either procedure or proportionality: it is the desire to shield the hangman from public view, to insure that the severed head falls neatly into a basket and is securely covered, to muffle gasps and groans—in short, to push the condemned gently into that good night. In the twentieth century, both opponents and supporters of capital punishment have generally agreed that death, if it is to be inflicted, should at least be concealed from public view and should not cause any undue pain. Walter Berns recognizes that "the effect of this concealment was to prolong the practice of capital punishment."[23]

In the past, much of the exemplary value of capital punishment was thought to rest upon the public nature, and public gruesomeness, of executions. This assumption may have been well founded when the aim of the death penalty was simply to demonstrate the overwhelming power of the state—when an occupying army, for instance, was trying to deter acts of rebellion on the part of the populace. The rationale for capital punishment in such cases is deterrence through retribution—revenge as a tactic to achieve a larger goal. Such tactics do eventually lose their usefulness, and even become counter-productive if carried on indefinitely, but they have been utilized effectively for limited periods by occupiers with a generally benign attitude toward the quiescent sector of the populace. By most accounts, though, the public execution of ordinary criminals does not inspire awe, or respect, or even fear. Pity, revulsion, excitement, and glee have all been reported, and none of these states of mind is exactly what the proponents of capital punishment hope to achieve.

After witnessing the beheading of three robbers in Rome, Byron wrote that "the first turned me quite hot and thirsty—& made me shake so that I could hardly hold the opera-glass (I was close—but was determined to see—as one should see every thing once—with attention), the second and third (which shows how dreadfully soon things grow indifferent) I am ashamed to say had no effect on me—as a horror—though I would have saved them if I could."[24] The thousands of people who gathered to witness public executions in London derived, by all accounts, a positive enjoyment from the spectacle. William Makepeace Thackeray, in a famous description of an execution which was constantly cited by reformers during the fight to restrict the use of capital punishment in nineteenth-century England, confessed that "the sight has left on my mind an extraordinary feeling of terror and shame.

> It seems to me that I have been abetting an act of frightful wickedness and violence, performed by a set of men against one of their fellows; and I pray God that it may soon be out of the power of any man in England to witness such a hideous and degrading sight. Forty thousand persons (say the Sheriffs), of all ranks and degrees—mechanics, gentlemen, pickpockets, members of both Houses of Parliament, street-walkers, newspaper-writers, gather together before Newgate at a very early hour: the most part of them give up their natural quiet night's rest, in order to partake of this hideous debauchery, which is more exciting than sleep, or than wine.[25]

In 1868, public hangings were finally abolished in England, and the *Times* of London published an editorial recalling Thackeray's description:

We shall not in the future have to read how, the night before an execution, Thousands of the worst characters in England, abandoned women and brutal men, met beneath the gallows to pass the night in drinking and buffoonery; in ruffianly swagger and obscene jests; how they hooted the hangman and cheered the criminal; how, at the very foot of the gallows, they committed with impunity deeds of lawless violence, scarcely less reprehensible than the crime of which they had come to witness the expiation.[26]

Questions of propriety and aesthetics seem to have been uppermost in the minds of those who attacked only the institution of public executions (rather than the practice of capital punishment itself). In both England and America, this polite distaste for the unaesthetic aspects of death was apparent in later efforts to change the way in which executions were carried out. In 1886, a parliamentary committee authorized to conduct inquiries into the manner of executions noted that "among murderers condemned to death there are occasionally some whose physical condition makes it undesirable that the execution should take place because it could not be done in a seemly manner, or because some scandalous thing might happen—a person's head might come off because the jaw was shot away or some other gruesome development might happen which would *shock public opinion rather than show it the law had been vindicated*" (italics mine).[27]

Sir Ernest Gowers, chairman of a Royal Commission on Capital Punishment established in 1949 (a commission that was explicitly forbidden to take up the question of whether the death penalty should be abolished), noted that condemned prisoners must be reprieved if their physical condition was such that they could not be hanged in "seemly" fashion. Under English law, it was illegal to carry out executions except by hanging. Nicholas Ogarev's nineteenth-century description of the botched hanging, for the crime of attempted suicide, of an unfortunate man who had tried to slit his throat exemplifies the sort of execution that was eventually considered too unseemly to be carried out. A condemned man who repeatedly returned to life because his wounded throat flapped open and allowed him to breathe with the noose around his neck would definitely have administered a shock to public sensibility. Reprieves on grounds of potential unseemliness were not, Gowers noted, as unusual as one might have expected; at the time the royal commission was established, five such reprieves had been granted in the preceding fifteen years. "A future student of the strange customs of the natives of Britain in the twentieth century," Gowers observed, "will find few that will seem to him more quaint than that the decision between the death penalty and a less severe punishment should sometimes have depended not on the gravity of the offense but on the shape of the offender's neck."[28]

Apart from requiring that hangings be shielded from public view and that they be conducted in a seemly, i.e., efficient and unbloody, fashion, the English were reasonably straightforward about calling an execution an execution until they abolished capital punishment in 1970. English debates on the subject of the executions were distinguished by an absence of esoteric language—particularly in comparison to the oratory of Americans (whose fondness for euphemisms in any death-related situation was first pointed out by Jessica Mitford in *The American Way of Death*).

In the history of capital punishment, no country has been more dedicated than the United States to the quest for a discreet, sanitary, painless (as far as the living are concerned) mode of execution. Only in America was there an immediate move, after the harnessing of electricity for domestic and industrial use, to replace the gallows with the electric chair. Although the United States is not the only country to have tried electrocution as a means of execution, it is the only country to have made systematic use of the fearsome contraption known as the "electric chair." Like Thomas Edison, many nineteenth-century Americans assumed that electrocution was a more humane way of doing away with condemned prisoners than the gallows or the firing squad; its chief appeal, though, seemed to reside in the fact that there was no blood involved. Electrocution, as anyone who has ever received an unexpected jolt of high-voltage electricity knows, is far from painless; moreover, death comes more slowly than it does by means of a guillotine, a firing squad, or even a skilled hangman. Death by hanging, although it has been known to take as long as fifteen minutes, can be accomplished in less than three minutes by a hangman who knows his business—at precisely what angle, and with what degree of force, to tighten the rope so as to cause a minimum of suffering. The electric chair, with the relatively primitive technological accoutrements of its heyday in the 1920s and '30s, frequently took longer than the more traditional modes of execution.

It was inevitable, then, that the new wave of public support for capital punishment in the 1970s would be accompanied by demands for a still more "humane"—seemly, as the English put it—mode of executing the condemned. And it was equally inevitable that a generation accustomed to relying on a variety of chemical substances would turn to the pharmacopoeia for the answer. The lethal injection, according to its advocates, is far more humane than the gas chamber (which makes the dying choke and gasp) or the electric chair (which leaves visible burns on the body). The condemned man or woman is simply transported into a chemical haze—an "altered state of consciousness"—and never wakes up. The governor of Illinois acted against the current trend when he vetoed a bill to change the state's method of execution from electrocution to lethal injection, arguing that opponents of capital punishment would not be placated by a change in the means of putting prisoners to death and that supporters of capital punishment could already depend on the efficiency of the electric chair.

One of the first politicians to express support for the idea of lethal injections was Ronald Reagan when he was governor of California. "Being a former farmer and horse raiser," Reagan declared in 1973, "I know what it's like to try to eliminate an injured horse by shooting him. Now you call the veterinarian and the vet gives it a shot and the horse goes to sleep—that's it. I myself have wondered if maybe this isn't part of our problem [with authorizing executions], if maybe we should review and see if there aren't even more humane methods than now—the simple shot or tranquilizer."[29] In the late 1970s and early 1980s, as executions resumed after the Supreme Court decision in the *Gregg* case, a number of states either passed laws mandating lethal injection as the means of execution or allowing condemned prisoners to make the choice of injection versus the gallows or electric chair. (Several states already allowed the prisoner to choose among the more conventional means of execution.) The State of New Jersey, displaying the greatest solicitude for the feelings of the condemned, provided that prisoners, in order to quell their fear of death, be given general anesthesia an hour before the lethal injection. Predictably, hard-line supporters of executions objected to this procedure, on the ground that condemned killers, already exempt from physical pain, ought at least to experience fear until the final moment of their lives.

On December 7, 1982, the first formal execution by lethal injection in the world took place in the State of Texas. Charles Brooks, Jr., a convicted murderer, was executed in a setting every bit as tawdry as the one described by Thackeray, though involving fewer people. Brooks's girlfriend was one of the official witnesses at the execution; outside the prison walls, members of a college fraternity turned up to cheer the proceeding as if it were an athletic event. The execution provoked debate in medical circles about whether it was ethically appropriate for doctors to assist in the preparations for or to actually administer "the ultimate high." The prison doctor in Texas inspected Brooks's veins to make sure that they were suitable conveyor belts for the lethal chemical but declined to administer the shot; that task fell to a medical technician. The American Medical Association declared that any doctor who participated, directly or indirectly, in such an execution was in violation of the Hippocratic oath, but Dr. Ralph Gray, medical director of the Texas Department of Corrections, disagreed. He suggested that a doctor who tries to help society cure itself of crime by helping to execute a criminal is performing a function analogous to that of a surgeon who removes malignant living tissue in order to save the rest of a patient's body. Most doctors, however, seem unpersuaded by this argument; the State of Idaho found it necessary to reinstitute the firing squad when no physician in the state would agree to administer a lethal injection. It would seem that executions, however performed, are difficult to conduct in a seemly manner. That is why supporters of capital punishment today are so deeply concerned about decorum.

Advocates of the death penalty, from politicians like President Reagan to academics like Berns, Ernest van den Haag, and Sidney Hook, have devoted considerable attention to the question of how death can be administered in the most dignified manner possible—administered in such a way as to teach a moral lesson rather than appeal to the prurient interests displayed by the crowds outside Newgate and the Texas penitentiary. Berns offers a particularly curious formula for dignified executions when he suggests they be conducted with official witnesses—but that certain categories of citizens be prohibited from attending them. "No ordinary person can be required to witness [executions]," Berns cautions, "and it would be better if some people not be permitted to witness them—children, for example, and the sort of persons who would, if permitted, happily join a lynch mob. Executions should not be televised, both because of the unrestricted character of the television audience and the tendency of television to make a vulgar spectacle of the most dignified event."[30]

One wonders how it would be possible to identify those among us who would, if given the opportunity, join a lynch mob. History suggests that, given a heated emotional climate and a symbolically terrifying crime, those who decline to join lynch mobs are the exceptions rather than the rule. And executions are supremely vulgar events, regardless of whether or not they are beamed into the TV rooms of America in living color. The newspaper photographs of Brooks's weeping girlfriend on her way to witness the execution and of the sterile setting, complete with medical gadgetry, in which the condemned man was to receive his shot were vulgar. So was the press speculation about the details of the execution. What would happen if the injection inexplicably failed to work? Would the technician try to insert the needle a second time? What if the chemicals caused irreversible brain damage but not death? (Even in this age of measurement, calculating the appropriate dosage for an individual is an inexact art.) Would another court decision be required to turn off the life-support systems of a condemned man who had crossed the river of Lethe but stopped short of the Styx? One recalls the London aldermen who assembled to bind the neck of the condemned man below his throat wound so that the noose would finally work.

Berns does have one excellent suggestion to enhance the dignity of executions. He insists that executions, though shielded from the general public, must be witnessed by its official representatives. (In this respect, he is more consistent and straightforward than many other capital-punishment advocates, who prefer to avoid the details of executions.) The official witnesses to executions, Berns insists, should not be chosen specifically for that purpose; that is, they should not be the sort of people who volunteer because they expect to derive a positive pleasure from watching others die. Rather, they should be ordinary legislators. "They represent the people when they enact the statutes permitting the penalty of death, and they can represent the people when they witness its carrying out. As [James] Madison said in the tenth *Federalist,* they are a 'chosen body of citizens' who can be expected to 'refine and enlarge the public views,' and we have a right to expect them also to represent the public's moral indignation. If they cannot do this, they are not justified in enacting death-penalty statutes. The abolitionists make this point and they are right."[31]

In the decade after the *Furman* decision in 1972, thirty-seven states carefully constructed new laws to meet the largely procedural criticisms that had led the Supreme Court majority to invalidate virtually all of the old capital-punishment statutes in the United States. Many of the legislators who voted, either out of genuine conviction or political expediency, to reinstitute the death penalty would no doubt be appalled by the suggestion that they be required to witness what they have wrought. In a psychological sense, it is one thing to endorse capital punishment and quite another to witness an execution conducted with premeditation, deliberation, and formality—and to have impressed on one's senses in the most graphic way possible the mortal consequences of an "aye" spoken in the familiar, dignified halls of a legislative body. Most human beings do not have the stomach for the task (a fact for which we can all be grateful). There is, however, something mystifying about the intensity of public emotion expended in favor of the death penalty when juxtaposed against the reluctance of the majority —of legislators, judges, and jurors as well as the general public —to act on the cherished principle that the state must have the right to execute its most vile criminals.

By the end of 1982, only six executions had actually taken place as a result of the widespread post-*Furman* restoration of death-penalty laws. This reluctance to execute is not attributable solely to procedural safeguards mandating extensive judicial review of virtually every case in which a defendant is condemned to die. Both judges and juries tend to give the defendant the benefit of every doubt when death is the issue. Most juries find it impossible to impose a death sentence unless the criminal is someone who, like Charles Manson, lends himself to being characterized as a beast rather than a human being. It also helps if the defendant either disclaims responsibility, as Eichmann did, or glorifies acts of criminal violence, as the Manson "family" did. After the Manson trial, several jurors said they had tried to find a way of rationalizing a lesser penalty for Manson's three female followers than for their leader but were unable to do so. One of the jurors said she was particularly shocked when none of the three girls showed the slightest sign of remorse, even when recounting Sharon Tate's pleas for the life of her unborn child.[32] Thus, it takes a truly exceptional, outrageous, grisly crime to merit the death penalty—even in an era when an overwhelming majority of the public expresses strong support for capital punishment. This suggests that the psychological appeal of the death penalty rests not upon any practical benefits it is thought to confer upon society but on its importance as a symbol of just retribution or, as seventeenth-century theologians put it, righteous vengeance.

It is a fact that a majority of the population—and an overwhelming majority of those who support capital punishment—believe that the death penalty is a deterrent to the crime of murder (which is, in western nations, the only offense for which most people now wish to execute their fellow human beings). Politicians generally express this popular belief with the "common-sense-tells-us" formulation, ignoring Voltaire's observation that "common sense is not so common." The force of "common-sense" belief in the deterrent value of executions is such that one would expect those who attempt a defense of capital punishment on rational, rather than purely emotional, grounds to make extensive use of social-science research on the deterrence question. In fact they do not, and the reason is that most of the studies—flawed as they are—do not support the popular notion of the death penalty as an effective deterrent to crime. That is the main reason why those who have made the intellectual case for capital punishment in recent years have come to rely increasingly on an argument that emphasizes retribution rather than deterrence.

It would serve no useful purpose to re-examine the data presented in numerous studies attempting to establish the deterrent effect of the death penalty. The studies generally fall into two categories—those comparing jurisdictions with similar populations and criminal-justice systems, differing only in whether or not they authorize the death penalty, and those comparing crime rates over time in jurisdictions that have abolished capital punishment after maintaining it for some years or have reinstituted the death penalty after abolishing it. A third type of study, widely quoted in the arguments over the Supreme Court decision in the *Gregg* case, was conducted by Isaac Ehrlich, a University of Chicago econometrician who used an extremely complicated technique called "multiple regression analysis." One of the purposes of Ehrlich's study was to offer a more careful statistical control for the many variables, apart from the death penalty, that might have affected the results of previous studies. Ehrlich's conclusion—more optimistic than most other studies with regard to the potential deterrent effect of capital punishment—was that one execution a year *may* have resulted in seven or eight fewer murders during the period in question.[33] It is not surprising that serious advocates of capital punishment are unwilling to base their case on such studies; words like *may* and *might,* when the issue is life or death, have a feeble ring.

I do not, however, agree with opponents of capital punishment who insist that research "proves" the death penalty lacks any deterrent value. Even in the physical sciences, proof of a negative is difficult to establish. In the social sciences, which focus on behavioral phenomena that tend to defy quantitative analysis, the task of obtaining negative proof is even more problematic. One cannot state with certainty that because people continue to kill one another at roughly the same rate after passage of a death-penalty bill, the law has therefore exerted no deterrent effect; it is, of course, always possible that still more murders would have been committed had the state continued to prohibit capital punishment. However, it seems even more ludicrous to assert that the possibility of execution may have changed the minds of seven or eight—or seven or eight thousand—potential murderers. When something fails to happen, there is no way to determine what the chances were of the event's occurring in the first place. There are, obviously, statistical methods of determining probabilities, but the administration of law is concerned not with general probabilities but with individual cases.

On the matter of deterrence, the burden of proof ought to rest with advocates of the "activist" approach to criminal violence, as exemplified by the death penalty. Because proponents of capital punishment cannot prove the case for deterrence—at any rate, to the satisfaction of those who distrust "common sense"—they must rely on retribution as a justification. And retribution is really the heart of the issue, for common sense does tell us that deterrence is not the only legitimate aim of punishment. If deterrence afforded the only rationale for criminal law, each of us would be entitled to one "free" crime. This idea was expressed by Bonnie Garland's mother in her bitter reaction to the relatively light manslaughter sentence received by her daughter's killer: "If you have a $30,000 defense fund, a Yale connection, and a clergy connection, you're entitled to one free hammer murder."[34]

In discussing any type of punishment, it is difficult to separate moral from utilitarian rationales. The concepts of punishment as an example to the populace and as a means of correcting the offender are both indicative of the ways in which moral and utilitarian rationales become inseparable. The exemplary justification for punishment is so closely related to the general deterrence rationale that the two are virtually indistinguishable. By making an example of the offender through some form of punishment, society demonstrates to all of its members that certain acts are serious breaches of the civil compact; that they are morally detestable; and that they will result in unpleasant consequences for those who commit them. The deterrent aspect of this concept of punishment (consequences) is thoroughly intertwined with the exemplary aspect (the public statement of values).

In recent years, officials at a number of American prisons have agreed to an experiment that attempts to combine the exemplary and the deterrent aims of punishment in an unusually specific way. Groups of schoolchildren—for the most part, young adolescents from urban areas with high crime rates—are taken on "field trips" to prisons, where they meet with convicts who speak to them about the extreme unpleasantness of prison existence and warn the youngsters against embarking on a criminal life. (Watching the embarrassed giggles of children asked to summarize their reactions to prison for the television news, I felt profoundly grateful that I grew up in an age when a school field trip meant a visit to a dull museum.) One wonders when someone will come up with the bright idea that children should be taken to witness executions. Such visits might be restricted to youngsters who have already demonstrated their antisocial tendencies by being arrested for minor crimes—as the prison visits seem, insultingly, to be reserved for children from schools in black and Hispanic neighborhoods.

The concept of punishment as correction is, in most respects, as utilitarian as the deterrent-exemplary notion, but it also has an avowedly moral aim. The idea of "correction" has both a punitive and a rehabilitative side. Penitentiaries, it must be recalled, were seen at the end of the eighteenth century as an alternative both to executions and to less severe forms of corporal punishment. Benjamin Rush, whose activities led to the establishment of the world's first penitentiary in Pennsylvania in 1790, conceived of prison as, literally, a "house of repentance"—a place where convicts might be led to recognize the error of their ways and returned, after their sentences were served, to useful lives in the community. Rush was not opposed to punishment per se, but he was opposed to punishment for purely retributive purposes.

The sad history of dashed hopes for "correction" through imprisonment has been amply documented; however, it seems to me that the reasons for this failure are not yet fully understood. Most critics of prisons focus on the physical and psychological brutality of the institutional community, which consists primarily of society's most violent members (on the guards' as well as the prisoners' side of the bars). In such a community, it is logical that most convicts will receive a higher education in crime rather than repentance. Such criticism is accurate enough as far as it goes, but it misses a fundamental point: a purely correctional concept of punishment attempts to apply principles to a pathological community that are valid only in a healthy environment.

A mother punishes a child found playing with matches not to exact retribution for a "crime" but to stop the child from playing with matches again and, if possible, to make the child understand the dangerous nature of fire. The short-range goal is deterrence, and the long-range goal is correction; that is, the child who comprehends the dangers of fire will not have to be controlled by external intervention. The combination of limited punishment and reasoning works perfectly well with a normal child whose act is not intrinsically "wrong" but is simply perilous at a particular stage in life. This same concept, embodied in the rehabilitative model of imprisonment, does not have the same impact when applied to criminals whose acts are intrinsically "wrong" as well as dangerous. The corrective model of punishment would certainly offer more hope to a receptive minority of prisoners if institutions were run in a different manner, but even a reform of the most brutal and stupid prison practices would not address itself to the issue of the "wrong-ness"—as distinct from utilitarian destructiveness—of criminal behavior. To deal with the question of evil, one must turn to a moral rather than a utilitarian rationale for punishment.

Clearly, there are many cases in which correction of an offender is either unnecessary or impossible. Jean Harris, now serving at least fifteen years in prison for the murder of Dr. Tarnower, is a case in point. Harris's remorse over her role in Tarnower's death is unquestionable; she loved the doctor. (Of course, she also hated him—something she will not acknowl-edge, although both the killing and the angry letters she wrote him when she felt he was slipping away from her attest to the fact.) Under pressure of circumstance and her own tangled emotions, Harris acted in a way she never had before and—insofar as it is humanly possible to judge—is unlikely ever to act again. Ruling out the possibility of future violence on psy-chological grounds is always risky, but one need not turn to a psychiatrist to make reasonable projections about Harris's fu-ture should she be released from prison. An aging woman who killed her long-time lover, and who was tried and convicted in a glare of publicity, is hardly likely to find herself in a similar situation again; even if she had the desire, she would not be afforded the opportunity. Jean Harris requires neither correc-tion nor deterrence, and she has already been treated as an example—of the consequences of self-debasing love as well as of violating the law. But none of these facts is relevant to the question of retribution. A man is dead; Harris killed him. Are we to say that no further punishment is required because she is sorry?

At the opposite end of the criminal spectrum are those whose callousness and lack of remorse place them outside any possibility of correction. There are people who are totally be-yond the possibility of redemption—Christian teaching and humanitarian optimism notwithstanding. Eichmann was one. Manson is another. They are human, but the nature of their humanity induces, or ought to induce, fear and loathing. It is a comfort to regard them as beasts, but it is a true delusion. What, then, is society to do about those whose actions and character defy the ordinary aims of punishment? In quite a different way from Jean Harris, the Eichmanns and the Mansons of the world require a retributive answer. The critical question is not the legitimacy of retribution but the particular kind of retribution.

It is particularly difficult to consider the question of retribution with any degree of dispassion and lucidity when it is linked to the issue of the death penalty. Capital punishment arouses strong passions on the part of both its supporters and opponents. The depths of those passions, Jack Greenberg observed in an analysis of Supreme Court decisions on capital punishment during the past fifteen years, may explain why each of the nine justices felt obliged to write a separate opinion in the controversial *Furman* case.

> A separate opinion by each of the nine Justices in a single case is extremely rare and perhaps reflects the intense personal feeling involved in voting either to condemn more than 600 persons to death or to spare them. The variety of opinions validly conveyed the sense of disquietude about capital punishment which affected even the dissenters and presented to the country a perhaps appropriate array of reasons, among which anyone might select those most persuasive to him. It could be that the infliction of death, sanctioned by society, so roils the emotions, that no single argument can be universally satisfying.[35]

Justice Potter Stewart, in an opinion concurring with the majority in the *Furman* decision, emphasized his disagreement with those justices who regarded retribution as an impermissible ingredient of the criminal-justice system. "The instinct for retribution is part of the nature of man," he declared, "and channeling that instinct in the administration of criminal justice serves an important purpose in promoting the stability of a society governed by law."[36] (Four years later, in the *Gregg* case, Justice Stewart joined the majority that upheld the constitutionality of a number of state laws that had been redrawn to satisfy the court's objections to existing death-penalty statutes in the *Furman* decision.)

Finely drawn distinctions between one sort of retribution and another are not, as a rule, respected by either the opponents or the advocates of capital punishment. The anti-capital-punishment forces generally equate the death penalty with all forms of retribution, or revenge, and rest their case on the illegitimacy of vengeance. Camus, writing shortly after World War II, asserted that "the great argument of those who defend capital punishment is the exemplary value of the punishment. Heads are cut off not only to punish but to intimidate, by a frightening example, any who might be tempted to imitate the guilty. Society is not taking revenge; it merely wants to forestall." But, Camus insisted, such arguments are merely smokescreens for the real desire: revenge.

> Whoever has done me harm must suffer harm; whoever has put out my eye must lose an eye; and whoever has killed must die. This is an emotion, and a particularly violent one, not a principle. Retaliation is related to nature and instinct, not to law. Law, by definition, cannot obey the same rules as nature. . . . Now, retaliation does no more than ratify and confer the status of a law on a pure impulse of nature.[37]

The supporters of capital punishment are now much more forthright in their defense of retribution than they were thirty years ago, but most opponents of the death penalty have not shifted their ground. Like Camus, they simply attack the principle of retribution (always calling it vengeance) and rarely examine the question of whether the death penalty is desirable *even from a retributive standpoint*. A *New York Times* editorial on the occasion of New Jersey's becoming the thirty-seventh state to restore the death penalty exemplifies the general "anti-vengeance" thrust of the rhetoric:

> "Why is it [the death penalty] morally blameworthy?" asks a reader. "Vengeance is a compensatory and psychologically satisfying reparation for an injury or a wrong."
>
> It certainly seems so from a reading of history. Throughout the 18th century execution, often preceded by torture, was the penalty for many crimes. As a dramatic public spectacle, it symbolized the state's power to enforce its laws and gratified outrage at their violation. . . .
>
> Vengeance, widely declared, is rarely achieved, for it is an ugly satisfaction. The long search for humane justice expresses a higher yearning. To revive symbolic brutality by the state is to give up on those ideals. Their loss could be as damaging as the worst of crimes.[38]

I believe Camus and the editorial board of the *New York Times* are right in their conviction that vindictiveness, not deterrence, is the most important factor in the unslaked public demand for executions. But the death penalty will continue to be applied as long as revenge, and not the executions themselves, remains the focus of public debate. It is impossible to control any undesirable manifestation of a powerful human impulse by attacking the impulse rather than the manifestation—impossible, at any rate, in a reasonably libertarian society. To say that capital punishment is wrong because it is motivated by vengeance and vengeance is wrong is no more useful than to say that sexual assaults of children are wrong because they are motivated by a combination of lust and aggression and lust and aggression are wrong—vengeance being as closely related to the thirst for justice as lust is to erotic love. There are better moral grounds for opposing the death penalty than a blanket condemnation of revenge.

There are, in my view, two grounds on which retribution may legitimately be incorporated in a system of criminal punishments. The first is relatively narrow and applies to cases like that of Jean Harris, in which the offender can arguably be viewed as no longer in need of correction. The second, more broad justification applies to cases like that of Eichmann, in which correction is unimaginable. Graham Hughes, a professor of law at New York University, set forth the narrower justification for retribution.

> Being a citizen imposes obligations in return for the benefits of social living. Assuming the system to be minimally just, one of these obligations is to comply with the criminal law. Failure to do so is taking an unfair advantage by allowing ourselves a license that membership in a community assumes we cannot allow to others. Punishment redresses the unfair advantage and, for this reason, the act of committing a crime is a sufficient justification for punishment even if the offender is in no need of rehabilitation.[39]

This narrow definition of retribution, Hughes notes, justifies punishing criminals in general but it does not justify any particular form of punishment; one may accept the validity of the retributive principle without extending it to cover every conceivable form of "legalized revenge."

Hughes's definition of retribution is essentially political in nature; its only moral aspect involves the concept of unfairness in breaking a social compact whose rules one has implicitly promised to accept by assuming the privileges of citizenship. A broader retributive justification is, it seems to me, needed to encompass the most serious crimes of which men and women are capable. In dealing with an Eichmann or a Manson— criminals demonstrably in need of correction but unable or unwilling to accept it—civilized societies need something more than a retributive principle that addresses itself to the "unfair advantage" they have taken in violating the law. There is a ludicrous inadequacy attached to any description of such actions as mere violations of the law; certain acts are so evil that ordinary words, or laws, can hardly encompass them. But that is all the more reason for society to heed the way in which it uses law to retaliate on its own behalf.

Neither the criminal's remorse nor the public's anger should have anything to do with the assessment of retribution for particularly grave crimes. It is natural for jurors like the ones in the Manson case to be influenced by a criminal's apparent lack of remorse when it is time to determine the severity and duration of a penalty—natural, but legally unjustifiable. It need hardly be said that the public has access only to the surface indicators of remorse. Tears and protestations of sorrow are not difficult to summon—especially when the criminal may in fact be extremely sorry that he or she was caught, quite independently of the degree of genuine sorrow for the original offense.* Nor should real remorse—if it were possible to enter the mind of the defendant—materially affect the nature of retribution. Had Eichmann been found flogging himself in a penitential cell, or devoting himself to caring for Jewish orphans, instead of maintaining a normal bourgeois life in Argentina, his behavior would in no way have mitigated his responsibility for past crimes. This is simply a restatement of the old issue of religious purification versus secular atonement; an inner change of heart and a reformed life may restore the personal integrity and self-respect of the offender, but they do not discharge the debt to past victims. By the same token, lack of remorse—and society's anger and repulsion at the unmasked face of evil—ought not to be the standard for public retribution.

In his brief for capital punishment, Walter Berns relies heavily on the argument that only the death penalty can ade-

---

*The Roman Catholic Church, in pre-Vatican II days, drew a nice theological distinction between the two types of remorse. "Perfect contrition" referred to pure sorrow derived from the awareness of having offended God. "Imperfect contrition," by contrast, meant one was sorry because one feared hell. Either brand of contrition was sufficient to save a sinner from the flames if he or she had managed to receive the sacrament of penance before death, but only perfect contrition would suffice without the last-minute assistance of a priest.

quately represent, and discharge, the public's anger toward criminals who are responsible for the gravest offenses against human dignity. It is certainly true that any system of criminal punishments is based, at least in part, on public outrage. The feeling that murderers—at any rate the most callous among them—"deserve" to die is widespread; that is why it is so difficult to engage public concern over brutal prison conditions or trigger-happy police officers. Even in communities where the police have traditionally been perceived as enemies, popular outrage over "police brutality" is seldom expressed unless the victim is perceived as "innocent." The shooting of a respected businessman or honor student is usually required to touch off demonstrations of hostility toward the police in black neighborhoods; the use of excessive official force against a teenaged hoodlum who was known as a mugger, thief, and dealer in drugs is not regarded in the same light. In similar fashion, few members of the public would shed tears upon reading that a convicted murderer serving a life sentence had hanged himself in a prison cell. However, this private feeling of "good riddance"—understandable if not laudable—hardly justifies the transformation of emotional anger into a calculated policy of state-ordered executions.

Nor does the principle of proportionality justify the death penalty. The frequency with which advocates of capital punishment cite their specific interpretations of the Biblical "eye for eye" passage is one of the great ironies of the debate over executions, for the most vile crimes afford the most convincing evidence that the principle of proportionality is useful primarily as a limitation on rather than an exhortation to legalized revenge.

After the first murder, proportionality becomes literally impossible to achieve. Broadly speaking, proportionality may be attained by imposing a lighter punishment for stealing ten dollars than for stealing ten thousand dollars; for robbery without violence than for robbery accompanied by physical assault; for rape than for murder; for murder committed in the heat of passion than for murder committed by a professional assassin. But there is no way of imposing a more severe penalty on Manson than on another psychopath who has committed only one "stranger murder," no way of treating Eichmann, who was responsible for the deaths of millions, more severely than a concentration-camp Kommandant who was personally responsible "only" for the deaths of five hundred thousand. The response of those who support capital punishment is: "All right, your crimes are so terrible that we can't possibly give you what you deserve; there is no way of making you suffer in any way comparable to the way you have made others suffer. All the same, we will do the worst within our power. We will kill you. You can't die more than once, but you can at least die once."

The difficulty with this approach, which undeniably elevates anger to a moral imperative, is that it ignores the unique impact of revenge by death not on the criminal but on society in its role of avenger. Death, unlike any other form of retribution presently employed in civilized nations, shifts the focus from the crime to the punishment. Those who support the death penalty on retributive grounds ignore the fact that executions are by definition so "unseemly" that they cast the general principle of just retribution in a questionable light. One wonders what noble moral lessons were drawn from the television footage of the beer-swilling thugs who gathered outside the Texas penitentiary to cheer on the state as it administered a lethal injection to Charles Brooks.

International reaction to the execution of Adolf Eichmann on May 31, 1962, offers an instructive lesson in the capacity of the death penalty to intrude upon moral sensibilities that ought to have been totally focused on the horror of the man's crimes. (I keep returning to Eichmann, as do many capital-punishment advocates from their perspective, precisely because he is the classic "worst-case" possibility. If the execution of anyone can ever be justified, Eichmann's certainly qualifies. And if the state ought never to put human beings to death, Eichmann strains the principle to its outermost limit.) It should be recalled that Eichmann's trial and execution took place at a time when popular opinion, on both sides of the Atlantic, was beginning one of its cyclical swings against the general practice of capital punishment. A century earlier (had pre-technological society been able to produce the particular tools and modes of bureaucratic organization that facilitated Eichmann's crimes), there would probably have been little general debate over his sentence. There was, of course, a large segment of the public that felt Eichmann deserved to die and there was no more to be said on the issue, just as a large proportion of the public were totally unimpressed by the debate that raged in legal circles over Israel's right, as opposed to that of an international or a German tribunal, to try Eichmann. And there were a number of newspapers, public officials, religious leaders, and legal experts who approved of the sentence. However, there was also a surprisingly extensive and sometimes angry debate over the death sentence itself—a debate suggesting that the execution was the least constructive aspect of the otherwise constructive process of bringing an arch-criminal to justice.

Some of the objections to Eichmann's execution were so far-fetched and bizarre as to be ascribed only to the emotional perplexity that naturally assails anyone who tries to come up with a sound reason why such a man should be permitted to live. A Michigan newspaper argued that Eichmann's execution deprived his six million victims of their individual dignity because it meant that each murdered Jew was only one six-millionth of a human being. (This is unquestionably the most literal interpretation of proportionality I have ever seen.) The *St. Petersburg Times,* a newspaper that had unequivocally declared its opposition to capital punishment at the time of the execution of Caryl Chessman, condemned the execution of Eichmann on the ground that it was too humanitarian—"too quick and easy a way out."[40] This "death-is-too-good-for-him" argument is in fact used in many contexts by opponents of capital punishment, and it is both disingenuous and unconvincing. If one is to reject capital punishment without rejecting the general concept of just retribution, one must judge the issue in terms of its effect on society rather than on the malign members awaiting sentence.

A number of American newspapers attacked the Eichmann sentence on more substantial grounds. The *Atlanta Constitution,* then the leading liberal newspaper of the American South, observed that "humankind is really quite glad [about Eichmann's execution]. . . . And that is just the trouble with this hanging, as it is with most capital punishments. It gets what they did off our consciences and frees us to feel clean and nice. We aren't, and we need living lessons to remind us of it instead of strangling the dark vision of ourselves with a rope."[41] Martin Buber had suggested that Eichmann be imprisoned in Israel to perform useful labor, and this proposal was noted with approval by the *New York Times* and newspapers in many European capitals.

Many commentators in France, England, Scandinavia, and the United States (the Germans were prudently silent on this point) lamented the loss of a "golden opportunity" for Israel to demonstrate her superiority to Eichmann and everything Nazism represented. One major newspaper remarked that many people had expected the Israeli judges to sharpen the contrast between Nazism and civilization by a "spectacular gesture of mercy."[42] These arguments induce a queasiness in the stomach, for one wonders why anyone thought it necessary for Israel to demonstrate her superiority to Eichmann or to Nazism.* This

---

*In reading these comments from more than two decades ago, one gains a certain insight into the current Israeli intransigence in response to international criticism of its policies with regard to the Palestinians and the West Bank Arabs. It must be exceedingly difficult to acknowledge the possible validity of new criticism that comes from those who have long held your country to standards expected of no other nation.

viewpoint was summarized in a long article decrying the sentence in a Protestant journal.

> It would do great honor to the state of Israel and to the Jewish community throughout the world if the High Court in Jerusalem were to . . . reverse the verdict, not because of extenuating circumstances, for there were none, but as a noble rebuke to the very idea that Eichmann represents, that men may choose to kill their fellow men. . . .
>
> It is almost certain that this great opportunity will be missed, that the powers-that-be will let it slip by. Perhaps many of us will be glad to see it go by. For if Eichmann were spared for an experiment in redemption, and the experiment succeeded, it might well spring the lock on our own Pandora's box of guilt and force us to face up to our own sins.[43]

This last quotation embodies all of the errant nonsense associated with the notion that the guilty party is not the criminal but the collective "we." We are all guilty of moral transgressions, and some of us are guilty of legal transgressions, but none of us is guilty of the particular crimes with which Eichmann was charged.

It will doubtless be said—I can hear the capital-punishment advocates raising the objection—that those who fail to recognize the distinction between general moral culpability and specific responsibility for specific crimes would have remained equally obtuse in their judgments had Eichmann been sentenced to life imprisonment instead of death. That may be true, but those who advanced the ludicrous (ludicrous on the basis of Eichmann's own testimony) proposition that he was capable of either repentance or rehabilitation represented only an insignificant minority of popular opinion throughout the world. The preponderance of objections to the Israeli court's decision was based not on opposition to criminal punishment but on opposition to executions. In some measure, the death penalty shifted the focus from what Eichmann had done to what the Israelis were going to do to him. That is regrettable, even scandalous. In retrospect, it is painful to realize that so much concern was wasted on Eichmann's punishment when his crimes were the real horror. For Eichmann was not a beast, to be disposed of as President Reagan disposes of sick animals. Like all other criminals, he embodied a decidedly human possibility. If criminals are beasts, modern society might logically follow the example of the ancient Greeks, who put rocks on trial for fracturing human skulls. (This approach would no doubt arouse the ire of the National Rifle Association, which clings to its slogan that "guns don't kill people, people kill people.")

To classify the worst criminals among us as alien beings is to evade the real question of how to give such men and women their "just deserts"; both justice and revenge lose their customary meanings when they are aimed at objects rather than human beings. The principle of the sanctity of human life (although I adhere to it) is too broad to offer a retributive justification for criminal punishment that stops short of capital punishment. Like the Supreme Court majority in the *Gregg* case, I regard retribution as a legitimate objective of criminal justice, but I do not agree with the conclusion that belief in the permissibility of retribution confers legitimacy on the death penalty. For those who accept the principle of retribution while rejecting the practice of the death penalty, the moral fabric of a society that is willing to conduct executions—not the sanctity of the criminal's life—is the fundamental issue.

Although even the most grievous criminal acts do not strip an offender of his or her humanity, they do shift the burden—and the right—of determining the offender's fate from the individual to society's representatives. Convicted murderers do not lose all of their rights, but they do lose the freedom to choose their own destinies. When Gary Gilmore, the protagonist of Norman Mailer's *The Executioner's Song,* was fighting in the courts to prevent any further stays of execution, the American Civil Liberties Union was sharply criticized for conducting a legal battle—against Gilmore's wishes—to prevent him from becoming the first person executed in the United States since 1968. This protest against the ACLU action by advocates of the death penalty was paradoxical: while insisting that the state has the right to take life, they opposed the ACLU's intervention because Gilmore himself preferred death to life in prison. By their extreme acts of violence, Gilmore and his ilk have forfeited their right to a voice in their own fate. There is no legitimate reason why society should concern itself with whether the Gilmores, the Mansons, the Eichmanns of the world want to live or die (and most of them want to live). What should concern us is the values that we, as a people, wish to represent—whether or not we wish to declare ourselves a civilization that can only satisfy its need for retribution by conducting executions. It is true that most civilizations of the past have declared themselves for the *embarras de richesse* available to public executioners: the gallows, guillotine, electric chair, gas chamber. The only answer to those whose support for the death penalty is grounded in the collective "common sense" of the past is Beccaria's observation that "the objection vanishes in the face of truth, which triumphs over all prescription; that the history of mankind appears a vast sea of errors, among which there float a few confused truths, each far from the next."[44]

Advocates of the death penalty are absolutely right, however, on one point: popular support for capital punishment is grounded in the conviction that criminals ought to be paid back for their violent deeds and that they are not now being punished in sufficient measure. This conviction is neither illegitimate nor childish; to deny it the respect it deserves is to encourage the boundless outrage that generates demands for boundless retribution.

VIII On Crimes and Punishments

No punishment has ever possessed enough power of deterrence to prevent the commission of crimes. On the contrary, whatever the punishment, once a specific crime has appeared for the first time, its reappearance is more likely than its initial emergence could have been.

HANNAH ARENDT, *Eichmann in Jerusalem: A Report on the Banality of Evil*

The severity of the punishment must also be in keeping with the kind of obligation which has been violated, and not [only] with the interests of public security.

SIMONE WEIL, *L'Enracinement*

On the television screen, a middle-aged woman is telling a reporter about the death of her daughter; her voice and facial expression oscillate between tremulous grief and controlled rage. Three years ago, on a spring evening, her twenty-year-old daughter was walking home from the bus stop after a day of college classes. A young man stopped her at knife point and demanded her purse; she gave it to him and then started to scream. He stabbed her in the chest, piercing her aorta. She was dead on arrival at the nearest hospital emergency room. Because there were several witnesses, the police were able to arrest the killer on the same night. Six months later, he pleaded guilty to a reduced charge of manslaughter and received a sentence of zero-to-seven years. In just thirty months, he was released from prison for good behavior.

"I just can't get over this," says the slain girl's mother. "I will never get over this. To know that the price of my child's life was less than three years, that this man is free now to do the same thing to someone else—I can't reconcile myself to it. I can't believe any more that there is such a thing as justice in the world. Everything I tried to live by, everything I brought up my children to respect: things just don't work that way." The woman tells the reporter she is active in an organization for crime victims and their relatives. "We all know we have to get on with our lives," she says, "but that isn't easy to do under the circumstances. I felt as though my girl was killed twice— once by that scum, and once by the judge who said, *well, you only have to go to jail for a few years.* They killed her memory, saying that was all her life was worth."

The outraged mother spoke of justice, not revenge, but revenge was obviously one element in an ideal of justice to which she had adhered, without giving the matter much conscious thought, until the day when the issue was transformed from an abstraction into a painful personal reality. This sense of justice is so fundamental to our psychological well-being that it rarely intrudes upon our consciousness; like many basic assumptions, it remains largely unexamined unless and until it is sorely violated. The symbolic "scales of justice" have a real meaning for most citizens, who believe that the legal system exists to maintain a moral and social equilibrium, and to restore that equilibrium when it has been violently disturbed.

There is, of course, a wide range of opinion on what constitutes appropriate redress. For those whose concept of justice is concerned primarily with the criminal's rights and prospects for rehabilitation, any extended punishment is simply another crime. For those focused totally on the victim's rights, only executions or other severe penalties will suffice to restore a sense of moral balance. Between these extremes lies a broad concept of justice that demands a greater measure of mercy than the death penalty and allows a greater measure of retribution than the American legal system currently dispenses—a spectrum of retribution that excludes both execution and the release of a killer from prison in less than three years. This intermediate sense of justice—one that is, I believe, shared by the largest proportion of the public—has been outraged by the inadequate response of the legal system to the rising incidence of violent crime during the past twenty years. Such outrage is unquestionably the single most important factor in the emotional resurgence of support for capital punishment today; it must be addressed by those who refuse, as I do, to include death in their concept of retributive justice.

It is true that a measure of popular enthusiasm for the death penalty exists independently of the general level of crime and violence in society. Otherwise, there would be no support for capital punishment in Western Europe, England, and Canada, whose crime rates make them appear as near-pastoral realms in comparison to the United States. (Although it is difficult and probably inaccurate to make comparisons among nations regarding certain crimes—rape, for instance, is much less likely to be reported in cultures that consider the crime a total dishonor for both the woman and her family—there is no question that the United States enjoys the dubious distinction of leading the West in murders. Year after year, the proportion of murders per 100,000 population in the United States is seven to eight times higher in the United States than in England, three times higher than in France, and twice as high as in West Germany, which has one of the worst homicide rates on the European continent.) In view of the relatively greater personal safety they enjoy, it is not surprising that those Europeans who favor capital punishment expend less passion on the issue than Americans do. One would assume, for instance, that an overwhelming majority of adults old enough to remember the taste prefer vine-ripened tomatoes to the blandness of today's artificially ripened fruits, but few citizens would be willing to expend their energies on throwing politicians out of office for failing to resolve the tomato crisis. In Canada, England, and most of Europe, the death penalty is something of a tomato issue; although people have definite opinions on the subject, those opinions do not translate into the sort of powerful emotions that influence public policy.

A significant exception to this lack of passion is apparent when Europeans begin to talk about the need to "get tough" with perpetrators of political violence. The United States has been relatively unaffected by the kind of highly visible terrorist acts that have influenced public opinion in England, France, Italy, and West Germany. Even our most traumatic political assassinations have generally been perceived (not always accurately, as white America demonstrated most notably in its limited understanding of the social significance of Martin Luther King's murder) as isolated acts rather than as full-scale ruptures in the fabric of society. This perception of violence as a phenomenon for which the instigators are *personally* and *individually* accountable reflects a characteristically American attitude that extends far beyond issues of crime and punishment.

Every comparative examination of American and European attitudes, from Tocqueville through modern social-science research, shows that Americans are far more disposed than Europeans to believe that individuals are largely responsible for their successes or failures. Since the 1930s, an increasing number of Americans have modified (but not abandoned) their traditional view that the poor are responsible for their own poverty, but few will concede the principle that criminals—even those from the most discouraging environments—may not be responsible for their crimes. This is not to suggest that Europeans reject the concept of individual responsibility—on the contrary, European courts are much less disposed than American ones to delay the disposition of notorious cases with endless psychiatric examination and testimony—but to mark the particularly sharp disparity between American attitudes and the current state of the criminal-justice system.

(The success of pro-gun lobbyists in repeatedly defeating proposals to restrict the sale of firearms—laws which have long been taken for granted in Europe—is based not only on the lobby's enormous financial resources but also on a perverse appeal to traditional American concepts of individualism. In this strangely consistent mindset, belief in individual responsibility for crime is linked with the conviction that individuals have a "right" to carry guns.)

A system of jurisprudence that tends to diffuse, in seemingly limitless ways, the process of assigning criminal responsibility could hardly be less suited to the political requirements of a people disposed to believe that individuals rise or fall primarily on their own merits. This disparity is an important factor not only in the current wave of support for capital punishment but also in the shift from a utilitarian to a retributive rationale, and the regressive trend is not likely to reverse itself until public officials begin to address themselves, in a realistic way, to the legitimate aspects of the popular desire for retribution. However, most politicians have avoided the difficult task of separating legitimate from illegitimate expressions of the need for redress and have simply offered the fraudulent sop of a possible handful of executions—whose "unseemly" details they have no intention of witnessing themselves.

In a society of laws, popular feeling cannot be allowed to dictate either a particular form of punishment or the application of that punishment to a specific individual. This principle is valid not only insofar as it applies to the ultimate penalty of death but also as it applies to all lesser punishments. Popular support alone is not sufficient to confer legitimacy on a legal penalty, whether that penalty is extremely cruel or extremely mild. However, popular opinion must be taken into account in devising and administering a general system of punishments— and particularly in devising penalties that reflect society's estimation of the seriousness of crimes. If it is morally acceptable and socially prudent to release a killer from jail after only thirty months, what penalty might reasonably be imposed for the relatively less heinous crimes of rape, child molestation, or a beating that stops short of death? For the seriousness of such crimes diminishes only in relative terms; they are all grievous insults to individual rights as well as social order.

The crucial concept of proportionality as a limitation on punishment emerged in the law codes of the ancient Hebrews as an advance over the boundless vengeance that had characterized more primitive stages of culture, but proportionality has no meaning as a barrier to cruelty if it does not also place some restrictions on compassion. In order to attain respect as a civic principle, proportionality must set limits at both ends of the spectrum of punishment, just as a complete concept of justice must consider obligations to the past as well as the future. If, as Judge Learned Hand observed, justice is "a tolerable accommodation of the conflicting interests of society," the prospective aspect of the judicial process is of chief concern to the accused criminal, while the retrospective aspect is the primary concern of the victim. Society, however, represents both the criminal and the victim in its judicial institutions, although a substantial segment of the public remain unconvinced of the validity of this basic principle of Anglo-American law. (Sobering evidence on this point is provided in surveys showing that a majority of Americans would reject many of the provisions of the Bill of Rights if they were proposed in Congress today.) In part, support for the death penalty proceeds from the mistaken assumption that convicted criminals lose all of their rights as citizens. In fact—unless they are put to death—criminals do not lose all of their rights. They lose some of them. In determining appropriate degrees of retribution, society decides which rights the criminal will lose and for how long they will be withheld. As far as a great many Americans are concerned, its institutions of justice are not withholding enough rights from violent criminals for a long enough period of time.

Fear of crime, it is sometimes argued, is greatly exaggerated.

There are, after all, "only" about 22,500 murders a year in a population of more than 240 million—fewer than 10 per 100,000 population.[1] Such statistics are bad, to be sure—even one murder is too many—but they are not as bad as people think they are. Such reasoning enrages ordinary citizens who are not impressed by academic distinctions between "real" and "perceived" crime. This reasonable distinction—reasonable when one looks at the statistics on paper—ignores the obvious point that the fear of crime, when violence reaches a generally unacceptable level, becomes inseparable from the reality of crime. Indeed, "real" crime feeds on such fears, and one need not be a victim or the relative of a victim to share them. In 1981, there were more than thirteen million FBI "index crimes." Each of these thirteen million victims of murder, rape, assault, robbery, auto theft, presumably has a number of friends and relatives. When friends and relatives hear about any sort of assault on someone they know, crime acquires a personal meaning that can never be attached to a strange face on the evening news. And FBI crime statistics record only the most serious offenses. An ordinary purse snatching, unless the victim is injured, is not likely to turn up in these reports, but ordinary purse snatchings are very much a part of both the real and the perceived crime problem.

Today, it is a rare resident of a metropolitan area who does not personally know someone victimized by crime. Children learn about crime when their lunch money is snatched from them in school bathrooms. When I was growing up, I did not know a single man, woman, or child who had ever been the victim of a crime. This does not mean that violence was nonexistent in the decidedly non-idyllic decade following the end of the Second World War; it simply means that crime was not common enough to be a daily topic of conversation or an expectable experience in middle-class life. Perceptions of crime today may be worse than reality, but the fear is generated by a reality that has in fact become more violent and more threatening.

The "ripple effect" of an individual crime is not always dramatic, nor is it invariably expressed in shrill, unequivocal cries for vengeance. For friends and relatives of a crime victim, the aftermath of violence frequently brings an unfocused sense of loss, a feeling that "something is missing" from the familiar fabric of everyday life. A New York newspaper described the reaction of a young woman who emerged physically unscathed from the sort of crime that impels people to say, "You were really lucky." Meaning: "You didn't get raped or stabbed or shot." The crime was over in an instant. A young man stepped out of the shadows at the girl's bus stop in a middle-class Italian-American neighborhood, put his knife to her throat and took her engagement ring and the twenty dollars in her purse. Then the mugger disappeared. All possibilities considered, the victim was lucky—but she doesn't feel lucky.

> Her life changed in large and small ways. After the incident, she lost weight dramatically—down from 112 to 103 pounds on an already slight frame. A respiratory problem that makes her breath come in spurts when she gets upset reappeared after the attack. Even a year later, when she recalls the events, she starts gasping slightly. . . .
>
> Her sense of vulnerability has been heightened by her mother's reaction—the predictable blend of anger and relief that a parent feels when a child escapes—just barely—from danger. . . .
>
> "Every time I left the house, it was, 'What time are you coming home? Who are you going to be with?' And if I ever wore jewelry, she'd say, 'So you haven't learned once?' "
>
> Renee loves jewelry; even today, she feels there's little point in having nice things if you can't wear them. But reluctantly, she avoids flashy stuff.

So do many of her friends. Even in this world, where you're not really engaged until a diamond glistens on your finger, some of her girlfriends, shocked by her experience, no longer wear their diamonds when they go out.

During dinner, Renee pointed out a young woman at a nearby table. "She's engaged," Renee whispered, "but she's not wearing her ring, either." These days, she notices such things.[2]

Renee's assailant was twenty-one-year-old Douglas Bruson, a man with eleven previous arrests on charges including armed robbery, assault with a deadly weapon, and rape. In all of these instances, he was allowed to plead guilty to a lesser charge and either released or sent to jail for only a few weeks. His longest jail sentence, for assault and attempted robbery, was set at four months. As a result of his most recent victim's testimony and identification, he was finally tried and sentenced to five years in state prison. She, at least, had the satisfaction of knowing that her assailant would be punished; one wonders how the previous rape and assault victims felt upon learning that their attacker had been allowed to plead guilty to lesser charges and released in only a few weeks.

Deterrence is obviously an issue in this all-too-ordinary account; such a dangerous man should have been removed from the streets at a much earlier point in his criminal career. But retribution, particularly from the victim's standpoint, is also an important issue. The desire to "strike back" at one's assailant —to return evil for evil—represents only the most primitive level of the victim's desire for revenge. Retributive desires also flow from a need to restore "something missing"—a sense of physical and emotional integrity that is shattered by violence. The punishment of criminals provides some measure of assurance to the victim that the assault was an exception to the rule, a violation of an order that society is determined to uphold. Retribution alone cannot provide such assurance—nor should it become the single determinant of criminal punishments—but it is an indispensable element in the process of restoration. The absence of sufficient retribution becomes a twofold attack on the sense of moral order that most people require to sustain their existence, as the mother of the slain girl suggested in her comments about the swift release of her daughter's murderer from prison. Her reaction recalls Elie Wiesel's observation that "at Auschwitz, not only man died but also the idea of man." When a killer's term of punishment is concluded in so short a time (short in absolute terms, and even shorter in relation to the time wrested from the victim), our most cherished concepts of the value of human life are called into question.

The public demand for "legalized revenge" generally focuses on crimes of violence rather than so-called "white-collar" crimes. Murder, rape, beatings, knifings, shootings: these are the crimes that arouse the loudest cries for retribution. The revulsion and indignation engendered by violent crime is sometimes viewed as a product of middle-class bias against the poor (whose criminal tendencies, for obvious reasons, are most likely to be expressed in muggings on the street, while the criminal tendencies of their more affluent fellow citizens are apt to manifest themselves in embezzlement and stock frauds).

But class and racial biases have relatively little to do with the visceral anger aroused by violent crime; the black members of the audience for *Death Wish* cheered with the same gusto as whites while Charles Bronson conducted his one-man rampage against outlaws. The particular aversion to violent assault, and the feeling that such crimes should be punished most severely, reflects a natural and admirable hierarchy of values. What sane man or woman would not prefer to be swindled rather than raped or beaten? Who would not regard the keeper of crooked books, or the gentlemanly jewel thief who tricks a security system with wits instead of a gun, with less loathing than the callous young man who, enraged that his victim has only twenty dollars in his wallet, shoots him through the head before resuming the search for more affluent prey? Only those who are foolish enough to place a higher value on money than on life are as angered by nonviolent as by violent crime.

It would, of course, be a mistake to deny the existence of a general relationship between the level of racial and class conflict and public attitudes toward crime. The United States, with its multiracial, heterogeneous population, has a well-documented history of interaction between majority prejudice—especially white prejudice against blacks—and discriminatory imposition of criminal penalties. White fear of crime is influenced by the undeniable fact that the poor (and blacks and Hispanics are disproportionately represented among the poor) are responsible for a disproportionate share of violent crimes. This phenomenon is neither native to nor exclusive to America. In England, the intensity of public concern over "the crime problem" is directly related to the rise in immigration, over the past twenty years, of blacks and Asians from former colonies that are now members of the British Commonwealth. The National Front, an arch-conservative political movement that many liberals regard as bordering on neo-Nazism, has called for a restoration of the death penalty and deportation of the "new" immigrants back to their native lands. (By "new," the Front means black or brown or yellow; its leaders have never suggested that Australians and New Zealanders be sent back where they came from.) In northern Europe, concern over crime has followed upon the migration of millions of "guest workers" from the poorer, less economically developed regions of the continent's southern tier. Eager for immigrant workers to fill the labor shortages of the booming 1960s, the previously homogeneous nations of northern Europe are notably unenthusiastic about meeting the educational and economic needs of a polyglot population in the leaner economy of the 1980s. Around the world, violent crime is more common among the poor than among the middle class—and the migrants, as a group, are poorer than the citizens of their host nations.

To suggest that only the rich want tougher action against criminals is to ignore the fact that the poor are at much greater risk than the well-off of becoming crime victims. Black Americans, aware of the long history of discriminatory imposition of death sentences on members of their race (especially for rape), are opposed to capital punishment in far greater percentages than whites are. But there is absolutely no evidence that black opposition to the death penalty is accompanied by opposition to lesser punishments. Blacks are overrepresented in relation to their presence in the population among criminals convicted of murder, rape, and robbery, but they are even more heavily represented among the victims of these crimes. In black communities, anger at the police and the courts stems not only from the feeling that some black criminals are treated too harshly but from the conviction that crimes against *black victims* are treated too lightly. All too frequently, the "repeat killer" who murders again after a speedy release from prison is put away for a long sentence only when his next victim is white. "Some of these cases hit the newspapers," observed one writer on criminal justice, "usually when the second victim is white. Nathan Giles slipped into prison with the murder of a woman in Harlem and came out to make headlines for shooting and burning a [white] nurse named Bonnie Ann Bush on West 102nd Street. Grant Minor made news when he followed the strangling of a [black] waitress in Queens with the strangling of a [white] lawyer in Fort Greene."[3]

In rape cases, black women are much less likely than white women to see their rapists brought to trial, convicted, and sentenced to lengthy prison terms. As a rule, the crime of rape is punished most harshly when the rapist is black and the victim white and, while the proportion of rapes by blacks against white women has increased in recent years, the overwhelming majority of rapes are committed by blacks against blacks or by whites against whites. Black women raped by black men account for the largest single percentage of rape victims.[4] A detailed study in the *Pennsylvania Law Review* reported that Philadelphia police considered rape complaints by black victims against black assailants to be "unfounded" 22 percent of the time, while only 12 percent of white-on-white complaints were assessed as unfounded.[5]

The same pattern holds true for most other crimes committed by blacks against blacks. Blacks receive lighter sentences and earlier parole for crimes committed against other blacks than they do for crimes committed against whites, or than white criminals do for offenses committed against either whites or blacks. A number of criminologists and sociologists have suggested that this pattern is attributable mainly to the overload of criminal cases in high-density crime areas—areas in which most crimes are committed by poor blacks and Hispanics against other poor blacks and Hispanics. There is a good deal of truth to this explanation, but it is far from the whole truth. The American criminal-court system is not organized on a neighborhood-by-neighborhood basis, and, if the sheer volume of crime were the only problem, violence committed by blacks against blacks would be treated in precisely the same manner by the overloaded courts in metropolitan areas as violence committed by blacks against whites. The glare of publicity surrounding so many of the most serious black-against-white crimes attests to the fact that all lives are not treated with equal respect.

There is something deeply repellent about demands for retribution that focus not on the injury to the victim but on the victim's spotless reputation or high social status.

In New York City, one of the most widely publicized crimes in recent years was the particularly brutal rape of a nun: she was not only assaulted sexually but had twenty-seven crosses cut into her body with a nail file. Many of the news reports concentrated as much on the fact that the victim was a nun as on the horrible nature of the crime itself. A newspaper reported that one of the suspects had been described by a veteran police officer as a "real bad guy" and indicated that both men "knew they were assaulting a nun."[6] The police officers presumably found it necessary to underline this point because the nun, like many members of religious orders today, was clad not in a traditional habit but in blue jeans. Would the crime have been less reprehensible if the suspects thought they were only raping an ordinary woman? The commanding officer of the Manhattan Detective Area, while acknowledging that "rape is a particularly heinous crime for any woman," went on to maintain that "when it [rape] involves a woman who has taken a vow of chastity, it is especially vile."[7]

The police mounted a full-scale effort to find and arrest the rapists, amid newspaper reports that the Mafia had put out a $25,000 contract on the men. The East Harlem area in which the crime was committed is primarily black and Hispanic but it was once an Italian immigrant neighborhood, and a small enclave of streets around the convent retains its reputation as a center of organized crime activity—but not of violent street crime. "This neighborhood is comparatively free of violent crime because the Mafia wants it that way," one merchant was quoted as saying. "When they heard this nun was raped in their own backdoor [sic] they had to take vengeance." According to another source, "They're talking about stringing the rapist from a lamp post. These guys are dead men."[8] In five days, the police did arrest the two rapists—one of whom already had a long criminal record. The florid publicity, the particularly brutal nature of the crime, and the victim's race and status as a member of a religious order may all have spurred the police to unusual efforts to find and charge the criminals.

In all of the publicity surrounding the case, there was a notable lack of commentary from black and Hispanic residents who make up an overwhelming majority of the population in the area. Explained one black minister: "How could you say anything negative about the enormous efforts being made by the police in this case without being misunderstood? Of course this is a deeply revolting crime, and as far as I'm concerned the men who did it should be behind bars for the rest of their lives; no one is safe when such criminals walk the streets. But as a black man, I can only ask where is the outcry, where is the special police task force, when a black woman is raped. One of my parishioners, a nurse and a mother of four children, was brutally raped by five teenagers as she was walking home from the night shift in her hospital. None of those 'boys'—I use the term with irony—was ever caught. Was the same effort made on her behalf as it was on behalf of that poor nun? We know the answer.

"Anyone who thinks black people don't want to see criminals of their own race punished simply does not know the black community. Most of the time, we are the victims. Too often, our rage and our demand that these criminals be paid back go unheard. But how can you say this in public? It would look as if we were indifferent to the sufferings of that particular victim, who happens to be a white nun. But we are not indifferent. We know that suffering all too well, and there is too little redress for us."

Too little redress. The white majority in America tend to view minority concern over "equal justice" as a movement to protect the civil rights of blacks and Hispanics accused of crimes. Although the rights of accused criminals are certainly, and properly, a matter of concern within minority communities, concern over the needs of victims is much greater.

The widely publicized case of the raped and tortured nun had an ironic ending. After all of the outrage expressed in the press and the community, the rapists were allowed to plead guilty to lesser charges of burglary and oral sodomy, for which they received, respectively, sentences of five to fifteen and ten to twenty years. The prosecution had no choice, because the victim refused to testify against her attackers in court. She was quoted as saying she had no desire for revenge and hoped that her attackers would come to understand the harm they had done to a fellow human being. Fair enough, from a personal and religious perspective. From a public perspective, though, this expression of religious compassion—"private forgiveness," in Beccaria's phrase—is troubling. Had the victim testified, her assailants would undoubtedly have received much longer prison terms—sentences commensurate with the especially brutal nature of the infliction of rape and aggravated assault (not burglary and sodomy). As the sentence stands, one of the rapists could be released from prison in only five years. This, of course, is likely to pose a new danger to the community.

Beyond the question of individual deterrence, though, there is the matter of justice and retribution. It simply defies commonly understood standards of decency and justice that men who raped and tortured a woman for an hour-and-a-half—with nail files, broomsticks, crucifixes, candles—should receive anything less than the maximum sentences prescribed by law for the crimes they actually committed. In this case, the victim herself was responsible, by virtue of her refusal to testify, for the relatively light penalty meted out to her attackers. In most cases, however, plea bargaining has nothing to do with the unwillingness of the victim to testify and everything to do with the general failure of the criminal justice system to mete out appropriate retribution.

The use of plea bargaining, in which the accused pleads guilty to a lesser charge and therefore receives a lighter sentence than would have been the result of a trial and conviction for the crime originally charged, is most common in areas with the highest crime rates. It is primarily a device to save the state the expense of a trial. Cries for retribution in the form of the death penalty are, to a significant degree, influenced by the general public knowledge that most criminals are not prosecuted to the full extent of the law. There is nothing isolated about the miscarriage of justice signified by plea bargaining in urban areas. In the mid-1960s and early 1970s, when FBI statistics show that the crime rate nearly doubled, both the courts and the prisons were overwhelmed. In New York City, it took more than two years to dispose of the average criminal case. Plea bargaining was an answer, but the effect of that answer on crime victims was to make them feel doubly wounded—first by their assailant and then by the society that is supposed to punish those who break the law. Consider this statement from a former prosecuting attorney: "First you looked to see who died. If it was a lowlife, you offered zip to four, maybe zip to seven. On sale days, they might get probation."[9] In 1981, only 13 percent of the criminal cases in which indictments had been handed down were actually taken to trial in New York City. Nearly three-quarters of those indicted struck a plea bargain with the prosecutor's office before trial. Sometimes, as in the case of the raped nun, the criminal pleads guilty to a lesser charge—burglary instead of rape, petit larceny instead of grand larceny, manslaughter instead of murder. In other instances, the accused pleads guilty to the original charge but strikes a deal for a sentence less than would have been handed down after trial and conviction. The "deal-for-sentence" plea bargain is extremely common. In the same month that the newspapers were demanding the arrest of the nun's rapists, another, much more typical case was reported in much smaller type.

Glen Steward, a convicted rapist who was released on parole after serving four years of his sentence (his parole officer said he had been a model ex-convict), walked into the lobby of an apartment building and shot sixty-two-year-old Luis Arias Perez, a doorman, after he had given up his money and offered no resistance. "I had no particular motive," he told the judge at his sentencing.[10] He then walked a few blocks and killed another doorman, fifty-year-old Edward Cruz, in the same fashion. The day before his case was to go to trial, he pleaded guilty to premeditated murder in return for a promise of a maximum sentence of fifteen-years-to-life (meaning he would be eligible for parole in fifteen years).

The Manhattan District Attorney's office allowed Steward

to plead guilty in return for a lighter sentence because, according to one source, "one of the psychiatrists who examined Steward found him 'not responsible.' " What the state gained from this bargain—a bargain that, to the average citizen, would seem to benefit only the killer—was a sure fifteen-year sentence as opposed to the uncertainty and expense of conducting a proper trial. One dissent by a psychiatrist means that the prosecution must produce its own psychiatric testimony. From the standpoint of the state, the bargain was not untirely unreasonable—it was, after all, better than "zip-to-seven." From the standpoint of the relatives of two hard-working doormen, the bargain must have seemed an obscenity. Had the man been tried and convicted, he would have received a life sentence and would not have been eligible for parole until he had served fifty years. Fifty years is an alternative to the death penalty that many people can accept. Fifteen years, or five years, or three years, is not.

The frequency with which parole is granted to criminals serving sentences for extremely serious offenses—like plea bargaining, a response to the increased incidence of crime that has taxed the resources of prisons as well as the courts—is another element in both the real and the perceived problem of inappropriate retribution. The concept of parole, as instituted in the prison reforms of the nineteenth century, was understood by the public as a way of mitigating the punishments of criminals whose behavior in prison provided convincing evidence of a change of heart and those who, because they had something or someone to come home to, might have a reasonable hope of making it outside the prison walls. Parole has also been—although it was not intended to be—a tool to ameliorate the condition of those who, though guilty under the law, are seen as less culpable than others convicted of the same crime. One would expect that Marianne Bachmeier, the German mother who shot her child's killer in a courtroom, will be treated more sympathetically in prison than the original killer would have been had he lived to go to jail. Such distinctions—although there is a strict legal case to be made against them—do not offend the common sense of justice. The public wants a criminal-justice system that makes distinctions, after prison as well as before, between those who display some moral awareness and those who do not, between those who make some attempt to display socially acceptable behavior (even if the attempt is motivated only by a desire to be released from prison) and those who do not. One cannot say with any certainty that a "model prisoner" will become a model citizen on the outside, but one can say that a prisoner who is trouble on the inside will probably continue to be trouble on the outside.

Parole, as granted in today's crowded prison system, has nothing to do with civilized notions of mitigation; its main purpose is to free prison cells for new prisoners. Since parole today is a matter of economic necessity for the state, it has only the most tenuous relationship to a prisoner's good behavior, or the absence of it. California law requires that prisoners who are serving their first sentence for murder be automatically considered for parole after fourteen years. This law does not guarantee that a convicted murderer will be released, but parole is extremely common for those who maintain a clean disciplinary record in prison. The routine nature of parole after fourteen years for "ordinary" murderers was underlined when Sirhan Sirhan, the convicted assassin of Robert Kennedy, made an angry plea for parole on the ground that he was being denied his "rights" because he had killed a famous man. Kennedy, Sirhan reminded the public, was a political leader who identified with the poor and oppressed. He, Sirhan, felt himself eminently qualified on that score. Kennedy would have been the first to insist that his murderer receive equal treatment under the law, and Sirhan saw no reason why his name should not be added to the list of first-time murderers released from prison on parole. In 1982, the state parole board turned down Sirhan's request—for the time being—partly because he had

been overheard making threats against the life of the only surviving Kennedy brother, Senator Edward Kennedy. The
sophistry of Sirhan's appeal to civic compassion—and to his
victim's legacy of sympathy for the oppressed—was nauseating
enough; still more nauseating is the accuracy of his contention
that he probably would have been released had he killed someone "ordinary."

One of the curious effects of the impassioned controversy
over the death penalty, combined with the uncertainties attached to sentencing and parole practices, has been to make
prison appear less of a punishment than it actually is—or ought
to be in a consistent criminal-justice system. Imprisonment,
except perhaps in those minimum-security institutions designed
specifically for convicts who have no record of violence, is most
assuredly a severe punishment. Supporters of the death penalty
sometimes suggest that prison is nothing more than an all-
expenses-paid vacation. This point of view is represented in a
description of the incarceration of Richard Speck, who was
convicted in the late 1960s of the brutal murder of eight student
nurses in Chicago. "Richard Franklin Speck," the author in-
toned, "is today contentedly watching television in an Illinois
penitentiary, at the taxpayers' expense. The eight student
nurses whom he murdered have been in their graves for ten
years, all but forgotten. There is an imbalance here that must
be corrected."[11]

Anyone who has spent any time around prisons—even in
relatively lenient institutions reserved for white-collar criminals
like the Watergate defendants—knows that few prisoners are
content with their lot, even if it does include nightly doses of
television. Only those who have always been free to come and
go as they please underestimate the degree of suffering inherent
in any deprivation of liberty—quite apart from additional punishments a penal institution may inflict on its inhabitants. Imprisonment is not as bad as death but it is, if equitably administered, a punishment that unquestionably makes violent

criminals suffer for their actions. The problem is that current parole practices, like the widespread use of plea bargaining, work against the principle of equitable and proportional retribution. A murderer or rapist in a high-crime district will probably be able to plead guilty to a reduced charge. If he is sent to a crowded prison, he will be paroled to make room for others, regardless of his behavior or his prospects for life on the outside.

Sirhan will remain in prison for the foreseeable future, and Charles Manson may remain in prison for the rest of his life— or at least until he is so old that penal authorities do not have a vivid memory of why he was sent to prison in the first place. The killers of doormen and taxi drivers and young women walking home from bus stops—"ordinary" murderers—are another matter altogether. The record of one such commonplace murderer, a man who killed again after he was released, made it clear that prison authorities had little hope of his staying out of trouble. In 1970, Milton Jones had stabbed a youth counselor to death—a counselor with whom he was staying because he had been thrown out of his own apartment for refusing to look for work. In 1980, Jones became eligible for release under a program known in New York State as the "good-time law." A prisoner becomes eligible for release after serving two-thirds of his maximum sentence, assuming he has not added any new offenses to his criminal record while in prison. Before Jones' release, his prison record flatly stated that he "did not indicate any plans for the future that were realistic. This inmate without therapy, which he consistently refused to accept, presents a major risk."[12] Six months later, Jones killed Olga Rodriguez, a mother of two young children who, with her husband, ran a successful freight-forwarding business. The Rodriguezes were a classic immigrant success story, parents who had worked their family's way out of poverty into a middle-class life. Mrs. Rodriguez was buried in the same cemetery as the youth counselor whom Jones had murdered eleven years earlier.

In one sense, the use of plea bargaining, parole, and early release is a pragmatic response to a high crime rate. There is a circularity to the process: we return dangerous criminals to the streets because there is not enough room for them in the prisons, and they commit more crimes, thereby aggravating the situation that led to their release in the first place. But this process is not understood in pragmatic terms by the public nor, in truth, does it represent a totally pragmatic approach on the part of public authorities. Like most matters of public policy, the current state of the criminal-justice system reflects a value judgment, and the judgment is that there are matters far more important than protecting the innocent and punishing the guilty. While it is ridiculous to suppose that the general public will embark on blood vendettas if murderers are not put to death by the state, it is all too plausible that the public will lose confidence in the law if it believes criminals suffer not at all—or not enough—for their violent assaults on others. Plea bargaining and early parole are systematic practices—not exceptions to the rule. There is a legitimate place for both in a compassionate system of criminal justice, but not as a routine substitute for just retribution.

The role of psychiatry in the criminal-justice system is even more problematic. Psychiatric justice, as it is practiced today, is not a matter of expediency but of philosophy—a philosophy that rejects the principles of personal innocence, guilt, and retribution. John Hinckley's acquittal, by focusing enormous public attention on only one aspect—the insanity plea—of the relationship between psychiatry and the law, has obscured a multitude of legal and ethical questions arising from the engagement of "physicians of the mind" in the process of criminal justice. Judging from the outcry over the Hinckley verdict, a large segment of the public seem to regard psychiatrists primarily as witch doctors who are dedicated to helping criminals escape the legal consequences of their deeds. The truth is a good deal more complicated, although it does not necessarily cast the alliance between legal and mental-health professionals in a more flattering light.

Psychiatrists in the courtroom today are sometimes viewed as advocates of crime without punishment but there is also a strong historical association between psychiatry and punishment without crime. The entanglement of psychiatry and law began with the general professionalization of medicine in the mid-nineteenth century. Psychological labeling was practiced as a means of social control long before the dissemination of Freud's theories led to the emergence of psychiatry as a coherent intellectual discipline and the development of "talking" and drug therapies to treat those suffering from mental disorders. The commitment of Elizabeth Packard in the 1860s for defying her husband's religious authority exemplifies the primitive use of psychiatry as an instrument of control. (Packard was most fortunate that the medical officer in charge of her insane asylum was a bureaucrat who followed orders but did not actually believe the fictions upon which they were based—as demonstrated by his suggestion that she should forgive her husband because the balance of *his* mind was disturbed.)

The use of what we now call psychiatry in this manner was as common in England and northern Europe as in the United States. In 1860, regulations promulgated for admission to the Salpêtrière, the Paris insane asylum, authorized confinement for children of poor Parisians up to age twenty-five if they "used their parents badly" or refused to work due to laziness. For girls, confinement was also mandated for those "debauched or in evident danger of being debauched."[13] The latter definition might easily have been applied to girls whose sexual conduct did not meet with their parents' approval or to those whose presence in the house proved to be too great a sexual temptation for their male relatives. The punitive misuse of psychiatry has frequently involved the application of differential standards of sanity to the poor and to women who fail to conform to their expected social roles. (I do not mean to imply by this statement that conformity to certain middle-class standards is illegitimate as an objective of voluntary psychotherapy. Indeed, many men and women seek treatment because of a failure, whether real or perceived, to live up to what they regard as desirable standards of behavior.) There is, however, a world of difference between enforced treatment as an unacknowledged form of punishment and voluntary treatment.

In recent years, the most prominent example of an unholy alliance between psychiatric medicine and governmental control mechanisms has been offered by the Soviet Union's practice of confining selected political dissidents to mental institutions. In 1970, the internationally known biologist Zhores Medvedev (who has since been permitted to leave the Soviet Union) was committed to a mental institution as a result of activities that included protests against restrictions on the international contacts of Soviet scientists. Because Medvedev was well-known in both the Soviet and international scientific communities, his professional colleagues demanded and got a meeting with the state-appointed psychiatrists who had examined him. The chief psychiatrist told the assembled scientists that he had diagnosed Medvedev as a schizophrenic because he was a biologist who wrote political tracts—in effect, because he refused to limit himself to one scientific specialty. Pyotr Kapitsa and Vladimir Engelhart, both famous Soviet scientists and winners of the Lenin Prize, congratulated the state's psychiatrist for having discovered a new disorder—"the Leonardo da Vinci syndrome."[14]

Compulsory psychiatric confinement as an adjunct to the criminal-justice system has not been relegated to the status of witch burning, nor is it employed exclusively by totalitarian governments. The civil rights of mental patients confined against their will, whether as a result of publicized criminal cases or unpublicized commitments by relatives, are a source of lively legal debate in both England and the United States. At first glance, it would appear that the punitive use of psychiatry to achieve social conformity has little in common with—indeed, runs directly counter to—employment of psychiatric testimony on the part of defense attorneys to exculpate those accused of crimes. On closer examination, these seemingly antithetical phenomena are really two sides of the same coin: they involve attempts to apply a medical-therapeutic approach to conflicts that demand other forms of resolution. The question of responsibility is subordinated to other social needs—for Soviet society, the need to find extra-legal ways of controlling behavior that is offensive to the authorities but not in technical violation of the law; for American society, the need (increasingly at odds with the public desire that criminals be punished) to exculpate those whose violent acts are seen by the therapeutic establishment as sick rather than evil.

A straightforward insanity plea like the one put forward in the Hinckley case is comparatively rare, but psychiatric involvement in criminal cases manifests itself in a wide variety of other ways. In the wake of the Hinckley verdict, there were angry demands that the insanity plea be abolished altogether; in an attempt to counter this extreme reaction, defenders of the legal-psychiatric status quo pointed to statistics like those released in a national survey in 1978, which showed that only 3,100 people confined in mental institutions had been acquitted of crimes as a result of insanity pleas.[15]

Such statistics minimize, in misleading fashion, the full impact of psychiatry on the criminal-justice system. In the first place, they do not include those acquitted of crimes by reason of insanity and subsequently released from confinement—like Francine Hughes, whose plea of temporary insanity persuaded a Michigan jury to acquit her of setting fire to her husband. Within a month, Hughes was examined by psychiatrists, declared to be fully recovered from her recent bout of insanity, and released with no requirement that she receive further psychiatric treatment. In Hughes's case, the implicit prediction that she would now endanger no one would seem to be well founded, in view of the fact that her only act of violence resulted from a long-term relationship with a husband who was brutal to her.

However, such releases—or transfers from maximum-security institutions to "open" hospitals that allow residents to leave on passes—also occur in cases where the patient has a long, well-documented history of criminal violence. In 1982, public prosecutors in suburban Long Island, New York, vigorously protested the transfer to a minimum-security hospital of a man who had rammed a stolen car into an ice-cream stand, killed three people, and injured twenty others. He was declared mentally incompetent to stand trial and diagnosed as a paranoid schizophrenic, but a panel of state-appointed doctors approved the transfer to a minimum-security hospital because they said the man was in remission. A fourth psychiatrist, who considered the patient still dangerous, was dismissed from the panel after he opposed the transfer. In "open" hospitals, patients can and frequently do walk out the door in the absence of strict security. In just such an institution in the same suburban setting, a psychopath named Adam Berwid made good on his repeated threats to kill his wife in 1979. The Berwid case embodies some of the most troubling issues arising from the relationship between psychiatry and the law. Like Francine Hughes's husband, Adam Berwid was a violent man; his attacks on his wife, had they been directed toward a stranger, would have sent him to jail many times over. His estranged wife, Ewa, sought legal help after he broke into her house and threatened repeatedly to kill her. The judge who found Berwid incompetent to stand trial, in an order committing the defendant for observation in a mental hospital, included a note to the authorities stating his belief that Berwid definitely intended to kill his wife and would do so if released. "But, under the law, that was all I could do," the judge said after Berwid did murder his wife. "And, in finding him incompetent to stand trial, the

maximum I could do, since he was charged with a misde-
meanor, was to remand him for observation for 90 days. If I'd
asked that I be notified if he was released or escaped, I couldn't
do anything except tell the police in case they wanted to put a
24-hour guard on the house."[16]

After the murder, psychiatrists continued to disagree on
Berwid's mental competence to stand trial. Under the law, a
defendant must be deemed to have the mental capacity to assist
in his own defense, another reason why statistics on those who
actually employ the insanity defense are misleading. If defendants are found incompetent to stand trial, they do not enter
insanity pleas—and yet they belong to the category of those
whose responsibility for crimes is never assessed. When Berwid
finally did stand trial, he quickly dropped his plea of not guilty
by reason of mental disease, and was convicted of murder and
given a sentence of thirty-five years to life. (The fact that Berwid
insisted on acting as his own attorney was adduced as evidence
of his incompetence to stand trial. In other instances, the refusal
of defendants to go along with a plea of insanity or diminished
mental capacity is viewed as proof that they are indeed too
disturbed to be guilty of a crime.)

By authorizing the release of mental patients who were
either acquitted of crimes by reason of insanity or who were
declared mentally incompetent to stand trial, state-appointed
psychiatrists are, in effect, making predictions of future behavior—something that respected psychiatrists in private practice
are loath to do. Eminent psychiatrists—however strongly they
may disagree with colleagues on explanations of human behavior and modes of treatment—are virtually unanimous in their
reluctance to make predictions about the behavior of patients.
"We have hopes," a respected psychoanalyst told me in an
interview, "and, because we are human and because the mind
is still *terra incognita*—however ardently we may wish to understand its workings—our hopes are sometimes dashed. Ask
any psychiatrist how he feels when a patient commits suicide

after seeming to have made excellent progress in overcoming emotional difficulties. If a psychiatrist still knows so little about a patient he has been seeing three times a week for years, how can a physician in a large state institution conclude that a man who killed someone two years ago is now 'cured' or 'in remission'? And if the violent patient is in remission, who is to say how long that remission will last?"

The unreliability of behavioral forecasts by psychiatrists may have extremely painful consequences for both patient and doctor, but the consequences generally remain private when they occur in an ordinary therapeutic setting. When psychiatrists guess wrong about the behavior of those committed to their care through the criminal-justice system, the consequences become public and potentially dangerous. (Of course, inaccurate psychiatric assessments of dangerously psychotic patients, like the one made by John Hinckley's private doctor, can eventually have serious public consequences. Hinckley's psychiatrist had seen him as an immature and irresponsible, but harmless, neurotic instead of a "walking time bomb" enmeshed in violent fantasies and largely divorced from reality.) As far as the state of public justice is concerned, the issue is not the accuracy of psychiatric predictions—the study of the human mind was never intended to be a mathematical formula—but rather the legitimization of this adventurous, highly imprecise exploration of the psyche as a tool for assessing the responsibility of criminal defendants and for treating them if they are found to be insane or mentally incompetent. Even if psychiatric forecasts were totally reliable, their dependability would not speak to the issue of how society ought to repay those who have violated its laws in the past.

The concept of insanity in law is not, as some harsh critics of modern psychiatric justice have mistakenly implied, the product of twentieth-century psychiatry. The idea that accused persons cannot be held criminally responsible if they are—or were at the time of the act in question—mentally incapable of understanding the nature of the crime is as old as written law. In English common law, madness was recognized as a legitimate defense by the beginning of the sixteenth century. In both England and America, limited versions of the insanity defense were far from uncommon in the eighteenth century. Then as now, the question of madness was most frequently raised in "domestic" cases—not that the matter of responsibility was any less problematic in the age of traditional religious faith than it is in the age of psychiatry. Possession by demons, for instance, was regarded as a mitigating or exculpating factor in the judgment of acts that would ordinarily have been regarded as criminal. However, the alliance with demonic forces had to be judged involuntary for the defendant to be acquitted; voluntary alliance with the devil was, of course, considered witchcraft.

In Anglo-American law, the modern standard of insanity is rooted in the 1843 decision of a British jury acquitting Daniel M'Naghten, who had attempted to kill Prime Minister Robert Peel. The decision concluded that M'Naghten, at the time of the assassination attempt, had been "laboring under such a defect of reason from disease of the mind as not to know the nature and quality of the act he was doing, or if he did know, that he did not know he was doing what was wrong."

"Defect of reason" is a specific concept—specific, at least, in comparison to the broader definitions of mental disease that have evolved during the past century. Under the M'Naghten rule, one might infer—and both American and English juries generally did infer—that a defendant could be found insane only if he or she was so deranged as to have virtually no understanding of the real nature of the crime. Under this guideline, Hinckley might conceivably have been acquitted had he been convinced that President Reagan was his rival for Jodie Foster's love, but not because he saw assassinating the President as a way of capturing her attention. Both the former and the latter beliefs fall under the heading of delusions—as delusions are understood in ordinary life rather than law. They are, however, quite different types of delusions insofar as the legal definition of insanity is concerned. The idea that President Reagan—or Satan, or a leopard—is Jodie Foster's suitor is a delusion in the most narrow sense of the term. The idea that it might be possible to attract Foster's attention by killing the President—by making, in Hinckley's own words, "some kind of statement or something on her behalf"—is a delusion of a different order. Hinckley knew that Reagan was Reagan and he knew he was trying to kill him; the psychiatrists who testified in his defense never asserted otherwise. What Hinckley did not know was that the kind of attention he wished to attract was not what he would be likely to receive as a result of his act. This lack of comprehension surely qualifies Hinckley as "crazy" in the colloquial sense, but the furor over his acquittal turns, quite properly, on the question of whether this craziness ought to absolve him of guilt. It is possible to be both sick and evil—just as it is possible to be mentally ill without being a criminal.

The M'Naghten rule, especially in the United States, was frequently expanded to encompass forms of mental aberration far more ambiguous than a literal inability to comprehend the nature of an act. The concept of "irresistible impulse" found its way into many American laws during the first three decades of the twentieth century—well before Freud's theories were generally known, much less accepted, in this country. This variation on the classical insanity defense was frequently applied to defendants in cases involving crimes of passion and was sometimes linked to crude physiological concepts of brain disorders, as in the case of Harry K. Thaw, who was said to have murdered Stanford White in a "brainstorm."

In 1954, Judge David Bazelon of the U.S. Circuit Court of Appeals in Washington handed down his now-famous decision in the Durham case, which expanded the concept of irresistible impulse. Bazelon's decision argued that defendants could not be held responsible for criminal acts if their violation of the law was "the product of mental disease or mental defect." This decision, handed down during a decade when psychotherapy had begun to gain a more widespread acceptance in American society than it had earned in the European birthplaces of psychoanalysis, forged new links between psychiatry and the law.

Public skepticism about the value of psychiatric justice, which has become so marked in recent years, began to surface in the early 1970s—at roughly the same time as resurgence of popular support for the death penalty. Like the movement in support of capital punishment, the demand for a return to narrower standards of insanity is attributable mainly to fear generated by the increased incidence of crime—and to the feeling that criminals are escaping the punishment they deserve. Criticism of the alliance between psychiatry and the law cannot be attributed to any lack of American enthusiasm for psychological exploration and experimentation. Although the 1970s saw a diminution of interest in classical psychoanalysis (largely as a result of the time and expense involved), the decade was characterized by an extraordinary proliferation of therapies and "consciousness-altering" movements—some of them of a bizarre and authoritarian nature. When a social history of the 1970s is written, it will no doubt be seen as a curiosity that, while millions of Americans clamored for a return to strict personal accountability under the law, other (and perhaps some of the same) millions paid hundreds of dollars each to attend est sessions conducted by "leaders" who promised to transform their outlook on life by calling them "garbage" and "assholes" and by refusing to allow them access to toilets.

Psychiatrists themselves have evinced a growing concern about the involvement of their profession in the criminal-justice system, in part because they fear a return to an old-fashioned view of the mentally ill as a danger to society. The publicity focused on the small but highly visible proportion of violent psychotics tends to obscure the fact that those thought to be mentally ill exhibit as wide a range of behavior patterns as those considered sane. Shortly after Hinckley was acquitted, I clipped a small newspaper item about a man in France who decided to win back his sweetheart by baking the world's largest *croquembouche* (a cake, frequently served at weddings, of cream puffs in a pyramid) and leaving it on her doorstep. She stepped out her front door into the cake and was predictably furious with him. No doubt the neighbors shook their heads and said, *"Quelle folie,"* but this young man merely chose to express his *folie* by baking an oversized cake, not by shooting François Mitterrand. Judaeo-Christian tradition may have overestimated the possibilities for free choice, but—to the extent that the possibility of choice exists—it is certainly not limited to those who are free of mental diseases or defects. For who among us would confidently declare ourselves, much less our neighbors, to be free of all mental defects?

In 1972, the same federal appeals court in Washington overruled the *Durham* decision and applied the somewhat narrower standard that was ultimately used in the Hinckley case—a combination of the "defect of reason" set forth in the M'Naghten rule and the concept of "irresistible impulse" embodied in many criminal statutes. In practice, juries still find themselves in a quandary when competing squads of psychiatrists take the stand and offer diametrically opposing interpretations of a defendant's state of mind and actions. If any defendant can ever be said to have acted on an "irresistible impulse," Hinckley would seem to fit the description. And yet, if one assumes the existence of an emotional stage at which Hinckley's admittedly deviant impulses might have been "resistible," did he not, at some point, make a decision to abandon resistance? What we know—and it may be all we know—is that he ultimately found the impulse impossible to resist because he did in fact try to kill the President. By that standard, any impulse is irresistible simply by virtue of its having been acted upon. This seems to me the heart of the conflict between psychiatric justice and the public demand that society punish those who break its laws. Dr. Harvey Lomas suggests that the persistent abdication of responsibility is both a mental disorder and a choice.

> Those of us who have undertaken the lengthy and difficult treatment of psychotic patients know that there are no simple answers to the question of responsibility. We are familiar with the "not guilty by reason of insanity" plea as a daily occurrence in the treatment of patients. For example, conflicts between physicians and nurses, between therapists and other members of the treatment team often occur when decisions are made about such things as privileges, responsibility levels, passes, and discharge planning. Such conflicts can easily be traced to divergent attitudes toward the patient and his/her degree of responsibility. . . .
>
> My own clinical experience and treatment philosophy hold that the great majority of our most disturbed patients are capable of achieving degrees of freedom of will and the exercise of choice, but that a substantial number of them refuse to make the choice or exercise their will. They choose not to choose. Their psychic economics are better served by shifting the responsibility for their lives to others and many of them decide on this course of action not out of helplessness, but out of a passionate sense of revenge.[17]

This abdication of responsibility is noticeable in many interviews with prisoners who have not been acquitted by reason of insanity but who have been convicted on lesser charges as a result of diminished capacity or "extreme emotional stress." California's diminished-capacity test and New York's extreme-emotional-stress defense—concepts replicated in many state laws—have essentially the same effect: defendants do not go free but receive substantially lighter sentences than they would have if convicted of premeditated crimes. Dan White, who killed San Francisco Mayor George Moscone and supervisor Harvey Milk in 1979, was treated by the criminal-justice system in essentially the same fashion as Richard Herrin was for the killing of Bonnie Garland: neither man was declared incompetent or insane but both were convicted of manslaughter instead of premeditated murder and sentenced accordingly. The arguments in White's case acquired the disdainful label of "the Twinkie defense" because his lawyers claimed his reasoning ability had been eroded by a diet of junk food. White's motive, however, was no secret. He hated homosexuals and Harvey Milk was a leader of the San Francisco homosexual community. Mayor Moscone had been elected by a coalition of liberal supporters, including gay activists, and had made good on campaign pledges to end discrimination against homosexuals in public employment.

Although a large segment of the public believe such men have "gotten away with murder," many of the convicts express resentment about the length of their manslaughter sentences. In referring to the crimes that sent them to prison, such men and women implicitly deny responsibility by referring to their actions in the third person. They use locutions like "the tragedy," "the incident," "this painful trauma." They *never* say, "I shot" or "I stabbed." Willard Gaylin's post-trial interviews with Richard Herrin exemplify this detached quality. "I would rather that she [Bonnie] had survived as a complete person," Herrin tells Gaylin. He never says, "I wish I hadn't killed Bonnie." He explains, at great length, why he feels his sentence of eight to twenty-five years is too heavy a punishment.

> Considering all the factors that I feel the judge should have considered: prior history of arrest, my personality background, my capacity for a productive life in society—you know, those kinds of things—I don't think he took those into consideration. He looked at the crime itself and responded to a lot of public pressure or maybe his own personal feelings, I don't know. I'm not going to accuse him of anything, but I was given the maximum sentence. This being my first arrest and considering

the circumstances, I don't think I should have been given eight to twenty-five years.

Herrin clearly regards himself as a victim, but *he* is not going to accuse the judge of anything.

Gaylin asks Herrin, "How would you answer the kind of person who says, for Bonnie, it's her whole life; for you, it's eight years. What's eight years compared to the more years she might have had?" Herrin replies, "I can't deny that it's grossly unfair to Bonnie, but there's nothing I can do about it. . . . She's gone—I can't bring her back. . . . It's sad what happened, but it's even sadder to waste another life. I feel I'm being wasted in here." Again, Gaylin asks, "But what about people who say, Look, if you got two years, then someone who robs should get only two days. You know, the idea of commensurate punishment. If it is a very serious crime it has to be a very serious punishment. Are you saying two years of prison is a very serious punishment considering what you did?" Herrin answers, "For me, yes."[18]

Richard Herrin, unlike Charles Manson and Sirhan Sirhan, is quite likely to be paroled after serving the minimum term specified in his sentence—eight-and-a-third years. Viewed solely in terms of the danger he may pose to society in the future, there is a more rational argument for releasing Herrin after eight years than for releasing the killers of the two doormen after twenty years. But such a release does not address itself to the question of whether eight-and-a-third years is adequate retribution for the deliberate taking of a human life.

The public outcry against psychiatric justice is characterized by a significant anomaly that is also apparent in the demand for restoration of the death penalty. People are afraid of crime and they want—in theory—more punitive treatment of criminals. In practice, when confronted with an individual defendant, jurors are not so eager to be the agents of retribution. As Anthony Amsterdam noted in his argument in the *Furman* case, verdicts resulting in death sentences had become increasingly rare long before the emergence in the 1960s of a broadly based movement to abolish capital punishment.

Where ordinary citizens are not awed by the responsibility of condemning a specific human being to death (as distinct from telling a pollster that yes, they believe murderers should be executed), it is a sure sign that a society is in the grip of a compulsion that overrides customary doubts, hesitation, and compassion. (The unifying obsessions of Nazi Germany and the post-Reconstruction American South come to mind.) In a relatively normal society, men and women are not so eager to condemn their fellow creatures to death. In similar fashion, there is a gap between what people say about their opinion of the insanity defense and what they actually do when the fate of an obviously disturbed defendant is in their hands.

If an opinion pollster were to ask one hundred parents what they considered an appropriate punishment for a man who killed a twenty-year-old girl because she wanted to end their relationship, I doubt that most respondents would consider eight years in jail a sufficient penalty. But juries confront a flesh-and-blood defendant, not a hypothetical case. If Bonnie Garland might have been anyone's daughter, Richard Herrin might have been anyone's son. And, as I have already noted, juries are most receptive to psychiatric defenses when recognizable human passions are at stake. A well-known forensic psychiatrist summed up the phenomenon in this way: "Juries do not tend to buy insanity in multiple-murder cases. They do in cases that do not involve social outrage. For killing a wife and kids, insanity may be okay. But not for killing a dozen neighbors."[19] If this psychiatrist is right—and I believe the legal record supports his judgment—his observation about the lack of social outrage attached to domestic murders is an unsettling commentary on contemporary social values.

In short, the muddled relationship between psychiatry and the law is not the consequence of a conspiracy on the part of psychiatrists to usurp the prerogatives of judicial institutions representing the public will; rather, it is symptomatic of a general cultural confusion regarding the appropriate role of retribution in our system of justice. There have been many suggestions that statutory law should restrict the insanity defense to the narrow standard of the M'Naghten rule, requiring a defect of reason so great that defendants either do not know what they are doing or do not understand the moral significance of their acts. The state of Idaho passed a law in 1982 that went even further, banning the insanity defense except in cases where defendants *literally* did not know what they were doing. Under this law, a woman might be acquitted of a charge of murder if she strangled her baby under the misapprehension that it was a teddy bear, but not, as has occurred in a number of recent cases, if she thought the baby deserved to die because it was carrying out the devil's work. This law is in fact far more rigid than M'Naghten, which at least raises the possibility of acquitting defendants on the less literal ground of a defect of reason that distorts the capacity for moral judgment.

In the wake of the Hinckley trial, The American Psychiatric Association issued a lengthy position paper urging more specific requirements for insanity defenses—but not so specific or narrow as those in either the old M'Naghten rule or the new, stringent laws modeled after the Idaho statute. The association urged that insanity acquittals be granted only for severe psychoses and not for more ordinary personality disorders defined *ex post facto* by the defendant's antisocial behavior. As a possible standard, the group suggested the existence of "severely abnormal mental conditions that grossly and demonstrably impair a person's perception or understanding of reality."[20]

Another frequently proposed solution to what is perceived as the overuse of psychiatric defenses is the verdict of "guilty but mentally ill," following which defendants are sent to mental institutions and transferred to prisons after psychiatric treatment. Such proposals, already enacted into law in many jurisdictions, raise serious problems from both a civil libertarian and a therapeutic point of view. How much treatment is needed to satisfy the intent of the law and restore a convict to reasonable mental functioning? What effect would a transfer to prison have on a person who had made progress under treatment in a mental institution? Would this system simply have the effect of expanding the influence of psychiatry on the criminal-justice system? In any event, one might expect that the prospect of transfer from a psychiatric institution to a maximum-security prison would be more effective as a deterrent to mental "recovery" than it has ever been as a deterrent to crime. Public psychiatric institutions are not, to be sure, the most agreeable residences in western society, but all but the most inhumanely administered mental hospitals are preferable to all but the most humanely run prisons. If Hinckley were in prison, he would certainly not be granting telephone interviews to reporters and speculating about the ominous possibility that he might "have a problem" with Jodie Foster should he eventually be released. It hardly seems necessary to judge a man "guilty but mentally ill" in order to impose more restrictions on mental patients who have committed acts of violence than on those who have not. Moreover, allowing Hinckley to continue his threats from the security of a mental institution would seem to raise a number of therapeutic as well as legal questions.

A more basic problem with the guilty but mentally ill formulation is its violation of the common-law principle that defendants cannot be held criminally responsible if they are incapable of understanding the nature of their crimes. This is not only a question of law but of psychiatric definition. What does the term "mentally ill," as distinct from "insane," really mean? Psychiatrists have never been able to agree on a definition of mental illness, but they are unanimous in their belief that there is no sharp dichotomy between the sane and the insane, the normal and the abnormal. One of Freud's greatest contributions to our understanding of human behavior was his demolition of the idea that "sick" and "healthy" impulses are locked away in separate compartments of the mind. Indeed, one definition of mental health is the ability to tolerate the existence of conflicting impulses. This tolerance of ambiguity, so necessary to the reasonable conduct of everyday life, is disastrous when translated into legal assessments of responsibility. The law simply cannot declare, "There's so much good in the worst of us/And so much bad in the best of us/That it ill behooves any of us/To talk about the rest of us."

The verdict of "guilty but mentally ill" is a contradiction in terms under traditional legal standards. Although the Idaho law takes too drastic a step backward in its exceedingly rigid concept of insanity, there is unquestionably a need to narrow the scope of psychiatric justice in order to satisfy the public's desire that those who violate the law be called to account. The desire for accountability is not a punitive whim of the moment; it is one of the foundations of all law. It ought not to be beyond the capacity of society to devise a standard of mental incapacity that falls somewhere between the "Twinkie defense" and a virtual abolition of any insanity defense, just as it ought to be within our capacity to set forth a consistent system of criminal penalties that neither reverts to the death penalty nor allows murderers to be released from jail in a few years.

There is a need—as even the American Psychiatric Association implies in its vaguely worded, politically cautious statement—to establish a distinction between the catchall concept of "mental illness" and the overwhelming insanity that truly renders a person incapable of volition. Such a distinction is no more artificial than all laws, which impose a structure of rules whose acceptability and applicability to human beings in a state of nature is irrelevant. Psychiatrists who are worthy of respect are extremely reluctant to throw up their hands and declare a patient "insane" in private therapy, and that is all the more reason why their role in the courtroom, and their legal power over criminal defendants confined in mental institutions, should be greatly circumscribed. Psychiatrists who command the greatest respect within their profession are exceedingly reluctant to make definitive statements, or to testify at all, regarding the mental condition of defendants in criminal trials. Therapists who make frequent appearances on witness stands are generally "hired guns" who profit financially by testifying in criminal cases either for the prosecution or the defense. One psychoanalyst, in a variant of the old saying, "Those who can, do; those who can't, teach," suggests that "therapists who can't treat, testify." Even if it were philosophically and legally appropriate to impose a therapeutic sensibility on the process of criminal justice, it is sobering to realize that those psychiatrists who are most eager to take on the task of diagnosing defendants from the witness stand are quite possibly the least-qualified members of their profession to do so.

Although Hannah Arendt may be correct in her contention that no punishment has ever possessed enough power of deterrence to prevent the commission of a specific crime, it has never been doubted that a general system of punishments acts as a general deterrent to crime. The possibility of punishment did not enter into Nazi calculations until very late in the day—too late for the millions who had already been reduced to ash. But Hitler himself had, in fact, already drawn his own conclusions from past crimes that most closely resembled what he had in mind for the Jews of Europe. "Who, after all, speaks today of the annihilation of the Armenians?" he asked his General Staff. This remark underlines the error of trying to isolate the question of deterrence from the question of retribution in discussing the general relationship between crimes and punishments. Insofar as any system of punishments can be said to possess deterrent value, its power depends in large measure on demonstrable evidence that society regards a crime as morally reprehensible and deserving of consistent retribution. It may be true, for instance, that the prospect of a prison sentence would not deter every brutal husband from battering his wife, but the well-known reluctance of western societies to impose punitive measures in family disputes virtually rules out any possibility of deterrence. The absence of a system of predictable punishments —whether as a result of foggy ideas of insanity, ineffectual penal and judicial procedures, or a willingness to excuse "hot-blooded" crimes—implies an absence of both retribution and deterrence. Moreover—and this point is generally ignored by those who insist that justice can incorporate no element of revenge—the elimination of retribution as a legitimate social value also rules out any possibility of genuine atonement and forgiveness.

IX   The Quality of Mercy

That which is past is gone, and irrevocable; and wise men
have enough to do with things present and to come: therefore
they do but trifle with themselves, that labor in past matters.
FRANCIS BACON, *Essays,* "Of Revenge"

We may not have to live in the past, but the past lives in us.
SAMUEL PISAR, *Of Blood and Hope*

If justice is customarily portrayed as an ideal that has replaced
lex talionis as a standard of public morality, forgiveness is seen
as the antipode of revenge in private life. The "better angels of
our nature" are presumed to keep watch over forgiveness; in
considering this highly esteemed human possibility, it is easy,
and reassuring, to overlook the reciprocal relationship between
the capacity to forgive and the capacity to avenge one's
wrongs.[1] Nadezhda Mandelstam, in discussing the qualities
shared by her husband, Osip, and his great contemporary Boris
Pasternak, observed that antipodes are by definition located at
opposite poles of the same sphere. Mandelstam and Pasternak,
she insisted in reply to those who saw the two poets as inhabitants of different universes, dwelled in a common realm of
ethical and cultural values in spite of their vast differences of
temperament and style—differences that condemned the former to die in the purges and allowed the latter to die in bed.
Neither poet could ever have been described as the antipode of
those conscienceless "literary workers" who lent their talents,

such as they were, to the Stalinist subjugation of true culture.[2]

So it is with forgiveness and vindictiveness, which touch reciprocal chords within the injured spirit, as well as between the sufferer and the agent of suffering. This reciprocity lies at the heart of the evolution of revenge. It is central to the resolution of both private and public conflicts; it informs spiritual and temporal passions. Unlike revenge, forgiveness has rarely exerted so forceful an influence on human affairs as to require the restraints of law and religion. Forgiveness is seen as an expression of the noblest possibilities of human nature, revenge of the basest—and we have become all too accustomed to the ascendancy of the base.

This perceived opposition between forgiveness and revenge omits at least two crucial elements of the moral equation. The first is a willingness to acknowledge culpability on the part of the man or woman who has wrought the suffering of others. The second goes beyond culpability and involves the offender's degree of remorse; "I did it and I'm glad" is not an admission of responsibility calculated to inspire forgiveness. A third factor comes into play when the injury is a public matter—the pressure applied by society to restore some sort of equilibrium between victim and victimizer. This equilibrium is called justice, and it is far from irrelevant even in private spheres of existence which cannot be reached by law. Fairness is to private disputes as justice is to public ones. Even in the context of profound love—affording compassion far beyond the point where it is extended or expected in other social contexts—forgiveness becomes impossible if a basic sense of fairness is repeatedly assaulted: the act is meaningless unless both parties realize there is something to forgive.

Just as there is a chasm between the desire for just retribution and the vulgar prescriptions for getting even and "winning through intimidation" offered by bestselling "self-help" (more self than help) books, so is there a vital distinction to be drawn between the forgiveness that flows from a timorous nature and

the willed transcendence of suffering that proceeds from
strength. The former brand of forgiveness rests on uncertainty
about one's rights or fear of defending them, the latter on a
fearless character that is able to forgive evil without condoning
it. A Protestant theologian summarizes this distinction in a
discussion of a hypothetical case of one who has suffered the
pain of a friend's betrayal and has been called upon to forgive.

> When by self-conquest which even bystanders can see to be
> noble the injured man (or, as it may be, woman), refusing to
> ignore moral realities, yet reaching over and beyond the wrong
> to knit up the old ties of communion, attains the act of pure
> pardon, the act presupposes and is mediated by costly suffer-
> ing. It is an exacting thing to pardon a great wrong; assuredly
> it is not with a heart of stone that an act so brave and loving
> can be carried through. A man engaged in it is conscious of
> wrench and agony in proportion as on the one hand he feels
> the shame of his friend's evil and on the other sympathy brings
> him close to the guilty life, actually by intense feeling putting
> himself where the other is.[3]

This highly elevated concept of forgiveness is far removed
from the platitudinous advice to "forgive and forget." Such
forgiveness is always attained at a high personal cost (and not
only to the one who forgives). To forgive a real injury requires
a conscious suppression of the instinct to make others suffer as
we have suffered; to accept such forgiveness is to incur the guilt
of having, in the most obvious sense, escaped our "just deserts."
The pain endured on both sides means that true forgiveness is
rare. In the course of long and intimate association, in which
injuries are inevitably inflicted and sustained, men and women
are repeatedly asked to forgive; in the absence of forgiveness,
the only alternatives are vindictive hatred or indifference. The
fact that many people prefer the latter alternatives confirms the
difficulty of attaining true forgiveness.

In its deepest moral and emotional meaning, forgiveness is

always a personal and private act. It should never, as Beccaria rightly argued, be used as a standard for the resolution of public conflicts. The value of private forgiveness is not demeaned by arguing its irrelevance to the maintenance of public justice. On the contrary, it is precisely because forgiveness is so exalted and difficult to attain that it cannot serve as an effective public alternative to unrestrained vengeance. One may speak of compassionate—as opposed to cruel—rulers, laws, and societies, but the embodiment of compassionate values in public institutions has little to do with their expression in private lives. Public compassion is, rather, an expression of the social philosophy of "the greatest happiness for the greatest number," as opposed to the promotion of maximum satisfaction for an elite.

Confusion between public and private spheres of action characterizes many modern discussions concerning the question of forgiveness. "It's easy to fake a reconciliation," argued Doris Donnelly, a lecturer at the Princeton Theological Seminary, in an article inspired by the enormous critical and popular success of the biographical movie *Gandhi.* Donnelly observed that "our language enshrines the idea [of false forgiveness] in phrases like 'kiss and make up.' We're programmed to bypass real forgiveness among people and nations. A peace treaty is the same: forget that you bombed our orphans and hurt our people; sign a treaty and all will be forgiven. But they [treaties] really mean, 'How can we pretend we're reconciled?' It's easy to sign a peace treaty or shake hands. It's not easy to forgive."[4]

If only it were easy to sign a peace treaty! True reconciliation and forgiveness may sometimes be possible within the framework of an international agreement to keep the peace, but they are not the primary aims of what is a formal, public structure of reciprocal obligations and prohibitions. Treaties attempt to halt the process of vendetta and destruction, to establish a zone of detachment in which people may once more enjoy individual and collective safety. To conclude a treaty, it is not necessary that peoples and nations love one another—if, indeed, love can ever be assigned a collective identity—but simply that they agree to stop killing one another. Unfortunately for the human species, there is nothing simple or easy about abandoning murder as a means of resolving disputes. International agreements break down not because they are based on "fake" forgiveness—since they are not based on forgiveness at all—but because no international body has sufficient authority to punish those who break the agreements. One returns, inevitably, to the delicate balance between retribution and compassion that is required to achieve a just and viable social order. Unrestrained retribution destroys the noblest human hopes along with human bodies; the absence of measured retribution leaves vindictive force in the hands of those who are unable or unwilling to restrain themselves.

The movements led by Gandhi and Martin Luther King, Jr., embodied a near-perfect balance of retributive and compassionate impulses in their successful resistance to colonial and racial tyranny. Gandhi and King would not have viewed their movements in this light and many of their admirers (of whom I am one) will regard the coupling of their philosophies with the concept of retribution as an insult to their noble ideals as well as to their historical reputations. I do not believe it is necessary to regard Gandhi and King as "secular saints" (a peculiar expression of recent provenance which I take to mean that sainthood is not restricted to those who devote their lives to traditional religious rituals) in order to view them as great leaders who changed their world for the better. Nor is it necessary, in order to admire the use of nonviolence to attain social justice, to see the process exactly as King and Gandhi saw it, or to see their ideals as unalloyed triumphs of love over hate and forgiveness over revenge.

"If everyone took an eye for an eye," Gandhi once said, "the whole world would be blind." But Gandhi did not want to take anyone's eye; he wanted to force the British out of India. In his Nobel Peace Prize acceptance speech, King declared that "nonviolence is the answer to the crucial political and moral questions of our time; the need for man to overcome oppression and violence without resorting to oppression and violence. Man must evolve for all human conflict a method which rejects revenge, aggression and retaliation. The foundation of such a method is love." In King's Christian philosophy, love means forgiving one's enemies unconditionally—regardless of whether they acknowledge wrongdoing or want forgiveness. Unsought forgiveness is, of course, a powerful weapon against enemies who would prefer to reduce you to the status of an object.

Nonviolence and nonaggression are generally regarded as interchangeable concepts—King and Gandhi frequently used them that way—but nonviolence, as employed by Gandhi in India and by King in the American South, might reasonably be viewed as a highly disciplined form of aggression. If one defines aggression in the primary dictionary sense of "attack," nonviolent resistance proved to be the most powerful attack imaginable on the powers King and Gandhi were trying to overturn. The writings of both men are filled with references to love as a powerful force against oppression, and while the two leaders were not using the term "force" in the military sense, they certainly regarded nonviolence as a tactical weapon as well as an expression of high moral principle. The root meaning of Gandhi's concept of *satyagraha,* as he explained in 1923 in his famous defense against the charge of sedition by the British colonial authorities, is "holding on to truth" or "force of righteousness." Gandhi also called *satyagraha* the "love force" or "soul force" and explained that he had discovered "in the earliest stages that pursuit of truth did not permit violence being inflicted on one's opponent, but that he must be weaned from error by patience and sympathy. . . . And patience means self-suffering. So the doctrine came to mean vindication of truth, not by the infliction of suffering on the opponent, but on one's self."

King was even more explicit on this point: the purpose of

civil disobedience, he explained many times, was to force the defenders of segregation to commit brutal acts in public and thus arouse the conscience of the world on behalf of those wronged by racism. King and Gandhi did not succeed because they changed the hearts and minds of southern sheriffs and British colonial administrators (although they did, in fact, change *some* minds) but because they made the price of maintaining control too high for their opponents. This tactic would not have worked with opponents who were prepared to pay any price or, at any rate, a higher price to maintain their coercive power; there are governments, today as yesterday, that would have turned machine guns on as many people as necessary to quell the rebellion. In the absence of outside intervention, systematic terror does work—not forever, perhaps, but for a longer period than the span of one man's life. The success of nonviolent resistance presupposes not only enormous discipline on the part of those who practice it but a point beyond which the other side is not willing to go to maintain its power.

On the whole, this process seems to me to have less to do with the intrinsic power of love and forgiveness than with the determination of those who are willing to die rather than take up the weapons of their enemies. Civil disobedience is itself a form of aggression—a particularly effective form in that it places the onus on the oppressor rather than the oppressed. Unless one regards aggression as evil by definition, this statement is no criticism of the movements led by King and Gandhi. They were not only more compassionate but more clever than their opponents. In this regard, it is instructive to recall the failure of King's tactics when they were directed against the more subtle forms of racism in the North. Northern police did not cooperate by providing the violent aggressive response that had been a critical factor in the southern equation. Moreover, large numbers of Americans refused to accept any guilt for keeping blacks out of their neighborhoods and schools; they did not seek forgiveness because they did not feel they had done anything wrong. Like retribution, forgiveness can never be a one-sided transaction.

All social movements, whether they embody the noble goals of King and Gandhi or the despicable aims of Hitler and Stalin, involve calculations of risks, costs, and benefits. A decent society—one in which men and women are able to enjoy both liberty and safety—can be based neither on limitless forgiveness nor on limitless retribution. I am aware that this statement can be interpreted as cold and parsimonious in spirit, but that interpretation is simply another consequence of the mistaken assumption of a dichotomy between retributive and compassionate impulses.

The development of an either-or view of mercy and retribution has been immeasurably influenced both by the genuine spiritual differences and the artificially stimulated antagonisms between the two great religions of the West. In Christian theology through the middle of the twentieth century, this idea was often expressed as a distinction between New Testament love and Old Testament justice—justice meaning, in this context, adherence to the letter rather than the spirit of the law. The "justice/love dichotomy," a term frequently used by Jewish scholars defending their Talmud against charges of being rigidly concerned with the letter of the law, is an idea of social significance extending beyond theological quarrels. Portia's famous speech in *The Merchant of Venice,* after she acknowledges that Shylock is legally entitled to his pound of flesh, embodies the full significance of the justice/love split in western attitudes toward public questions of mercy and retribution that are analogous to private questions concerning forgiveness and vindictiveness.

> The quality of mercy is not strain'd,
> It droppeth as the gentle rain from heaven
> Upon the place beneath: it is twice blest;
> It blesseth him that gives and him that takes:

'Tis mightiest in the mightiest: it becomes
The throned monarch better than his crown;
His sceptre shows the force of temporal power,
The attribute to awe and majesty,
Wherein doth sit the dread and fear of kings;
But mercy is above this sceptred sway,
It is enthroned in the heart of kings,
It is an attribute to God himself;
And earthly power doth then show likest God's
When mercy seasons justice. Therefore, Jew,
Though justice be thy plea, consider this,
That in the course of justice, none of us
Should see salvation: we do pray for mercy;
And that same prayer doth teach us all to render
The deeds of mercy. I have spoke thus much
To mitigate the justice of thy plea;
Which if thou follow, this strict court of Venice
Must needs give sentence 'gainst the merchant there.[5]

The caricature of the Jewish sense of "justice" in this scene embodies the social attitudes that make Judaic scholars extremely sensitive to any suggestion of a justice/love dichotomy between the Old and New Testaments. "There is plenty of both in both" is the general position adopted by Jewish and Christian leaders today. This is essentially a political posture, the outgrowth of an altered relationship between Judaism and the Christian churches that has emerged in the decades since the Holocaust. On one level, the statement is of course true: there is plenty of mercy in the Old Testament (there is plenty of everything in the Old Testament), and Jesus was not averse to dispensing justice, either by driving the moneychangers out of the temple or by confounding those who would stone an adulteress by citing the rabbinical law in which they—and he—were so well versed. But there are major differences of emphasis between the Jewish "story of stories" and the Christian gospel, and those differences are chiefly concerned with the matter of justice—not as the carelessly used pejorative "strict legalism" but as a blend of forgiveness and retribution. The term "Judaeo-Christian heritage," with its implication of common values, is appropriate to many cultural traditions, but it is not appropriate here. Justice is a far more troubling issue in the Old Testament than in the New, while forgiveness is the central mystery of Christianity. These concerns are complementary but are so far from being identical that they are sometimes seen as opposites. Today, they continue to express themselves in distinct strains of thought in a culture no longer based on religious faith.

The Jews were the first people to raise, in terms comprehensible to the modern mind, the question of how it is possible to keep faith with the idea of justice (in their universe, a just God) when suffering and retribution seem undeserved. To modern men and women, this seems an obvious and universal question, but one need only turn back to Greek tragedy to realize it was not always so. Oedipus does not cry out at the injustice of his fate or question the retribution visited upon him for a crime he committed unwittingly. "It was Apollo, friends, Apollo, who brought fulfillment to all my sufferings," he says. "But the hand that struck my eyes was mine and mine alone. What use had I for eyes? Nothing I could see would bring me joy." Retribution is simply in the nature of existence, however we struggle and try to escape our appointed fate. The final choral ode underlines the futility of searching for a justification of suffering that is comprehensible to the human mind:

> Citizens who dwell in Thebes, look at Oedipus here, who knew the answer to the famous riddle and was a power in the land. On his good fortune all the citizens gazed with envy. Into what a stormy sea of dreadful trouble he has come now. Therefore, we must call no man happy while he waits to see his last day, not until he has passed the border of life and death without suffering pain.[6]

The Jews, however, were not content with this fatalism. Chosen by a God whose vengeance seemed as capricious as his favor, they searched for a just explanation for their sufferings. And they cried out when God's retribution seemed so arbitrary as to call his justice and goodness into question. The most resonant of these outcries—still painful to read, still unanswered—was made by Job. He does not ask for forgiveness in this passage; he asks to know the meaning of revenge.

My soul is weary of my life; I will leave my complaint upon myself; I will speak in the bitterness of my soul. I will say unto God, Do not condemn me; shew me wherefore thou contendest with me. Is it good unto thee that thou shouldest oppress, that thou shouldest despise the work of thine hands, and shine upon the counsel of the wicked? Hast thou eyes of flesh? or seest thou as man seeth? Are thy days as the days of man? are thy years as man's days, That thou enquirest after mine iniquity, and searchest after my sin? Thou knowest that I am not wicked; and there is none that can deliver out of thine hand. Thine hands have made me and fashioned me together round about; yet thou dost destroy me. . . . If I sin, then thou markest me, and thou wilt not acquit me from mine iniquity. If I be wicked, woe unto me; and if I be righteous, yet will I not lift up my head. I am full of confusion; therefore see thou mine affliction; For it increaseth, Thou huntest me as a fierce lion; and again thou shewest thyself marvellous upon me. Thou renewest thy witnesses against me, and increasest thine indignation upon me; changes and war are against me. Wherefore then has thou brought me forth out of the womb? Oh that I had given up the ghost, and no eye had seen me! I should have been as though I had not been; I should have been carried from the womb to the grave. Are not my days few? cease then, and let me alone, that I may take comfort a little, Before I go whence I shall not return, even to the land of darkness and the shadow of death; A land of darkness, as darkness itself; and of the shadow of death, without any order, and where light is as darkness.[7]

Shew me wherefore thou contendest with me, Job cries. The demand for justice could hardly be more explicit; there is nothing like it in the New Testament. Of course, Job does not get justice; what he gets is a restoration of God's favor and mercy as arbitrary as the withdrawal had been. But the question of justice never faded into the background for the children of Israel, a people bound by the most elaborate code of laws in human history yet locked into a covenant with a God whose forgiveness and vengeance were the equally unpredictable acts of an omnipotent being who did not have to justify himself to his creatures.

The problem surfaces repeatedly in Jewish history, confounding even the most pious believers. In the ghettos of eastern Europe, there were many instances in which the most devout and observant Jews prepared for their deportation to the concentration camps by fasting, reading Psalms, and convoking a *din Torah,* a rarely enacted ritual of the utmost gravity in which the Ark is opened and man accuses God of committing injustice. The deity is then enjoined against visiting any further retribution on his people. Unfortunately, God gave his people in the ghettos a different answer from the one he gave Job. (One of the few religious jokes I have heard told by both observant Roman Catholics and Jews begins with a child asking the rabbi or priest how it is possible to know whether God is listening if he does not answer our prayers. "God always answers our prayers," is the reply. "Sometimes the answer is no." I remember thinking, when I first heard the joke as a child, that it was no laughing matter.)

In the New Testament, the problem of undeserved suffering is never fully resolved, but it does not torture the authors of the gospels and the apostolic letters as it did the authors of the Old Testament. In the Christian universe, temporal suffering does not call into question the certainty of ultimate forgiveness—and forgiveness is the end of Christ's atonement on the cross for the sins of humanity. The Christian understanding of the meaning of the cross—of the relationship between suffering and forgiveness—hinges upon the belief that Jesus was both God and man. If God himself chose to suffer and die as a human being suffers and dies, Job's reproach—*seest thou as man seeth?*—loses its meaning. The believing Christian need not fear that human suffering casts doubt on the prospect of God's final forgiveness. The dual-natured God, speaking not out of a whirlwind but from the familiar wooden cross, demonstrates with his own mangled flesh that heavenly pardon is the end of earthly pain. Among the many prophets of religious history, Jesus was unique in declaring that he had the power to forgive sins, and this promise of forgiveness can hardly have been an insignificant factor in the eventual triumph of Christianity over the multitude of competing religious sects in the early Christian era. Paul, in the fateful passage in which he insists that Gentiles need not be circumcised in order to be received as Christians, declares that Jesus' ultimate act of love and forgiveness supersedes all legalistic questions of who is a Christian and who a Jew.

I said unto Peter before them all, If thou, being a Jew, livest after the manner of Gentiles, and not as do the Jews, why compellest thou the Gentiles to live as do the Jews? We who are Jews by nature, and not sinners of the Gentiles, Knowing that a man is not justified by the works of the law, but by the faith of Jesus Christ, even we have believed in Jesus Christ, that we might be justified by the faith of Christ, and not by the works of the law: for by the works of the law shall no flesh be justified. . . . I am crucified with Christ: nevertheless I live; yet not I, but Christ liveth in me: and the life which I now live in the flesh I live by the faith of the Son of God, who loved me, and gave himself for me. I do not frustrate the grace of God:

for if righteousness come by the law, then Christ is dead in
vain.[8]

As long as one accepts its basic theological premise, Christianity has an answer to the question that is truly unanswerable as
posed by Job to the God of the Jews.

> We are constantly under a temptation to suppose that the
> reason why we fail to understand completely the atonement
> made by God in Christ is that our minds are not sufficiently
> profound. And doubtless there is truth in the reflection that for
> final insight into the meaning of the cross we are not able or
> perspicacious enough. But there is a deeper reason still. It is
> that we are not good enough; we have never forgiven a deadly
> injury at a price like this, at such cost to ourselves as came
> upon God in Jesus's death. We fail to comprehend such sacrifi-
> cial love because it far outstrips our shrunken conceptions of
> what love is and can endure.[9]

In Christian theology (as distinct from the fallible practices
of societies categorized as "Christian"), forgiveness is an absolute value. In his sacrifice on the cross, Jesus personified—and
deified—the Christian belief that no act, however terrible, excludes a human being from the possibility of God's grace, redemption, and forgiveness. From the point of forgiveness and
atonement—and Christians do differ among themselves about
the conditions for atonement—the sins of the past lose their
hold on individual destiny and future behavior is all that matters. This message is reinforced repeatedly in the Gospels—in
Jesus' forgiveness of the woman taken in adultery, of the "good
thief" on the cross, of his apostle Peter's cowardice in denying
him—and it is one of the most consistent themes in subsequent
lives of the saints. Ecumenical propaganda notwithstanding,
the Christian view of forgiveness differs significantly from the
Judaic view, and it differs on a matter of fundamental importance to the organization of human society: the claims of the

past in ordering the present and imagining the future.

In the western world today, these two strains of thought present themselves not as religious conflicts but as distinctive, and sometimes antagonistic, moral and political philosophies. Pope John Paul II was speaking very much from his religious tradition when he issued a statement—the first ever made by a Roman Catholic pontiff—criticizing capital punishment. The Pope did not call for the abolition of the death penalty; he recommended "clemency and mercy for those condemned to death," especially for those condemned on political charges. Clemency from above has quite a different meaning from abolition of capital punishment by duly constituted representatives of people. Clemency is a God-like gesture of mercy; like Jesus' act of forgiveness on the cross, it is not necessarily "deserved" by the condemned. Opponents of the death penalty have been generally critical of the use of clemency as a substitute for the outright abolition of capital punishment (though not as a last resort for the condemned in societies that do authorize executions) because clemency always depends, in the last instance, on the benevolence of those who rule. Legal abolition, by contrast, does not rest on any appeal to human goodness—humans being far from Christ-like in their capacity for forgiveness—but on statutory restraint of the ultimate weapon of earthly vengeance.

Elimination of the persistent pejorative meaning attached to the term "legalism" in western culture is long overdue. Although it is clear that some laws, and some administrators of laws, are inadequate or evil, legalism—the stricter the better—affords a far more hospitable environment for the spread of liberty and decency than does hopeful reliance on the loving potential of the human heart. One of the most important features of well-established democratic legalism is a system of checks and balances that guards against perversions of law like those in Hitler's Germany and Stalin's Russia. "Legalism" and "legalist" deserve to be regarded not as terms of opprobrium but as titles of honor.

The legalistic approach to questions of justice does not exclude compassion any more than it excludes retribution, but it does pose a question unthinkable to those for whom forgiveness is an absolute value: are there some actions that ought never to be pardoned by society, even though God and individuals may forgive as they see fit? By "pardon," I do not of course mean what the Pope meant by clemency; I refer to the absolute renunciation of retribution implied in the locution "justice, not revenge." If one does not acknowledge forgiveness as an absolute good, it follows that retribution is not an absolute evil. There is undeniably an element of score keeping in the legalistic, secularist approach to forgiveness and revenge; the legalist is unapologetically preoccupied with the terms and conditions of justice. To the legalist, the following exchanges between Hermine Braunsteiner's lawyer and the survivors who testified at her deportation hearings are unrealistic in substance and surrealistic in tone:

> Lawyer to witness: You came here to tell the truth?
> W: Yes, I came here to tell the truth.
> L: And you have no hate for anybody.
> W: No, I know many bad people but I have no hate in my heart.
> L: No hate. Can you say you love these people?

In another exchange, the lawyer asks, "Can you sit here now and forgive the person who hit you?"

> W: I testify only the truth, that's all.
> L: And you have no hate. . . .
> W: She could kill me, but I am still alive.
> L: I didn't ask whether she could kill you. Would you forgive her?
> W: Yes.
> L: With all your heart?
> W: That's right, forgiveness is my religion.[10]

More is at stake in these astonishing exchanges than the conventional effort of a lawyer to impugn the motives of witnesses testifying against his client. To raise doubt about the reliability of the testimony, the attorney need only have asked something like "Do you honestly feel that you can be fair—I don't mean to suggest that you would deliberately lie about so serious a matter—toward a woman for whom you feel such anger?" But the lawyer did not ask the witnesses about fairness; he held them to a standard of *love* and *forgiveness.* And it was clear that the survivors felt it incumbent upon them to repudiate any hatred and assert their ability to forgive. It would no doubt have shocked the spectators had a witness spoken the truth—that there was no reason at all why any victim of Hermine Braunsteiner's should be expected to forgive her. If a victim wanted to partake of divine charity and grant forgiveness, well and good, but such forgiveness has nothing to do with public justice.

In society, there are limitations and conditions associated with both forgiveness and retribution. Both private and public forgiveness require two essential conditions: acknowledgment of responsibility on the part of the wrongdoer and a willingness to make amends based on genuine remorse. When both parties are culpable, the conditions must obviously be fulfilled on both sides.

Without contrition on the part of the offender, forgiveness is simply a state of mind—a condition that may be emotionally or morally meaningful to the one who forgives but has no significance as a social bond, as a medium for restoring civilized relations between the injured and the injurer. The absolute importance of reciprocity is apparent in considering the process of reconciliation as it applies to every offense from the most mundane violation of domestic order to the most grievous crimes against humanity. In our private lives, we are all familiar with the difference between a friend or lover who simply says, "I'm sorry you're hurt," and one who says, "What I did was wrong; you have every right to be hurt and I'm sorry." The former personality somehow manages to place the entire burden of forgiveness on the one who has already been hurt. In her novel about a pathological marriage, Joy Fielding captures this quality to perfection in a scene in which a woman discovers, quite by accident, that her husband-to-be has lied to her about a previous marriage and about the fact that he has a living mother (he had told her his entire family was dead). She confronts him and he responds:

"The ball is in your court, Donna. . . . Nobody's talking about blame. Who said anything was anybody's fault? Why do you have to assign blame? We're talking about truth. Either you're interested in hearing it or not." . . .

"I thought marriage was a fifty-fifty affair," she said quietly.

"Who told you that?" he asked, trying to smile. His voice was gentle again. "Certainly no one with any brains." He touched her face. "You try meeting someone halfway and see where it gets you. It gets you halfway."[11]

Failure of the offender to take responsibility for wrongdoing is a serious problem in attempts to confront the issues of domestic violence and sexual child abuse—acts punishable by law in theory but avoided by social institutions in practice. A. Nicholas Groth, an expert on sexual abuse of children, has observed that one of the main problems in attempting to change the behavior patterns of men who molest children, especially if the victims are members of their own families, is that they are rarely willing to accept responsibility for having done anything wrong.[12] Remorse or shame is extremely unusual among men who have sexually molested their daughters, although it is extremely common among wives and mothers who blame themselves for having failed to satisfy their husbands' sexual needs or for having failed to detect signs that a daughter was being subjected to her father's sexual advances. Forgiveness, as the term is understood by either theologians or psychoanalysts, clearly has no relevance to such situations; the concept is meaningful only to a man or woman who feels the pangs of conscience.

In public settings, failure to acknowledge culpability makes a mockery of the legal concept of clemency. Former President Richard Nixon's refusal to acknowledge any wrongdoing in the Watergate affair (apart from having picked the wrong associates) was one of the most unsettling aspects of the unconditional pardon granted him by his successor, Gerald Ford. Such a pardon is a favor that imposes no reciprocal obligations on the wrongdoer; it is analogous to forgiveness as a one-sided state of mind rather than as a meaningful reconciliation in private disputes. The difference between forgiveness as a state of mind and as true reconciliation was succinctly described by Sylvia Salvesen, who spent the last eighteen months of the war in the Ravensbrück concentration camp, in her bluntly titled memoir, *Forgive—But Do Not Forget.* Salvesen, who was sent to Ravensbrück as a result of her activities in the Norwegian resistance, was also the wife of the personal physician to Norway's King Haakon VII. Because of her status as an Aryan and her connections with highly placed officials whom the Nazi occupation authorities wished to placate, Salvesen did not suffer as cruel a fate as most of her comrades in Ravensbrück. She was able to use her experience as a doctor's wife to work as a camp nurse and, insofar as camp officials would allow, she attempted to ease the suffering of those who had been used by the Nazi doctors for medical "experiments." After the liberation, she had a final conversation with the camp matron before leaving to return to her home in Norway. The matron refused to acknowledge any responsibility for the horrors suffered by the women in her charge and insisted that she had no choice because all of the inmates were enemies of Germany.

"She had persecuted me for a year-and-a-half like an evil spirit," Salvesen reflected. "Did she realize what I wished her was peace within herself and that neither she nor Germany would be able to gain peace until they realized their guilt and took the responsibility for it?"[13] Later, when she testified at the war crimes trials of the Ravensbrück "medical staff," Salvesen was still shocked by the refusal of the Nazi doctors to acknowledge their guilt—and she was equally shocked that no one, as she saw it, seemed to be trying to make amends to the victims. Commenting on the creation of international funds to aid Germans injured or impoverished by war, she observed that the "victims of German pseudo-science were enough to make the very stones weep, and it seemed to me an international duty to look after them in every possible way. Would it not be better to start a fund for these victims of German brutality than for the Germans themselves, even if the latter were in need?"[14] Salvesen was not suggesting reparation as a substitute for retribution but as a decent, complementary act on the part of society.

In distinguishing between appropriate private and public responses to wrongdoing, the function of restitution is extremely important. A just society ought to declare its sentiments by making some tangible amends, however inadequate these may be in relation to the injury, to those who have suffered as a result of its incompetence, negligence, or complicity. Walter Berns speaks contemptuously of this concept as a kind of social insurance policy "embodied in statutes whereby the sovereign (or state), being unable to keep the peace by punishing criminals, agrees to compensate its contractual partners for injuries suffered . . . injuries the police are unable to prevent. . . . There is no anger in this kind of law and none (or no reason for any) in the society."[15] I do not share Berns' contempt for this sort of restitution, but he is quite right in his contention that it does not cancel out the need for retribution.

In private life, the making of amends, coupled with acknowledgment of guilt, may indeed overcome the desire for retribution. The making of amends follows naturally upon remorse in the resolution of private disputes. If one is truly sorry for having inflicted an injury, the desire to "make it up" to the other person arises without external coercion. Although some wrongs are so painful they can never be forgotten, the evidence of remorse implicit in attempts to offer restitution goes a long way toward making forgiveness possible. Even so, vindictive needs are strong, and a high degree of self-mastery is required to overcome punitive anger. For the one who is asked to (or wants to) forgive, an offering of remorse softens the heart, while restitution salves wounded pride. Indeed, the absence of a serious effort to make amends is likely to cast doubt on the sincerity of any private expression of contrition. When serious private as well as public injuries are involved, forgiveness in the absence of either remorse or restitution is not only difficult; it may not even be desirable.

Both modern psychological wisdom and traditional religion argue that forgiveness is, invariably, good for mental (or spiritual) health and that vindictiveness is bad. While acknowledging that it may sound ludicrous to advise a battered wife to turn the other cheek, Doris Donnelly goes on to emphasize her belief that "ultimately, when that battered wife is out of danger, at some point she's going to have to address the question of forgiveness—or hang on to her outrage for the rest of her life."[16] Karen Horney put it another way:

> In simplest terms the vindictive person does not only inflict suffering on others but even more so on himself. His vindictiveness makes him isolated, egocentric, absorbs his energies, makes him psychically sterile, and, above all, closes the gate to his further growth.

This finally brings me back to the beginning, to the warning against revenge expressed in the Bible. The more we understand of neurotic vindictiveness, the more this warning reveals its profound wisdom. The self-effacing—"masochistic"—vindictiveness is merely more obviously at the person's own expense. Every vindictiveness damages the core of the whole being. Repressing it makes it worse. Not "liberating vindictive aggression" but overcoming it is our therapeutic goal."[17]

These statements of commonly accepted psychological wisdom confuse specific acts of deserved forgiveness with a policy of unconditional forgiveness—and they confuse specific acts of retaliation with vengefulness as a way of life. It is not the question of forgiveness a battered wife must address—unless she plans to go on living with the same husband—but the question of how to free herself from the power of vengeful rage. One step toward such freedom, I believe, is the admission that forgiveness may, on occasion, be as inappropriate and self-destructive a response to injury as overweening vindictiveness. There are people who, in denying responsibility for their actions, abandon their claim upon human compassion. Evildoers may be banal characters, but the effect of evil on the individual victim is always striking, always unique.

Boundless vindictive rage is not the only alternative to unmerited forgiveness—in either private or public life. A wife need not forgive an unashamedly brutal husband in order to avoid dousing him with gasoline and setting him on fire; a concentration-camp survivor need not pray for God's blessings on the Nazis in order to refrain from personally settling scores in the manner of spy-novel avengers; a society need not set murderers free if it refuses to put them to death; the leaders of adversary nations need not throw their arms around one another in order to restrain themselves from destroying the world in a nuclear holocaust. Once the possibility of a balance between compassionate and retributive impulses is acknowledged, individuals and societies turn their attention to the question of which forms of retribution, and which forms of forgiveness, afford the opportunity of an existence that encompasses both justice and love.

Just as the generally accepted meaning of "retribution" is less pejorative than that of "revenge," so too does "vindication" have more positive connotations than "vindictiveness." In dictionary definitions and in colloquial usage, vindictiveness is a virtual synonym for vengefulness—the desire to inflict trouble, pain, injury, humiliation, or annoyance on a person who has been a source of injury. Vindication suggests the process of clearing oneself of a false charge, or of overcoming injury and humiliation by proving oneself to the world. The two qualities (like the words) have common roots. All forms of vindication arise from the same powerful urge to demonstrate mastery over the people or forces that have been the agents of our suffering. Some men and women aim at vindication by attempting to build themselves up, others, by trying to tear down their enemies. It is a psychological commonplace that forceful leaders of great compassion have a number of personality traits in common with savage dictators; the difference lies not so much in their native abilities and instincts as in the ethical structures through which those abilities are refined and expressed.

In the biography of nearly every great political leader, egotism and self-aggrandizement are recurrent motifs; so, too, are humiliations and setbacks the leader must overcome. And yet neither subjective personality traits nor objective, external obstacles fully account for the emergence of leadership based on negative vengeance rather than positive vindication. Franklin Roosevelt's battle against polio, for instance, is generally regarded as the crucible in which his personal ambition was transformed into a larger and more compassionate vision of public leadership. One can easily imagine—indeed, history offers countless examples of—men whose style of leadership becomes more negative and vindictive as a result of personal adversity. Hitler, of course, affords the prime example of such a leader. Another man, wounded and temporarily blinded by mustard gas in the trenches of the First World War, might have turned his energies to the cause of peace. For Hitler, the war crystallized the sense of grievance that was already present in his character and fostered dreams of vengeance that would, only fifteen years later, be realized in public policy.

Even in extremity, the nature of retributive responses is infinitely various. Many survivors of Nazi camps have described their feelings when, immediately after liberation, they were presented with the opportunity to fulfill a cherished fantasy—to torture or kill their guards. Most reported that they were unable to do so—not because their desire for vengeance had been replaced by forgiveness but out of ethical restraints that had survived the camps. "I have heard people say that when they saw Nazis stripped of their power, they lost their hatred," a camp survivor once told me. "I don't believe them. As for me, I tell you the hardest thing I have ever done in my life was not to beat one of the camp nurses who helped the doctor in his medical experiments. I decided, I will become like them if I do this and then they might as well have killed me. But I have testified at many trials, and sometimes it has interfered with my present life. I have friends from camp who don't agree with me about this; they say it is not healthy. How can I answer them? I know I cannot live with myself if I do not go on telling what I know, as long as anyone will listen, until the day I *do* die. It is my revenge, and I am not ashamed to say it."

Bearing witness is perhaps the most common twentieth-century form of socially sanctioned revenge, but it is sanctioned only up to a point. Sanction ends when the witness appears to be motivated by personal animus rather than by an abstract concern for justice. At first glance, this widespread cultural attitude poses something of a mystery; it should be self-evident that suffering in the mass is personally experienced and that one may testify on one's own behalf as well as on behalf of others. Scholars who have addressed themselves—and their number is growing—to the puzzle of ambivalent cultural attitudes toward witnesses generally come up with the relatively simple explanation that the world does not want to hear what survivors have to say. Terrence Des Pres expounds this view eloquently:

Refusal to acknowledge extremity is built into the structure of existence as we, the lucky ones, know it. More perhaps than we care to admit, spiritual well-being has depended on systems of mediation which transcend or otherwise deflect the sources of dread. . . . Too close a knowledge of vulnerability, of evil, of human insufficiency is felt to be ruinous. And therefore we assert that death is *not* the end, the body is *not* the self. The world is *not* a film upon the void, and virtue is *not* without Godhead on its side. So too with the survivor. The ostracism of outsiders, of bearers of bad news, is a very old practice. In order to gain momentum the human enterprise bought time and assurance by taking refuge in myth, in numbers, in any makeshift strategy of distance of denial. But what was wisdom once is not so now. The gates of pearl have turned to horn, and the appearance of the survivor suggests—indeed, this is his message—that we embrace illusion at our peril.[18]

This analysis is perceptive as far as it goes, but it does not account for the particular unease generated by survivors who are angry and say so, who have not learned to modulate their voices and enumerate horrors with a dispassionate air. It is not the survivor per se who is rejected and labeled "unbalanced" but the survivor who insistently raises the issues of accountability and retribution. The anger that proceeds from unredressed suffering can be more terrifying than the original facts of suffering; moreover, the outraged, as distinct from the ostensibly detached, witness not only expects us to listen but also to *do something* about the wrongs that have been enumerated. If only it were as easy to address the demand for retribution within the constraints of civilization and law as it is to cheer movie avengers who specialize in the shedding of ketchup! We prefer to obscure the nature of these demands by falling back on the formula of "justice, not revenge." We prefer to experience revenge as metaphor, and the survivor who seeks retribution by bearing witness disturbs the peace by demanding that we face the issue in its concrete reality.

Anna Akhmatova, in her poem *Requiem,* lays bare the connection between the retributive impulse and the determination to bear witness. In her long lament for the victims of Stalinism, the survivor's uncompromising rejection of symbolism is evident in every line and is particularly noticeable by virtue of being expressed in a genre that does not lend itself to a documentary approach. But the documentation is there, and Akhmatova makes it clear that retaliation by bearing witness was her intention from the beginning, even as she stood outside a prison in the hope of finding out whether her son had been executed or was still alive. The long poem opens with a stark prose foreword, dated April 1, 1957.

> During the terrible years of the Yezhovshchina* I spent seventeen months in the prison queues in Leningrad. One day someone recognized me. Then a woman with lips blue with cold who was standing behind me, and of course had never heard of my name, came out of the numbness which affected us all and whispered in my ear—(we all spoke in whispers there):
> "Can you describe this?"
> I said, "I can!"
> Then something resembling a smile slipped over what had once been her face.[19]

In the poem's closing stanzas, Akhmatova is even more explicit in her invocation of concrete memory and in her rejection of abstract tributes to an idealized image of suffering.

> I would like to call them all by name,
> but the list was taken away and I can't remember.

*Nikolai Yezhov was Stalin's secret police chief during the great purges of 1937–38. *Yezhovshchina* is the term older Russians used for the height of the terror, which took place under his administration. Yezhov was in turn purged and replaced by Lavrenti Beria.

For them I have woven a wide shroud
From the humble words I heard among them.

And if they gag my tormented mouth
with which one hundred million people cry,

then let them also remember me
on the eve of my remembrance day.

If they ever think of building
a memorial to me in this country,

I solemnly give my consent,
only with this condition: not to build it

near the sea where I was born;
my last tie with the sea is broken;

nor in Tsarsky Sad by the hallowed stump
where an inconsolable shadow seeks me,

but here, where I stood three hundred hours,
and they never unbolted the door for me.[20]

"Survivors" and "witnesses" have become almost inter-changeable in the popular mind, but many survivors do not have either the ability or the will to bear witness. In an account of her unsuccessful attempt to ascertain the exact circum-stances of her husband's death, Nadezhda Mandelstam ob-served that the determination to keep one's memory intact in order to testify to the truth required a concentration of energy much rarer than the will to live (which was difficult enough to maintain).

It was a feature of almost all the former camp inmates I have met immediately after their release—they had no memory for dates or the passage of time and it was difficult for them to distinguish between things they had actually experienced themselves and stories they had heard from others. Places, names, events and their sequence were all jumbled up in the minds of these broken people, and it was never possible to disentangle them. . . . I was horrified at the thought that there might be nobody who could ever properly bear witness to the past. Whether inside or outside the camps, we had all lost our memories. But it later turned out that there were people who had made it their aim from the beginning not only to save themselves, but to survive as witnesses. These relentless keepers of the truth, merging with the other prisoners, had bided their time.[21]

To assume the burden of being a relentless keeper of the truth is to place a higher value on righteous anger and remembrance than on forgiveness. Such people arouse antagonism not only because the world is unprepared to hear what they have to say but also because the personality traits that lend themselves to a sharp recollection of past injustice are not considered the most appealing qualities in ordinary social intercourse. "Thorny," "abrasive," and "vindictive" are the adjectives most frequently applied to those who devote a substantial portion of their lives to detailing the facts of pain and injustice. Who would not prefer Jesus to Jeremiah as a dinner guest? Bacon was quite right to link revenge and preoccupation with the past; there is a trace of Michael Kohlhaas in every survivor who self-consciously defines himself or herself as a witness. Unbounded rage is, however, restrained and directed at appropriate objects; in the act of bearing witness, the survivor's testimony is to unbounded vindictiveness on the Kohlhaas model as the conviction of a murderer is to the retaliatory slaughter of the killer's entire family. But there is no question that the act of bearing witness is rooted not only in devotion to justice but also in the psychological need for vindication. But the witness, unlike the destructive avenger, places the drive for vindication in the service of justice rather than in opposition to it.

The concept of the triumphant life as a form of vindication

—"living well is the best revenge"—opens the gate to a maze of emotional and ethical dilemmas that make the act of bearing witness appear, by comparison, to be a thoroughly straightforward matter. Most of us are accustomed to thinking of the "positive" aspects of our lives—the acquisition of an education, professional achievement, the rearing of happy and accomplished children—as unrelated to the dark impulses associated with revenge. Only when life overwhelms us with sorrow that cannot be denied—and sometimes not even then—do we acknowledge the connection between our "better angels" and the dark inner forces that threaten hard-won pride in triumph over adversity.

Insightful biographies always deal with this subject; autobiographies almost never do. One of the few autobiographies concerned with the relationship between the desire for vindication and high achievement is *Of Blood and Hope,* by the well-known international lawyer Samuel Pisar. Pisar, who was deported to Auschwitz from the ghetto of Bialystok when he was only twelve years old, is one of the youngest survivors of the Nazi camps (most children of that age were either gassed immediately or soon collapsed because their bodies were not developed enough to withstand the rigors of camp life). His memoir, while it belongs to the literature of survival, is unusual in that it focuses not on what happened to him in the camps but on the effort to build a life after the war. In and of themselves, his dilemmas are unremarkable; they involve the choices any man must make—of a school, a profession, a wife, a place to live. But, because Pisar is a survivor, he is forced consciously to weigh every decision against the claims of the past—and to assess every action in terms of whether he is winning or losing the battle against the early injuries inflicted on him. He sees life, always, as a struggle, and the choice for him is not one of justice versus revenge but of which forms of vindication are appropriate to a civilized life.

My life, I now understood, had been at a dead end. Physically I had escaped, I was breathing, but Hitler had programmed my mental and moral destruction from the grave. The struggle for survival was going on once more, survival through study. It had to be waged with the same determination, the same fury. . . .

I still was given to flashes of violence. One day, in chemistry class, when I dug into my jacket pocket for a piece of chalk, I pulled out instead a banana peel. At the desk behind, a boy named Bill Downey grinned, chomping on a banana. With the blood rushing in my head, I swung a Landsberg jailhouse punch at him; he was knocked from his chair to the floor. . . .

I was mortified. Fool, I said to myself, what have you done? You have reacted as if he wanted to kill you. Have those Nazis succeeded after all? It's no life to remain a savage. If you really want to make a life for yourself, you've got to become civilized. It's not enough to pass exams. You've got to learn some self-control as well. You have got to lock up the hoodlum in you and throw away the key. . . .

We decided that continuing the moral and intellectual rehabilitation we had begun, the undoing of Hitler's destructive work, even on the infinitesimal scale of two individuals, was *perhaps the only meaningful form of vengeance.* It seemed the best way to begin discharging our duty toward the Jewish people and toward humanity as a whole. . . .

So impressed was I, in fact, by the Anglo-American commitment to the rule of law, equitably administered by trusted judges and random juries, and the infinite value attached to human life, that I decided I would be a lawyer, not a scientist after all. Who could better devote himself to the defense of the weak than someone who had seen the helpless condemned with no more judicial ceremony than the whim of a kapo or the order of an SS? [Italics mine.][22]

Pisar's memoir might serve as a textbook on the constructive uses of vindictiveness. There is nothing unusual in the urge to high achievement—whether in service to others, a profession, or the creation of art—as a way of redeeming past suffering and restoring a damaged identity. What is unusual is the emotional intelligence to recognize this hunger for what it is: a blend of altruism and egotism, in which the need to transcend one's injuries expresses itself not in vindictive rage but in work of individual merit and social importance. Pisar remarks that he chose the law over science not only out of intellectual fascination but because the law was better suited to his emotional needs as a survivor—one of them being the need to do battle with forces that might, in future generations, lead to a reenactment of the horrors inflicted on him and his contemporaries. The passage in which he admonishes himself to "lock up the hoodlum in you and throw away the key" is both emotionally revealing and evocative of a consummate legalist's attitude toward violence and revenge.

To the legalist—in the deservedly positive sense of the word —it is a true delusion to suppose that the human capacity for good might flourish in the absence of well-defined, carefully constructed restraints on the capacity for evil, to imagine that it might be possible to create a brighter future without settling the accounts of the past. Legalists do not denigrate the value of mercy and forgiveness; on the contrary, they believe it is precisely because these qualities are so rare and precious that it is dangerous to rely on them as a sustaining force for public good.

"Forgive and forget" is, in this view, not only an impossible admonition but an undesirable one; it implies a lack of respect for the profound sense of moral equilibrium impelling us to demand that people pay for the harm they have done to others. The entire modern argument over the relationship between revenge and justice turns on this question of the equilibrium between memory and hope. With moral and legal balance firmly in mind as a social goal, the formula of "justice, not revenge" has the same absurd ring as "justice, not forgiveness." True justice partakes of both qualities.

In one sense, it is a curiosity of recent history that a taboo has been attached to the subject of revenge in a century that has witnessed the fearful union of mass vengeance with technology. In another sense, the taboo is entirely understandable: with our illusions about the moral progress of the human species in shards, it is natural that we, like Euripides' Orestes, wish to throw the mantle over our eyes. But this self-willed blindness is exceedingly dangerous. Dismissing the legitimate aspects of the human need for retribution only makes us more vulnerable to the illegitimate, murderous, wild impulses that always lie beneath the surface of civilization—beneath, but never so deep that they can safely be ignored.

Notes

I. Taboo

1. Dorothy Rabinowitz, *New Lives* (Knopf, New York, 1976). For a discussion of the Braunsteiner deportation hearings and of attitudes toward Holocaust survivors who expressed any emotions that might be considered vindictive anger, see Chapters I and IV.
2. *New York Times*, August 14, 1964, as cited by Joseph Lelyveld. In 1981, after a five-and-a-half-year trial of eight former Maidanek guards in West Germany, Hermine Braunsteiner Ryan was convicted of murder and sentenced to life imprisonment. Ryan was the only defendant at the trial, which aroused enormous political controversy in West Germany, to receive the sentences requested by the prosecution. The other defendants all received shorter prison terms.
3. *New York Times*, February 8, 1983. The quotations from the president of the Jewish Federation and Ugo Iannucci are cited by E. J. Dionne, Jr. The observation about "settling old scores" versus "establishing the truth" is Dionne's.
4. Romans 12:19. Unless otherwise noted, all Biblical quotations are from the King James version.
5. *Gregg v. Georgia*, 428 U.S. 153, 183.
6. *New York Post*, January 19, 1982.
7. After Abbott was convicted of manslaughter rather than murder, the family of the victim filed a civil suit to obtain damages for wrongful death. Pending disposition of the case, Abbott's royalties from *In the Belly of the Beast* were frozen by judicial order.
8. Albert Camus, "Reflections on the Guillotine," *Resistance, Rebellion, and Death*, translated by Justin O'Brien (Knopf, New York, 1961), pp. 230–31.
9. Karen Horney, "The Value of Vindictiveness," *American Journal of Psychoanalysis*, Vol. 8 (1948), p. 3.

II. Written in Blood

1. Milton, *Paradise Lost*, Book II, lines 99–105.
2. Cited by Lily B. Campbell, "Theories of Revenge in Renaissance England," *Collected Papers of Lily B. Campbell*, with an introduction by Louis B. Wright (Russell

& Russell, New York, 1968), p. 155, from *Hamlet,* edited by Joseph Quincy Adams (Houghton Mifflin, Boston 1929), p. 211.

3. Mario Praz, "Machiavelli and the Elizabethans," *Proceedings of the British Academy,* Annual Italian Lecture (London, 1928), Vol. XIII, p. 24.

4. Moses Hadas' introduction to *Ten Plays by Euripides,* translated by Hadas and John McLean (Bantam, New York, 1981), p. ix.

5. Ibid., p. 32.

6. Aeschylus, *Agamemnon,* from *The Plays of Aeschylus,* translated by Philip Vellacott (Penguin, Harmondsworth, 1959), p. 97.

7. *Sophocles,* Vol. II, translated by David Grene, edited by David Grene and Richmond Lattimore (University of Chicago Press, Chicago, 1957), pp. 138–39.

8. Euripides' *Electra,* from Hadas-McLean edition, p. 214.

9. Ibid., p. 228.

10. Ibid., p. 236.

11. Campbell, "Theories of Revenge in Renaissance England," p. 164.

12. *Paradise Lost,* Book I, lines 92–105.

13. *Paradise Lost,* Book IV, lines 386–392.

14. William Blake, note to "The Voice of the Devil," *The Marriage of Heaven and Hell,* 1790–93.

15. *Othello,* Act V, Scene 2, lines 16–20.

16. *Othello,* Act I, Scene 3, lines 159–170.

17. Philip Massinger, *The Fatal Dowry,* Act I, Scene 2.

18. Ibid., Act V, Scene 2.

19. Goethe, *Wilhelm Meister: Apprenticeship and Travels,* translated by R. O. Moon (G. T. Foulis, London, 1947), Vol. I, pp. 211–12.

20. *The Merry Wives of Windsor,* Act V, Scene V, lines 124–27.

21. Racine, *Phèdre,* translated by John Cairncross, Act II, Scene V (Penguin, Harmondsworth, 1970).

22. See Chapters 1 through 4 of *Jane Eyre.*

23. Heinrich von Kleist, *Michael Kohlhaas,* translated by James Kirkup (Blackie & Son, London, 1967), p. 1.

24. Ibid., p. 325. The "quotation" from Luther is Kleist's invention. His version of *Michael Kohlhaas* might reasonably be classified as a "nonfiction novel."

25. Mario Puzo, *The Godfather* (Putnam, New York, 1969), pp. 363–64.

26. Robert Littell, *The Amateur* (Dell, New York, 1982), p. 54.

27. Ibid., p. 297.

28. Puzo, p. 31.

29. Ibid., p. 325.

30. Barbara Abercrombie, *Good Riddance* (Harper & Row, New York, 1979), pp. 79–80.

31. P. D. James, *Innocent Blood* (Scribner's, New York, 1980), p. 69.

32. Ibid., p. 275.

III. In the Beginning Was the Word

1. The concept of pollution appears in Biblical accounts relating to much earlier periods of Jewish history, and it is an essential element of Mosaic law. However, the pollution doctrine existed side by side with earlier tribal customs for many centuries after the exodus of the Israelites from Egypt—just as monotheism was periodically challenged by belief in older gods. The seventh century B.C. marks the period during which the pollution doctrine finally supplanted earlier practices—just as the Babylonian exile marked the final death of polytheism for the children of Israel.

2. Hubert J. Treston, *Poine: A Study in Greek Blood-Revenge* (Longmans, Green, London, 1923), p. 1.

3. Homer, *The Iliad,* translated by E. V. Rieu (Penguin Books, Harmondsworth, 1950), Book IX, pp. 177–78. I have used this prose translation because it portrays religious and legal customs with great clarity; for purely literary reasons, I would have selected a verse translation.

4. Genesis 4:10–13.

5. *The Collected Works of Sophocles,* translated by Lewis Campbell (Oxford University Press, London, 1906), p. 96.

6. *Ten Plays by Euripides,* translated by Moses Hadas and John McLean (Bantam, New York, 1981), p. 237.

7. *Eumenides,* from *The Plays of Aeschylus,* translated by Philip Vellacott (Penguin, Harmondsworth, 1959), pp. 169–70, 172.

8. Maimonides, *The Book of Torts,* translated by Hyman Klein (Yale Judaica Series, New Haven, 1954), p. 195.

9. Treston, p. 118.

10. Sister Mary Bonaventure Mroz, *Divine Vengeance* (Catholic University Press, Washington, D.C., 1941), p. 67.

11. Exodus 21:22–25.

12. Deuteronomy 19:2–6, 10.

13. Deuteronomy 19:11–13.

14. Dan Jacobson, *The Story of Stories: The Chosen People and Its God* (Harper & Row, New York, 1982), p. 83.

15. Ibid., p. 84.

16. Ibid., p. 157.

17. Psalm 137:1–6.

18. Ezekiel 18:2–4, 14–20.

19. Niddah 16b, cited by George Foot Moore in "Fate and Free Will in the Jewish Philosophies According to Josephus," *Harvard Theological Review* (Cambridge, 1929), Vol. XXII, p. 371.

20. John 8:3–11.

21. Matthew 5:17. The familiarity of this viewpoint to the Pharisees is underlined by the fact that although execution by stoning or strangulation is the penalty for

adultery in Mosaic law, exaction of the penalty was extremely rare in Biblical and rabbinical times. Not a single case of execution for adultery is recorded in either the Old or the New Testaments, although there are frequent warnings about this form of retribution. For a full discussion of this subject, see Louis M. Epstein, *Sex Laws and Customs in Judaism* (Bloch, New York, 1954).

22. Matthew 5:43–48.
23. Luke 10:30–36.
24. Luke 12:42–48.
25. John Reynolds, *The Triumphs of Gods Revenge against the crying and execrable sin of wilful and premeditated murder* (London, 1704), p. 207.
26. Ibid., p. 209.
27. Ibid., p. 10.
28. Peter de la Primaudaye, *The French Academy, wherein is discerned the institution of manners, and whatsoever concerneth the good and happy life of all estates and callings, by precepts of doctrine, and examples of the lives of ancient sages and famous men,* translated by Thomas Bowes (London, 1594), Vol. II, pp. 326–27.
29. Matthew 18:7.
30. Lily B. Campbell, *Shakespeare's "Histories": Mirrors of Elizabethan Policy* (Huntington Library Publications, Berkeley, 1947), p. 122.
31. Cited by Campbell in "Theories of Revenge in Renaissance England," p. 165.
32. Primaudaye, p. 603.
33. Cited by Antonia Fraser, *Mary Queen of Scots* (Delacorte, New York, 1978), Chapter 25.
34. Matthew 27:25.
35. Eugene Fisher, *Faith Without Prejudice* (Paulist Press, New York, 1977), p. 37.
36. John 18:28–40.
37. Luke 23:34.
38. Luke 23:28–31.
39. Léon Poliakov, *The History of Anti-Semitism: From the Time of Christ to the Court Jews,* translated by Richard Howard (Vanguard Press, New York, 1965), Vol. I, p. 41.
40. Cited by Poliakov, pp. 132–33, from *Mistère de la Résurrection de Nôtre-Seigneur, Jésus Christ,* Antoine Vérard Edition, Paris.
41. Marc H. Tannenbaum, unpublished paper on "The Role of the Passion Play in Fostering Anti-Semitism Throughout History," delivered on November 19, 1978, before the Bavarian Katholische Akademie symposium on "The Passion of Jesus —Then and Now."
42. Cited by Poliakov, p. 215, from *Augenspiegel* folio 32b.
43. Cited by Poliakov, p. 215, from Erasmus letter as quoted by L. Geiger in his 1870 biography of Johannes Reuchlin.
44. Martin Luther, *Works: The Christian in Society,* edited by Franklin Sherman, translated by Martin H. Bertram (Fortress Press, Philadelphia, 1971), Vol. IV, pp. 138–39.
45. Ibid., pp. 264, 267.
46. Armas K. E. Holmid, "Martin Luther: Friend or Foe of the Jews?" (National

Lutheran Council, Division of American Missions, 1949), p. 27.

47. *The Eichmann Case in the American Press* (Institute of Human Relations, the American Jewish Committee, New York, 1961), p. 51.

48. *The Witness,* March 8, 1961, as cited in AJC study.

49. *The Standard,* June 12, 1961, as cited in AJC study.

50. *The Unitarian Register,* October 1960, as cited in AJC study.

51. *St. Louis Review,* March 10, 1961, as cited in AJC study.

52. "Nostra Aetate: Declaration on the Relationship of the Church to Non-Christian Religions," October 28, 1965.

iv. Letters of the Laws

1. Cesare Beccaria, *On Crimes and Punishments,* translated by Jane Grigson, in Alessandro Manzoni, *The Column of Infamy* (Oxford University Press, Oxford, 1964), p. 14.

2. Beccaria, in Manzoni, p. 37.

3. Cited by Judy Freed, "Notes On Getting Even," *The Dial,* October 1981.

4. See Hubert J. Treston, *Poine: A Study in Greek Blood-Revenge* (Longmans, Green, London, 1923) and Sister Mary Bonaventure Mroz, *Divine Vengeance* (Catholic University Press, Washington, D.C., 1941).

5. Abraham A. Neuman, *The Jews in Spain* (Jewish Publication Society of America, Philadelphia, 1944), Vol. I, pp. 138–39.

6. The uses of public revenge as a cover for private vindictiveness in a police state are discussed with particular insight by Roy A. Medvedev, a Marxist historian living in Moscow, in *Let History Judge* (Knopf, New York, 1971). See Chapter III, on the period of collectivization and industrialization; Chapter VI, on the party purges, and Chapter XIV, on the impact of Stalinism on science and art. Also Aleksandr Solzhenitsyn, *The Gulag Archipelago,* Part II (Harper & Row, New York, 1975) and Part III (Harper & Row, New York, 1978).

7. *New York Times,* November 18, 1981.

8. Maimonides, *The Book of Torts,* translated by Hyman Klein (Yale Judaica Series, New Haven, 1954), p. 195.

9. Philip Rush, *The Book of Duels* (Harrap, London, 1964), p. 58.

10. The Reverend Lyman Beecher, "The Remedy for Dueling," a sermon delivered before the Presbytery of Long Island, April 16, 1806, printed in 1809 by J. Seymour, pp. 22–23.

11. The Reverend James B. Britton, "The Practice of Dueling in View of Human and Divine Law," preached before the Congregation of Christ Church, Indianapolis, March 25, 1838, published in 1838 by Livingston and Comingore.

12. See Susan Brownmiller, *Against Our Will: Men, Women and Rape* (Bantam, New York, 1976), Chapter 2.

13. St. Augustine, *Works,* edited by the Reverend Marcus Dods (Edinburgh, 1872–1876), Vol. XIII, pp. 168–69.

14. A brilliant account of the pre-Enlightenment religious rationale for legal cruelty is offered by Marcello T. Maestro in *Voltaire and Beccaria as Reformers of Criminal*

Law (Columbia University Press, New York, 1942). I am particularly indebted to him for his observations concerning the substantive differences between the theories of the leaders of the early Christian church and the harsh religious prescriptions for legal revenge that prevailed in Christian Europe from the medieval period well into the nineteenth century. In Maestro's view, clerical opposition to Voltaire's and Beccaria's proposals for legal reform were indicative of the ways in which the institutional church had departed from early Christian teaching.

15. Maimonides, p. 161.
16. From *The Writings of Benjamin Franklin,* edited by Albert Henry Smyth (Macmillan, New York, 1905–1907), Vol. IX, p. 292.
17. Cited by Maestro, p. 7.
18. Cited by A. Alvarez, *The Savage God* (New York, 1972), from E. H. Carr, *The Romantic Exiles* (Penguin, Harmondsworth, 1949), p. 389.
19. Beccaria, in Manzoni, p. 49.
20. Beccaria, in Manzoni, pp. 72–73.
21. Beccaria, in Manzoni, p. 69.
22. Maimonides, *The Book of Torts,* pp. 207–208.
23. Plato, *The Laws,* translated with an introduction by Trevor Saunders (Penguin, Harmondsworth, 1970), Book IX, Chapter xvii, p. 362.
24. Ibid., Book IX, Chapter xvii, p. 372.
25. Beccaria, in Manzoni, pp. 17–18.
26. Machiavelli, *The Discourses,* edited by Bernard J. Crick, translated by Leslie J. Walker, S.J., with revisions by Brian Richardson (Penguin, Harmondsworth, 1970), p. 278.
27. Machiavelli, p. 173.
28. Isaiah Berlin, *Against the Current: Essays in the History of Ideas,* "The Originality of Machiavelli" (Viking, New York, 1980), p. 75.
29. Ibid., pp. 77–78.
30. Ibid., p. 78.

v. Revenge as Metaphor: New Image Makers

1. Willard Gaylin, *The Killing of Bonnie Garland* (Simon & Schuster, New York, 1982), p. 255.
2. Nadezhda Mandelstam, *Hope Abandoned,* translated by Max Hayward (Atheneum, New York, 1972), p. 572.
3. Gaylin, p. 155.
4. Heinz Kohut, "Thoughts on Narcissism and Narcissistic Rage," *The Psychoanalytic Study of the Child,* Vol. 27, 1972, pp. 377–78.
5. Jacob A. Arlow, "The Revenge Motive in the Primal Scene," *American Journal of Psychoanalysis,* Vol. 28, 1980, p. 523.
6. Cited in "The Insanity Plea on Trial," *Newsweek,* May 24, 1982.
7. Cited by Maya Pines, *New York Times,* May 14, 1982.
8. Karen Horney, "The Value of Vindictiveness," *American Journal of Psychoanalysis,* Vol. 8 (1948), p. 4.

9. Rose Nader, *New York Times,* December 3, 1982.

10. Horney, p. 4.

11. Cited by Gaylin, pp. 171–72, from People's Exhibit 15D, trial of the State of New York v. Richard Herrin.

12. Ibid., p. 176, from People's Exhibit 15G, 15H, and 15I.

13. Harvey D. Lomas, chief of psychiatry, Veterans Administration Hospital, Cincinnati, Ohio, from an unpublished paper presented on September 30, 1982.

14. Horney, p. 3.

15. See Harvey Lomas on "Graffiti: Some Observations and Speculations," *The Psychoanalytic Review,* Vol. 60, No. 1, 1973.

16. Daniel 5:1–7.

17. Dorothy Thompson, *Harper's Bazaar,* December 1934.

18. Cited by Lucy S. Dawidowicz, *The War Against the Jews* (Holt, Rinehart & Winston, New York, 1975), p. 149, from "Trial of the Major War Criminals," Document 1919 P.S.

19. Cited by Eric Pace, *New York Times,* June 6, 1982.

20. Lomas. From an unpublished paper presented on September 30, 1982.

21. Karl Menninger, *Whatever Became of Sin?* (Hawthorn Books, New York, 1973), p. 62.

22. Horney, p. 12.

23. See *Totem and Taboo.*

24. Kohut, p. 364.

VI. Sexual Revenge

1. For a discussion of the disproportionate attention accorded the relatively small number of violent female criminals, see Ann Jones, *Women Who Kill* (Holt, Rinehart & Winston, New York, 1980), pp. 1–14 and 177–237.

2. *Othello,* Act IV, Scene III, lines 87–104.

3. In 1974, Inez Garcia was convicted of second-degree murder in spite of her self-defense plea. Three years later, another jury overturned the verdict and acquitted her.

4. See Willard Gaylin, *The Killing of Bonnie Garland* (Simon & Schuster, New York, 1982), Chapters 1, 2, and 8.

5. Susan Brownmiller, *Against Our Will: Men, Women and Rape* (Bantam, New York, 1976), p. 7.

6. See Genesis: 34:27–29.

7. II Samuel: 13:1–39.

8. Dan Jacobson, *The Rape of Tamar* (Weidenfeld and Nicolson, London, 1970), pp. 90–91.

9. Christine de Pizan, *The Book of the City of Ladies,* translated by Earl Jeffrey Richards (Persea Books, New York, 1982), pp. 162–63.

10. See Louis M. Epstein, *Sex Laws and Customs in Judaism* (Bloch, New York, 1948), pp. 180–200.

11. *New York Times,* April 30, 1967.

12. *New York Times,* October 3, 1979.
13. *Washington Post,* February 4, 1973. I interviewed Irene Papas, and her comparison between Medea and Othello struck me as singularly apt.
14. *Ten Plays of Euripides,* translated by Moses Hadas and John McLean (Bantam, New York, 1981), pp. 37–38.
15. In her account of the Lizzie Borden trial, Ann Jones draws on contemporary sources as well as the accounts that continued to appear for fifty years. Her excellent description combines hindsight with the temper of the time in which Borden was tried for and acquitted of murder.
16. Edmund Lester Pearson, *Trial of Lizzie Borden: Edited, With a History of the Case* (Doubleday, Doran, Garden City, N.Y., 1937), pp. 306–307.
17. Jones, *Women Who Kill,* p. 218.
18. Ibid., p. 288.
19. Trial Record, The State of New York v. Richard Herrin, Vol. V, pp. 1419–1421.
20. Trial Record, The State of New York v. Richard Herrin, Vol. V, p. 1490; pp. 1493–1494.
21. Gaylin, p. 13.
22. Elizabeth P. W. Packard, *The Prisoner's Hidden Life* (published by the author, A. B. Case, printer, Chicago, 1868), p. 65.
23. Ibid., p. 191.
24. Ibid., p. 245.
25. Brownmiller, *Against Our Will,* pp. 423–24.
26. Ibid., p. 425.
27. Paul Zimmerman, "Kubrick's Brilliant Vision," *Newsweek,* January 3, 1972.
28. John Irving, *The World According to Garp* (Pocket Books, New York, 1979), p. 429.

VII. Life for Life

1. Walter Berns, *For Capital Punishment: Crime and the Morality of the Death Penalty* (Basic Books, New York, 1979), pp. 38–40.
2. Willard Gaylin, *The Killing of Bonnie Garland* (Simon & Schuster, New York, 1982), p. 336.
3. Ibid., p. 346.
4. From a speech by Prime Minister Pierre Trudeau, delivered on June 15, 1976, in the Canadian House of Commons. Parliament passed the bill to abolish capital punishment in Canada.
5. See annual Uniform Crime Reports of the Federal Bureau of Investigation.
6. Vincent Bugliosi with Curt Gentry, *Helter-Skelter* (W. W. Norton, New York, 1974), p. 448.
7. Cited by Berns, p. 37, from American Friends Service Committee's "Struggle for Justice" (New York, 1971), p. v.
8. *Gregg v. Georgia,* 428 U.S. 153, 183 (1976), majority opinion.
9. *Gregg v. Georgia,* dissent of Justice Thurgood Marshall.

10. William J. Bowers, *Executions in America* (Lexington Books, Lexington, Mass., 1974), p. 176.

11. Berns, p. 13.

12. Jacob J. Vellenga, "Is Capital Punishment Wrong?" *Christianity Today,* October 12, 1959, pp. 7–9.

13. George Foot Moore, *Judaism* (Harvard University Press, Cambridge, 1927), Vol. II, p. 186.

14. Torahs Sanhedrin 37b, cited by Israel J. Kazis, "Judaism and the Death Penalty," from *Man's Right to Life,* one of the "Issues of Conscience" pamphlets issued by the Commission on Social Action of Reform Judaism, reprinted in *The Death Penalty in America,* edited by Hugh Adam Bedau (Doubleday, Garden City, N.Y., 1964), p. 173.

15. Ibid., p. 174.

16. Cited in *Judicial Process and Social Change,* edited by Jack Greenberg (West Publishing Co., St. Paul, Minn., 1977), p. 468.

17. See James B. Christoph, *Capital Punishment and British Politics* (University of Chicago Press, Chicago, 1962).

18. Bedau, ed., *The Death Penalty in America,* p. 4, cited from Leon Radzinowicz, *A History of English Criminal Law* (New York, Macmillan), pp. 151–53.

19. Cesare Beccaria, *On Crimes and Punishments,* translated by Jane Grigson, in Alessandro Manzoni, *The Column of Infamy* (Oxford University Press, 1964), pp. 17–18.

20. Bedau, *The Death Penalty in America,* p. 4.

21. Alexis de Tocqueville, *Democracy in America,* translated by Henry Reeve as revised by Francis Bowen, with new additions by Phillips Bradley (Knopf, New York, 1960), Vol. II, p. 166.

22. Bedau, *The Death Penalty in America,* p. 12.

23. Berns, p. 25.

24. *Lord Byron: Selected Letters and Journals,* edited by Leslie A. Marchand (Harvard University Press, Cambridge, 1982), p. 161, letter from Byron to his publisher, John Murray.

25. William Makepeace Thackeray, "Going to See a Man Hanged," *Fraser's* Magazine, August 1840, p. 156.

26. *The Times* of London, August 14, 1868.

27. Cited by Sir Ernest Gowers, *A Life for a Life* (Chatto & Windus, London, 1956), p. 12.

28. Ibid., p. 12.

29. Quoted from Associated Press dispatches by Henry Schwarzschild, "Homicide by Injection," *New York Times,* December 23, 1982.

30. Berns, pp. 187–88.

31. Ibid., p. 188.

32. Bugliosi with Gentry, *Helter-Skelter,* p. 456.

33. Isaac Ehrlich, "The Deterrent Effect of Capital Punishment: A Question of Life and Death," *American Economic Review,* No. 65 (June 1975), p. 414.

34. *New York Post,* June 19, 1978.

35. Greenberg, p. 534.

36. *Furman v. Georgia,* concurring opinion by Justice Potter Stewart.

37. Albert Camus, "Reflections on the Guillotine," *Resistance, Rebellion, and Death,* translated by Justin O'Brien (Knopf, New York, 1961), p. 236.

38. *New York Times,* July 2, 1982.

39. Graham Hughes, "License to Kill," *New York Review of Books,* June 28, 1979, p. 23.

40. *St. Petersburg Times,* December 16, 1961.

41. *Atlanta Constitution,* June 2, 1962.

42. *Chicago Daily News,* December 16, 1961.

43. William Robert Miller, *The United Christian Herald,* January 25, 1962.

44. Beccaria, in Manzoni, p. 47.

VIII. On Crimes and Punishments

1. In 1981, the last year for which FBI crime statistics are available, there were 22,520 murders reported in the United States and 13,290,300 index crimes.

2. Constance Rosenblum, "Just Another Victim," New York *Sunday News Magazine,* October 18, 1981, pp. 28, 32.

3. Michael Daly, "Double Jeopardy: Freed Murderers Who Kill Again," *New York Magazine,* September 14, 1981, p. 35.

4. See Susan Brownmiller, *Against Our Will* (Bantam, New York, 1976), Chapter 7, "A Question of Race."

5. "Police Discretion and the Judgement That a Crime Has Been Committed—Rape in Philadelphia," *University of Pennsylvania Law Review,* Vol. 117 (December, 1968), cited by Brownmiller in *Against Our Will,* p. 410.

6. New York *Daily News,* October 25, 1981.

7. *New York Post,* October 15, 1981.

8. Ibid.

9. Daly, p. 36.

10. *New York Post,* October 15, 1981.

11. Frank G. Carrington, *Neither Cruel nor Unusual* (Arlington House, New Rochelle, N.Y., 1978), p. 14.

12. Cited by Daly.

13. Thomas Szasz, *The Manufacture of Madness* (Harper & Row, New York, 1970), p. 14.

14. For a full account of Zhores Medvedev's commitment to a Soviet psychiatric institution, see *A Question of Madness,* by Zhores Medvedev and Roy Medvedev, translated by Ellen de Kadt (Knopf, New York, 1971).

15. "The Insanity Plea on Trial," *Newsweek,* May 24, 1982, p. 56.

16. *New York Times,* December 19, 1979.

17. From an unpublished paper by Dr. Harvey Lomas, chief of psychiatry at the Veterans Administration Medical Center in Cincinnati, Ohio.

18. See Willard Gaylin, *The Killing of Bonnie Garland* (Simon & Schuster, New York, 1982), pp. 326–27.

19. Quote attributed to Dr. Ronald Markham of Los Angeles in "The Insanity Plea on Trial," *Newsweek,* May 24, 1982, p. 58.
20. *New York Times,* January 20, 1983.

IX. The Quality of Mercy

1. The full quote is from Abraham Lincoln's First Inaugural Address: "We are not enemies, but friends. We must not be enemies. Though passion may have strained, it must not break, our bonds of affection. The mystic chords of memory, stretching from every battlefield and patriot grave to every living heart and hearthstone all over this broad land, will yet swell the chorus of Union when again touched, as surely they will be, by the better angels of our nature."
2. See Nadezhda Mandelstam, *Hope Against Hope,* translated by Max Hayward (Atheneum, New York, 1970), Chapter 33, "The Antipodes."
3. H. R. Mackintosh, *The Christian Experience of Forgiveness* (Harper, New York, 1927), p. 190.
4. Cited by Glenn Collins, "Forgiving: A Kind of Freedom," *New York Times,* December 27, 1982.
5. *The Merchant of Venice,* Act IV, Scene I.
6. *Oedipus the King,* translated by Bernard M. W. Knox (Pocket Books edition, Washington Square Press, New York, 1972).
7. Job 10:1–8, 14–22.
8. Galatians 2:14–16, 20–21.
9. Mackintosh, p. 193.
10. These exchanges appear in a transcript of the U.S. Immigration and Naturalization Service hearings on the deportation of Hermine Braunsteiner Ryan, pp. 378, 380–381.
11. Joy Fielding, *Kiss Mommy Good-Bye* (Signet, New York, 1982), pp. 40–41, 45.
12. Cited by Florence Rush, *The Best-Kept Secret: Sexual Abuse of Children* (Prentice-Hall, New York, 1980), p. 14.
13. Sylvia Salvesen, *Forgive—But Do Not Forget,* translated by Evelyn Ramsden (Hutchinson & Co., London, 1958), pp. 218–19.
14. Salvesen, pp. 224–225.
15. Walter Berns, *For Capital Punishment: Crime and the Morality of the Death Penalty* (Basic Books, New York, 1979), pp. 174–75.
16. *New York Times,* December 27, 1982.
17. Karen Horney, "The Value of Vindictiveness," *American Journal of Psychoanalysis,* Vol. 8 (1948), p. 12.
18. Terrence Des Pres, *The Survivor* (New York, Pocket Books, 1977), pp. 44–45.
19. Anna Akhmatova, *Requiem,* from *Selected Poems: Anna Akhmatova,* translated by Richard McKane, Penguin Modern European Poets Series, 1979.
20. Akhmatova, pp. 104–105.
21. Nadezhda Mandelstam, *Hope Against Hope,* p. 379.
22. Samuel Pisar, *Of Blood and Hope* (Little, Brown, Boston, 1980), pp. 129–31, 133–34, 140.

Index

Abbott, Jack Henry, 7
Abercrombie, Barbara, 59–61
abortion, legality of, 80, 148–9
Adalbert, Bishop, 104
Adams, Joseph Quincy, 18, 34
adultery, 82, 88–9, 187, 222
  death penalty for, 252
  literary treatment of, 39–40, 41–2
  sexual revenge and, 39–40, 184, 187, 192
  see also sexual revenge
Aeschylus, 21, 23, 25–9, 30, 31–2, 57, 70
  pollution doctrine and, 73, 75–6
Against Our Will (Brownmiller), 128–9
"Against the Jews and Their Lies" (Luther), 108
Agca, Mehmet Ali, 155
aggression, relation to revenge, 166–8
Akhmatova, Anna, 356–7
Akiba, Rabbi, 254
alien cultures, projection of revenge onto, 17–20, 34, 41, 55
Amateur, The (Littell), 55–7
American Civil Liberties Union (ACLU), 288–9
American Jewish Committee, 106–7, 109
American Medical Association, 269
American Psychiatric Association, 165, 326, 328
American Way of Death, The (Mitford), 266
Amsterdam, Anthony, 256–7, 324–5
anti-Semitism, 200–1
  as form of revenge, 68–9, 99–112

in Himmler's speech to SS officers, 173
  see also Christianity; Judaism
Aquinas, Saint Thomas, 92, 143
Arab-Israeli relations, as example of tribal revenge, 84, 113, 247, 286n
Arendt, Hannah, 290, 329
Arias Perez, Luis, 306
Aristotle, 87, 143
Arlow, Jacob, 164
Augustine, Saint, 92, 130, 131–2, 135

Bachmeier, Marianne, 214, 307–8
Bacon, Francis, 1, 331, 358
Barbie, Klaus, 3–4, 247
Barzun, Jacques, 238–9
Bazelon, David, 319–20
bearing witness, as form of revenge, 354–8
Beccaria, Cesare, 142–3, 149, 203, 225, 253, 258–9, 305, 334
  death penalty opposed by, 135, 136, 236, 237, 238, 256, 257, 260, 289
  human conduct as viewed by, 116–17
  proportionality and, 134–8, 139
Becket, Saint Thomas à, 259
Bedau, Hugo Adam, 257–8, 259
Beecher, Lyman, anti-dueling sermon of, 114, 126–7
Begin, Menachem, 247
behaviorism, free will and, 152, 161
benefit of clergy, death penalty and, 259–60
Berlin, Isaiah, 146–8
Berman, Edgar, 220
Berns, Walter, 236, 237, 252, 263, 282–3, 350

Berwid, Adam, 315–16
Berwid, Ewa, 315
bestiality, as excuse for crimes, 162–3,
    288
Bible, 20, 64, 66, 79–86
    control of revenge in, 79–81, 85–6,
        88–92, 169–70
    "eye for eye" passage in, 79–80, 92,
        111, 129–32, 283
    Ezekiel, 85–6, 91
    forgiveness, comparison of attitudes
        toward in Old and New
        Testaments, 342–5
    Job, demand for justice of, 341–2
    justice, comparison of attitudes
        toward in Old and New
        Testaments, 340–5
    love-justice dichotomy in, 338–40
    New Testament of, 88–92, 96, 100–3,
        338, 339, 342–5
    Old Testament of, 67, 73, 77–9, 80–7,
        88–94, 339–42
    pollution doctrine in, 71–2
    rape in, 194–8, 202–3
    secular law influenced by, 139–140,
        141
    symbolic revenge in, 171–2
    see also Christianity; Judaism
Bill of Rights, U.S., 138, 255, 260, 295
Birch, Wayne, 191–2, 205
blacks, 122, 299, 300–5, 335–8
    death penalty for, 261, 301
    failures of social justice and, 9,
        301–2, 304
    sentencing of, 211, 302
    white fear of crime by, 300, 304
Blake, William, 37–8
blood atonement:
    "cities of refuge," as substitute for,
        80–1
    as form of revenge, 7, 10, 17–36,
        39–44, 46–8
    relation to tribal retribution, 67,
        69–71, 119
    see also Bible
blood revenge, in literature, 17–36,
        39–44, 46–8, 51–65
Book of the City of Ladies (Christine de
    Pizan), 200
Borden, Andrew, 210–11

Borden, Lizzie, trial of, 208–11, 244
bride capture, 2, 203–4
Brodsky, Joseph, 233
Bronson, Charles, 8, 174–5, 299
Brontë, Charlotte, 14, 49–50
Brooks, Charles, Jr., 268–9, 270, 284
Brownmiller, Susan, 128–9, 193, 194,
    202, 228
Bruson, Douglas, 298
Buber, Martin, 286
Bugliosi, Vincent, 244–5
Burgess, Anthony, 230
Burr, Aaron, 126–7
Bush, Bonnie Ann, 301
Byron, George Gordon, Lord, 183, 234,
    264

California, 322–3
    death penalty in, 245
    parole laws in, 308
Campbell, Lily B., 35, 39, 40–1, 96
Camus, Albert, 10–11, 279, 280
Canada, death penalty in, 239–40, 242,
    246, 292, 293
child abuse, 63, 161, 180, 186
    as extra-legal offense, 59, 128, 129,
        222–3, 348
    sexual, 184, 193, 214, 222–3, 348–9
    see also sexual revenge
child-custody cases, as form of revenge,
    61, 184, 222
Choëphoroe (Aeschylus), 26–9, 30
Christianity, 88–113
    controls on revenge in, 5, 34–8, 40–1,
        67–8, 88–92, 113, 170
    death penalty and, 95, 253
    Jewish attitudes to forgiveness
        compared to forgiveness in, 338–45
    Jewish teaching on revenge compared
        to revenge in, 20, 67, 68, 73, 77–9,
        82, 83, 88–94
    Machiavelli's views of, 144–5, 147
    natural law vs. situation ethics in, 92
    revenge encouraged by, 34, 68–9,
        99–112
    see also Bible
Christine de Pizan, 199–200
civil disobedience, as form of
    aggression, 337
clemency, practice of, 257–9, 345, 349

Clockwork Orange, A (movie), 230
comic revenge, 44–6
Commentaire sur le livre des délits et des peines (Voltaire), 137
contrition, perfect vs. imperfect, 282*n*
Coppola, Francis Ford, 176–7
Covenant Code, murder in, 125
crime, 290–330
  fear of, 242, 243, 244, 295–7, 300, 304
  increase in incidence of, 237, 242, 243, 246, 292, 305–6, 311, 320
  individual vs. collective responsibility for, 120–3, 139, 293
  by men against women, 185–6
  private forgiveness vs. public retribution and, 117–18, 125, 128, 129, 203, 304–5, 334
  racial and class elements in, 122, 299–304
  real vs. perceived, 244, 296–7
  "ripple effect" of, 297
  sin and, 77, 140–1, 148, 222
  in U.S. vs. Europe, 9–11, 185, 246–7, 292–3
  violent vs. nonviolent, 136, 151, 299–300
  see also victims; *specific crimes*
criminal justice, 114–49
  failures of, 9–10, 12, 53, 58, 60–1, 290–1, 298, 301–2, 304–9
  legitimate uses of revenge in, 280–9, 294
  role of psychiatry in, 150–73, 178–82, 307, 311–29; *see also* death penalty; insanity defense
criminals:
  abdication of responsibility by, 321–4
  intent vs. act, 140–2
  plea bargaining and parole as boon to, 298, 304–9
  rights of, 295, 304, 308
Crusades, anti-Semitism in, 103–4, 200–1
Cruz, Edward, 306
Curtis, Venira, 191–2

Daisenberger, Joseph Alois, 106–7
Darrow, Clarence, 242

Dawidowicz, Lucy, 162
death penalty, 5–6, 7, 10–11, 20, 114, 118, 126, 137, 142, 233–89
  abolition of, 138–9, 235, 242–3, 245, 246, 257, 261, 262–3
  anger underlying appeal of, 241–2, 243, 282–3, 284
  for attempted suicide, 134, 148, 266
  Barzun's defense of, 238–9
  Beccaria's opposition to, 135, 136, 236, 237, 238, 256, 257, 260, 289
  black opposition to, 301
  for crimes against property, 132–3, 137–8, 139, 251–2, 257
  demand for, as response to increase in crime, 237, 242, 243, 246, 292, 320
  deterrent value of, 11, 246–50, 263–4, 272–5, 279, 280
  humanitarian argument against, 285–6
  for murder, 5–6, 7, 124, 244–52, 277–8, 283–9
  opposition to, equated with opposition to all punishment, 235–7
  proportional punishment and, 240, 250, 262–3, 283–4, 285
  for rape, 228, 261, 301
  as real vs. theoretical power, 256–7, 324–5
  religion and, 79, 80, 81, 95, 252–6, 283
  resurgence of support for, 11, 237, 241–5, 248–50, 292, 320
  as shifter of focus from crime to punishment, 284–8
  terrorism and, 246–7
  see also executions
Death Wish (movie), 8, 174–5, 177, 178, 299
Death Wish II (movie), 174, 175
deicide, as rationalization for anti-Semitism, 68–9, 99–112
della Bella, Giano, 121
Demosthenes, 119
Des Pres, Terrence, 354–5
detached revenge, 166, 167
detective fiction, revenge and, 16, 26, 53, 55, 62–3

determinism, 57
  in Greek tragedy, 20–1, 23, 24, 33,
    57, 74
  psychiatric, 24, 153, 155–6, 160–1,
    169
  religious, 47, 69, 83, 223
Discourses, The (Machiavelli), 98, 114,
    144–6, 147
disemboweling, as penalty for treason,
    133, 236
divine vengeance, 5, 7, 47–8, 53, 54, 64,
    68, 72–3, 88, 92–5
  cyclical concept of, 82–4, 87, 92–6,
    104
  in Elizabethan literature, 35–6, 38,
    40–1
  psychiatric view of, 169–70
Doctorow, E. L., 52
domesticity, literature of, and revenge,
    59–61
Don Juan (Byron), 183
Donnelly, Doris, 334, 351
Dostoyevsky, Feodor M., 113
Dozier, James, 10, 155
Draco, laws of, 119, 251–2
dueling, as private settlement of
    revenge, 125–8

Edison, Thomas Alva, 241, 267
Ehrlich, Isaac, 273
Eichmann, Adolf, 240, 277–8, 281–2,
    284
  trial and execution of, 109–11, 247,
    252, 284–8
Eichmann in Jerusalem (Arendt), 290
Eleazer ben Azariah, 254
Electra (Euripides), 25–31, 74
Electra (Sophocles), 25–9, 31
electrocution, 241, 266–8
Elizabeth I, Queen of England, 35,
    98–9, 126
Elizabethan and Jacobean revenge
    tragedy, 7–8, 34–45, 134, 144
  Greek tragedy contrasted with, 21–2,
    33, 36, 40
  modern mass media contrasted with,
    174
  politics and, 19–20
  public vs. private revenge in, 18, 33,
    34–6, 40–4, 52–3

Engelhart, Vladimir, 313
England, 9, 95, 98–9, 293
  crime in, 300
  death penalty in, 126, 139, 246,
    257–9, 261, 264–6, 292, 293
  dueling in, 125, 126
  insanity defense in, 318
  rape laws in, 128–9, 200, 201–2
  use of psychiatry in criminal justice,
    312, 313–14
English, Christine, 219–20
Enlightenment, legal reform in, 116,
    120, 130, 132, 134–9, 236, 255
Erasmus, Desiderius, 107
Essays, "Of Revenge" (Bacon), 1,
    331
Eumenides (Aeschylus), 29
  misogyny in, 31–2, 75–6
  pollution doctrine in, 75–6
Euripides, 21–34, 61, 70, 143, 187,
    206–8
  death of, as revenge tragedy, 22
  misogyny attributed to, 24–5, 207
  modern sensibility of, 21–2, 23, 24,
    32–3, 48, 207–8
  pollution doctrine and, 73, 74
  Racine compared to, 46–7
  Shakespeare compared to, 44
executions:
  attempts to dignify, 269–71
  by electrocution, 241, 266–8
  by hanging, 133, 134, 264–6, 267
  incarceration vs., 234, 237, 275–7
  by lethal injection, 234, 241, 267–9,
    284
  official witnesses to, 268, 269, 270–1
  public, 134, 263–6
  search for "humane" form of, 266–9
  see also death penalty
exile:
  of Jews, 84–6
  as penalty for murder, 77, 124,
    251–2

Fatal Dowry, The (Massinger), 41–3,
    44–5
Federal Bureau of Investigation (FBI),
    crime statistics of, 243, 296, 305
feminist literature, revenge in, 49–50,
    53

feminists, 148, 198–9
  rape as viewed by, 193, 194, 221, 227–9
  sexual revenge as viewed by, 53, 185–6, 204–5
Fielding, Joy, 61, 348
For Capital Punishment: Crime and the Morality of the Death Penalty (Berns), 236, 237, 252, 263, 350
Ford, Gerald, 349
Forgive—But Do Not Forget (Salvesen), 349–50
forgiveness, 1, 20, 331–62
  abdication of responsibility and, 348–50
  difficulties in attainment of, 333
  false, 334
  Jewish vs. Christian attitudes toward, 338–45
  justice and, 332
  as personal and private act, 334
  public retribution vs., 117–18, 125, 128, 129, 203, 304–5, 334
  restitution and, 350–1
  revenge as antipode of, 331–2
  see also mercy
Foster, Jodie, 205–6, 318–19, 327
France, 34, 95, 103, 293, 321
  death penalty in, 132, 138–9, 247
  dueling in, 125–6
  legal reform in, 138–9
  use of psychiatry in criminal justice, 312
Franklin, Benjamin, 132
Frederick the Great, King of Prussia, 137–8
Fredreck, William, 217–18
free will, 33
  mental defects and, 321–4
  psychiatric views of, 153
  religious views of, 74, 87–8, 96, 153, 321
  see also determinism
French Revolution, legal reform and, 138
Freud, Sigmund, 74, 150, 151–2, 159, 312, 327–8
  oedipal conflict and, 163–4, 180
Furman v. Georgia, 242, 256–7, 278–9, 324–5

Gandhi, Mohandas K., 335–8
Garcia, Inez, 189, 204, 214
Garland, Bonnie, 160, 189–90, 205, 216–19, 227, 274, 323–4
  held responsible for her death, 216–17
Gaylin, Willard, 169, 323–4
  on crimes of passion, 218–19
  on psychiatric determinism, 153, 160
  on punishment, 237–8
Germany, Federal Republic of, crime in, 292, 293, 307–8
Giles, Nathan, 301
Gilmore, Gary, 142, 234, 288–9
Godfather, The (movie), 176–7
Godfather II, The (movie), 177
Godfather, The (Puzo), 1, 54–5, 58–9, 176
Goethe, Johann Wolfgang von, 43–4
Good Riddance (Abercrombie), 59–61
Gowers, Sir Ernest, 265, 266
graffiti, as symbolic revenge, 171, 172–3
Gray, Ralph, 269
Greeks, ancient, pollution doctrine of, 20, 67, 71–7, 118, 124, 251
Greek tragedy, 20–34, 340
  Elizabethan tragedy contrasted with, 21–2, 33, 36, 40
  modern revenge compared to, 57–61, 64
  sexual revenge in, 24–5, 61, 187, 206–7
Greenberg, Jack, 278
Greenlease, Bobby, 242
Gregg v. Georgia, 248–50, 268, 273, 279, 288
Groth, A. Nicholas, 348
guilt:
  hereditary, 99–112, 120–3
  Judeo-Christian view of, 73
  psychiatric view of, 153
  as punishment, 6
guilty but mentally ill, 326–8
Gustavus III, King of Sweden, 138

Hadas, Moses, 21, 24
Hamilton, Alexander, 126–7
Hamlet (Shakespeare), 18, 34, 38, 43–4
Hand, Learned, 295

hangings, 133
    descriptions of, 134, 264–6
    speed of, 267
Harris, Jean, 6, 116, 186, 187, 189, 190,
    191, 277, 281
Hearst, Patricia, 154, 155
Hedda Gabler (Ibsen), 49, 208
Henry II, King of England, 259
hereditary revenge, 69, 83, 120–3, 133,
    138
    deicide as rationale for, 99–112
Herrin, Richard, 160, 189–90, 191,
    216–19, 220
    manslaughter charge of, 190, 205,
        218
    movement from self-effacement to
        aggression in letters of, 168–9
    self-pity of, 190, 323–4
Hillel, Rabbi, 87, 90
Himmler, Heinrich, 173, 178
Hinckley, John, Jr., 164–6, 170, 327
    acquittal of, 155, 205, 311
    insanity defense of, 155, 205–6, 218,
        220, 311, 314, 318–19, 321
    psychiatric predictions about, 317
Hinckley, John, Sr., 164–5, 166
Hippolytus (Euripides), 46–7
Hispanics, crime and, 300, 302, 304
history, cycles of vengeance in, 96
Hitler, Adolf, 173, 180, 353
Holocaust, 2–4, 69, 86–7, 157, 299
    Eichmann trial and, 109–11, 247,
        252, 284–8
    forgiveness and, 346–7, 354
    symbolic use of, 162–3
    see also anti-Semitism; Christianity;
        Judaism
Holocaust literature, revenge and, 53,
    56
Holtzman, Elizabeth, 220
Homer, 69–71, 124
Horney, Karen, 12, 150, 179, 351–2
    types of revenge catalogued by,
        166–70
Howard, Henry, 7
Hughes, Francine, 211–13, 214, 215,
    216, 314–15
Hughes, Graham, 281
Hughes, James, 212–13

Iannucci, Ugo, 4
Ibsen, Henrik, 21–2, 49, 208
Idaho:
    death penalty in, 269
    insanity defense restricted in, 326,
        328
Iliad (Homer), 70–1, 124
Illinois:
    death penalty in, 267–8
    husband's ability to commit wife in,
        223–6
informers, exposure of, as revenge,
    158–9
In the Belly of the Beast (Abbott), 7
Innocent Blood (James), 62–5
Inquisition, long-term influences of,
    121–2, 133
insanity defense, 314–22
    in Hinckley case, 155, 205–6, 218,
        220, 311, 314, 318–19, 321
    historical evolution of, 317–18
    proposed solutions to overuse of,
        326–8
    sexual revenge and, 190–1, 205–6,
        211, 213, 214–16
    statistics on use of, 314
    temporary, 213, 215–16, 314–15
Irving, John, 230–1
Israel, 84, 113
    Eichmann trial and execution in,
        109–11, 247, 252, 284–8
Italy, 103, 192
    bride capture in, 2, 203–4
    death penalty in, 132
    terrorism in, 10, 293

Jacobson, Dan, 82–4, 86, 104, 196–7
James, P. D., 62–5
Jane Eyre (Brontë), 14, 49–50
jealousy, relation to revenge, 14, 15, 39,
    206, 222
Jews, 122
    "Against the Jews and Their Lies"
        (Luther), 108
    failures of justice regarding, 53,
        103–4
    see also anti-Semitism; Holocaust;
        Judaism; Talmud
John Paul II, Pope, 155, 345
Jones, Ann, 209, 210, 213

Jones, Milton, 310
Judaism, 77–88
  Christian attitudes to forgiveness
    contrasted with forgiveness in,
    338–45
  Christian teaching on revenge
    compared to revenge in, 20, 67, 68,
    73, 77–9, 82, 83, 88–94
  controls on revenge in, 67–8, 79–82,
    119–20, 170
  death penalty and, 81, 252–6
  murder in legal codes of, 119–20,
    124–5, 127–8
  pollution doctrine in, 67, 71–3, 77,
    80–1, 97, 251
  rape as viewed in, 200–1
  religious vs. civic prohibitions in,
    81–2, 125
justice, 331, 332
  differing public definitions of, 291–2
  equal, 301, 304, 308–9
  forgiveness vs., 338–42
  literary relationship between revenge
    and, 27–8, 31–2, 34, 38–40, 48–65
  mercy as element in, 116, 291
  revenge as element in, 27–8, 38, 48,
    49–50, 179
  revenge vs., 1–12, 31–2, 38–40,
    48–52, 54–5, 130, 151
  sexual revenge and, 206–7
  see also criminal justice; social justice

Kapitsa, Pyotr, 313
Kemmler, William, 241
Kennedy, Edward, 309
Kennedy, Robert, 308
kidnapping, 1–2, 61
  death penalty for, 242, 262
  in Lindbergh case, 208, 242, 262
  by terrorists, 10, 154
Killing of Bonnie Garland, The
  (Gaylin), 218
King, Martin Luther, Jr., 293, 335–8
kings, divine right of, 35, 95–7, 98–9
Kiss Mommy Goodbye (Fielding), 61
Kleist, Heinrich von, 50–2, 54, 57, 358
Kohlhaas, Hans, 50–1
Kohut, Heinz, 162–3, 181
Kubrick, Stanley, 230

law, 114–49
  equitable vs. inequitable, 115
  functions of, 5, 10, 115
  psychiatry contrasted with, 152–3,
    154, 156, 160–1
  rape, 128–9, 199–203, 228, 301
  religion compared to, 68, 152–3,
    160–1
  secularization of, 139–49
  unwritten, sexual revenge and, 184,
    189, 192–7, 204, 211
Laws (Plato), 124, 140–2
Lebanon, melding of religious and
  political revenge in, 112–13
"legalism," pejorative meaning attached
  to, 340, 345
Leopold, Grand Duke of Tuscany, 138
Leopold-Loeb case, 208, 242
Lindbergh kidnap-murder case, 208,
  242, 262
literature, 14–65
  blood revenge in, 17–36, 39–44, 46–8,
    51–65
  comic revenge in, 44–6
  misogyny in, 24–5, 31–2, 75–6
  rape in, 58, 59–61, 230–2
  relationship between justice and
    revenge in, 27–8, 31–2, 34, 38–40,
    48–65
  religious revenge in, 33–8, 40–1,
    47–8, 104–7
  women's revenge in, 21, 24–5, 27–8,
    31–2, 45, 49–50, 62–4, 187, 188,
    199, 206–7, 230–2
  see also Elizabethan and Jacobean
    revenge tragedy; Greek tragedy;
    specific works
Litman, Jack, 217
Littell, Robert, 55–7
Locke, John, 239
Lomas, Harvey, 169, 177, 322
Lombroso, Cesare, 122
Luther, Martin, anti-Semitism of, 107–9
Lysenko, Trofim, 122

McCarry, Charles, 14, 57–8
McDonough, J. Norman, 111
Machiavelli, Niccolò, 97–8, 114, 144–8,
  253
Madison, James, 271

Maestro, Marcello, 136
Mailer, Norman, 7, 288
Maimonides, 77, 140, 143, 252
  on murder, 125, 146
  on proportionality, 131–2
  on rape, 201
Mandelstam, Nadezhda, 157–9, 178,
    331–2, 357–8
Mandelstam, Osip, 157–8, 331–2
Manson, Charles, 244–5, 248, 272,
    277–8, 281–2, 284, 310
marriage, 12–13
  as substitute for criminal prosecution
    of rape, 2, 128, 202–4
  see also wife beating
married women, rape of, 201, 202
Marshall, Thurgood, 249–50
Mary Queen of Scots (Mary Stuart), 35,
    99
Massinger, Philip, 41–3, 44–5
mass media:
  revenge theme in, 8, 150–1, 174–8,
    179, 181, 203
  sex roles reinforced by, 175–6
  symbolism in, contrasted with
    psychiatric metaphor, 150–1, 178
matricide, 28–33, 72, 73, 74–6, 93
Measure for Measure (Shakespeare), 46
Medea (Euripides), 21, 24–5, 40,
    206–8
  emotional force of, 187
  women's despair in, 206–7
Medvedev, Zhores, 313
Melodia, Filippo, 203–4
Menninger, Karl, 178, 236
mental health, 12, 156, 327–8
mental illness:
  definition of compared with insanity,
    327–9
  revenge seen as form of, 12, 17, 59,
    156–7, 169, 179–81, 351–2
mental patients, 223–6
  release of, 314–15, 316
  rights of, 313
Merchant of Venice, The (Shakespeare),
    338–9
mercy, 331–62
  conflict between vengeance and, 66–8
  legal, 116

religious, 34, 66–8, 73, 78, 82–3, 87,
    88–9, 92
  see also forgiveness
mercy killings, 215
Merry Wives of Windsor, The
    (Shakespeare), 45
Michael Kohlhaas (Kleist), 50–2, 54,
    57, 358
Middle Ages, rape in, 199–202
Milk, Harvey, 322–3
Milton, John, 14, 15, 36–8, 47
Minor, Grant, 301
Mirror for Magistrates, A, 96–7
Mitford, Jessica, 266
M'Naghten, Daniel, 318
M'Naghten rule, 318–19, 321, 326
Montesquieu, Baron de la Brède et de,
    136
Moro, Aldo, 247
Moscone, George, 322–3
Moslems, 103
  Christian massacres of, 112–13
mothers, 61, 62–4
  children abandoned by, 49
  children murdered by, 21, 24–5, 186,
    187
  killing of, 28–33, 72, 73, 74–6, 93
murder, 7, 21, 24–5, 119, 140
  abolition of private settlement for,
    118, 123–5, 128
  death penalty for, 5–6, 7, 124,
    244–52, 277–8, 283–9
  imagination and, 234
  manslaughter vs., 124, 190, 205, 214,
    218, 323
  mass media portrayals of, 8, 174–7
  payments as private settlement for,
    70–1, 119, 124–5
  pollution doctrine of, 20, 67, 71–7,
    80–1, 97, 118, 124, 251
  as sexual revenge, 60–1, 168–9, 184,
    185–7, 189–92, 199, 204–5, 208–20
  stranger, 243–5
  in U.S. vs. Western Europe, 292
mutilation, as punishment, 118, 133,
    136, 138, 139, 236, 238, 241
  see also pollution doctrine; private
    settlement

Napoleonic code, 138
narcissism, revenge and, 162, 163–6,
    181
National Front, British, 300
National Lutheran Council, U.S., 109
National Rifle Association, 288
Nazism, 2–4, 86–7, 106, 159, 162–3,
    300, 325, 354
    Oberammergau Passion Play and
        (1934), 106, 172–3
    Sippenhaft and, 121
    symbolic revenge and, 172–3
Neier, Aryeh, 117
Nesbit, Evelyn, 219
neurosis, revenge seen as form of, 12,
    32, 156
New Jersey, death penalty in, 260, 268,
    279–80
New York:
    criminal case overload in, 306
    extreme emotional stress defense in,
        190, 322
    murder vs. manslaughter in, 189–90,
        218
    parole practices in, 310
    rape victims in, 229, 302–5
New York Times, 123, 165, 279–80, 286
nineteenth-century literature, revenge
    in, 48–52
Nixon, Richard M., 349
nobility, punishment of, 133, 136
Nuremberg rallies, 150–1, 172

Oberammergau Passion Play, 105,
    106–7, 172–3
Odyssey (Homer), 70–1, 124
oedipal conflict, 163–6, 180
Oedipus myth, pollution doctrine in,
    73–4
Oedipus the King (Sophocles), 26
Of Blood and Hope (Pisar), 331, 359–61
Ogarev, Nicholas, 134, 265–6
On Crimes and Punishments (Beccaria),
    116–17
Oresteia, 21, 25–33, 73–6, 187
"Originality of Machiavelli, The"
    (Berlin), 146–8
Othello (Shakespeare), 39–40, 42, 188,
    206

pacifists, death penalty as viewed by,
    260, 262
Packard, Elizabeth, 223–6, 227, 312
Packard, Theophilus, 223–6
Papas, Irene, on revenge in *Medea* and
    Othello, 206
Paradise Lost (Milton), 14, 37–8, 47
parole practices, 306–11, 324
Pascal, Blaise, 110
passion, crimes of, *see* sexual revenge
passion plays, 172–3
    anti-Semitism as form of revenge in,
        102, 104–7
Pasternak, Boris, 331–2
patriarchy:
    in classical Greece, 31–2
    mass media as reinforcer of, 175–7
    sexual revenge and, 187–8, 189,
        192–8, 211
patricide, Lizzie Borden trial and,
    208–11
Peel, Robert, 318
penance, sacrament of, as form of
    atonement, 78
Penn, William, 260
Pennsylvania, death penalty in, 260–1
Pennsylvania Law Review, 302
Pfefferkorn, Johannes, 107
Phèdre (Racine), 46–8
pickpockets, death penalty for, 257
Pisar, Samuel, 331, 359–61
Plato, 124, 140–2, 143
plea bargaining, 298, 304–7, 311
    "deal-for-sentence," 306–7
Plutarch, 124
Poliakov, Léon, 104
political crimes, 9–10, 151, 155–6
    death penalty for, 138–9, 246–7
    hereditary guilt and, 120–2
political metaphor, revenge and, 172–3
Portnoy's Complaint (Roth), 18
Praz, Mario, 19
predestination, 47, 69, 83, 223
pregnancy, torture and, 133
premenstrual syndrome (PMS), as
    criminal defense, 219–22
Primaudaye, Peter de la, 95–6, 97,
    145
Prince, The (Machiavelli), 98, 147

prisons, 118, 121
  as alternative to execution, 234, 237,
    275–7
  overcrowding of, 308, 311
  as punishment, 309–10
private settlement, 123–5
  dueling as form of, 125–8
  for murder, 119, 124–5
  for rape, 128–9
  as substitute for punishment, 117–19
property crimes, 119
  Beccaria's views on, 136
  death penalty for, 132–3, 137–8, 139,
    251–2, 257
  rape as form of, 193, 195, 200–1
psychiatry, 143, 150–73, 178–82
  American vs. European attitudes
    toward, 153–4
  complications in revenge-justice views
    due to, 53, 151, 152–3, 156, 166,
    169, 178–82, 311–29
  determinism and, 24, 153, 155–6,
    160–1, 169
  Greek tragedy and, 20, 32, 151
  negative view of revenge in, 12, 17,
    59, 156–7, 169, 179–81, 351–2
  omission of attention to revenge in,
    151, 163
  plea bargaining and, 307
  primitive state of, 154–5
  punitive misuse of, 223–6, 312–14
  responsibility question and, 53,
    152–3, 156, 162–3, 166, 169, 307,
    314, 321–4
  sexual revenge and, 156, 188, 190–2,
    197, 205–6, 211, 213, 214–16
  symbolism and metaphor in, 156,
    161–3, 166, 171–3
  unreliability of behavioral forecasts
    in, 316–17
  see also insanity defense
punishment, 233–330
  capital, see death penalty; executions
  in comic revenge, 45–6
  deterrence and, 9, 11, 115, 246–50,
    263–4, 272–5, 279, 280, 298
  disproportional, 132–4, 136–7, 301–2
  effect of crime rate on attitudes
    toward, 237, 246, 292
  guilt as, 6

  mutilation as, 118, 133, 136, 138,
    139, 236, 238, 241
  proportional, 10, 85–6, 88, 91–2,
    129–32, 134–9, 180–2, 240, 250,
    262–3, 283–4, 285, 295
  for rape, 128–9, 199–203, 228, 301
  torture as, 118, 121–2, 133, 136, 137,
    138, 236, 238, 241, 302, 305
Puzo, Mario, 1, 54–5, 58–9, 176

Quakers, death penalty restricted by,
  260

Racine, Jean, 46–8
Ragtime (Doctorow), 52
rape, 94, 184, 193–203, 227–32, 292,
    302–5
  Biblical accounts of, 194–8, 202–3
  blacks and whites, 301–2, 304
  damage payments for, 200–1
  feminist views of, 193, 194, 221,
    227–9
  legal punishment for, 128–9,
    199–203, 228, 301
  literary treatment of, 58, 59–61,
    230–2
  mass media portrayals of, 8, 174–5,
    176, 230
  private settlement and, 59–61, 128–9,
    193–8, 202–3, 230–2
  reporting of, 243, 292
  special legal status of, 227–9
  see also sexual revenge
Rape of Tamar, The (Jacobson), 196–7
Reagan, Ronald, 155, 268, 288, 318–19
reciprocity:
  divine vengeance and, 82–3, 87, 92–4,
    96
  historical cycles and, 96–7
  law and, 131–2
Red Brigades, 10, 154
"Reflections on the Guillotine"
    (Camus), 10–11
Reformation, religious revenge and,
    98–9, 100
rehabilitation of criminals, 178–9, 234,
    275–7, 291
  Platonic view of, 140–2
religious prophecy, as symbolic revenge,
  171–2

religious proselytizing, revenge and, 69,
101, 104, 107
religious revenge, 66–113, 152–3
anti-Semitism and, 68–9, 99–112
in literature, 33–8, 40–1, 47–8,
104–7
paradox of, 66–9, 83
political vendetta melded with, 69,
112–13
state control vs., 35, 69–77, 95–9,
113
see also divine vengeance
religious scholarship, Talmud
controversy and, 107
Requiem (Akhmatova), 356–7
retribution, as euphemism for revenge,
4
Reuchlin, Johannes, 107
revenge:
comic, 44–6
diminution of literary interest in,
16–17
emotional need for, 5–6, 11–12, 40,
152–3, 170–3, 298
Jewish vs. Christian teaching on, 20,
67, 68, 73, 77–9, 82, 83, 88–94
legalized, 5–6, 10, 11–13, 114–49,
152–3, 154, 235, 340, 345–7; *see
also* death penalty; punishment
literary views of, 7–8, 14–65, 104–7,
187, 188, 199, 206–7, 230–2
as metaphor, 150–82
pros and cons of, 14–15, 59, 157–9,
235
psychiatric views of, 12, 17, 59, 62–4,
150–73, 178–82, 351–2; *see also*
insanity defense
public vs. private aspects of, 14, 15,
33–6, 82, 40–6, 48–82, 94–9,
114–18, 123–9, 139, 144, 151,
202–4
religious views of, 5, 20, 21, 34–8,
40–1, 53, 59, 64, 66–113, 152–3
sexual, 24–5, 39–40, 45, 53, 59–61,
128–9, 156, 168–9, 183–232; *see
also* rape; wife beating
symbolic, 171–3
see also specific topics
Revenger's Tragedy, The (Tourneur),
16, 36, 44

revenge taboo, 1–13, 59
psychiatry and, 12, 17, 59, 156–7,
169, 179–81, 351–2
Victorian sexual taboos compared to,
12–13
revenge tragedy, 18–48
modern revenge contrasted with, 54, 62
see also Elizabethan and Jacobean
revenge tragedy; Greek tragedy
Reynolds, John, 66, 92–4, 121–2
Robinson, John D., 210
Rodriguez, Olga, 310
Roman law, 119, 124, 128
Roosevelt, Franklin D., 353
Roth, Philip, 18
Royal Commission on Capital
Punishment, British, 265
Rush, Benjamin, 257, 260, 275–6
Ryan, Hermine Braunsteiner, 2–3, 157,
346–7

sadism, Horney's views on, 166–7
St.-Foix, 125–6
Salpêtrière (Paris insane asylum), 312
Salvesen, Sylvia, 349–50
Sand, George, 183
Sanders, Lawrence, 150
satyagraha, Gandhi's concept of, 336
Second Treatise of Civil Government
(Locke), 239
Second Vatican Council, 78, 101
deicide charge repudiated by, 111–12
self-defense plea, sexual revenge and,
213–14, 230
self-effacing revenge, 166, 167, 168,
171
sexual revenge, 183–232
cold-blooded crimes vs., 184, 192,
222, 330
double standard of morality and,
186–9
insanity defense and, 190–1, 205–6,
211, 213, 214–16
legality of, 185–6
in literature, 24–5, 39–40, 45, 53,
59–61, 187, 188, 206–8, 230–2
male vs. female motives for, 185–6
murder as, 60–1, 168–9, 184, 185–7,
189–92, 199, 204–5, 208–20
news value of, 186

sexual revenge *(cont.)*
  patriarchal origins of codes for, 189,
    192–8, 211, 223
  PMS defense and, 219–22
  through private settlement, 59–61,
    128–9, 193–8, 202–3, 230–2
  psychiatric views of, 156, 188, 190–2,
    197, 205–6, 211, 213, 214–16
  religious influences on attitudes
    toward, 194–8, 202–3
  self-defense plea and, 213–14, 230
  unwritten law and, 184, 189, 192–7,
    204, 211
  see also rape; wife beating
Shakespeare, William, 18, 22, 36,
    38–40, 42, 43–4, 96, 188, 206, 338–9
  comic revenge in, 45, 46
  Euripides compared to, 44
Sicily, bride capture in, 2, 203–4
Simeon ben Shatah, 254
sin:
  crime vs., 77, 140–1, 148, 222
  Hellenic vs. Semitic view of, 73
  individual vs. collective
    accountability for, 68–78, 85–6, 88,
    91–2, 99–112, 123
  private revenge as, 34, 35, 68
  revenge for, 68–9, 72–3, 77–8, 82–96,
    99–112
Sippenhaft (kin-arrest), 121
Sirhan, Sirhan, 308–9, 310
Smith, Gerald L. K., 109
Smith, Sandie, 219
social justice:
  failures of, 9, 48–65, 103–4
  in nineteenth-century literature,
    48–52
  use of term, 48
Solon, 119, 252
Solzhenitsyn, Aleksandr, 157, 159
Sophocles, 21, 22, 23, 25–9, 31, 32, 57,
    70, 143
  pollution doctrine and, 73, 74
Soviet Union, 157–8, 356–8
  misuse of psychiatry in, 313, 314
  "political crimes" in, 121, 122
Spain:
  criticism of Jewish legal procedures
    in, 254–5
  torture in, 133

Speck, Richard, 309
Spirit of the Laws (Montesquieu), 136
spy novels, revenge theme in, 55–8
Stalin, Joseph, 121, 122, 157–8
Statutes of Westminster, 128–9, 202,
    203
Stern gang, 247
Steward, Glen, 306–7
Stewart, Potter, 278–9
Story of Stories, The (Jacobson), 82–4,
    86, 104
Stringfellow, William, 110
suicide, 63–5, 186, 316–17
  attempted, death penalty for, 134,
    148, 266
  as response to rape, 199–200
Supreme Court, U.S., death penalty
    and, 5–6, 242, 248–50, 256–7, 268,
    271, 273, 278–9, 288
Sutherland, Mary, 134
symbolic revenge, 171–3
Szasz, Thomas, 53

Talmud, 84–5, 338
  conception legend in, 87–8
  death penalty and, 81, 254, 255
  rape in, 200–1
  Renaissance controversy over, 107
Tannenbaum, Marc, 106–7
Tarfon, Rabbi, 254
Tarnower, Herman, 6, 186, 189, 227,
    277
Tate, Sharon, 209, 272
Tate-LaBianca murders, 244–5
Tears of Autumn, The (McCarry), 14,
    57–8
terrorism, political, 9–10, 151, 155–6
  death penalty as response to, 246–7
  as literary theme, 55–7
Texas, death penalty in, 268–9, 284
Thackeray, William Makepeace, 264–5
Thaw, Harry K., 219, 319
Thompson, Dorothy, 173
Thucydides, 22, 72
T. J. Hooker (television series), 175,
    176
"To Lycomedes on Scyros" (Brodsky),
    233
Tocqueville, Alexis de, 261, 293

torture, 136, 137, 236, 241, 302, 305
  abolition of, 118, 138
  in criminal interrogations, 121–2,
    133, 238
Tourneur, Cyril, 16, 36, 44
treason, as crime, 67, 121, 133, 236
Treston, Hubert, 77
tribal identity:
  death penalty and, 251–2
  revenge and, 58–9, 67, 69–76, 79, 90,
    124, 171
Triumphs of Gods Revenge, The
  (Reynolds), 66, 92–4, 121–2
Trojan Women (Euripides), 33
Trudeau, Pierre, 239–40, 242
twentieth-century literature, 52–65
  avengers as beyond the law in, 53–7
  Greek tragedy compared to, 57–61,
    64
  social change as influence on revenge
    in, 53

vendetta, 66, 69, 121–2
  modern survivals of, 84, 121–2, 123
  tribal, as advance over uncontrolled,
    69–71, 79
  tribal, evolution from, 67, 79, 123
  see also pollution doctrine; sexual
    revenge
victims:
  blacks as, 301–2, 304
  injury vs. reputation of, demand for
    retribution and, 302–5
  poor people as, 301

  revenge as viewed by, 1–4, 297–9,
    304–5
Victims (movie), 175–6
Victorianism, 50
  death penalty and, 257
  sex and, 12–13, 164
  sexual revenge and, 208–11
vindication:
  triumphant life as form of, 358–61
  vindictiveness vs., 352–3
Viola, Franca, 203–4
virgins, rape of, 200–1, 202
Volanakis, Minos, 206
Voltaire, 133, 135, 136–7, 139, 143,
  238, 272

Weil, Simone, 290
Wellington, Duke of, 126
Wergeld (restitution), 70–1
Westinghouse, George, 241
White, Dan, 322–3
White, Stanford, 219, 319
Wiesel, Elie, 299
wife beating, 9, 161, 184, 351
  deterrence of, 226, 329–30
  as extra-legal offense, 59, 128, 129
  murder as response to, 185–6, 190,
    205, 211–13, 314–15
Wilhelm Meister (Goethe), 43–4
World According to Garp, The (Irving),
  230–1

Yehiel ben Asher, 120, 255